Normandie

$20.00

Harvey Ardman

NORMANDIE

Her Life and Times

Franklin Watts/1985/New York/Toronto

Cover courtesy of Adolphe Cassandre: "Normandie" © by ADAGP, Paris 1985.

Photographic insert following page 84: (top and bottom) Compagnie Generale
Transatlantique; (top) CGT, (bottom left and right) Barrie Davis collection,
CGT; (top) Barrie Davis collection, (bottom) CGT; (clockwise from top left)
Barrie Davis collection, CGT, CGT, CGT; (top and bottom) CGT; (top and
bottom) CGT; (top and bottom) CGT.

Photographic insert following page 212: (top right and left) CGT, (bottom)
author's collection; (top and bottom) CGT; (top) Frank Braynard collection,
(bottom) Ray Farr collection; (top) Charles Winner collection, (bottom)
Barrie Davis collection; (top left) CGT, (top right) Frank Braynard collection,
(bottom) author's collection; (top) CGT, (bottom) author's collection;
(top) Theodore Sayler/Steven Emmons collection, (bottom) Ray Farr collection.

Photographic insert following page 340: (top) Victor Scrivens collection,
(bottom) Franklin D. Roosevelt Library; (top) author's collection, (bottom)
FDR Library, Frank Braynard collection; (top) FDR Library, (bottom) Ray
Farr collection; (top) Ray Farr collection, (bottom) Frank Braynard collection;
(top) Robert Russell collection, (bottom) U.S. Navy; (top and bottom)
Lipsett Corporation, Victor Scrivens collection.

Library of Congress Cataloging in Publication Data

Ardman, Harvey.
Normandie.

Includes index.
1. Normandie (Steamship)   I. Title.
VM383.N6A73   1985   387.2'432   85-668
ISBN 0-531-09784-6

CONTENTS

acknowledgments

A book like this could not be written without help—and a lot of it. And I've received assistance of all kinds, from literally hundreds of people.

These include former *Normandie* crew members: Maurice Coquin (former chief engineer), Armand Limdender de Nieuwenhove (former chief purser), Roger Marneffe (former chief quartermaster);

Former CGT employees: Peter Rossi, René Bouvard, Pierre de Laulignan, Gerard Blin;

Former *Normandie* passengers: Shirley Rosenberg, Gerard Burke, Sylvia Mandy, S. Oscar Boughner, Mrs. Donald H. Gleason, Mrs. I. T. Levin, Francelle Marcus, Kenneth Ripley, Margot Pekar, Mrs. Thomas H. Hall, Robert J. Newman, Petra Williams, Charles Colvin, Ellie Rogard, Robert C. Kennedy, Mrs. Kitty Lee, Frank Bishopp, Ronald Dendieval, Olivia de Havilland, James Tierney, Samuel Silvernail, Edwin Fisher, George Ehrlich, Oscar Williams, Wanda de Muth Hellpen, Jeannette Whitebook, G. W. Dean, Mary Sargent, Suzanne Braud, J. F. Painter, Frank Tack, Edna Paine Cohee, Mrs. Frank Charles Lee, Warnie Geiger, Dorothea Deans, Catherine Reed, Kent Genrich, Mrs. Edward Earley, Barbara Frost Shively, Mariette Vietz, Katherine Wharton, Mrs. Stanley Weinerman, Dr. Dorothy Withrow, Mrs. Donald Gleason, James Christensen, Fred Fechter, Ann Maxtone-Graham, Helen Balliet;

People associated with *Normandie* during her internment:

Victor Scrivens, Conrad Trahan, James Kane, Peter Altieri, Herman Wahl, Joseph Hines, R. M. Epstein;

People associated with *Normandie* during the attempted conversion: Robert Brunet, John Pyle, Fred Anechins, Joseph Curiale;

People who worked on her salvage: Lester C. Holmes, Leonard Greenstone, Louis Daddario, Salvatore Benelli, Anthony Savino;

Ship experts and collectors of ship memorabilia: John Maxtone-Graham, Walter Lord, Wayne LaPoe, Carl House, Ralph Whitney, Robert J. Russell, Everett Viez (also a passenger), Ted Hindmarsh, Thomas Blandford, Marco Behar, Barrie Roger Davis, Richard P. de Kerbrech, David L. Williams, Robert L. Scheina, Gary Spence, Christopher Sterling, William Donnell, Joseph G. McOrlly, Edward Epstein, Donald Stoltenberg, Bill Miller, Stanley Lehrer, Scott Seifert, Allen Jordan, Stephen Emmons, Dick Faber, Bob Miskey, David Powers, Mrs. Ellis Bell, Theodore Salyer, Hollis French, Goro Suzuki and Robert Forrest;

Museum people: Esther Brumberg (Museum of the City of New York); Wendy Shadwell (New York Historical Society); James Knowles (Smithsonian Institution); John Riley (Navy Historical Center); Mrs. Patty Maddocks (Naval Institute Photo Service), the staff of the Musé de la Marine in Paris, France; the staff of the National Maritime Museum in Greenwich, England; Michael Cook (Cunard Archives at the University of Liverpool); Paul Hensley, Ardie Kelley and the staff of the Mariner's Museum at Newport News; Barbara Edkins and the staff of the Peabody Museum; William Sherman, Ken Hall, Bill Sherman, Maida Loescher, Donald S. Post, Joel Buchwald and the rest of the staff of the National Archives (both in Washington, D.C., and in Suitland, Md.); J. E. Crow (Scottish Records Office—John Brown Archives); the staff of the New York Public Library; the staff of the Library of Congress; Jane Chermayeff (South Street Seaport Museum); William Emerson, director, Franklin D. Roosevelt Library; John Slonaker (Chief, Historical Reference Section, U.S. Army Military History Institute);

Art experts: Penelope Hunter-Steibel (Metropolitan Museum of Art), Alistair Duncan (Christie's auction house), Stewart Johnson (Museum of Modern Art), Tina Chow (of Mr. Chow's), Robert Littman (Grey Art Gallery, New York University), Dr. Irwin Berman, George Theofiles, Richard Oliver (Cooper-Hewitt Museum), Albert Brenet (*Normandie* illustrator), Hilliard Rentner (owner of some grand-salon panels), John Zupan (ship painter); Gertrude Stein (of the Gertrude Stein Galleries, New York), and Evan Blum and Miriam Novallo (of Irreplaceable Artifacts, New York);

And all kinds of others: George Yourke (son of Vladimir Yourkevitch), Lewis McEwen (a Cunard engineer in the 1930s and a Cunard spy on *Normandie*), Julius Lipsett (of Lipsett, Inc.), Paul J. O'Keefe (of Todd Shipyards), Dr. Pierre Thoreux (son of the *Normandie* captain), Henry Woodbridge, Richard Murphy, Ed Turner and Jonathan Peirce (all formerly with Raymond-Whitcomb), Mrs. John Kinley, George McKenna (New York City Fire Department Battalion Chief, the last man off the ship during the fire), William McGuire (who, in the late 1940s, wrote an extremely useful, almost book-length manuscript about *Normandie* for the *New Yorker*, which was never published and which he has allowed me to use as I pleased), Todd Sinclair, Mrs. Ludwig Bemelmans, Nigel Nicolson, Liz Smith, Gus Howard, William Hoisington, Jr., Senator William Cohen, Richard Cull, Joseph Butler III, Richard B. Schmitt, Rita Reiff, Harry J. O'Donnell, Gemma Trent (wife of Frank Trentacosta), Erika Fusco, John Rice, Paolo Locatelli, Walter Havighurst, George Geller (the Fire Chief in charge of fighting the *Normandie* blaze), Father Patrick Walsh (son of the New York Fire Commissioner), Mrs. Charlotte Boyce (she and her husband flew over New York on *Normandie*'s maiden arrival, playing French songs over a loudspeaker system), Patricia Nielson, Arthur Brookes, Frances Tate, Wynne Gibson, Klaas P. Dijkstra, Helen Gucker, Edward Crane and Barbara Smith.

Three other people deserve special mention for help above and beyond the call of duty. They are Charles Sachs, president of the Oceanic Navigation Research Society, who turned up many research leads and made a number of useful comments on the book while it was in its manuscript stages;

Frank Braynard, the *doyen* of American ship memorabilia collectors, who advised me at length, let me browse at will through his astonishingly voluminous accumulation of steam-ship artifacts, brochures, pictures, etc., and allowed me to bor-row whatever I wanted;

And Ray Farr, who loaned me the incredible collection of contemporary *Normandie* newspaper and magazine clippings he'd gotten from Ralph Whitney, a collection filled with forgotten gems of information and interest.

To all of these people, I owe my heartfelt thanks. Much would be missing from this book without their help. Of course, I am responsible for any of the book's errors or omissions—and if any reader discovers some, or has more information to tell me, I would be happy to hear about it.

Rockport, Maine, 1985

Normandie

pReface

This is the biography of a ship named *Normandie*. While using the word *biography* to describe the life of a ship may seem a contradiction in terms, ships have always occupied a special place in the pantheon of human affairs; to those who know them well, ships are *alive*. They have souls. But what raises a ship above the level of its component parts? What is the source of its spirit and its vitality?

More than hunks of wood and steel, ships, like human beings, are incredibly complex—especially large ships. And of these, ocean liners are probably our most complex creations.

Like human beings, ships are unmistakably individual. No two are exactly alike; not even sister ships.

Like human beings, ships are subject to fate—to accident, unforeseen happenstance, disaster, success and failure.

Like human beings, ships have ancestors, parents, siblings, descendants. They have friends and enemies, yet there are legions of people who are indifferent to them. And, like human beings, they have limited lifetimes. They are conceived and born, they have productive periods of varying lengths, they grow old, they die.

Ships have their own personalities and characters. They are cooperative or obstinate, proud or humble, eccentric or predictable. And, like people, they are also beautiful or ugly or somewhere in between. They're smart or dull, fast or slow. They're worse than average, better than average or outstanding.

They are repositories of hopes—of the designers, the builders, the owners, the crew, and of one set of passengers after another. And, like people, sometimes they live up to these hopes, sometimes not.

Ships are also one of humanity's greatest technological achievements. In fact, until the advent of aviation, they were without peer. Ships were invented not once but many times. Canoes, rowboats, galleys, barges, men-of-war, schooners, clipper ships—each required a separate act of imagination. And in the nineteenth century, when steamships appeared, their size, strength and power made them objects of awe and astonishment.

Ships gave us the ability to explore our planet, to gather food from the seas, to establish colonies on far-flung shores, to trade with distant countries, to do battle far from home and hearth. Even now, in one way or another we depend on them. They are an integral part of our lives. They have given us good reason to be endlessly fascinated with them.

But why *Normandie?*

Because she was the most inspired, most original, most imaginatively-conceived ship of her time—perhaps of all time—and becauser she is generally considered the most beautiful ocean liner ever to have sailed the seven seas;

Because in her day *Normandie* was the largest ship ever constructed and the fastest, and because she was the epitome of luxury and glamour in a world plagued by depression and portents of war;

Because she died at the hands of strangers in circumstances of unparalleled carelessness, stupidity, and greed;

And because she will always be loved by those who knew her.

This, then, is *Normandie's* story, her biography. It is also the story of her times—the period between 1928 and 1947—for she cannot be separated from them nor they from her.

It is the story of the determination that brought her to life in the depths of the Depression, of the extraordinary scientific breakthroughs that made possible her size and speed, of the remarkable artistic achievements that gave her beauty and grace and made her the last great expression of the Art Deco era.

It is also the story of her rivalry with the *Queen Mary*, of the celebrities who sailed aboard her and of the desperate and determined Americans who, hoping to use her as a weapon of war, destroyed her, resurrected her, then destroyed her again.

Normandie was one of those rare creations that approach perfection. And this book is her long-overdue celebration. She deserves nothing less.

1

OCTOBER 29, 1932

Coming from Paris by train, you could see her looming across the distant marshes of Montoir. From the heights above Pornichet, a good five miles from St. Nazaire, she dominated the entire city, 40,000 strong, towering over the cluster of red roofs, dwarfing even the Cathedral.

She looked like a big, black office building, an immense iron structure ten stories high and seven blocks long, sitting on the banks of the Loire, an odd building, unrelated to any other within view.

She was *Normandie*. And this windy, overcast Saturday, this gray day in the depths of the darkest depression the world had ever known, was her birthday, the day of her launch, when she would leave her awkward perch on dry land and enter her true element, the sea.

Despite the threatening weather, the grumblings that France's millions could be better spent and the unrest among the unemployed of unrelated industries, nearly 200,000 people—practically all of Brittany, plus thousands brought by special trains to St. Nazaire from Paris, dignitaries and commoners alike—had gathered at the mouth of the Loire to watch the Great Event.

Not everyone had come in a festive spirit, however. Some came openly anticipating disaster, even hoping for it, fighting for the best seat from which to see it, like spectators at the Indianapolis 500.

Some, like the group from John Brown's shipyard in Scotland and from the Cunard Steamship Co., came with a mixture of admiration and jealousy. Their own giant liner, known then only as number 534 (one day she would be the *Queen Mary*), lay rusting in her berth, all work on her having ceased ten months before when Cunard ran out of money.

Some—those responsible for *Normandie*'s launch and for the ship—came filled with nervous apprehension, and not without reason. Rarely does a ship undertake a more dangerous journey than the first brief trip from land to sea. As she slides down the ways into the water, a ship undergoes a condensed version of all the greatest stresses and strains she is ever likely to face during her lifetime.

During the launch there is that moment when the aft end of the hull extends out over the water, hanging in mid-air. This puts an extreme strain on the ship's midsection, which desperately wants to bend, to allow the stern to seek the water's support. In the very next moment, as the launch continues and the stern hits the water, the stresses are suddenly reversed. Now the unsupported midships area tries to sag, to find its own support. It's at exactly this moment, when the hull is half immersed, neither fish nor fowl, that it is most unstable. The slightest miscalculation, the smallest mishap, can send it tumbling.

A mislaunch is a shipbuilder's nightmare. It can occur in a number of ways:

- ☐ The launching ways may sink unevenly into the ground, sending the hull careening seaward at an angle, causing it to capsize;
- ☐ The oak cradle supporting the vessel may collapse, toppling the vessel;
- ☐ The lubricants used to grease the ways may freeze up, bringing the launch to an abrupt halt and leaving engineers with an unlaunchable ship.
- ☐ Storms can drive the newborn hull aground or out to sea before waiting tugs can corral it.

Normandie, larger and heavier than any other vessel ever built, faced not only these risks, but also the unpredictable risks that went with her unprecedented size. Is it any wonder that the local oddsmakers were betting three to one against a successful launch?

The man who had the awesome responsibility for launching this new ship was André See, chief hull engineer at Penhoet shipyard. He was a slender, handsome man in his early thirties with intelligent eyes and a bushy black mustache.

See and his colleagues had begun their complex launch calculations more than three years earlier, as soon as Compagnie Générale Transatlantique—CGT or the French Line—had finalized its plans to build the ship and decided on her general dimensions.

From the start See knew he was faced with a problem of a new order. This new ship would be the largest ever built—961 feet long at the waterline, 1,029 feet 4 inches long overall, with a maximum breadth of 119 feet 5 inches.

She would be launched, like all large ships, as an empty hull, her engines and interior fittings to be added later. But even at launch she would weigh 27,657 tons, about twice the launch weight of the *Ile de France* and 720 tons more than the newest American aircraft carrier, the stupendous *Lexington.*

See had surveyed Penhoet's slipways and decided it would be impossible to build the new ship at the Penhoet shipyard in St. Nazaire, at least not with the existing facilities. Even the 792-foot *Ile de France*'s old building berth was far too small.

And so in April 1929 construction began at Penhoet on a new building berth and slipway, the largest the world had ever seen. Situated on a sandy strip of land reclaimed from the Loire, Slipway Number One, as it was called, was built of reinforced concrete shaped like a shallow wedge 1,017 feet long (enough to accommodate the ship's length at her waterline) and 60 feet wide.

At its inland end this great concrete wedge rose to a height of about 60 feet. At the other end it actually extended into the Loire, to slightly more than 13 feet below low-tide level. It ended in an underwater stone wall.

It was here that *Normandie*—known at first only by her shipyard number, T6 BIS—took shape, the bow at the high end of the wedge, the stern near the low end, just out of the water. The 5-percent incline made the ship look as if she was impatient to be waterborne. But she could not do that until her hull was complete and then only at one of the two highest tides of the year. The chosen date and time: October 29, 1932, at 3:15 p.m.

At that moment, if all went well, the T6 would be officially christened by some dignitary or other, Monsieur See would give the signal, the last of the releasing devices would be let loose and the giant hull, riding on her wooden cradle, would slide down into the ways and into the water, coming to a quick, almost abrupt stop so that waiting tugs could bring her under control and tow her to her fitting berth. The entire event would take little more than a minute—if all went well.

In December 1931, ten months before the appointed moment, launch calculations went into high gear. See and his team did thousands of computations, designed the launch cradle, the gear that would send the hull sliding toward the water, figured out how fast she would travel and calculated the stresses she would experience, the pressure on the ways, etc.

By September the great ship was nearly ready for launch. Surrounded by scaffolding, she rested on an enormous wooden cradle 840 feet long, extending beyond it slightly fore and aft, where bow and stern curved upward.

The hull and its cradle sat together on the "sliding ways," which were built on the concrete wedge itself. These consisted of two timber tracks running from the head of the building berth down into the water. During the launch they would bear the entire weight of ship and cradle.

Until the launch, however, the ship also rested on several hundred keel blocks, stacks of oak beams much like railroad ties. She'd been built on top of these beams. As launch time approached, they'd be removed one by one until the hull was suspended on the cradle alone.

Four rows of timber shoring on each side of the hull kept the ship erect and in place, like a forest of telephone poles. All would have to be removed before launch. Three different types of apparatus kept the T6 from a premature launch: hydraulic triggers, "dog shores" and releasing "salt blocks."

See's team had built two hydraulic triggers on each side of the vessel, underneath the cradle. At the crucial moment they'd release metal levers that otherwise extended into slots in the cradle, holding it in place.

The "dog shores"—there were five on each side—were foot-square oak beams wedged between the bottom rail of the cradle and the top rail of the sliding ways. At launch time See's men would remove them one by one.

The releasing "salt blocks"—five on each side—were actually three foot by five foot salt-filled bags. So long as these were in place, the cradle pressed against the sliding ways, preventing movement. When See gave the signal, the salt bags would be ripped open, water would be pumped into them, the salt would dissolve and the blocks would disappear.

In addition See had four 100-ton hydraulic rams installed at the forward end of the ways. If necessary, they would *shove* the T6 into the Loire.

And what of the Loire itself? Was it prepared for the sudden entrance of the largest ship that had ever taken to water? See carefully calculated the trajectory of the hull to determine its deepest immersion as it plunged into the water. Then he had the river dredged a full meter deeper than absolutely necessary, to 52 feet 9 inches.

The single most crucial part of the launch was getting the ship moving down the ways and into the water. But it was also very important to *stop* the empty hull as quickly as possible once it was waterborne. For this reason See had 100 tons of drag chains bolted to each side of the vessel. The chains would stop this huge ship, See calculated, simply by dragging on the sandy soil beside the launching berth. Nevertheless, he tested their drag by pulling them over the ground behind a locomotive.

All told, See and his men had spent three years of their lives figuring out what would happen in the seventy-five seconds it would take to launch this monstrous hull.

In the middle of September the clanging and banging that go with building a steel hull gradually faded away. The eight giant Titan cranes that towered over the ship like doctors hovering over a very important patient ceased plucking hull plates from the building-berth floor.

Instead, the ship swarmed with thousands of workers whose

job it was to dismantle the incredible thicket of scaffolding that had surrounded the ship and hidden it from view, like a gigantic hedge.

Revealed frame by frame, the T6 was big. She was also black and streaked with rust and dirt. And yet she was beautiful, awe-inspiring.

On October 5, with launch just twenty-four days away, See's men took over, 600 strong. Their first job was to grease the ways. This was no simple task, for the complex cabinetry on which the ship rested was already in place. In order to grease the ways, practically every piece of this cabinetry had to be disassembled, section by section, lubricated with five separate layers of grease and tallow, soap and oil, and then replaced. That included the part of the ways that extended into the river.

This particular job required 42 metric tons of tallow, 4 metric tons of paraffin, 2.5 metric tons of lard/tallow, 3 metric tons of Marseilles soap and soft soap and half a ton of oleonapht oil.

While some of See's men greased the ways, others hammered loose the keel blocks on which the hull rested, substituting supporting sand bags which could easily be removed at the moment of launch. Bit by bit, the T6's grip on dry land was loosened.

Of course, when it came time to send her sliding down the ways to the sea, when the moment of her birth was upon her, she could no longer be known as the T6 BIS. She had to have a proper name, a euphonious name, an evocative name, one that would not only fit her perfectly, but also honor France and appeal to rich American passengers.

She needed a name that would satisfy everyone, but that was obviously impossible. Everyone in France, it seemed, had a different notion of what the ship should be called: La France (or La Belle France or Rayon de France), Napoléon, Charlemagne, Maréchal Joffre, Général Foch, Clemenceau, Pétain, Jeanne d'Arc, Marianne, La Paix, Victoire, La Patrie, La République, La Lorraine, Alsace-Lorraine, Champs-Elysée, Champagne and La Marseillaise.

Those who particularly favored America (or who were especially anxious to attract American trade) wanted to name the ship Benjamin Franklin. Those more sentimental than sensible held out for Mademoiselle from Armentières. The irreverent or bitter suggested La Dette or La Répudiation.

One very vocal group wanted the T6 named after Paul Doumer, the President of the French Republic who'd been gunned down by a mad Russian that May. And in fact, while See's legions were greasing the ways, French papers announced that this, indeed, was the name chosen, with Doumer's widow in full agreement. The next day, however, that name was officially withdrawn. After sleeping on it, CGT officials realized there was no magic to naming the world's greatest passenger liner after a decreased French politician of no special merit.

To placate Doumer's disappointed widow, a new China-route tea-trade ship was named after her husband. And to placate all of those who had suggested names, CGT officials announced that henceforth all French transatlantic *paquebots* (passenger ships) would be named after French provinces.

On October 19, just ten days before launch, with the official approval of French Premier Edouard Herriot, CGT announced that its marvelous new ship would be called *Normandie*, which, by happy coincidence (if that's what it was), was the very province represented in Parliament by William Bertrand, Minister of the French Merchant Marine.

The name was well received. For one thing, Normandy was typically French—a province of ancient towns of stone-and-timber two-story homes, of farms just large enough to support a single family, of apple orchards and herds of cattle and sheep.

The province was distinctive, too, for its world-renowned resorts at Deauville and Trouville, the beauty of its Gothic cathedrals at Rouen, Chartres, Amiens, Caen and Lisieux, and of the medieval tapestry at Bayeux.

In addition, the name echoed with historical significance. It was in Rouen, in front of the great clock, now four centuries old, that Jeanne d'Arc had made the ultimate sacrifice. It was to Normandy that the King of England, Henry II, had come to atone for the murder of Thomas à Becket.

Finally, Normandy was the home of William the Conquerer, the man who led a band of Normans across the Channel in 1066 and conquered England. Nothing could have delighted the French more than to hint at this event in the name of a ship, particularly a ship superior to anything the British had ever built.

But there was one problem with the name, and it was one with which the French were not unfamiliar: should the ship be called *La Normandie* (because the province has a feminine gender) or *Le Normandie* (because in France all ships take the masculine gender)?

Perhaps because of the Americans, and their fondness for calling ships "she," CGT and the Minister of the Merchant Marine insisted the ship be known as *La Normandie*. They even enlisted the support of a member of the prestigious French Academy, Abel Hermant.

But the *French Journal of the Merchant Marine*, the sailors' and shipbuilders' magazine, opposed the idea. "All ships," it wrote, "no matter what their names may be, are masculine in France. In spite of all the official circulars and all the grammarians of France, never can we be forced to say anything but *Le Normandie*."

A solution of sorts was found. The ship would be neither *La* or *Le*, but, quite simply, *Normandie*. That is how Edmond Lanier, later CGT chief, who began his career aboard her, refers to her in his company history, and that is how she shall be referred to here. Despite her size and power, *Normandie* was every inch a female.

In the fall of 1932 nobody in St. Nazaire, or in Brittany, or almost anywhere else in France could resist discussing the approaching launch of their glorious *Normandie*. Elsewhere, the world was proceeding as usual.

Well, not quite as usual.

In the United States the Dow Jones average had hit rock bottom: 41.22. And wages had fallen to their lowest level—$17 a week, on average. Thirteen million Americans were unemployed.

In England and Europe the situation was almost as bad.

Germany, in deep financial trouble, had defaulted on its reparations payments. That sent Britain and France reeling, since they were using that money to pay off their American war debts. The effect on U.S. banks was equally grim.

The depression was at its most severe. Passenger-ship traffic was hurt as badly as any other enterprise. Now, once-crowded liners routinely crossed the Atlantic less than half full. More than a fifth of the world's ocean-going vessels lay idle in port.

In the United States, FDR, campaigning for President, was promising voters a New Deal, while Hoover was offering a chicken in every pot. In Germany, Hitler was running against Paul von Hindenburg for state president.

At St. Nazaire the *Normandie* launch countdown continued.

On October 22, a week before launch, the last of the scaffolding was removed and *Normandie* finally stood fully revealed, an overwhelming spectacle even to those who had for twenty-one months watched her rise from the building-berth floor plate by plate and rib by rib.

See's men continued their greasing operations, removing keel blocks as they went. Four days before launch, only 153 oak blocks, supplemented by 22 large supporting sand blocks and 58 smaller sand blocks, remained in place beneath the hull.

Three days before launch, carpenters completed their work on the narrow, elevated VIP platform which led to the base of the bow.

According to See's timetable, all was on schedule. Then, two days before launch, the entire enterprise was threatened.

The cause was innocent enough. It was wind—a howling, buffeting, shrieking wind that whipped the Loire into an angry froth and sent huge waves crashing against the slipway.

The ship wasn't in any danger so long as she stayed where she was. But to launch her into these turbulent waters, to let gale-strength gusts slam against her slablike hull at her most unstable moment, was a gamble See and his superiors weren't willing to take.

If *Normandie* couldn't be launched on October 29, it would be six months before another attempt could be made, since there were but two days every year when the tides were at their high-est, when the water level in Penhoet basin was deepest and launch was safest.

A six-month delay might not sound crucial, but it was. In bad times like these it might have been enough to scuttle the entire project, since it would have delayed *Normandie*'s maiden voyage by at least that period, along with the first payment on her incredible cost, very likely causing Parliament to back out of the project entirely.

Wind or no wind, See's workers hammered loose another twenty-eight keel blocks that day, further weakening *Norman-die*'s link with land. There was nothing else to be done. Other workers rehearsed launch-day procedures, practicing every step.

Back in Paris at the CGT offices, the public-relations staff had a different sort of problem. Some bright young man had de-cided that the world's largest ship should be christened with nothing less than the world's largest bottle of champagne.

So, a double jeroboam (or eight-bottle bottle, known as a nebuchadnezzar in wine circles) had been duly ordered and filled. Then an older and wiser head realized that it would not be a circus strongman who swung the champagne bottle, but Ma-dame Lebrun, the wife of the French president—and a dimin-utive lady at that. Fearing she'd have trouble swinging the mon-strous bottle or that it might spray her with glass as it shattered against the steel hull, the senior CGT public-relations man can-celed the nebuchadnezzar and ordered instead a single jero-boam, or four-bottle bottle, a stock size.

He was about to dispatch this entirely adequate bottle to St. Nazaire on the special train from Paris, the very one that would carry President Lebrun and his wife, when the office genealogist pointed out that Madame Lebrun was related to the great cham-pagne-making Pommery-Greno family and the jeroboam was clearly labeled "Paul Bernard *brut*."

By this time the official party was clambering aboard the special train, orchids were being presented and the President had donned his official top hat. CGT sent a runner to the corner wine store and he came back with a magnum, a measly two-bottle bottle of something or other.

The senior CGT man tucked this final offering under his arm and left to board the special train.

The day before launch the winds blew unabated. Still the work continued. See's workmen took out another fifty-six keel blocks, leaving just sixty-nine in place, plus the salt bags, which, when ripped open, could be removed in moments.

At the same time dignitaries and common folk streamed into St. Nazaire by the thousands, from all directions, until there wasn't a vacant room in a hotel or boardinghouse within fifty miles. But not one in a hundred of them realized that their trip might be for naught, that if the winds continued, the ship would not be launched, that it might never even carry passengers.

See was up before dawn the next morning. One look out of his bedroom window told him what he wanted to know: October 29, 1932, was gray. And cold. But there was no movement in the trees. If anything, it was almost unnaturally still. If the weather held, there would be a launch today, at 3:15 in the afternoon.

At 6:00 a.m. work began again. Wielding mammoth wooden mallets, See's launch team attacked the remaining oak keel blocks. By 9:30 a.m. only forty remained underneath the ship. By 11:00 a.m. *Normandie* rested on eighty bags of sand, nothing more.

Madame Lebrun and her husband, Monsieur le Président, arrived on their special train at 9:30 that morning. They were met by CGT's and Penhoet's highest officials. They inspected a marine guard, toured the town by car, then came to the shipyard. At 11:45 they and 500 assorted guests sat down to a ceremonial lunch. The meal was followed by a series of speeches.

Last to speak was President Lebrun. In comparison to this masterpiece, this "super, floating cathedral," he said, all of CGT's earlier ships seemed archaic. He also insisted that, while there were too many ships idle in port, better times would come and "in the great international movement of travelers which united Europe and North America," *Normandie* would take a high place.

While the dignitaries were listening to speeches, See scanned the skies. The weather was still holding and, as predicted, the tide was beginning to rise. Working according to plan, his men began ripping open the sand bags beneath the keel and dragging them away, starting at the extreme aft end of the ship and following the rising tide toward the bow.

On the ground beside the slipway Madame Lebrun and her coterie of dignitaries were met by a priest and a handful of choir boys dressed in white and shepherded by a pair of choirmasters.

Together they paraded around the ways, the Lebruns gazing at the massive black hull rising above them, their faces filled with awe and trepidation. The priest, reinforced by his little choir, blessed the ship and the enterprise.

Standing in the midst of the crowd, the editor of *Shipbuilding and Shipping Record*, one of Britain's leading maritime journals, took in the scene with jaundiced eyes. He was thoroughly miserable.

In front of him loomed a ship the likes of which he had never beheld. She was even larger than hull 534, which lay rusting on the banks of the Clyde. Furthermore, she was streamlined to an incredible degree, with a graceful, curving bow that made her look more like a clipper ship than an ocean liner.

High above, the editor could see several men on her main deck—there, he knew, to ride the ship down the ways and into the basin, to help the tugs take hold of her. He could hear the sound of banging and hammering echoing beneath her, a sure sign that the launch procedures were well under way.

To either side of the ship, every square inch of the berth swarmed with people, from the head of the slipway almost to the water's edge. Some spectators were standing practically beneath the bilge keels.

Below the ship, the editor noted, a band lackadaisically played patriotic airs and popular songs. Souvenir hawkers worked the crowds with great skill, dispensing postcards, toy ships and pennants. Out in the bay a tugboat flotilla anxiously awaited its charge. A covey of fishing boats and sailboats hovered nearby, close enough to get a good view but not close enough to risk being swamped.

The editor, eyeing all of this, pulled his notebook from his pocket and began to make a rough draft of the article he planned to print in the November 3 issue of his magazine:

The distinction of launching the first ship over 1,000 feet long has not fallen to the greatest maritime nation in the world. This is not because British naval architects are incapable of designing a ship of these dimensions. It is not even because in this country, a British shipping line has lacked enterprise in ordering a vessel of such size. It is because the governments of other nations realize that in the creation and maintenance of maritime supremacy, they must lend a helping hand.

See, supervising the removal of the sand bags from beneath the keel, checked his watch. It was 1:00, two hours and fifteen minutes until launch. Everything was going exactly according to schedule. All was well. At that moment, however, he felt a gust of wind. Then there was another gust and another. Thick, dark clouds were rolling in. See looked at the river. The tide was moving in much more quickly than he'd anticipated. Suddenly the launch seemed chancy again.

Madame Lebrun, her husband and the other high officials had nearly completed their circuit of the ways when André See approached the group, took Penhoet President René Fould aside and whispered a few words to him. Fould consulted some of the other gentlemen. They reached agreement and informed Monsieur See of their decision: Don't wait for high tide. Don't wait for the winds to pick up and make it all impossible. Launch! Launch *Normandie* now, as quickly as possible.

In the crowd the editor continued to write. 'We are sorry,' he scribbled, to have to obtrude these despairing reflections during a moment of the triumphal entry of France as the great pioneer of the great ship. We are more sorry than ever to have to do so because we were an honoured guest at the historic ceremony which witnessed at St. Nazaire last Saturday the graceful sliding into the water of the Normandie. *We hope, therefore, in giving expression to a sense of national humiliation, our very generous hosts on that occasion will forgive us for expressing the acuteness of our feelings as we saw this wonderful ship make the first momentous stage of her entry as the Queen of the North Atlantic.*

Underneath the ship See exhorted his men to their utmost. By 2:15 p.m.—twenty-five minutes ahead of schedule—there were only three large sand bags left under the keel, and these at the extreme forward end. By 2:30 there were none. At that point the eight huge traveling cranes were run up to the top of the ways, leaving the berth open.

At the same moment other workers, swinging huge battering rams, hammered out the shoring timbers one by one, laying them beside the ways. That operation was completed by 2:35 p.m.—again, twenty-five minutes ahead of schedule.

Now Madame Lebrun and her party ascended the stairs to the ceremonial platform that abutted *Normandie's* bow, passing slowly along the walls of bunting so that the crowd would have ample time to cheer.

At 2:40 See's workers swarmed over the oaken dog shores and hammered and pounded them loose from between cradle and ways.

A few minutes later See gave the signal to empty the salt bags. A torrent of water flowed through them, and in less than a minute they were flat.

Now the wooden cabinetry beneath the ship began to creak and moan. Only four hydraulic triggers held the massive vessel in check, and then just barely.

At this instant See gave the launching signal. Below the ship the band struck up "La Marseillaise."

On the ceremonial platform Madame Lebrun stepped forward, grasped the magnum of champagne hanging from the ship's bow, drew it back with both hands and flung it against *Normandie's* hull with all of her strength. It shattered nicely, sending a spray of champagne over the vessel's bulbous tip.

"I baptize thee *Normandie*," she cried in a thin, reedy voice. And she blew the ship a kiss.

Underneath the hull the four hydraulic triggers fell out of their slots with a tremendous crash. Now nothing held the ship, nothing at all except habit. Would she move? See's hand was on the lever of the hydraulic rams, ready to give a push if necessary.

No push was necessary.

Freed of the restraints that had kept her on dry land, *Normandie* began to move, gently gliding toward the water, riding on her oaken cradle, backing out of the concrete parking place on which she'd been built, her enormous mass rumbling over the wooden slipway, the ways shuddering, crackling and screeching as if they might collapse at any moment.

Majestically, inexorably, she moved seaward, toward her natural medium, at the leisurely rate of 10 knots, 200,000 pairs of eyes hypnotized by her progress, 200,000 voices cheering her on, just as the Cape Kennedy crowd would urge Apollo missions to "Go! Go! Go!" thirty-seven years later.

After traveling 544 feet down the ways, *Normandie* reached her first dangerous transition, the pivot point, the moment when her aft end, her rudder, her propeller bossings, her stern began to float.

This put terrible pressure on her midships to bend, to fold up. But that did not happen. It also put a great strain on the wooden cradle, which now had to bear most of the ship's weight and keep her erect. It performed as planned.

It was now that *Normandie*'s hull penetrated the water to its greatest depth—49.2 feet, 13 feet beyond her normal draft. At that instant her hull came within 3.9 feet of the dredged-out channel, exactly as See had planned.

Normandie's next transition came 465 feet later, when she'd slid a total of 1,009 feet down the ways. It was now that she found herself fully afloat for the first time, a land creature no longer. It was also now that she was at her least stable. But she never wavered.

Some of the cheering crowd raced after the ship to the very

edge of the water. They did not realize that as *Normandie* slipped past the edge of her launching berth, she'd generate an enormous wave, a wave that would head shoreward with all the force of a class-ten roller at Waikiki.

All the while the ship continued into the basin, toward the flotilla of whistling and tooting tugboats. Some 656 feet later the four twenty-five-ton piles of drag chains that had been lying passively near the head of the ways suddenly came alive, like the broomsticks in *Fantasia*. Hissing and clanking across the sandy ground beside the ways, they chased after *Normandie* as though furious at being left behind.

They were to bring the massive hull to a quick, almost abrupt halt so waiting tugs could take charge. But they did not perform as expected. After only a few yards of travel the port chains popped a link and collapsed in a heap.

Normandie might have careened across the river as a result. But fate was on her side. Instead of floating loose, she came to a halt 985 feet later, in midriver, almost exactly as planned. She'd been stopped by the starboard chains and the fast-moving tidal current.

The entire trip had taken seventy-five seconds, less time than the Kentucky Derby.

At this moment the launch wave came flooding into the berth, swamping dozens of spectators, sending some well-dressed gentlemen clambering onto the shoulders of braver friends, dumping others into the drink, leaving them to struggle landward in water up to their chests.

Briefly it looked as though *Normandie*'s birth might be accompanied by tragedy. But the wave receded, leaving those who'd come too close merely sopping and bedraggled, everything intact but their dignity.

Back in Paris, the CGT's office genealogist and the bright young PR man, both of whom had been left behind to mind the store, had invited everyone in the building to come down, pull up a chair near the steam heat and join them in listening to the launching ceremonies on the radio. Once the launch was successfully concluded, the jeroboam of Paul Bernard was duly produced, the cork popped and a round of toasts begun, to *Normandie*, to CGT, to Madame Lebrun and, most of all, to France.

In the bay, tugboats sidled up to *Normandie*, their crews heaved lines to the men who'd ridden her down the ways and she was made fast. Seven minutes after See's launching signal the ship was firmly in hand and under tow.

It would be two and a half years before the new ship was ready for passengers, before her powerful engines were ready to propel her across the Atlantic, before her gorgeous staterooms, dining rooms and lounges were ready to accept the rich and famous. But the uncertainty of her birth was over. There was a new ship in the world, the largest moving object mankind had ever created. Her name was *Normandie*.

2

SETTING THE STAGE

Normandie was not an orphan. She came from a long line of passenger ships large and small, fast and slow, plain and fancy. She was, in fact, the culmination of that line, its finest expression.

Before the age of steam, transatlantic travel was slow, dangerous and uncomfortable. Packet companies did operate fleets of sailing ships, but schedules were irregular, thanks to the whims of wind and weather.

The steam engine promised to change all this. It offered the hope of regular schedules, faster, safer, more comfortable voyages and higher profits to shipowners. It offered a certain amount of freedom from the vagaries of nature.

Once steamships were reliable enough to provide regular transatlantic service—and large and fast enough to be profitable—steamship lines sprang up by the dozen in every country with a port on the North Atlantic.

These companies included most of the steamship lines that would play a part in *Normandie*'s history: Cunard (founded in 1840), Hamburg-Amerika Line (1856), North German Lloyd (1858), Compagnie Générale Transatlantique (1864) and White Star Line (1871).

Fortunately for steamships, their birth coincided almost exactly with the European potato famine. As a result, between 1840 and 1850 they found themselves sharing the unexpected bounty of 1.7 million passengers bound for the United States, the first great wave of immigrants to head for American shores.

Thus began the union of steamship and immigrant, a symbiosis destined to last for eighty years, providing transportation to the promised land for one, and profits and almost a *raison d'être* for the other.

As the years went by and as each line tried to outdo its competition, ocean liners steadily evolved into larger, faster, more luxurious, more comfortable and more beautiful vessels inside and out. Their engines were also changing, gaining in sophistication and efficiency.

When screw propellers and compound engines gained sway, with their advantages of reduced fuel costs and larger passenger quarters or cargo capacity, steamships became the dominant force on the Atlantic. They could cross it in either direction in ten days or less. They could keep to fairly strict schedules. They were distinctly safer, more reliable and more comfortable than their wind-driven competition.

These ships made possible the greatest mass migration the world has ever seen. They brought to America from Europe an average of a quarter of a million people a year during the mid-nineteenth century and even more in later years.

By the turn of the century, passenger liners, equipped with even more efficient turbine engines, were an important part of almost everyone's life either as a means of passenger transport or through the cargo they carried. At about this time an American decided to get into the steamship business, one of the few to exhibit a commercial interest. And this wasn't just any American—it was J. P. Morgan, the great financier, consolidator of the nation's railroads, creator of U.S. Steel.

In the early 1900s Morgan's International Merchant Marine (IMM) bought six shipping lines and concluded trade agreements with two more, the major German lines: Hamburg-Amerika and North German Lloyd. That left only two important steamship lines outside the IMM fold—Cunard and Compagnie Générale Transatlantique.

To the horror of the British government, Morgan had also

approached Cunard. The oldest and largest of all British steamship lines seemed about to be sold to an American. If that happened, it would leave "the world's greatest seafaring nation" without a single major steamship company.

Money solved the problem. The British government loaned Cunard 2.6 million pounds sterling so it would remain British-owned and build two new steamships to compete with Morgan's mighty IMM.

The names of these ships are still legendary. They were the *Lusitania* and the *Mauretania*. Cunard intended them to be so large, so fast and so incredibly beautiful and luxurious that it would take years for the competition to catch up. It was a familiar shipowner's goal, but this time Cunard was uniquely situated to achieve it.

First, it had that huge government loan. Second, it had a revolutionary power plant developed by a British inventor—the highly efficient turbine engine.

The resulting ships were astonishing. To begin with, they were 30 percent larger than any other existing passenger ship. The *Mauretania*, fractionally larger than her sister, measured 790 feet long and 88 feet wide. The entire Liverpool dock area had to be dredged to make room for her and the *Lusitania*.

In addition, the two ships were 75 percent more powerful than any previous ocean liner. The *Mauretania*, whose engines were slightly stronger than her sister's, developed 78,000 shaft horsepower (SHP)—an unheard-of output. Both were designed to cross the Atlantic at speeds of up to 24.5 knots, a full knot faster than previous record-holders.

Naturally, Cunard did not neglect the interiors of this fabulous pair. Each was decorated in a wildly eclectic variety of period styles.

The *Mauretania* had a library decorated in the style of Louis XVI, a main lounge and ballroom out of eighteenth-century France, a main dining room in the style of François I, a smoking room that might have existed in fifteenth-century Italy and a Verandah Café modeled after the Old English Orangery at Hampton Court.

Their exteriors were equally beautiful and much less a hodgepodge. They had knife-edge bows, counter sterns, four raked funnels and, in the case of the *Mauretania*, rows of cowled ventilators to provide fresh air below decks.

But two men were determined not to let Cunard and its new ships dominate the Atlantic unchallenged. They were J. Bruce Ismay, president of the White Star Line (part of Morgan's combine), and Albert Ballin, guiding genius of the Hamburg-Amerika Line.

Neither man was willing to surrender to Cunard the lion's share of the transatlantic trade, which in 1907 was greater than ever. Not only were there more wealthy travelers, but there were also more U.S.-bound immigrants, almost 1.3 million in that year alone. Ismay and Ballin both decided instead, quite independently of each other, to build not just two but three first-rate ships so they could offer weekly service to New York.

Ismay, with Morgan's backing, began immediately to plan his three ships: the *Olympic*, the *Titanic* and the *Britannic* (some say the original name was the *Gigantic*). Naturally, each of Ismay's three ships had to be larger than the *Lusitania* and the *Mauretania*, and they were almost 100 feet longer, a full 5 feet wider, with 30 percent greater gross tonnage. They were not, however, faster or even as fast. Ismay instead chose to emphasize comfort and decor.

In this great game of can-you-top-this, a winner emerged— Hamburg-Amerika Line and its brilliant chairman, Albert Ballin. In the years 1912, 1913 and 1914 he managed to launch a new ship every year. And each of these ships, successively, was the largest in the world.

They were the *Imperator*, the *Vaterland* and the *Bismarck*. The *Imperator*, the first ship to surpass 900 feet in length, measured 909 feet from stem to sterm, or more than three times the length of a football field.

Built with the immigrant trade in mind, at least on the lower decks the *Imperator*'s capacity was enormous. She could carry 1,772 in steerage and just under 1,000 in first class, second class and third class.

Ballin's second ship, the *Vaterland*, was forty feet longer than the *Imperator*, and his third, the *Bismarck*, was eight feet longer than the *Vaterland*.

Keeping a close eye on the competition, Cunard decided to add a third ship to the *Lusitania* and *Mauretania*, so that it, too, could offer weekly service to New York. It built the *Aquitania*, a ship slightly smaller than the *Imperator*, but with lines so graceful and flowing that she was immediately adjudged one of the most beautiful ships on the Atlantic.

"No other shipping route in the world has ever spawned such extravagances or such follies," wrote one marine historian. "Where else have ships had Byzantine chapels or Pompeiian swimming pools, dining rooms styled like the palace of Versailles, lounges decorated in mock Inigo Jones and Turkish baths like Eastern harems?"

The lifetimes of these ships, for the most part, overlapped *Normandie's*. They were her companions and her competitors.

In 1912, a serious new player entered the game: France, represented by Compagnie Générale Transatlantique. CGT had been plying the Atlantic for decades, but with ships that, for all their considerable elegance, couldn't match the size and speed of the British and German vessels.

Now, however, CGT put a truly first-rate ship into service. She was the *France*, a graceful, turbine-driven four-stacker. She wasn't a particularly large ship, but apart from the *Mauretania* and the *Lusitania* she was the Atlantic's fastest vessel. On one occasion she made the Le Havre–New York run in just 5 days and 17 hours.

The French government was so pleased with the *France* that it offered CGT a huge contract to carry mail—and an enormous government subsidy so it could build three more vessels. This was the initial inspiration for *Normandie*. Construction on the first of the new ships, the *Paris*, began in 1913. But it was interrupted, and her projected sister ships were put off by the onset of the Great War.

The outbreak of war caught both sides by surprise. The *Mauretania* and the *Olympic* were at sea, heading for New York. And dozens of German vessels were caught in American ports, among them Ballin's latest world-beater, the *Vaterland*.

Because of British warships, most of these German ships were trapped in the then neutral United States. But British liners were freely able to return home. A few, in fact, continued to make the North Atlantic run, transporting civilians to their respective homes on either side of the ocean. Among these was the *Lusitania*.

On May 8, 1915, a German submarine torpedoed the *Lusitania* off the Irish coast. She sank in twenty minutes. Some 1,200 men, women and children died, many of them Americans. That brought America a giant step closer to war.

By the war's end, transatlantic shipping had been transformed. The German merchant marine had ceased to exist, having surrendered all of its major units to the Allies.

The U.S. was awarded the *Vaterland* (renamed the *Leviathan*). A young naval architect by the name of William Francis Gibbs, who figures prominently in *Normandie*'s story, was given the job of changing the *Leviathan* from the U.S. troopship she was during the war into a modern liner suited to fly the American flag.

Cunard ended up with the *Imperator*. The company renamed her the *Berengaria* and immediately set about obliterating all traces of her Germanic origins. She was deemed compensation for the lost *Lusitania*.

The emerging postwar world was one deeply in debt—crushing, suffocating debt. Germany owed billions to France and England in war reparations. And France and England owed billions to the United States, which had financed their war efforts.

England and France had planned to use German payments to satisfy their American debts. But where was Germany to get the money to pay her debts? The answer was obvious and, given hindsight, ridiculous. American banks would lend it to her, out of the monies repaid them by France and England.

During the 1920s, then, the billions went round and round, everyone taking his cut with each revolution.

A second aspect of the postwar world was its profound fear of new armed conflict. This impulse was responsible for the League of Nations, the Washington Naval Conference (which limited the size of national navies), the Locarno Pact (in which the former combatants guaranteed peace in Western Europe) and the Kellogg-Briand Treaty (in which sixty-two of the world's largest and most important nations agreed to "outlaw war").

The United States made clear its loathing for war by edging toward isolationism. This expressed itself in at least two ways: (1) the rejection of membership in the League of Nations and (2) the Emergency Quota Act of 1921, commonly known as the "Three Percent Act." This limited immigration from any one foreign country to no more than 3 percent of the former nationals of that country living in the U.S. as of 1903, according to the census.

The Three Percent Act slammed the gates shut, the same gates that had admitted more than 35 million immigrants into the United States in the century between 1820 and 1920, and more than a million in 1913 alone, the last full year before the Great War. It also dissolved forever the symbiosis between immigrant and steamship, leaving shipowners with fleets of cavernous vessels and no one to fill them.

As if the Three Percent Act hadn't dealt a sufficiently heavy blow to the steamship companies, the tide of wealthy travelers was also at a low ebb in the years immediately following the war. The result: Total transatlantic passenger traffic was off by two thirds in 1924, compared with prewar figures.

There was a single ember of hope for the Atlantic ferry, however. And in the 1920s steamship companies fanned it so furiously that it eventually caught fire and enabled them to completely re-create the transatlantic travel business, even to expand it. Its name: tourism.

Following World War I, there was a surge of American interest in Europe, partly as a result of the war, as seen from afar, partly because more than two million American soldiers had visited the place and returned to regale friends and relatives with tempting stories about their Old Country adventures.

It didn't take steamship lines long to detect and exploit this new American urge, which cut across almost all social and economic classes. One by one, they sent their great liners into dry dock, where the dormitories and eating halls of steerage were refitted with decent, if modest, cabin accommodations and renamed "tourist third" or "tourist cabin."

The object was to attract the great American middle class—teachers, students, small businessmen, factory foremen, traveling salesmen, the newly widowed, veterans and their families, etc.

While tourism was the salvation of many a steamship company, it didn't quite fill ships or produce profits with the efficiency of mass immigration. For this reason steamship lines desperately sought ways to cut costs. What they found was the next major advance in ocean transport: oil fuel.

Actually, shipowners had started experimenting with oil as far back as 1870. But it had taken a world war to perfect the technology and to prove its efficiency and economy. It wasn't so much that oil was cheaper than coal. That varied, according to the supply of each. It was that oil-fired engines didn't need "black gangs"—the begrimed stokers who shoved coal into ship boilers. That permitted enormous crew reductions—in some cases, a third of the total number. (For instance, 403 members of the coal-fired *Vaterland*'s 1,234-member crew had been stokers.)

So, while the carpenters were installing tourist cabins on the upper decks, engineers were installing oil-fuel plumbing below. The conversion process took ships out of service for about eight months, but it was worth it. With business still slack, they were hardly missed. And when they reappeared, they'd been transformed.

Well, not completely.

Given their heavy, period decor, their paucity of bathrooms and their built-in class-consciousness, these old ships no longer fit the temper of the times. But, given the state of Atlantic passenger trade, steamship lines were reluctant to risk building new, more modern tonnage. There was one exception: Compagnie Générale Transatlantique.

When other lines were wondering about the viability of their largest and fastest ships, CGT decided to build a new vessel. She was the *Ile de France*, a ship of 43,000 gross tons and a designed speed of 23.5 to 24 knots (very slightly smaller and slower than *Aquitania*).

But the *Ile* was not distinguished by her size or speed. Four other qualities made her noteworthy: (1) she was the first major ship of the postwar era, (2) she was the first passenger ship *built* to burn oil, (3) she was the first liner *built* from the start to appeal to the tourist trade and (4) she was the first ocean liner designed not as a museum of ancient styles of interior decoration, but as a showcase of the best in modern decor.

When the *Ile de France* entered service on June 22, 1927, every other passenger liner suddenly seemed obsolete. She was an instant hit, not only with the tourist trade but also with the wealthy and glamorous.

As a result, at White Star, at Cunard, at Navigazione Generale Italiana, at Lloyd Saubado, at Flotta Riunite (all three Italian), at Compagnie Générale Transatlantique and even at North German Lloyd, committees were set up to plan new transatlantic liners.

Surprisingly enough, the first off the mark were the Germans. Even before the *Ile* was launched, North German Lloyd had decided to build two new major ocean liners. With these ships it hoped to leapfrog everyone else, making Germany once more the leader in transatlantic transportation.

The ships were the *Bremen* and the *Europa*. Laid down only a few weeks after the *Ile*'s maiden voyage, they were surely two of the most interesting vessels ever built.

Though both were slightly smaller than the prewar *Imperator-Vaterland-Bismarck* trio, they were the fastest passenger ships ever built. Their owner considered their speed a necessity, since NGL wanted to use them to provide weekly service between Bremerhaven and New York. This meant each had to cross the Atlantic, refuel, reprovision, reload and cast off all within seven days.

In the 1870s weekly service between Bremerhaven and New York had required five ships. Around the turn of the century four ships could do it. As World War I approached, that figure dropped to three. That NGL now thought two ships were enough was a measure of how far liner technology had come and of how much it expected from the *Bremen* and the *Europa*.

The two new German ships, built when German money was practically worthless and financed with American loans, were an almost complete break with the past, from the standpoint of decor. As one writer put it, "There were no longer any Louis XVI rooms, no rococo halls and no English country home style."

What there was, instead, was the geometric sterility of the Bauhaus, with mosaics and tapestries, it was said, on the level of calendar art, and an illuminated fountain in the middle of the dance floor that changed colors while couples in formal wear danced to the tune of "Yes Sir, That's My Baby."

Externally, the *Bremen* and the *Europa* were also revolutionary. Instead of presenting the traditional knife edge to the water, they had slightly raked bows, each with an extraordinary, illogical protrusion at the tip, below the waterline—a "bulbous forefoot," it was called, an innovation that tank tests had proven would decrease water resistance.

The German superliners were not beautiful. They both had a pair of squat, stumpy-looking funnels, a certain oval chunkiness amidships and a rounded bridge that tantalizingly hinted at streamlining. The overall impression was one of power.

And power they had aplenty—130,000 horsepower for the *Europa*, 135,000 for the *Bremen*. The then current holder of the Blue Ribbon, the symbol of transatlantic speed supremacy, was the *Mauretania*, with but 78,000 horsepower. It is no wonder, then, that each of the two new German ships, in turn, won the mythical Blue Ribbon on her maiden voyage.

In the first complete year for the two ships, each carried twice as many passengers as any other ship at sea—and more than three times as many as three of the most popular ships of the mid-1920s, the *Berengaria*, the *Mauretania* and the *Olympic*.

How could the other companies counter a breakthrough such as these two new German liners? How could they surpass vessels that represented, in every particular, state-of-the-art technology and design? Was it possible, in the face of such a spectacular advance, to trump it immediately with yet another?

For decades marine engineers, naval architects and steamship owners had nurtured a dream, a vision bordering on the inconceivable. They had imagined an ocean liner 1,000 feet long, a monstrous ship capable of carrying at least 3,000 people across the Atlantic in less than four days, at an average speed of 30 knots (34.5 miles an hour) or more. For the shipping world, this was tantamount to running the four-minute mile, breaking the sound barrier and landing a man on the moon simultaneously.

But for several reasons the 1,000-foot ship seemed unattainable:

1. *The power plant.* In terms of speed, the difference between a 28-knot ship, say, and a 30-knot ship was only 7 percent. But to achieve that slight extra speed the 30-knot ship's engines had to be 30 percent larger than those of the 28-knot ship—much bigger than any marine engine ever built. Could the turbine still do the job?

2. *The cost.* Cunard had been forced to ask the British government for help in order to build the *Lusitania* and the *Mauretania*, both 200 feet smaller and 4 knots slower than the dream ship. What steamship line, by itself, could afford to build the liner they all dreamed of?

3. *The construction.* The previous giants of the North Atlantic had apparently stretched shipbuilding facilities and technology to the limits. Could larger parts be cast? Could greater forgings be made? Could cranes lift them into place? Were berths strong enough to support the additional weight?

4. *The docking facilities.* Even if such a ship could be built and launched, there was nowhere on earth it could be docked. To be sure, piers had been extended again and again over the years, to accommodate larger and larger ships. But would New York, Southampton, Le Havre or Bremen be willing to go through the expense all over again to accommodate another country's ship?

Assuming all of these problems could be solved, building a 1,000-foot, 30-knot ship still entailed risks of enormous magnitude, since the steamship line that built it would very likely be putting all of its eggs in this one basket.

So far as can be determined, the first person to propose such a ship seriously was William Francis Gibbs, the same American naval architect who rebuilt the *Leviathan* after World War I and who, after World War II, created the remarkable *United States*.

In 1908 and 1909, when he was scarcely out of college, Gibbs dreamed up the idea of building two transatlantic liners, each with an overall length of 1,000 feet and a beam of 106 feet. Such a pair, he thought, would put the U.S. in the forefront of Atlantic shipping.

He took the notion first to the Navy, then to P. A. S. Franklin, head of Morgan's IMM steamship combine, then to Morgan himself. That great financier was so impressed with the earnest young man that in 1916 he put up the money to have plans drawn up and models tested. But the war killed the scheme.

The idea of a 1,000-foot liner was revived again in 1928 by Lord Kylsant, head of the reorganized White Star Line, now once more under British ownership. Though his company was in deep financial trouble, he ordered a "super-*Olympic*" on June 19, 1928. His ship, according to *Ill-Fated Liners*, by Richard de Kerbrech and David Williams, was to be 1,000 feet long, with a beam of 120 feet and a service speed of 30 knots. It was to be called the *Oceanic*.

But Lord Kylsant's ship wasn't the only 1,000-footer on the drawing boards. Faced with the same problem—the *Bremen* and the *Europa*—Cunard and Compagnie Générale Transatlantique had come up with the same solution. Impossible or not, they, too, would build 1,000-foot, 30-knot ships. Cunard would eventually call its ship the *Queen Mary*. And CGT's would be named *Normandie*.

3

THE UNLIKELY PARTNERSHIP

Although *Normandie* wasn't launched until October 1932, her beginnings date back to the mail contract Compagnie Générale Transatlantique and the French government signed in 1912.

This contract, in return for mail subsidies, required CGT to build four new vessels, one in 1916 or before, the second by 1921, the third by 1926 and the fourth by or before 1932. It also required that these vessels be the equals—better yet, the superiors—of any North Atlantic ship.

CGT did its best to meet this obligation. In 1913 it laid down the keel of the *Paris*, 10,000 tons larger than its former flagship, the *France*, whose career had begun only a year before.

But the outbreak of the Great War brought the *Paris'* construction to a halt. The company was not able to complete her until 1921, which was just as well, since she then was able to become the first modern postwar liner.

Recognizing the new postwar world, France amended her mail contract with CGT, allowing the steamship line to build only two more ships, not the three originally scheduled. One was to go into service no later than the summer of 1927, the other not later than the summer of 1932.

So in 1925 CGT began work on the first of this pair, the *Ile de France*. She, too, was 10,000 tons larger than her predecessor, the *Paris*, and was the largest ship that could easily be constructed at the Penhoet shipyard at St. Nazaire, where all major CGT vessels were built.

With the *Ile*, far more was involved than fulfilling a mail contract. Building her was also a matter of pride. CGT— and France—were tired of watching Germany and England contend for transatlantic supremacy and profits.

But by the time the *Ile* went into service on June 22, 1927, CGT officials were worried about the two great new German ships which in slightly more than a month's time would be laid down in Bremen and Hamburg. They were also concerned about the huge ship being planned by Britain's White Star Line.

Across the Channel, the venerable Cunard Line, long accustomed to transatlantic supremacy, was in even worse trouble. Cunard had not built a new ship to meet the *Ile*'s challenge, nor was it doing anything to match the coming German ships and the White Star liner.

Cunard had gotten used to being on top. But its Big Three were old-fashioned and showing signs of wear. They were the ponderous, German-built *Berengaria* (formerly the *Imperator*) of 1912; her British-built equivalent, the *Aquitania*, of 1914; and the Atlantic's elderly speed queen, the *Mauretania*, of 1907.

When the *Ile* was launched in 1927, these three ships were still among the Atlantic's most popular. But their future was not bright, and that was obvious to everyone, especially Cunard, which realized it would have to build two new ships, both larger and faster than the German competition, to regain its transatlantic leadership.

CGT, on the other hand, didn't need two new ships to maintain its competitive position. It already had the *Paris* and the *Ile de France*, both postwar, both modern, although neither large enough or fast enough to conduct a two-ship weekly service. What CGT needed to challenge the British and the Germans was a third modern ship.

Some CGT officials thought that should be a sister ship to the *Ile*, perhaps a few feet longer and wider. Others, especially CGT's associate managing director, Pierre de Malglaive, wanted to build a ship greater than anything afloat.

At about this time Vladimir Yourkevitch, a forty-two-year-old Russian emigrant to France, an assembly-line worker at a Parisian Renault factory, a short, slight man who rather resembled Charlie Chaplin, picked up a newspaper and read about the great success of the *Ile de France*, which had just completed its first season.

As it happened, Yourkevitch was anything but a typical Renault employee. In Russia he'd been a naval engineer at the Baltic Shipyard in St. Petersburg. In fact, he'd designed eleven Russian submarines between 1910 and 1917.

In 1912 the Baltic Shipyard and the Russian Admiralty were asked to submit competing designs for the new "Borodino class" of super-dreadnaughts—the largest, fastest, most powerful battle cruisers ever conceived. Yourkevitch, instructed to design their hull shape, produced a revolutionary form.

The prow of the ship he designed was its most unusual feature. It curved out over the water like the bow of a clipper ship. Its sides were deeply hollowed out, flaring up to the deck. And it was anything but the backward-sloping stem favored for warships, or even the straight, knife-edge bow of the world's fastest liners. It was beautiful.

Yourkevitch was certain that this shape would help a ship cut through the water more smoothly, either giving it greater speed without an increase in horsepower or maintaining its designed speed with less horsepower and lower fuel consumption.

The Russian Shipping Board thought Yourkevitch's hull shape was ridiculous—too big-bellied around the middle, too pointed at the ends. Besides, the Russian Admiralty had produced a conventional design the Shipping Board liked very much. But the Baltic Shipyard insisted a model of Yourkevitch's design be tested against the Admiralty design.

Two models were run through the experimental tanks at Kronstadt Naval Base. To everyone's astonishment but Yourkevitch's, his design proved far more efficient. It could maintain the required speed—26 knots—with 65,000 horsepower. The conventionally shaped Admiralty model needed 10,000 more.

The Admiralty refused to accept the results. It demanded that the models be tested in the larger, more sophisticated model basin at Bremerhaven. The tests were duly made. Yourkevitch's model won again.

In December 1912 the *Borodino*, the *Ismail*, the *Kinburn* and the *Navarin* were laid down at St. Petersburg, every one of them with a Yourkevitch hull. All four were launched in 1915 and 1916. Then came the Russian revolution. None were ever completed.

Yourkevitch himself fled Russia in 1919 and escaped to Constantinople, where he and some immigrant colleagues set up an auto-repair shop. In 1922, like thousands of other Russian refugees, he found his way to Paris. He gave up all thought of designing ships.

But now, reading about the *Ile*, Yourkevitch's curiosity was aroused. It was sixteen years since he'd developed his revolutionary hull design. Surely it must be in wide use by now, he thought. No doubt the *Ile* had a "Yourkevitch hull," since she was the most modern ship in service.

But, to his surprise, photos of the ship showed no soaring stem, no flaring bow. Instead, her cutwater was straight and knife-edged, her bow only slightly hollowed out. As for her hull, it might have been designed in 1895.

Yourkevitch simply didn't know what to make of this. Had his discovery been ignored? Disproved? Had no one put it to use after all these years? It was puzzling. But perhaps it was also an opportunity.

Meanwhile, Cunard made its decision. On March 28, 1928, the head of Cunard's operations in the United States, Sir Ashley Sparks, wrote to his boss, Sir Thomas Royden: "There should be no limitation on the type of ship we are to build," he said, "or we shall simply play into the hands of the Germans, Frenchmen, Dutchmen, Americans or whoever can build better."

Accordingly, Sir Thomas and his board ordered a preliminary design for a superliner—for the biggest ship the world had ever seen.

At CGT, Pierre de Malglaive had finally manged to convince his timorous colleagues that the company should build nothing less than the world's largest, fastest and most beautiful ocean liner.

But there was one serious obstacle. Penhoet, the shipyard that had built every major CGT ship since the company was founded, simply couldn't construct a vessel much larger than the *Ile de France* without expanding its biggest launching berth and building an entirely new dry dock—truly major undertakings.

CGT took the problem to André Tardieu, the Minister for Public Works, who approached his government. To its credit, the government immediately grasped what such a ship could mean, not only to CGT but also to the present administration and to France itself. It agreed to help.

On March 30, 1928, two days after Sparks wrote to Royden, the French Assembly approved the plan, putting up a first installment of $3.1 million to begin work on the new dry dock.

Once the government had committed itself, CGT's chief engineer, Paul Romano, brought CGT's ship proposal to the French Admiralty, at Grenelle, which designed most French liners, in addition to warships. Design us a ship, he said. Design us the greatest ship men have ever created.

At almost exactly this time the leaders of Germany's Nazi Party were campaigning to win the coming national election, their ranks thinned by the absence of Adolf Hitler, whom the Bavarian courts had forbidden to speak in public until 1929 as a result of his open threats against the state.

Without Hitler, the Nazis made little impact on the voters. In the election of May 30 they polled just 810,000 votes out of a total of 31 million cast. This gave them only a dozen of the Reichstag's 491 seats.

It would have taken a special kind of visionary to realize what a force they would become in the future.

In England the White Star Line began building its superliner, the *Oceanic*. Her first keel plates were riveted into place on June 19 at the Harland & Wolff Shipyard in Belfast, Ireland, where, sixteen years earlier, the *Titanic* had been built.

This new ship, said White Star, would be 1,000 feet long, 60,000 gross registered tons—5,000 more than anything else afloat or building—with the biggest Diesel engines ever installed in a ship, monsters capable of generating 100,000 horsepower.

But Cunard doubted its rival could afford the ship. Wrote Cunard chairman Sir Thomas Royden to his U.S. chief, Sir

Ashley Sparks, "It will put them in a very unhappy position, I think, and go near to financially crippling them."

The Germans, too, were busy building their superliners. And on successive days in August—the 15th and the 16th—they launched them, the *Bremen* and the *Europa*, both over 935 feet long, both about 50,000 GRT, both with a designed speed of 27 knots and a Bauhaus interior as modern as the *Ile's*.

In England, Germany's accomplishment settled the Cunard debate once and for all. Their new superliners must be built as quickly as possible. The Germans must be beaten. Planning went into high gear for the ship that would someday be known as the *Queen Mary*.

The French government reacted differently. It sent Pierre Laval, then Minister of Justice, to talk to German shipping officials about limiting the size and speed of passenger liners. (This was the same Pierre Laval who would head the Vichy French government during World War II and be executed for treason afterward.)

But as Laval negotiated, CGT accelerated its plans for the ship that would someday be known as *Normandie*.

This dichotomy—on one hand, trying to reach an agreement with Germany; on the other, attempting to somehow defeat it—was also reflected in the French foreign policy.

Less than two weeks after the *Bremen* and the *Europa* were launched, sixty-three nations, including France, Germany, Britain, Italy, Japan, the United States and Russia, signed the Kellogg-Briand Pact, which "outlawed" war altogether. But France, the nervous victor of World War I, needed further guarantees. So in 1928 she decided to build a system of defensive fortifications for her eastern border, an act which didn't exactly reflect self-confidence. This system was eventually known as the Maginot Line.

In Paris, Vladimir Yourkevitch's opportunity came even more quickly than he'd hoped. Late in 1928 he heard that Compagnie Générale Transatlantique was planning a huge new ship.

Yourkevitch decided that he was the perfect man to design it. The only question was how to tell CGT.

First, Yourkevitch wrote to Penhoet, briefly describing his accomplishments. He got no response. He sent a wire saying he could make the new ship more efficient than any previous liner. Still no answer. He even called, but without result.

Yourkevitch was undaunted. He contacted an old friend, Rear Admiral S. S. Pogulaiev, former chief of staff of the Russian Black Sea Fleet. Pogulaiev had also emigrated to France after the revolution and he'd been welcomed with open arms. In fact, France had made him an admiral.

Early in 1929 Pogulaiev and Yourkevitch met with Penhoet President René Fould. In broken French, Yourkevitch told the steamship-line official about his work at the Baltic Shipyard and about the battleships he'd designed. Pogulaiev backed him up.

Fould was suspicious. After all, who was this man? A common laborer. While he had actually accomplished something worthwile in Russia, that was in 1912, nearly two decades ago. Besides, the man was a Russian. Everyone knew that French naval architects led the world in marine technology.

But Yourkevitch and his ideas were impressive. Fould promised to study the Russian's papers and discuss them with Penhoet's technical experts.

By this time, however, the French Admiralty's designs for the new CGT ship were well advanced. They were based on the following specifications, which had been drawn up by Penhoet's chief engineer, Monsieur Pinczon:

Length: 902 feet 3 inches on the waterline (overall length: about 960 feet, more than 20 feet longer than the new German ships);

Breadth: 105 feet (compared with the *Bremen*'s 101 and the *Europa*'s 102);

Draft: 36 feet 1 inch. This was almost uncomfortably close to the maximum, given the low-tide depth at St. Nazaire, where the ship would be built, and at Le Havre, Plymouth (or Southampton) and New York, her prospective ports.

These dimensions would make CGT's vessel the world's

largest except for the White Star *Oceanic*. (And CGT didn't know the *Oceanic*'s exact specifications when it drew up its own plans.)

Based on these specifications, the French Admiralty had made preliminary blueprints of several alternate hull shapes. They were now preparing to make models and run them through the test tanks at Grenelle, near Versailles, to choose the most efficient shape.

Suddenly CGT changed its mind, scrapping all previous specifications. It now wanted a larger ship—a considerably larger ship, with a waterline length of 951 feet 5 inches and a beam of 111 feet 7 inches. (The draft, out of necessity, remained the same.)

Why the change?

The official documents insist it was caused by a "more detailed study of the engine and boiler arrangement." But that wasn't it. CGT's directors had discovered the *Oceanic*'s dimensions and they weren't about to start building a giant new ship they knew would be almost immediately surpassed by the competition.

In April 1929 the French naval architects began testing the best of their new hull designs at the Grenelle tank, running dozens of twenty-eight-foot paraffin models through a lengthy series of trials. In the process they made a surprising and alarming discovery: models built to CGT's new specifications were dangerously unstable. The only way to correct that was to widen the beam still further to 116 feet 6 inches. CGT gave the okay.

While the French Admiralty tested its models at Grenelle, Cunard engineers did exactly the same at the John Brown experimental tank at Clydebank, Scotland. If they kept on this way, the two steamship lines might very well launch their superliners within a few days of each other.

But something was happening on the French side of the Channel that would ultimately disrupt the CGT schedule. To their surprise, Penhoet's engineers found they liked Yourkevitch's hull designs.

So, in the early summer of 1929 Fould summoned Yourkevitch to Penhoet headquarters. This time Fould had called in André Lévy, his second in command, along with several other senior Penhoet engineers. By the meeting's end Penhoet had decided to let Yourkevitch produce a liner design of his own.

Fould gave Yourkevitch his company's most carefully guarded secrets: the latest specifications for the new CGT superliner: length, breadth, draft, displacement and required top speed—30 knots. Yourkevitch returned to his small Parisian apartment, a ship designer once more.

At Grenelle, Romano's team continued its model-testing. They'd heard talk about a Russian naval architect, but didn't take it seriously.

When it came to ship design, the French had a self-confidence bordering on arrogance, as did the British. But designers in both countries must have quailed that July when the *Bremen* completed her maiden voyage. She eclipsed the *Mauretania*'s twenty-two-year-old crossing records in both directions.

Westbound, the *Bremen* made the voyage in 4 days, 17 hours and 42 minutes, averaging 27.83 knots. Eastbound, she did it even faster, averaging 27.92 knots.

The British press was thunderstruck. "This is a direct blow to national pride," the London *Daily Telegraph* whined. And *The Times* asked, "What is England going to do about her sullied pride?"

CGT, however, responded with bravado. Said that company's U.S. director, Jean Tillier, "The French Line will need to apologize to no one" when its own new ship was launched. But the Germans had clearly won the day.

If the *Bremen*'s spectacular debut had been an unpleasant surprise for France and Britain, it was only the first in a series of disturbing events.

In France the old guard was passing away. Marshal Foch, who more than any other man was responsible for France's victory over Germany eleven years before, had died that spring. That fall saw the death of Georges Clemenceau, defender of lost causes and Premier of France during the last part of the Great War. That winter he was followed by Marshal Joffre, "Victor of the Marne."

In Britain, meanwhile, a twenty-two-year-old Royal Air Force flying officer named Frank Whittle was figuring out how to adapt the principle of jet propulsion to airplanes. It would be decades before his invention had any effect on steamship travel, but eventually it would inflict a mortal wound.

In Germany, Hitler's court-enforced silence had come to an end. And, largely due to his oratory, the Nazi Party was once again showing signs of life. In 1929 alone 70,000 people joined its ranks, an increase of nearly 65 percent.

In the United States the stock market came crashing down in a single day, carrying with it the prosperity of the entire nation. Across the sea Europe hoped this dangerous new virus would not prove contagious.

In his Paris apartment Vladimir Yourkevitch spent months doing battle with the specifications Fould had given him and finally came up with a hull design that satisfied him.

At least on paper Yourkevitch's hull cut through the water so much more smoothly than previous ships that it could hit the required 30 knots with only 160,000 horsepower. By all conventional standards that speed should have required 180,000 horsepower. If Yourkevitch was right, his design would save CGT a fortune. The smaller engines would cost less to begin with—nearly $2 million less, Yourkevitch figured. And they would use less fuel—$200,000 less each year, he calculated.

Yourkevitch made another appointment with Fould.

But French Admiralty designers had also been at work. Using model tests, they'd narrowed down their choice of hull shapes to two, then, finally, to one. So far as they were concerned, this was it: the hull of the "Super-*Ile*," or whatever the ship would be called.

Penhoet and CGT's staff engineers now worked out the other details of the ship—the number of staterooms, the number and location of the public rooms, the type of engines and boilers, the deck and funnel design, etc.

CGT's managing directors had told their staff to be as imaginative as possible within the bounds of good sense.

Following these instructions, CGT's naval architects drew up what may justly be called the first truly streamlined superstructure ever designed for an ocean liner.

According to their plan, she would begin, at the bow, with

something never before seen on a major ship: a "whaleback," a shell that covered the forward part of the deck, concealing the usually untidy deck machinery—capstans, winches, piles of rope and chain—under a clean, smooth surface.

This whaleback would come to an end halfway to the bridge, in a dramatic, upsweeping breakwater both beautiful and useful, since it would keep heavy waves off the deck so the ship could maintain high speed even in rough seas.

The front bulkhead of the superstructure would be a broad, curving white wall from which graceful "bridge wings" would protrude on either side to provide ship's officers with a better view during docking.

The funnels were also unique. Three huge, oval, somewhat stumpy affairs raked at a 10-degree angle to give the impression of speed. They would sit on more or less circular bases which would conceal all of the ship's ventilating equipment, which was usually scattered around the decks in apparent disarray.

The first two funnels would be real and functional. The third would be a dummy, designed to make the ship look more balanced and to distribute wind pressure evenly over the length of the superstructure.

The rest of the deck space would also be practically clear of the normal deck machinery, with a minimum of masts, derricks and kingposts. The result: unprecedented areas of uncluttered teak, enough for a full-sized tennis court between the second and third funnels.

Aft of the funnels the decks—still clean and clear—would descend in tiers, six of them, the last three connected by pairs of stairways. There would be a small outdoor swimming pool on the next-to-lowest tier. The bottom one, which on most ships was crowded with mooring equipment, would be free of all obstructions.

The ship's stern would not be the usual type either. In the conventional design, the "cruiser" type later used on both the *Queen Mary* and the *Queen Elizabeth*, the rudder joined the rudder stock below the waterline. In the event of rudder damage such a ship had to be dry-docked for repairs, an arduous and time-consuming task.

Instead, CGT designers chose the spoon-shaped "yacht" stern

for their new ship. It not only avoided the disadvantages of the "cruiser" stern, but was also best suited for housing a stem anchor, which CGT felt was essential. Besides, it was beautiful.

In all, it was the cleanest ship design anyone had ever seen.

But there was another innovation that was even bolder—the engines.

Ever since the *Mauretania* and the *Lusitania* had come into service, every major ocean liner had been propelled by turbine engines connected to propeller shafts via reduction gears. (These last were a necessity since turbines spun at 2,000 to 3,000 rpm for greatest efficiency, whereas propellers had to revolve at 175 to 275 rpm for the same reason.)

For their new "Super-*Ile de France*," however, CGT's engineers decided on a different method of transmitting power to the propeller shafts: electric motors. Each of the four steam-driven turbine engines would be shafted directly to an alternator. The alternators would turn four electric motors. And each electric motor would turn a propeller shaft at the required speed.

This system was almost as old as turbine engines themselves, having first been used by two fire tenders built for the Chicago Fire Department in 1908. It had also been used on a number of smallish passenger liners such as the *Monarch of Bermuda*, the *Morro Castle* and the *California*.

Mainly, however, turbo-electric propulsion, as it was called, was the pride and joy of the U.S. Navy, which had installed turbo-electric engines in the battleship *New Mexico* and the aircraft carriers *Langley*, *Saratoga* and *Lexington*. (And more or less the same system could be found in most of the world's land-based power stations.)

But never before had turbo-electric propulsion been chosen for a major North Atlantic liner. It was a bold, almost risky decision for CGT.

CGT chose turbo-electric propulsion because it would let the ship use full power in reverse, it would allow all four propellers to be driven even if a turbine had to be shut down and it would give greater freedom in engine-room layout (since perfect alignment wouldn't be necessary).

On the other hand, turbo-electric propulsion wasn't quite as efficient at high speeds and it was slightly heavier.

CGT told everyone that the deciding factor was passenger comfort. Turbo-electric drive, it claimed, was quieter and smoother than reduction gear.

Maybe so. But the real reason CGT chose turbo-electric, after weighing all the pros and cons, was that it was another way of saying the new ship was the most advanced in the world.

By the time Yourkevitch and Fould met again, the "Super-*Ile*" was nearly complete, on paper anyhow. So was Cunard's new ship.

Fould took one look at Yourkevitch's plans and ordered that a model be made and tested against the Admiralty's best at Grenelle.

While CGT was putting everything on hold to test out Yourkevitch's hull design, Cunard was proceeding full speed ahead. In accordance with its instructions, the Cunard design team had followed the conservative path, drawing up plans for a ship that looked like a larger version of the 1914 *Aquitania*.

On March 12, 1930, the company asked for bids from Britain's leading shipyards: John Brown, Vickers-Armstrong and Swan, Hunter & Wigham Richardson. Only Harland & Wolff, White Star's favorite shipyard, where the *Oceanic* was taking shape, was left off the list.

In France just as Yourkevitch's design had once bested the Russian Admiralty model, so another Yourkevitch design now outperformed the French Admiralty's model.

The Admiralty ran the tests again. The results were the same. They decided to try once more, just to be sure.

On May 28, in Great Britain, Cunard's directors chose John Brown to build their new express liner. The ship would cost between $22.5 and $25 million. If everything went according to schedule, she'd be launched in May or June of 1932 and go into service in spring 1933.

There were a host of details to be settled before a final contract could be signed, but, to be prepared when the go-ahead came, the shipyard started readying its facilities. It began by lengthening its largest building berth by 300 feet. It was the mirror image of what was happening at Penhoet.

Even though model-testing at Grenelle was still under way, CGT responded to Cunard's announcement the only way it could—with an announcement of its own, a statement designed to please its friends and confuse its enemies.

On June 22 CGT told the world it was ordering a new ship, a ship 991 feet long, with a 110-foot beam. The engines of this new ship, said CGT, would develop 120,000 horsepower and drive the vessel through the Atlantic at a speed of 28 knots. It would go into service in April 1933.

Not a word of this statement was true. The best explanation is that CGT was putting out what is now called "disinformation"—"facts" designed to mislead its rivals, perhaps to encourage them to scale down their own vessels in the mistaken belief that CGT did not intend to build a 1,000-foot ship.

By now the French Admiralty had done everything possible to prove its hull design superior to Yourkevitch's, but without success.

At this moment the Grenelle model basin obligingly sprang a leak and had to be closed down for repairs. CGT decided to continue the testing in Germany.

This time the French headed not for Bremerhaven, but for Germany's other test tank, at Hamburg, where the great Blohm & Voss ships had been built, including two of Ballin's Big Three, the *Vaterland* and the *Bismarck*.

In August 1930 the testing began again, Yourkevitch's hull, with its flaring prow and bulbous bow, vs. the Admiralty hull, with its conventional knife-edge entry. The results were the same.

But now each model was altered in a variety of ways. Large and small bulbs were tried on the Yourkevitch design. Eventually a medium-sized bulb was chosen, since it produced the minimum hull resistance regardless of pitching and heaving or changes in draft.

When those in Germany had finally agreed on a hull design, CGT once again changed the rules. Its designers, given more time to work over the ship's internal layout, had made the superstructure larger. That raised the vessel's center of gravity, which made it necessary to widen the hull again, from 116 feet 6 inches to 117 feet 9 inches. (This actually translated into a maximum width of 119 feet 5 inches, because of overhang at the Promenade Deck.)

Yourkevitch and the Admiralty team changed the model appropriately, but it wasn't as stable as before. The ship had to be lengthened at the waterline in proportion to her greater beam. They argued the point with CGT and finally got the go-ahead to add 10 feet. That brought the ship's waterline length to 961 feet 11 inches. Yourkevitch and the French Admiralty changed the model once more and tested it again. This time it was perfect.

Incidentally, two years later, while *Normandie* was being built, no less an authority than the *New York Times* reported that her stern was being left unfinished until the last moment so that she could be lengthened, if necessary, to surpass Cunard's 534, the ship that would eventually be named the *Queen Mary*. Other publications have since repeated this statement. Actually, *Normandie*'s final dimensions were settled in August 1930, before a single keel plate of either ship had been laid. There were plenty of rumors after that, but that's all they were.

Normandie's final dimensions would be 1,029 feet 4 inches (not on the waterline, but from stem to stern) and 119 feet 5 inches at her widest point. The *Queen Mary*'s final dimensions: 1,019 feet 6 inches long, overall; 118 feet 1 inch wide at her greatest breadth.

Of course, during the summer of 1930 these dimensions were as secret as the design of the H-bomb. And during the next three years Cunard and CGT would do their very best to fool each other and the public about which ship would be the largest.

Before leaving Germany, the French design team consulted Dr. Kempf, the model tank director who'd supervised the *Bremen*'s tank tests, and Dr. Ernest Forster, Blohm & Voss's chief naval architect and designer of the *Vaterland*. Both agreed that Yourkevitch's hull form was superior.

After a month of anguished deliberation CGT made its decision. It would build the ship with a Yourkevitch hull. Compagnie Générale Transatlantique, facing the strongest, most determined competition in its history, had decided to risk everything on a hull design that had never been used on any ship of any size save the *Borodino*-class battleships—none of which had ever been completed.

Decades later, in an attempt to determine a ship's ideal hull shape, the famous American naval-architecture firm of Gibbs and Cox put all of the factors into a computer. Out came almost precisely the design that Vladimir Yourkevitch had developed through instinct and experience.

If *Normandie*'s story were fiction, Yourkevitch might have reacted to this vote of confidence by being forever grateful to CGT and loyally risking everything to keep his discoveries out of the hands of the competition, the German or British shipbuilders.

The truth, however, is not quite so neat.

Yourkevitch was indeed ecstatic about CGT's decision to use his design. He felt vindicated. But he now believed he could preside. over a revolution in hull design that would change the history of passenger liners, warships, merchant vessels and every other craft that plied the seven seas.

So, as soon as CGT notified him that it had accepted his design, Yourkevitch contacted a certain Mr. E. Bloomfield, formerly a "Russian expert" in the British Foreign Office, now a French textile manufacturer. He asked Bloomfield to act as his agent. He needed an agent for what he had in mind. He had decided to design *Cunard's* new superliner as well as CGT's.

On August 7, 1930, Bloomfield met with J. H. Cahill, the British Ambassador to France, to press Yourkevitch's case. He cited patriotism—British patriotism. Thanks to Yourkevitch's ideas, Bloomfield said, the French had made a very significant breakthrough in ship design. But the British could still catch up if Cunard acted before CGT made an exclusive deal with Yourkevitch and before Cunard's own design was finalized.

Cahill was impressed by Bloomfield's argument and Yourkevitch's technical papers. On the very next day he wrote to Sir Edward Crowe, head of Britain's Department of Overseas Trade, forwarding Yourkevitch's papers, which, it must be said in Yourkevitch's favor, revealed nothing about CGT's new ship.

Crowe immediately contacted Sir Percy Bates, the head of Cunard. Bates asked that copies of Cahill's letter and Yourkevitch's papers be passed on to a well-known marine engineer, J. E. Petavel, at Britain's National Physical Laboratory in Teddington, Middlesex, and to G. M. Paterson, Cunard's chief naval architect, a man of unimpeachable integrity, whom Bates knew he could trust to deliver an honest opinion.

Less than a month later both men had finished their evaluations. And on September 3 the issue came before Cunard's shipbuilding committee.

Yourkevitch's claims were "not improbable," Petavel reported. But their importance depended on the "degree of skill and knowledge possessed by the original designers." Translation: The French weren't very good naval architects to begin with, so it wouldn't be surprising if this Russian immigrant could come up with a more efficient hull than they could.

Paterson said he'd tested many Yourkevitch-type hull forms during Cunard's model-basin experimental program. He even presented the committee with a photo of his version of the Yourkevitch bow, which bore only the faintest resemblance to the original. Said Paterson, the bow he'd chosen for Cunard's new ship was far superior to Yourkevitch's.

"No action to be taken," said the committee.

Yourkevitch persisted. He asked another friend, a Mr. E. J. Foley of London, to write Bates directly and restate the case. Bates soon wrote back. "I am not a technical expert myself," he said, "but I understand that our advisors are satisfied that they can do as well as Mr. Yourkevitch."

And there the issue rested, at least temporarily.

That summer the newspapers were filled with items about the French and British superliners.

On August 18, perhaps hoping to twist the tail of its British rival, CGT announced that its new ship would be an enormous 1,170 feet long. Two days later the firm coyly denied this report, saying that its new ship would be "only" somewhere between 1,000 and 1,050 feet. It declined to be more specific.

Before the week was out, Cunard struck a public-relations blow of its own. It announced its plan to build a second superliner, once the first had been finished.

In retrospect, it seems amazing that CGT and Cunard, two responsible firms, would proceed with their superliners despite what was quickly becoming the world's most serious depression. But there is an explanation.

France entered the 1930s free of depression. Throughout 1929 French industrial output had increased and unemployment, never very high, had fallen still further. The French thought they were immune to this economic malaise.

Britain had been hit hard and early by the depression. But Cunard was unafraid. In fact, it hoped to take advantage of the situation. Sir Ashley Sparks put it this way to Sir Thomas Royden: "We ought to get our boat cheaper if we place the order now than we are likely to . . . if we defer until after the horizon clears."

In Germany the depression had another sort of effect. In the election that fall Adolf Hitler's Nazi Party became the nation's second largest, polling 6.4 million votes and winning 107 seats in the Reichstag.

In New York, municipal authorities, aware of the coming influx of superliners and the lack of docks large enough to accommodate them, decided to build some new piers uptown from the old ones. Every major European steamship company immediately applied for space.

Then, suddenly, after two and a half years of intermittent work on the enormous *Oceanic*, White Star dropped out of the race. It was out of money, done in by the depression.

On December 1 Cunard signed a contract with John Brown to build what immediately became known as job number 534. That very day the first keel plate went down at John Brown's Clydebank shipyard.

Simultaneously the British steamship company revealed some details about its new ship. It would be 1,018 feet long, overall (an understatement—the actual figure was 1 foot 6 inches longer). It would be registered at 73,000 gross tons (also an understatement, but perhaps an honest error, since this figure is difficult to calculate in advance). It would be launched in May or June of 1932—a sincere statement, no doubt, but, as it turned out, a wildly optimistic one.

On January 16, six weeks after Cunard had laid down the first keel plate of job 534, CGT at last ordered her new ship, which until her launch would be called job number T6 BIS. The new building berth at St. Nazaire was finished and ready for action. French government financing was secure, or so CGT thought.

Ten days later the T6's first keel plate was lifted into position. *Normandie* was under way. The race was on.

The *New York Times*, impressed by the twin keel-layings in Britain and France, ran an editorial on the subject on January 30:

"One industry which seems convinced that the world is not coming to an end economically is the shipping industry. It's a testimony to the faith that there will yet be prosperous times . . . and great crowds of people traversing the seas for business and pleasure."

4

A SUPERLINER COMES TO LIFE

By the end of January 1931 two different 1,000-foot superliners were under construction, one on either side of the English Channel. The Cunard ship was six weeks ahead of her CGT rival.

Vladimir Yourkevitch had his eye on both ships. In early January 1930, even before the T6's first keel plate was laid down, he drafted a second letter to Cunard.

Once more he offered to show that old-line company how his revolutionary ideas could be applied to its new ship, making it faster and more efficient. He told Cunard that CGT had given him permission to deal with other shipyards, so long as he revealed nothing about its new ship. He also said that he'd made a tentative deal with Blohm & Voss to work out the design of a new German superliner.

Yourkevitch sent this letter via three different channels: his new British agent, a Mr. B. Perlowsky; a contact in the British War Office, Lord Marley; and a Member of Parliament, the Honorable Mrs. Bethell.

Once again Cunard's shipbuilding committee found itself considering a Yourkevitch proposal. It decided that Mr. Perlowsky should be informed that his client's proposals had come too late to affect the 534 and that they were too vague to be properly evaluated anyhow.

But Yourkevitch kept on. When Cunard's shipbuilding committee met again two weeks later, it had another Yourkevitch letter to consider. This one came complete with drawings showing test results of a Yourkevitch model hull and graphs showing how much more efficient the *Bremen*, the *Maure-tania*, the *Ile de France* and the *Ausonia* (an Italian ship) would have been with his design.

Cunard "acknowledged the letter with thanks" and took no further action. By this time the British steamship company was just too consumed with its own dreams, now coming true on the banks of the Clyde, to concern itself with this Russian immigrant's wild ideas.

Job number 534 was progressing faster than expected. The keel was finished and work had begun on the double bottom. With a little imagination one could look at the rusty steel girders sitting on the building berth and picture a great ship that before long would be transporting thousands of passengers across the Atlantic in remarkable luxury and comfort.

To the south, across the Channel and down to the Bay of Biscay, this scene was repeating itself in detail on the banks of the Loire at St. Nazaire, the location of the Penhoet shipyard. St. Nazaire sits on France's Atlantic coast, near Nantes, about 250 miles southwest of Paris.

Penhoet was by far France's largest shipyard. When operations were at their peak, it employed as many as 10,000, half that number on T6 alone. Hardly a family in St. Nazaire didn't have at least one member working there. Now Penhoet was engaged in its greatest undertaking, the construction of T6. But what sort of a structure was it, this monstrous ship on which so much effort was being lavished?

Let's begin where the construction itself began—at the bottom. Job number T6 started off as a single line of steel plates running from stem to stern, from the head of the building berth to the water's edge, assembled atop stack after stack of wooden keel blocks. On top of these plates a giant girder was laid down along the vessel's entire length.

And on top of this girder and others like it, running lengthwise, and scores of steel ribs running crosswise, a second set of steel plates was laid down, forming a double bottom. This turned the corner of the bilges and extended upward along the whole length of the ship, well past the waterline.

Subdivided by bulkheads, the T6's double skin created fifty-four separate watertight compartments for storing fuel oil, boiler water, drinking water and ballast water. It also protected the ship against accidents of the sort that sank the *Titanic*.

Eventually eleven decks would be built on top of this double bottom, nine within the hull and two above it, in what's called the superstructure. These decks would be divided vertically into eleven large watertight compartments, considerably surpassing the safety standards of the day.

In planning the T6's hull, decks and superstructure, her designers had tried to make her both as strong as possible, assuring safety and a long, maintenance-free career, and as light as possible, giving her the highest speed and best fuel economy. To accomplish this, they'd used two rather novel construction techniques.

First, they'd made sure that practically every square inch of steel that went into her contributed to her longitudinal strength, to eliminate any chance that she'd crack open when she confronted the gales of the North Atlantic.

T6's unique shape simplified this task. She was much fuller amidships than most liners. Her fullness continued for a much greater part of her length than usual. This meant most of her weight was concentrated amidships with relatively little at either end. The T6 would experience less hull stress than most ships, not more, as her size and length might lead one to believe.

Second, her engineers specified more high-tensile steel than had ever before been used in an ocean liner. They chose high-tensile steel because thinner, lighter sheets of it provided as much strength as much heavier and thicker sheets of mild steel. That saved another 900 tons of weight.

In all, the T6 used about 6,400 tons of high-tensile steel, made at the Siemens-Martin factories in the Saar. It was used on both layers of her double bottom, on her Promenade and upper decks (the ones just below the superstructure) and in her main girders.

All of this was put together with 11 million rivets, according

to a publicist's final tally. Laid end to end (which is something
only a publicist would think of), they would stretch 406 miles.

At its height the construction was an incredibly noisy business. The staccato rattle of riveting machines and compressed-
air drills on heavy steel plates, the clatter of traveling cranes, the
snort of donkey engines, the clanging of the shell plates as they
were hoisted into place, the shouts of the workmen and the tat-
too of thousands of hobnailed shoes on the ringing metal decks
as the men moved from one task to another all created an enormous cacophony.

While the T6's shell was being assembled at Penhoet, Skoda
Works in Prague was casting her steel rudder frame and shaft.
Her boiler shells were being built by Press-u. Walzwerk in Düs-
seldorf. Her turbine blades were being cut in Sheffield, England, the davits that would hold her lifeboats at the ready were
under construction in Glasgow and her aluminum-frame bridge
windows were being built in America.

Back in Paris, Monsieur Yourkevitch asked his agent, Mr. Perlowsky, to propose again that Cunard test his ideas on a model.

This time, surprisingly, Cunard appeared to give Yourkevitch a green light. "Submit a concrete proposal," Cunard suggested on April 20. The British firm was no doubt hoping it could
get Yourkevitch to reveal some of the details of the new CGT
ship he'd designed.

Yourkevitch believed Cunard's response showed genuine interest. He replied quickly, asking that Cunard supply him with
the specifications of its second superliner.

Then, on second thought, as if he'd realized Cunard might
not be willing to reveal such secrets, especially to someone so
close to CGT, he said, "Should Cunard consider it undesire-
able to communicate to me their data and dimensions . . . I
will go into the problem thoroughly myself in order to establish
my own conception."

By May the T6's double bottom was practically complete. But
construction had not yet begun on any of the eleven decks or
on the shell that would hold them.

In the coming months, when the decks would be laid down

one by one, they would all be pierced by funnel uptakes—huge tubes leading from the boilers to the smokestacks, providing an outlet for the ship's exhaust gases, her smoke.

From the moment steamships had been invented, funnel uptakes had been the bane of naval architects. The problem was this: Funnel uptakes had to run right up through the center of the ship, the very best part of it, where the beam was greatest, where the sea's motion was least felt, where the passengers most wanted to be. It was as though car exhausts, for some reason, had to run out through a car's dashboard, across the seats at chest level and out the side windows.

In small ships those uptakes weren't much of a problem, since they were little more than narrow stovepipes. But in vessels like the T6, which needed ducts as broad as a house, they were an architectural catastrophe. Not only did they take up an enormous amount of prime space, they also interrupted, subdivided or reduced the size of the ship's showplaces, its public rooms: the main dining room, the smoking room, the grand lounge, etc. The result was a cramped or disjointed feeling even on the largest liners, no matter what architects did.

The problem was first solved—so far as it could be solved— before World War I in two of Ballin's Big Three, the *Vaterland* (later the *Leviathan*) and the *Bismarck* (later the *Majestic*).

In these two ships the uptakes were spilt in two down their length and routed not through the center of the ships, as usual, but as close to the sides as possible. The two sections were rejoined just below the funnels.

This innovative approach permitted the construction of truly enormous public rooms between the divided uptakes, creating spaces of unheard-of size and impact. Later the *Bremen* and the *Europa* used the same scheme, but it was not copied by British, Italian or American shipbuilders.

In fact, *Normandie* would be the only major non-German ship ever built with divided uptakes. And because of her remarkable size, the resulting public rooms were the biggest ever seen at sea, before or since, and larger than practically any similar rooms on land.

By using divided uptakes, *Normandie*'s designers could create a first-class dining room 305 feet long, 46 feet wide and 28 feet high. That comes to 14,030 square feet, making it the largest single room ever put into a ship.

(Some *Queen Mary* partisans claim that honor for that Cunarder's main dining room. But, according to Cunard's own figures, its main dining room measured only 13,627 square feet. If you compare the two rooms in terms of cubic feet, the disparity would be even greater, since only about half the *Queen Mary*'s dining room—the central part—was three stories high, whereas the entire *Normandie* dining room was that height.)

Normandie's dining room wasn't the only public space to benefit from the divided uptakes. Above it, on the Promenade Deck, the divided uptakes would allow more gigantic public rooms to be built: a grand lounge 85 feet wide by 110 feet long and a smoking room 85 feet wide by 55 feet long, to name just two.

Workers at St. Nazaire soon finished the T6's double bottom and began erecting the structural members for the vessel's eleven transverse bulkheads.

In Liverpool, at Cunard headquarters, naval architect Paterson finally reported back to the shipbuilding committee with his evaluation of Yourkevitch's most recent proposal. "In order to assess the value of Mr. Yourkevitch's ideas," he said, "it would be necessary to give him *accurate data* of the design of No. 534 and ask him whether he can produce a better form within the limits laid down. . . ." But, "In view of Mr. Yourkevitch's association with the French line, it is considered inadvisable to take any further action in the matter, at any rate for some considerable time to come," he concluded.

It was a Mexican stand-off. Cunard had failed to pry any information out of Yourkevitch about the T6 and it would be damned if it were going to tell him about number 534.

Cunard finally notified the Russian naval architect of its decision on July 17, after keeping him dangling for nearly three months.

At John Brown's shipyard, number 534 was beginning to look like a ship. The decks were put in, and the shell plating was going up port and starboard.

There was a cloud on the horizon, however: money. Transatlantic passenger traffic was down more than anyone had anticipated, as was income. But Cunard was sure the banks would provide it with all the funds it needed.

Business was just as bad for CGT, but the French steamship line was supported by the French government. There could be no better security than that, or so it seemed.

By September the T6's lower decks were in place and work was beginning on the shell plating. Viewed from above, she looked like the corpse of a skyscraper recently laid to rest.

At the same time the firm of Christiani and Nielsen was busy building a giant new combination lock and dry dock not far from the T6's building berth. Once the ship was launched, she'd be taken there to outfit her interior and finish her exterior.

In Belfort, that small part of Alsace-Lorraine that had not been ceded to Germany after the Franco-Prussian War, the T6's enormous turbine engines and electric motors were being built at the Als-Thom factory, with the guidance of General Electric. (GE's William Emmett was the principal inventor of turbo-electric propulsion.) One of the chief supervisors on this job was Jean Hazard, who would one day be *Normandie*'s chief engineer.

Fall 1931 arrived with no let-up in the economic and political bad news. On September 21 England abandoned the gold standard. And almost overnight the pound dropped from $4.86 to $3.49.

That same day Japanese troops invaded southern Manchuria after months of tension. It was the first time the two nations had fought each other since the end of the Great War.

Three weeks later Field Marshal Paul von Hindenburg, Germany's eighty-four-year-old President, received Adolf Hitler in his private chambers for the very first time, no longer able to ignore the growing Nazi power.

CGT continued to do battle with Cunard on the playing fields of public relations, trying simultaneously to deceive the competition and win the hearts and minds of the public.

In its last announcement Cunard had revealed that number 534 would be 1,018 feet long, with a beam of 115 feet—a slight understatement, though CGT couldn't have known that. CGT decided to take its turn in the game. The T6, it announced, would be 1,020 feet long, with a beam of 117 feet.

This was enough of an understatement about *Normandie*'s planned size—nine feet in length, two in width—to mislead Cunard and to delight the traveling public when the truth became known. And yet it clearly exceeded the 534's announced dimensions, giving everyone the impression that the French, not the British, were building the world's largest ship.

In Liverpool, Cunard's money worries were now causing its directors to wonder if they'd be able to continue with their remarkable project at all.

Percy Bates had gone to Cunard's friendly bankers, asked for a loan of three million pounds sterling—about $10.5 million—and been turned down flat. The bank couldn't see how Cunard would ever be able to pay off the loan, given the current state of transatlantic travel. Bates decided to try other banks.

The shipbuilding committee, now under orders to economize in every way possible, began cutting back on number 534's luxuries. The November 3, 1931, committee minutes are full of examples:

"Delete pedestal fans from tourist accommodations, also from captain's, officers', doctor's, pursers' and chief steward's rooms. Delete also oscillating and ceiling fans from first and tourist public rooms. Delete the luminous call system from tourist accommodation and substitute the ordinary drop-shutter system. Delete the second quarter-inch model. . . ."

While the shipbuilding committee was economizing, Bates was making the rounds of the big British banks and being rebuffed time after time. He finally realized that if the company itself was to survive, it would have to call a halt to number 534. On December 10 the company did just that. It looked as though number 534 was going the way of the *Oceanic*.

The shutdown caused an enormous outcry throughout the British Isles. It wasn't just a matter of jobs. It was that everyone knew how much the 534 meant to British pride, prestige and self-confidence, all three of which had been deeply eroded by the depression.

Said Sir Percy Bates, "If the government will give us a contingent guarantee of three million pounds sterling for a period not exceeding six years, the work will immediately be resumed. My bankers formerly did this for me for nothing."

His Majesty's government flatly refused. This was not the time, it said, for a luxury liner to be financed out of the public coffers—however the government of France might feel about the same subject.

The 534's cancellation had an effect in France, however. By this time about $12 million had been spent on the T6, 36 percent of her total cost. Most of her decks had been laid down and a good deal of her shell plating was in place. Every day an average of 1,500 workers per shift riveted another fifty-five tons of steel into position. But now, suddenly, the French Chamber of Deputies decided to debate the ship's future.

It began with a routine request by Premier Pierre Laval for a $12 million subsidy that would allow CGT to continue building the T6. The Chamber had approved a similar request two years earlier without serious debate. Laval expected a repeat performance.

Instead, Jules Moch, the Socialist Deputy from Drôme, rose to attack CGT and its administration, saying that the company had "falsified its balance sheets, distributed fictitious dividends and embarked on engagements difficult to estimate," whatever that meant. "There was," he charged passionately but inarticulately, "culpable complacency on the part of the treasury and influence by subsidiary firms."

A member of the merchant-marine committee then rose to say that unless the CGT loan was guaranteed immediately, the company and the T6 project would be in serious trouble.

The Minister of the French Merchant Marine, a man named De Chappedelaine, appealed to French pride. He suggested that France tell Great Britain it would give up the T6 if Cunard scrapped number 534. He hoped for a patriotic outcry against his suggestion, but there was none.

Instead, the debate was gaveled to a halt and the vote was

called for. When the final tally was in, it was 265 for the subsidy, 275 against. The T6 seemed about to follow the 534 into limbo.

That night Laval demanded that the finance committee revise the bill and vote again the next day. That day, two days before Christmas 1931, the Chamber of Deputies approved the revised subsidy bill, taking control of the company out of private hands and turning it over to the government.

Across the Channel, Cunard officials watched all of this with great interest. Once the French subsidy had gone through, they again asked the British government to do the same for number 534. But the Chancellor of the Exchequer, Neville Chamberlain, at that time an ascending star in his party, responded with a flat turndown.

The year 1932 didn't start out any better for the Western World than the year before. In Germany, unemployment had reached 5.6 million. In the United States, it was triple that. In Great Britain, His Majesty's government decided that, to protect jobs, it would have to abandon free trade. This ended a policy begun in 1849.

The economic news wasn't good for steamship lines either. Transatlantic traffic had fallen from 1.3 million passengers in 1930 to 939,468 in 1931—and the drop was even worse than it looked, since many of those who did cross in 1931 did so on less expensive tickets, dropping down a class or even two.

During this period the political news was almost uniformly bad, at least in retrospect. True, on January 21 Franklin Delano Roosevelt announced that he would be a candidate for President of the U.S. But a month later Joseph Goebbels announced that Hitler would be a candidate for President of Germany. His chief opponent would be the eighty-four-year-old Field Marshal von Hindenburg.

The German election was held on March 13. When the polls closed, Hindenburg had won 18.6 million votes, or 49.6 percent, and Hitler had gotten 11.4 million votes, or 30.1 percent.

Minority candidates got the rest. Since no one had received an absolute majority, a run-off was scheduled for a month later.

At St. Nazaire the T6 was just about on schedule. At her bow, steelworkers were beginning to piece together what would be one of her most distinctive features: the whaleback that would conceal her deck machinery and protect her from heavy seas. Down below, deep inside, other workers were starting to frame out the walls of her vast first-class dining room.

The frantic activity at St. Nazaire was in stark contrast to the pall that had settled over Clydebank, where flocks of birds had nested in the dirty, rust-streaked skeleton of number 534.

On April 10 Germany held its run-off presidential election. Field Marshal von Hindenburg won again, adding about three quarters of a million votes to his previous total. But Hitler, in losing, managed to pick up two million additional votes from the minority candidates, polling 36.8 percent of the electorate. People began to wonder what would happen when Hindenburg died.

During the summer of 1932 steelworkers finished the T6's whaleback and completed the walls of her dining room. They plated B Deck, laying the floor of what one day would be the chapel. Then they went on to A Deck, which would be occupied largely by first-class staterooms. After that, they started on the Upper Deck, the site of *de luxe* cabins forward and tourist-class public rooms aft.

In the United States, Rockefeller Center was opened to the public. A masterpiece of Art Deco interiors, Rockefeller Center was, at least in the decorative sense, perhaps the closest American equivalent to *Normandie*.

In Britain nothing was happening to number 534 now, although there were rumors aplenty. One of them found its way into *Fortune* magazine. Number 534, it said, would be launched "as is," for advertising purposes and to save shipyard rental.

But it was politics—especially German politics—that dominated the news that summer, not shipbuilding. In late May, Chancellor Brüning was forced out of office, and on July 31 Germany held its third national election in five months. It was a resounding victory for the Nazis. They polled 13.7 million votes, winning 130 seats, making them easily the largest party in Germany.

In Paris, CGT announced that the T6 would be launched on October 29, 1932, on one of the year's two highest tides. The company also announced the liner's estimated final price: $30 million.

In August, Paul Conard of Penhoet and Pierre de Malglaive of CGT visited New York to help Jean Tillier negotiate pier space for the huge new vessel. As they came off the *Ile de France*, they were cornered by a covey of New York newspapermen.

"Does the French Line plan to build even larger ships than the T6?" one reporter asked.

Jean Tillier answered. "It would come as no surprise if a ship big enough to fill the proposed 1,200-foot ways at St. Nazaire is laid down within a year or two," he replied.

Pierre de Malglaive then interrupted with a note of reality. "While we do intend to build a larger ship someday soon, to serve as the T6's running mate," he said, "the line is not certain of the French government's attitude toward its subsidy. We must consider that fact in making plans."

By mid-October the T6 was structurally complete. Except for her superstructure and her funnels, which would be added later, she looked pretty much finished. But of course she wasn't.

What her builders had created, after twenty-one months of work, was the bare bones of a ship, fine-lined and structurally sound, but minus all of her opulence and interior beauty and all of her remarkable machinery, which were just as much a part of her as her frame and steel plating.

Ahead lay her launch. And after that, her fitting out, when her engines would be installed, when her naval engineers and steelworkers would give way to architects, interior decorators, carpenters and artisans.

She was half done, but splendidly so.

On October 18 CGT announced that her captain could be René Pugnet, former captain of the *Paris*, a multi-talented man who happened to be the nephew of Frédéric Auguste Bartholdi, creator of the Statue of Liberty.

And on October 19, after much speculation, CGT announced the T6's name. She would be called *Normandie*, after the province.

On October 29 France's great new transatlantic express liner *Normandie* was successfully launched into the Loire and towed through the giant new lock nearby to the fitting-out dock that had been built to receive her. The world's first 1,000-foot ship had been born.

Fate had worked overtime, you might say, to save this honor for the French, for CGT and for *Normandie*. It has scuttled the boyhood dreams of William Francis Gibbs. It had dashed the hopes of Lord Kylsant, director of the White Star Line, who thought the *Oceanic* would save his company but saw it do just the reverse. It had frustrated the well-laid plans of the North Atlantic's oldest and most prestigious steamship line, the Cunard company, saddling it with a hulk that seemed destined never to carry passengers.

What was this honor, exactly, that fate had reserved for *Normandie*? Aside from the enormous expense and great difficulties in construction, what was the real significance of creating a liner 1,000 feet long?

By achieving the unequaled length of 1,000 feet, *Normandie* won a special place in our hearts and minds, for her achievement was not only hers and her builders' and France's, it was also ours. She was a measure of what the human race could do when it really set its mind to the task. Looking at her, it must have been hard for even the average man not to feel just a little bit of pride.

5

fITTINg OUT

Normandie's successful launch was celebrated throughout France. Even those newspapers which, for political reasons, had sniped at her government-subsidized financing now allowed that "we French have reason to be proud of our accomplishment."

There was no joy in England, however.

For one thing, France—who would have imagined it—had become the first nation to launch a 1,000-foot ship, snatching the honor away from Britain and altering the natural order of events. For another, Cunard's own monster, number 534, now seemed doomed. Nevertheless, Cunard continued to act as though its ship would eventually be ferrying the rich and famous across the Atlantic in competition with her sister superliners from France, Italy and Germany.

Until Normandie was launched, Cunard's Sir Percy Bates had tried to get his government subsidy with the "unemployment argument." Now he stressed the "foreign competition" argument.

This argument—and the reality of Normandie—finally swayed His Majesty's government. Chamberlain asked Lord Weir, a well-known industrialist, to give him a report on Cunard's competitive situation. Finally, it seemed, there was a ray of hope for number 534—and for Cunard.

Immediately after her launch Normandie had been turned around in the Loire by a fleet of tugs, backed through the giant lock/dry dock made to accommodate her and brought into her fitting-out basin, a land-locked channel a few hundred yards inland from her launching berth.

At this point *Normandie* was only an empty hull. Now more than 3,000 workers—men and women—swarmed over her, aided by three giant, derrick-mounted cranes and by every other kind of shipbuilding machinery imaginable. Their task was to turn this empty hull into a finished ship.

Their first job was to install *Normandie*'s machinery, the engines and motors slated for her lowest decks. These had to be put in position before any of her amenities could be brought aboard.

Included in this machinery was a full-scale electric power plant to drive the ship, big enough to power the city of Boston, and a smaller auxiliary power plant to provide electricity for *Normandie*'s lights, air-conditioning, elevators, steering mechanism, etc.

To generate all this electricity, *Normandie* had twenty-nine water-tube boilers, each weighing nearly ninety-nine tons, plus four auxiliary Scotch boilers of forty-nine tons each, with 3,500-square-foot heating surfaces. The steam they made would produce the electricity needed to run the electric motors which turned the propeller shafts.

Once the turbines had wrung every last bit of energy from the steam, it would be collected and transformed once again into water to repeat the process in still more large pieces of equipment: condensers—four main ones, each the size of a Patton tank, and six slightly smaller ones.

Installing all of this equipment was a prodigious, exacting and time-consuming task. It took months.

During this process *Normandie* was practically an inferno of banging, clanging and hammering, of dust and dirt, and of freezing winters and boiling summers. Inside, she was filled with scaffolding, lit only by bare bulbs strung along temporary wooden beams.

Through it all walked men in dungarees and women in black aprons and black berets. They groped through the passageways, their arms filled with tools or equipment, traversing an apparently bottomless Grand Canyon of pipes and machinery, into which, it seemed, someone might disappear and be lost forever.

Here and there, in the dust and heat, in that racket of hammering and riveting, worked the women laborers of St. Nazaire, standing over charcoal braziers, heating rivets. When the rivets were red hot, they'd seize them with tongs and toss them to the men who were fastening the engines to the ship's floor.

While *Normandie*'s machinery was being installed, preparations were being made on both sides of the Atlantic to receive her when her traveling career began.

The French government had decided that this was the moment to completely revamp the harbor of Le Havre, which had been designated as *Normandie*'s French port.

This began with the enlargement and deepening of the outside channel which led to the harbor itself. While the dredging was under way, a new boat dock was begun. It would be nearly 2,000 feet long, long enough to accommodate *Normandie* and the *Ile de France* simultaneously.

Construction also began on a new portside railway station, a reinforced concrete structure 1,048 feet long, with automatic doors at both ends to keep out cold weather. It would be called *Gare Maritime*.

On top of this station would be erected an extraordinary tower 262 feet high, which would display tidal readings in numbers 10 feet tall, on a scale that looked like a giant thermometer. Topping it all off was a clock with a dial 20 feet across.

Something similar was happening at *Normandie*'s other "home" port, New York. The city's piers and docks had been kept in excellent condition and expanded to fit each new generation of ocean liners. But when the flood of immigrants became a trickle, the passenger piers gradually became less important to the city.

By the time *Normandie* was launched, some of them were downright dilapidated. They were no longer conveniently located, since the center of the city had moved farther and farther uptown, and they were much too small to accommodate the new European superliners on the way.

In the early 1930s Cunard, CGT, North German Lloyd and other lines threatened to shift to Boston or even Montauk Point, on Long Island, if New York didn't improve its docking situation.

Despite the drop in transatlantic passenger traffic, New York wasn't about to give up its ocean-liner business, so it began planning five new piers in the midtown area between 47th and 52nd Streets.

There was only one problem: If the new piers were extended farther into the Hudson than the old ones, they'd intrude into the channel and strangle the very traffic they were intended to serve.

Early in 1931 Secretary of War Patrick J. Hurley held open hearings on the subject. After listening to all parties, he ruled that the pierhead line could be extended seventy-five feet into the Hudson.

Unfortunately, seventy-five feet wasn't enough to accommodate the huge new piers the New York City dock authorities had in mind. They had to satisfy the steamship lines, which meant piers no less than 1,100 feet long by 125 feet wide, with 400 feet of berthing space between them.

There was only one way to build piers that size, given Hurley's decision: Cut back on the Manhattan side of the Hudson by about 325 feet. It was either that or lose the steamship trade.

And so, in 1932, an enormous coffer dam began to take shape on the New York side of the Hudson, enclosing the area where the five new piers would sit. This would temporarily create dry land, allowing steam shovels to carve slips into the floor of the Hudson.

Meanwhile, plans went ahead on an elevated highway, the West Side Highway. It would connect the second stories of the pier buildings with each other and carry traffic heading uptown or downtown.

The piers were expected to cost $4.1 million, the highway many millions more. All in all, the project rivaled the reconstruction under way at Le Havre.

While *Normandie*'s engines were being installed and her ports were being enlarged and revamped to receive her, world politics and economics continued on their mainly downward spiral.

In Germany the Weimar Republic, such as it was, was in its last days. And on the wintery morning of January 30, 1933, Hindenburg appointed Adolf Hitler Chancellor of Germany.

What was happening in the United States at this time was no less significant. By the morning of FDR's inauguration every bank in the country was closed, as were the New York Stock Exchange and the Chicago Board of Trade. General Mac-Arthur, in command of the inauguration parade, anticipated trouble. He ordered Army machine guns mounted at strategic points in the Capitol.

Then Roosevelt took the oath and began to speak. "Let me first assert my firm belief that the only thing we have to fear is fear itself. . . ."

Four days later Congress passed FDR's Emergency Banking Act, which provided prison terms for gold-hoarders, appointed "conservators" (receivers) for failing banks and authorized the printing of $2 billion in new bills, based on bank assets. The sense of panic receded.

Despite the swirling tides of world politics and economics, work on *Normandie* continued unabated.

By the beginning of summer 1933 most of *Normandie*'s engine machinery was in place and thousands of engineers and mechanics were connecting it all together. At the same time other workers were installing kitchen equipment, deck machinery, elevators and other mechanical fittings.

In all, *Normandie* would have four kitchens: one serving all passengers and officers, one for the crew, one for the grill room and one kosher kitchen for the ship's orthodox Jewish passengers.

The main kitchen was on D Deck, immediately below the cavernous main dining room. It occupied a space 108 feet wide by 197 feet long.

This kitchen would have to prepare 14,100 meals every day— 14,100 *delicious* meals—not counting breakfasts and the steady stream of incidental refreshments that had to be available at all hours of the day. To create this enormous cooking capacity, enough kitchen equipment was installed in the ship to handle an army:

□ An electric range 56 feet long, with 32 roasting ovens and 8 stoves;

- ☐ A 56-foot steam table for first-class passenger service;
- ☐ Six electric grills;
- ☐ Two 80-quart mixers;
- ☐ Three 66-gallon boilers, one 33-gallon boiler and one 22-gallon boiler;
- ☐ A pastry oven 8'2" by 6'10";
- ☐ A confectionery oven 4'11" by 3'3";
- ☐ A double oven with a capacity of 2,260 pounds of bread a day;
- ☐ A battalion of freezers, refrigerators and other food containers.

To make sure the kitchen worked efficiently, it was connected to the dining rooms by a pneumatic-tube dispatching system, a telephone system and three service elevators.

While *Normandie* remained in her fitting-out basin, many months away from service, the other European superliners fought tooth-and-nail for the Blue Ribbon and the lion's share of the remaining passenger traffic.

At the time, the *Europa* held the Blue Ribbon. In March 1930 she'd crossed the Atlantic in 4 days, 17 hours and 6 minutes, averaging 27.91 knots.

This record stood for three years. Then, in July 1933, the *Bremen* eclipsed her sister's record by a fairly substantial 51 minutes. But *Bremen*'s new record was not long for this world.

In August an Italian superliner, the *Rex*, turned in an even better performance, with a westbound passage 3 *hours* and 5 minutes faster than the *Bremen*'s voyage the month before, at the average speed of 28.92 knots—nearly half a knot better than her German rival.

Ordinarily, it would have been about a year before *Normandie* was ready to challenge the *Rex*'s record. But these were not ordinary times.

1931 had been a terrible year for the transatlantic trade and 1932 was worse. The total number of passengers carried had slipped to 642,000—the lowest in the twentieth century, not counting war years. The first half of 1933 was at least 20 percent worse than 1932. Even the *Bremen* and the *Europa* were suffering.

At this point Marcel Olivier, the new head of the French Line, a government appointee who'd previously been Governor General of Madagascar, announced that *Normandie*'s completion would be delayed by a full year, until Spring 1935—to coincide with a hoped-for upturn in tourist travel.

Ironically, just when CGT was delaying *Normandie*, Cunard was beginning to make progress on a government aid package that would resurrect the abandoned number 534.

The British Chancellor of the Exchequer, Neville Chamberlain, had decided to use Cunard's crisis to strengthen British commercial shipping. He would loan Cunard the money it needed not only to complete number 534, but also to build a sister ship. But there was one condition: Cunard must absorb the nearly defunct White Star Line's few remaining ships and routes.

On February 8 His Majesty's government advanced three million pounds sterling to Cunard–White Star, the new company, to complete number 534.

During the long construction moratorium Cunard had continued work on the plans and blueprints of number 534's interior layout, partly in response to what it had learned about *Normandie*.

Among other things, the company had decided to boost the ship's horsepower to 150,000 and her service speed to "at least 30 knots."

When work resumed on number 534, CGT knew it must also resume work on *Normandie* in earnest. The workers began to return—men in mufflers, on foot and on bikes; women in black aprons, sabots clicking on the cobblestones; dogs pulling carts heaped high with bread. In this land even the dogs worked.

The next order of business was to install *Normandie*'s fireproofing, a serious and important job, the more so because during the two previous years two French ocean liners had burned: the *Georges Philippar*, on May 16, 1932, while returning on her maiden voyage from Aden, and *L'Atlantique*, which burned in the English Channel on January 4, 1933.

Normandie's designers approached the fireproofing problem from four different directions simultaneously. First, they specified fireproof materials wherever possible—glass, plaster of paris, slag wool, duralumin, etc. To check the flammability characteristics of various materials, an experimental furnace was set up at the shipyard. In all, nearly 10,000 square feet of paneling was tested inside it, plus 250 different types of paints and varnishes and thirty-five different floor coverings, from linoleum to carpeting. Plywood was extensively used in the ship, particularly in the partitions between rooms, but it was painted with fireproof paint and asbestos sheets were inserted in its core.

Second, the ship was divided into four main fire zones by fireproof bulkheads. Each of these was subdivided by the decks into thirty-six "minor zones," then into smaller compartments and even smaller "cells." The main fireproof bulkheads were designed to withstand fire indefinitely. Secondary bulkheads could withstand 1,500° F. for an hour. Even the cell bulkheads could contain fires for at least half an hour.

Third, *Normandie* was also fitted with the most complete system of warning devices ever installed on board a ship. Over 1,000 heat-detectors were built into the passenger quarters alone, along with 224 fire-alarm sirens. All were wired into a central security station on A Deck, amidships, on a lighted display board that showed the entire ship, deck by deck. This room would be manned continually after the ship went into service. It was located right beside the fire-brigade quarters, which would house forty-six men whose job it would be to patrol the ship constantly.

If they found fire, they could break out hoses at any one of 504 fire hydrants. These were connected to three sets of fire pumps, two in the main engine room and one in No. 2 boiler room. They had a total output of 300 tons of water an hour.

If a fire broke out in a passenger's cabin, a fire hose with a specially designed swiveling nozzle could be inserted into a hole in the ceiling and the entire room soaked in a matter of moments. This hole was the invention of *Normandie*'s first commander, René Pugnet.

Fourth, if it became necessary to evacuate the ship because of fire or some other emergency, passengers could go to any one of twenty-six lifeboats, each with an 88-passenger capacity, or twenty-two other lifeboats with a 46-passenger capacity, or four motor boats that could each hold 42 passengers, or two other motor lifeboats able to transport 32 passengers each, or two whaleboats with a capacity of 25 passengers each. The lifeboats, in all, could carry 3,582 people. The total capacity of the ship, assuming every bunk was occupied both in crew and passenger quarters, was 3,317. In the event of disaster even the stowaways would have a lifeboat seat.

The lifeboats were mounted high on the Boat Deck, on gravity davits. They could be launched by a single man even if the ship were listing 15 degrees in either direction, even if she were still making 16 knots.

Finally, one additional safety feature was built into the ship, a feature unique to *Normandie*: all portholes pivoted outward and they were big enough for passengers or crew members to use as exits if normal routes were blocked.

Fortunately, this elaborate fire-protection and safety system was never put to a test while *Normandie* was at sea, although there's every reason to believe it would have worked splendidly. There's also every reason to believe it would have saved the ship on that fateful day in New York harbor in 1942, had it been properly maintained and used. But that's getting ahead of the story.

When all of her machinery and technical equipment was in place, it was time to bestow upon *Normandie* the beauty, glamour and magnificence for which she would be remembered long after her demise, by former passengers, ocean-liner *aficionados* and art historians alike.

6

THE ART dECO SHIP

From the beginning Pierre de Malglaive and his associates had intended their superliner to be both the world's largest and fastest passenger ship and the most beautiful, the most glamorous, the most magnificent vessel ever created.

When the French government took over the direction of CGT, it set out to create a ship of state, a vessel that represented all of France's virtues, real and imagined. It intended the ship to be a floating, semi-permanent exhibit of France's arts and sciences in that World's Fair of shipping known as the North Atlantic.

France was well served in the scientific part of this exhibit by *Normandie's* unique hull shape and by her unusual engines. But to make the package complete, France also had to demonstrate that her artistic prowess was just as awesome as her scientific prowess.

Happily, she had the means at hand—a style of artistic decoration and interior design as beautiful as any ever conceived, a style developed and perfected in France by French artists of world renown, a style Americans openly admired, a style that could be found on no other ship. That style was Art Deco.

Art Deco was a reaction to the exaggerated stylized forms of Art Nouveau. Its colors were inspired by the Russian Ballet, particularly Léon Bakst's settings and costumes for *Shéhérazade*, which had opened in Paris in 1910. Its shapes were inspired, in part, by Paris's leading couturier, Paul Poiret. Its decorative themes came largely from Munich and Vienna. Its furniture was a simplified version of Louis XVI style, in particular the Directoire and Consulate styles and the more ponderous Empire designs.

Art Deco was elegant and luxurious. It delighted in ornament for its own sake. It exuded sophistication, class and quality.

Where possible, its designers used only the finest materials—ebony, amboyna, ivory, delicate wrought-iron work, molded, cast and hammered glass, pewter, gilded and enameled metalwork, lapis-lazuli. All of this often made Art Deco objects extremely expensive, which was just fine with its artists and artisans, for theirs was an art meant for those who could appreciate and afford it.

Art Deco was developed almost exclusively in France, mainly between 1910 and 1920. It reached its peak in 1925, in Paris, at the exhibit from which the style took its name: Exposition Internationale des Arts Décoratifs et Industriels, the most successful show of its kind.

The Paris exposition featured the works of all the great figures of Art Deco: Emile-Jacques Ruhlmann, Jean Dunand, Jean Dupas, Lalique, Leleu, Raymond Subes, Max Ingrand, Ivan da Silva Bruhns and others, many of whom contributed to *Normandie*'s interior decoration.

The marriage of Art Deco to *Normandie* benefited both sides. The art endowed the ship with all the qualities most likely to attract the rich and famous, those most interested in (and most capable of) escaping the era's economic and political turmoil. And *Normandie* helped Art Deco and the French artists who worked in this style by showing wealthy passengers what interior decoration could be at its best.

In addition to style *Normandie* also had a decorative theme: the province of Normandy itself—its people, its countryside, its industry, its agriculture, its architecture, its history.

While *Normandie* had no single interior decorator, it could be said that her interior was inspired by a single man, perhaps *the* seminal Art Deco figure: Emile-Jacques Ruhlmann. Ruhlmann didn't actually design much for *Normandie*—only the interior of a single suite and some birdcages for the winter garden.

In fact, he died in November, 1933, before most of the ship's interiors had been designed. But many of those chosen to decorate *Normandie* were Ruhlmann's friends, associates and collaborators, people like Jean Dunand, Jean Dupas, Pierre Patout, F. DeJean, Jean and Joel Martel. What they created was, to a large extent, the interior Ruhlmann might have designed.

Not all of *Normandie* was Art Deco, however. That style was reserved mainly for first-class public rooms and accommodations and tourist-class public rooms. Third class had only the faintest touch of it, and the crew quarters were strictly utilitarian.

In a way *Normandie* was four separate ships. They left the same port at the same moment, traveled across the Atlantic at the same speed and arrived at the same destination at the same time. Other than that, they didn't have much in common.

Normandie number one, or the first-class *Normandie*, was the *Normandie* of fame and legend, the *Normandie* on which investment bankers, important businessmen or industrialists, celebrities, high public officials, members of Royalty and the merely wealthy traveled. No other ocean liner, before or since, has devoted so much of its space to this class. In terms of square footage, more than 75 percent of the ship's public area was occupied by first-class cabins, public rooms or promenades. Of a total of 1,972 passenger berths, 864 were in first-class or de luxe staterooms.

First-class passengers entered *Normandie* on A Deck, through port or starboard foyers, each with its own information desk. Behind this was a set of doors, through which passengers walked to a short flight of stairs that led to the main entrance hall, a breathtaking gallery three decks high, 66 feet long and 70 feet wide.

This gallery was designed by Pierre Patout, who created Ruhlmann's pavilion at the 1925 Paris Exposition. Its walls were sheathed in Algerian onyx, upon which were mounted gilded, hand-wrought bronze "embellishments" by Raymond Subes and strips of hammered glass.

Two pairs of elevators, with facades of gilded bronze by Subes, provided an exit, as did six sets of stairways leading down to the next level. A wall-sized cloisonné bas-relief of a mounted and armed Norman knight, by Monsieur Schmied, adorned the landing at the bottom of the stairs. The knight's costume was copied from the Bayeux tapestry, which was woven in Normandy in the days of William the Conqueror. This panel also served as a sliding door leading to the chapel.

On to the passengers' rooms. As in cruise ships today, the better located rooms were more expensive, for even in first class, some passengers are more equal than others.

The *creme de la creme* suites were positioned about two-thirds of the way to the ship's stern, on the uppermost deck, the Sun Deck. These were the Trouville and the Deauville Suites. Each had four bedrooms, a living room, a dining room, a pantry, a servant's bedroom and five baths or half-baths. Adjoined to each was a two-room suite suitable for servants, assistants or secretaries. Both suites also had private promenades 45 feet by 15 feet, an amenity unique to *Normandie*.

The Trouville, which was designed by Leleu, was distinguished by a drawing room carpeted with a dark, velvety broadloom, most of which was covered by white area rugs interwoven with graceful patterns of tiny flowers. At the room's center stood a table with a thick glass top on a three-legged white wooden pedestal. A flared-back satin-covered couch sat against one wall which was covered by Aubusson tapestries depicting Greek hunting scenes. Against another wall sat a large white cabinet and a white grand piano against a third. Floor-length translucent white drapes covered the doors which led out to the promenade.

A folding black enameled door decorated with garlands of flowers led to the dining room—a study in gleaming black woods, except for its white ceiling and white, geometric-patterned area rug. (An American passenger who frequently used this suite fell in love with the dining room's decor and eventually created an exact duplicate in his New York apartment. Captain Pugnet and Chief Purser Niewenhove were invited to the first meal he served there.)

The other *grand luxe* suite, the Deauville, was just as big and as beautiful as the Trouville, although its layout and decor were entirely different.

There were two other suites on the Main Deck, three levels down, that almost rivaled them: the Caen and the Rouen.

Like the more expensive suites on the Sun Deck, the Rouen was the work of an Art Deco master, Monsieur Dominique. The classic lines of its bedroom were set off by a blue lacquer mural sprinkled with silver and decorated with panels of etched glass, "a fitting setting," said one promotional booklet, "for its furniture, which is covered in Chinese sharkskin." The sunken living room was every bit the equal of the sleeping quarters. Its parchment walls contrasted strongly with the trim—dark, polished macassar wood and gleaming metal bands. Against one wall sat the inevitable grand piano, varnished to the point of luminescence.

The Caen was the creation of an interior decorator named Montagnac. Like all the *grande luxe* suites, the Caen was filled with masterpieces. The *objects d'art* included a bronze by Guenot, a pewter vase by Daurat, handwrought iron doors by Subes and painted wood pieces sculptured and gilded by Gallot.

One step down from these sybaritic accommodations were the ten apartments *de luxe*, all of which were on the Main Deck. Each had a living room, two or three bedrooms and two-and-a-half or three bathrooms.

Each suite *de luxe* was decorated by a different designer, mostly in variations of Art Deco. But two were done in period decor—Bayeux (by Carlhian) was in the style of Louis XVI, in tones of cameo blue and white; and Jumeigues (by Nelson) took its inspiration from the apartments of Madame de Pompadour, Louis XV's favorite lady.

For those first-class passengers unable or unwilling to engage one of these remarkable suites, there were plenty of other luxurious accommodations—four different types of "ordinary" first-class staterooms in forty different interiors.

Initially, CGT invited thirty interior designers to submit plans for the first-class staterooms. Half the contestants were eliminated. The winners built thirty-seven completely outfitted model staterooms in the Exhibition Park of the Porte de Versailles in Paris. These were examined by the staffs of CGT and Penhoet and either altered to suit prevailing tastes or approved as they stood. Later three more designs were added.

There were a total of 431 first-class staterooms on *Normandie*, which might lead you to believe that there were about ten cabins of each design. Actually, there were *no* identical cabins, thanks to color-scheme variations. Furthermore, similar cabins were not adjacent to each other. The effect was one of great variety.

Of the four basic types of first-class staterooms there were:

1. *Verandah.* There were twenty-four of these, most of them at the after end of the promenade deck, and each with a private verandah overlooking the ocean.

These twenty-four rooms had nine basic decors. In some a decorator named Madame Klotz specified walls covered with leather. In others, Monsieur Groult covered the walls with woven straw. Still others, designed by Monsieur Rapin, used glass panels etched by Max Ingrand. Ruhlmann himself contributed a design in which practically everything was made of metal.

2. *Outboard sitting room.* These usually had one sofa bed and one disappearing Murphy-type folding bed and were intended for quick conversion into sitting rooms. Though smaller than the verandah staterooms, they were nonetheless lavishly decorated. There were 81 of these.

3. *Outboard bedroom.* There were 209 of these: 37 singles, 160 doubles and 12 two-room triples. The smaller rooms could be joined if necessary.

4. *Inboard.* These were the smallest, least expensive and least desirable of *Normandie*'s first-class cabins. It is impossible to eliminate inside rooms in a ship as big as *Normandie*, but she had remarkably few of them: 117 in first class, compared to 322 outside rooms.

In all, there were 69 inboard singles, mainly intended for business people traveling alone, and 48 doubles, for couples somewhat shy on funds but still wishing to travel—and especially to eat—first class. The inboard rooms shared nine different decorative schemes.

The main problem with inside rooms is that they don't have portholes. For those who yearn to see the Atlantic, this is a serious drawback. On the other hand, for those inclined to *mal de mer*—and remember, *Normandie* predated Dramamine—it's a blessing.

Of course, those passengers subject to seasickness were better off avoiding the 30 inside first-class staterooms that shared communal bathrooms. (This would be inconceivable today, but

(Top) The first hull plate is laid down on the stocks,
with VIPs from Compagnie Generale Transatlantique
and Penhoet looking on, Jan. 26, 1931. (Bottom)
After six months work, the double bottom is almost
finished and the framework is taking shape.

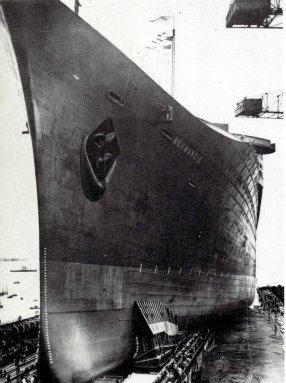

Under the scaffolding (top), the hull shape is well filled out, even though launch is still seven months away. Launch day (left). (Above) Madame LeBrun hits her mark. Champagne splashes against Normandie's hull. She pauses a moment before starting down the ways. (Facing page) Normandie enters the water for the first time, the sliding ways creaking, groaning and smoldering.

Normandie *in dry dock in 1935,
with her original three-bladed
propellers that had caused
a troublesome vibration*

*These new four-bladed propellers
ended the vibration problem once
and for all. Note that the bossing
tables—the appendages that connect
the propeller shafts to the ship—have
also been substantially changed.*

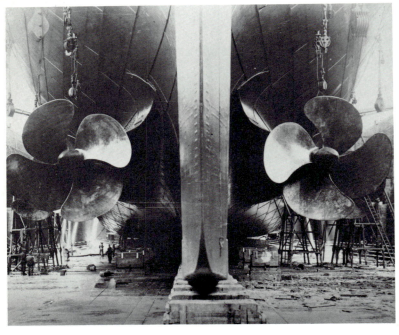

The Lorna Doone, *the little tender that transferred* Normandie *passengers and luggage to and from the Southampton pier. The ship herself was too large to dock there.*

René Pugnet (left), *the first* Normandie *commander;* Henri Villar (top), *the legendary* Normandie *chief purser;* Jean Hazard (bottom), Normandie's *first chief engineer.*

The control board area of the engine room. Clean and cool, it was a great contrast with the same area in pre-1920 coal-burning vessels.

The main fire station. When Normandie caught fire, it was in operation, but the rest of the fire-fighting system had been disconnected.

The livingroom of
the "Trouville" suite,
one of the two
most luxurious
accommodations
on the ship

The bathroom of the
"Rouen," one of the suites
just below the "Trouville"
in extravagance

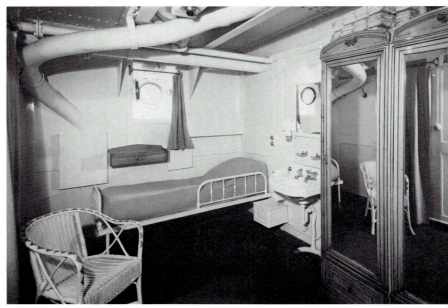

(Top) *A fairly typical first-class terrace suite.*
(Bottom) *Standard accommodations in third class.*

it was a fact of life even on the most luxurious ship of the time. Still, 93 percent of *Normandie*'s first-class cabins did have bathrooms.)

Undoubtedly the worst room in first class was number 211. A tiny cubicle (about eight feet square) on the Main Deck, it abutted the tourist-class lounge, which made it more than a little noisy during the night hours. Furthermore, it contained no plumbing but a sink. The nearest bathroom was a good thirty-five feet down the corridor. On the other hand, if one had no intention of sleeping in it—and there were plenty of *Normandie* passengers who rarely ruffled the covers on their own beds—this room was the least expensive way to travel first class.

A verandah stateroom on the Main Deck, however, lived up to *Normandie*'s reputation for luxury. Handsomely outfitted in Art Deco style, perhaps designed by Ruhlmann himself, it was equipped with a full-length wardrobe (to keep a tux or evening gown wrinkle-free), plenty of mirrors, several chests of drawers, enough comfortable chairs for any guests the occupants might invite in for a drink, a telephone, a clock, a genuine Beautyrest mattress, and a large, handsomely-outfitted bathroom, including tub.

After first-class passengers found their cabins, unpacked their steamer trunks with the help of an ever-present but never obtrusive steward, and freshened up and dressed for the evening meal, they'd head toward the main dining room, the ship's most famous public area.

Leaving a Main Deck cabin, passengers walked forward, along a corridor, to the ship's shopping center—a gallery with a bookstore, a small branch of Paris's famous Bon Marche department store, a flower shop, a drugstore/bookshop/travel agency and an information desk, an area not unlike Rockefeller Center's lower-level shopping promenade. On either side of the large combination barber shop and beauty salon were elevators by which passengers could descend to C Deck, three levels down, the location of the main dining room.

The elevator doors opened into the main embarkation hall, where a crush of first-class passengers gathered nightly, all of them elegantly attired and coiffured. At one end were the twenty-foot tall gilded bronze doors that lead to the dining room. Designed by Raymond Subes, a master of metalwork, they were decorated with ten circular medallions, five on each door, each a bas-relief of a Normandy scene—with churches, ancient clocks, turreted castles and, on the Le Havre medallion, the *Ile de France*.

A few broad stairs brought first-class passengers into what must have been one of the most sumptuously appointed rooms ever created. *Normandie's* main first-class dining room was a vast gallery, more than 300 feet long and three decks high, a palace chamber fit for a great king accompanied by his entire entourage.

This remarkable room was designed by Pierre Patout, who was assisted by his partner, Pacon. Its walls glittered with tiles of molded glass and vertical strips of hammered glass. Its coffered and gilded plaster ceiling was set off at each end with an Art Deco chandelier of etched glass.

The room's center was dominated by a giant gilded statue of a toga-clad woman, one arm raised and offering an olive branch. "La Paix" by Dejean, a sculptor whose work was a sensation at the Paris Exposition, stood nearly eighteen feet high (the statue was thirteen feet tall, the pedestal four and a half feet), in keeping with the room's scale.

The brilliant decoration was matched by the brilliant lighting. Dozens of glass fixtures mounted on the glass-paneled walls caused them to shimmer and glow. These were supplemented by twelve glass "light fountains" illuminated from within. Created by that master of glass design, René Lalique, they stood gleaming among the tables like sentries, in two rows of six fountains each.

Within this huge chamber, distributed over a floor of highly-polished blue rubber tiles in geometric patterns of the Art Deco style, there were 157 tables. Each was set with the finest linen, with silver designed by Puiforcat and executed by Christofle, with crystal by Daum, with custom-made china and with crystal bud vases filled with fresh flowers. Art Deco chairs covered in Aubusson needlepoint completed the picture.

Bordering the ceiling, a gilded valance of vents marked a real innovation for ocean liners, artifically cooled and dehumidified air conditioning. It chilled the dining room to such a degree that ladies sometimes wore their fur coats to dinner, pleased with the opportunity to show them off.

Today we take air conditioning for granted in public places. It's more of a necessity than a luxury. But it was also a necessity in *Normandie*'s dining room; despite its size, it had no portholes or windows to admit air and light.

Normandie's designers chose to make her dining room long and relatively narrow (46 feet wide) rather than creating the usual square chamber found in many ships' dining rooms. This was done to maximize the number of outside first-class staterooms.

In older liners (and in some ships that came long after *Normandie*) designers resorted to some seedy tricks to keep inside rooms to a minimum. Their favorite ploy was cabins shaped more or less like the state of Oklahoma. Beds, chests and wardrobes were put in the square, wide part. At the end of a sometimes very long panhandle there was a single porthole. *Voilà*, an outside room. It was an awkward and silly solution to the problem and everyone knew it, especially the passengers who had to walk down a kind of alley to get a look at the sea. But it did wonders for a ship's gross income, since outside rooms commanded a higher price than inside rooms.

Normandie's designers were determined to avoid this particular architectural mendacity, in first class anyhow, and the ship's narrow dining room helped them. It allowed them to run two rows of first-class outside staterooms along the entire length of the dining room, one on either side of the ship, not only on C Deck, the dining level, but also on B and A Decks, where the central part of the ship was occupied by the open space below the high dining room ceiling.

The result, as *Normandie*'s publicists were so fond of saying, was a room "slightly longer" than the famous Hall of Mirrors at Versailles. Despite its size, the dining room was a bit crowded. Having dinner with 583 other people at the same time isn't exactly an intimate experience. But there were many other places first-class passengers could eat if privacy was their chief goal.

VIPs were often invited to a large dining room behind the bridge, which, according to Armand de Niewenhove, a former *Normandie* purser, the crew called "The Ritz."

A passenger ensconced in a *de grand luxe* or *de luxe* suite could eat in his or her own dining room. And first-class passengers who wanted to throw a private party for, say, eight persons, could arrange to eat in one of the eight small, private dining rooms adjoining the main one.

For those willing to spend extra money on a meal, there was the café grill, five floors above the main dining room on the Boat Deck, behind the third funnel. A comfortable, unpretentious room, the café grill was a nice change of pace from the magnificence of the main dining room.

The café grill was *Normandie*'s nightclub, *à la carte* restaurant, dance hall, observation lounge and first-class bar. A more or less oval room about seventy-five by ninety-two feet with lots of floor-to-ceiling windows, it afforded first-class passengers a splendid view of the sea and the ship's wake which stretched back across the Atlantic into infinity. It was a popular spot too, for a midnight snack.

The café grill was more Bauhaus than Art Deco. Stainless steel tables and thickly upholstered chrome-framed chairs counterpointed the luminous columns of cast glass and swirling, ceiling-mounted strip lighting. The room was carpeted, except for a central illuminated glass oval which served as the dance floor. Its walls were covered in varnished pigskin.

Just forward of the café grill, portside, were a private bar and a card room. On the starboard side, forward, a small dining room offered privacy to those who liked café grill fare but wished to dine incognito.

A special attraction of the café grill was its delightful terrace, a large, more-or-less rectangular expanse of teak at the after end of the Boat Deck. Two rows of Art Deco-style wooden benches, with glass panels mounted atop them to keep away the Atlantic's cool breezes, provided seating. In the evening, the area was lit by six Art Deco-inspired pole lights.

According to early artist's renderings, the aftmost part of the café terrace—the very end of the ship—was to have been presided over by a giant green copper Neptune rising from a dolphin-filled sea and holding a trident aloft. But the statue proved too heavy for the deck, so it was mounted instead on a Le Havre pier.

None of *Normandie*'s first-class eating places, numerous though they were, was really appropriate for two special types of first-class traveler: young children and servants. The maids, valets, chauffeurs, nannies, secretaries or other servants of first-class passengers ate in a special dining room on B deck, below the main dining room. A dining room for young children was next door.

Exiting the café grill, a passenger en route to *Normandie's* renowned first-class public rooms came first to the top of the grand staircase, a flight of steps almost as broad and imposing as those of the Lincoln Memorial. Here stood "La Normandie," by Baudry, a lacquered bronze statue, 7 feet 8 inches tall and weighing 1,000 pounds, of a simple peasant woman, her hands filled with the fruits of the field.

From this vantage point, passengers could look forward through the smoking room, the grand lounge, the gallery salon, the upper hall and the theater, all the way to the backdrop at the rear of the stage (assuming all the doors were open). There had never been such a view in any ship before *Normandie* and there probably never will be again.

Descending the magnificent stairway, first-class passengers found themselves in the smoking room, an enormous chamber 55 feet long, 85 feet wide, with a 22-foot high ceiling. The room's walls were its most striking feature. Entirely paneled in Coromandel lacquer with gilt overlays, they were the work of Jean Dunand, the world's greatest lacquer craftsman and one of Art Deco's originators.

When *Normandie's* decorative contracts were given out, Dunand was told to create designs on the theme of "the games and pleasures of humanity." To his mind, that included "sport," "hunting and fishing," "the conquest of the horse by man," "dancing," and "the grape harvest." Brown Morocco leather settees or easy chairs and lacquered card tables completed the decor. It was to this room that the after-dinner set retired to puff on their cigars or pipes and play a few friendly hands of gin or poker.

Passengers inclined to visit the grand lounge passed through a sliding wooden partition 27 feet wide and 22 feet high, also by Dunand. On one side, it was carved with hunters and animals in jungle scenes and lacquered in brilliant colors. On the other, it was covered in stucco, which was decorated with clouds and heavenly figures. Two sets of doors were set into this partition, although it could also be completely opened to join the two rooms.

The grand lounge (also called the main lounge, grand salon, main saloon or grand saloon) was as wide as the smoking room (85 feet) but twice as long (110 feet) with a ceiling that reached 30 feet at its center. Such height made it the loftiest room ever installed in an ocean liner, the shipboard version of the waiting room at Grand Central Station.

The grand lounge's walls were almost entirely covered with glass panels etched and painted on the back in gold, silver, platinum and palladium. They were the work of Jean Dupas, Ruhlmann's friend and collaborator. These panels, which tell the story of navigation—or at least a mythological version of it—are populated with golden ships, gods and goddesses, sea serpents and other legendary beasts, and islands dotted with classical temples and lighthouses.

The four corners of the room held four ruffled glass Lalique lighting "fountains," similar to those in the main dining room and to the artist's fountain at the 1925 exposition. Each stood about 12 feet high and had a circular settee as its base. There were also two massive pewter urns by Daurat, one forward, one aft.

A warm gray rug covered most of the floor; in the center was a parquet dance floor which exactly reproduced the pattern of the floor of the Fontainebleau throne room. During the day, the parquet area was covered by perhaps the largest hand-woven carpet ever made, an Aubusson masterpiece 27 feet wide and 40 feet long, decorated with a magnificent flower basket pattern.

The grand lounge was the most stunning room on the ship, with the possible exception of the main dining room, and some passengers found it overwhelming. For them, two smaller lounges in the room's forward port and starboard quarters, concealed behind Dupas' glass panels, offered a retreat.

The grand lounge was large enough to hold every first-class passenger aboard, at such gala events as costume balls, boxing matches, fencing exhibitions, ballets, charity bazaars and fashion shows. At sea these events were presided over by the ship's most famous passengers. At one time or another they were hosted by Fred Astaire, Marian Anderson, Arturo Toscanini and Jascha Heifetz. In less frenzied hours, the lounge was the perfect place in which to play cards, nibble canapés, or sip a drink.

Forward, past the grand lounge, an elegant connecting hallway called the gallery salon led to *Normandie*'s theater/cinema, the first genuine movie house ever installed in an ocean liner. ("Talkies" were just seven years old when *Normandie* went into service.) This was also the first ship's theater to be equipped with first-rate stage equipment, lights and dressing rooms.

The theater had more than 380 folding red velvet seats, plus room for twenty or thirty standees along the back. Its silver-colored plaster of paris walls and ceilings were illuminated by recessed lighting fixtures. The curtain was a pearly rose velour interwoven with strands of spun cellophane. Its acoustics equaled those of Radio City Music Hall, which it somewhat resembled. Children's films were shown here every morning, while more adult fare was screened in the afternoon. These screenings were always crowded, partly because tourist-class passengers were allowed to attend. In the evenings, the offerings included plays, ballets and other spectacles.

There were four other public rooms on the Promenade Deck: a 5,000-book library; a writing room (the transatlantic radio-telephones were there, too); a shooting gallery; and the renowned winter garden.

To reach the winter garden from the theater, passengers entered the covered promenade, either port or starboard. The covered promenade—a perfect place for strolling—was 450 feet long on both sides of the ship, and it passed most of the major public rooms. The flower-filled winter-garden was located at the extreme forward end of the superstructure, running the full width of the ship, about 119 feet.

This remarkable room was alive with rare and beautiful flowers and plants, some strung out on swirling loop-the-loop trellises. Against a background of bubbling fountains, brilliantly-colored tropical birds twittered and sang in enormous crystal and bronze birdcages, designed by Ruhlmann.

The forward wall of this room, which followed the curved shape of *Normandie*'s streamlined superstructure, was fitted with twenty-eight super-strong windows, each more than a yard square. Through them passengers could see the ship's unique whale-back bow and, beyond it, the ocean itself.

For the first-class passengers who craved exercise that went beyond promenade strolling, salvation lay six decks below in a fully equipped gym and a large swimming pool.

At that level, the elevator doors opened on *Normandie's* first-class swimming pool, *la piscine des premieres classes*, a remarkable sight, considering its location deep in the bowels of an ocean liner.

The equal of many a land-based indoor pool, *Normandie's piscine* was 75 feet long and 18 feet wide, and was surrounded by a tiled platform 4 feet wide. That made it the largest swimming pool ever built into an ocean liner. In addition to its size, it had another unique feature, five different depths, from very shallow to fairly deep, to provide swimming pleasure for everyone from Olympic hopefuls to toddlers.

The entire area was designed by Patout and Pacon, the men responsible for the main dining room. Its walls, ceilings, which were two decks high, and surrounding terraces were covered by pale blue enameled sandstone tiles. A decorative frieze of mosaic tiles ran around the room. At the pool's after end there was a tiled bar and directly behind that, a large, fully-equipped gymnasium, decorated with murals of skiers, golfers and tennis players.

There were other places about *Normandie* a first-class passenger could get some exercise. Eight decks above the swimming pool, a vast, open recreation area between the first of two funnels was marked for such games as shuffleboard and badminton. There was also a full-sized tennis court between the second and third funnels, on a platform above the sun deck. To play on it, however, one had to be an excellent judge of how tennis balls behaved in thirty-five-mile-an-hour winds!

All told, *Normandie* provided some 46,000 square feet of open deck space for first-class passengers.

Behind the tennis courts there were accommodations for the only first-class passengers not yet mentioned: pets—dogs, cats, birds and the occasional monkey. Except for some animals whose owners couldn't bear to be parted even for a moment, the pets of first-class passengers were housed in a room within the casing of the third funnel, the dummy funnel. There were about three dozen tiled cages here, surrounding a two-level drinking fountain and phony fire plug. A dog-walking promenade was situated directly aft of the tennis courts, on the roof of the grand lounge.

At the base of the first funnel there was another surprise: a delightful children's playroom outfitted with a miniature three-pony merry-go-round, some rocking horses and the inevitable Punch and Judy puppet stage.

This, then, was the first-class *Normandie*. But it was only one of four *Normandies*, so to speak. Tourist-class passengers—owners of small businesses, department store buyers, college professors, well-heeled students, factory executives and the like—experienced a very different *Normandie*.

A tourist-class traveler (who was not called "second-class," even though tourist is between first and third), was one of a maximum of 654 passengers or 33 percent of the ship's capacity. About 29,000 square feet were allotted to their needs—a fraction of the first-class section, to be sure, but quite sufficient for most purposes.

Tourist-class passengers boarded *Normandie* on A Deck, aft, near a barber shop, a combination bookstore/drugstore/travel agency/florist shop, the purser's and head steward's cabins, the baggage master's room and the information desk. The embarkation hall did not equal the one in first class, but it was nevertheless beautifully decorated in oak paneling.

Here was the tourist elevator—a *Normandie* "first." Here also was a wide, curving stairway to take tourist-class passengers to their rooms, if the rooms were on another deck, or to the tourist-class public rooms. Tourist-class cabins might be on any deck, although usually aft of the third funnel.

On the Promenade or Main Decks, tourist-class cabins were inside rooms. They had no portholes, but each had a shower, a sink and a toilet. Passengers had to go down the hall to find a bathtub, however. On the other hand, those tourist-class passengers lucky enough (or smart enough) to book an A Deck stateroom had a good chance of getting an outside cabin. The best tourist-class rooms were either #376 or #375, both on A Deck. Made for conversion to first-class, if there was sufficient demand, each contained two beds and a complete bathroom.

Lesser tourist-class quarters could be found on B Deck. Here *Normandie*'s designers yielded to their baser impulses and laid out quite a few "Oklahoma" rooms. The strangest of these were #874 and #869, where the panhandles jogged as they approached the portholes, so that the only way an occupant could look out was to walk down their entire length (six feet or so).

On C Deck, the tourist-class cabins were all far aft, with many "Oklahoma" rooms. D Deck rooms were similar—and D Deck was the location of probably the worst tourist-class room on the ship, #1015.

This was a tiny, L-shaped cubbyhole big enough for an upper and lower bunk, a chest, a sink and nothing else. Its occupants could stand erect or lie down, but walking around was out of the question. The bathrooms were a good thirty feet away, down a long corridor. And the cabin was directly above the third-class pantry and directly below the tourist-class dining room. Chances for an afternoon nap here weren't good.

More typical, perhaps, was stateroom #227, a tourist-class room on the main deck. Approximately nine feet square—perhaps two-thirds the size of the average first-class accommodation—it had nicely decorated walls and a carpeted floor. The furnishings, which had a slightly Art Deco look, consisted of one comfortable chair, a chest of drawers, and two beds, one bed on the floor and one that folded up, all in handsome, polished dark woods. It was the equivalent of a good 1980s motel room.

The tourist-class dining room was three levels below, immediately aft of the main first-class dining room. A large handsome room, 103 feet wide by 66 feet long, it was remarkable for its central dome two decks high, supported by five massive glass-tiled columns. A huge glass chandelier hung from the center of the dome. The room's walls were paneled in ash.

After dinner, tourist-class passengers often retired to the tourist-class lounge, three levels up on the Main Deck, a short elevator ride away. This room, the equal of all but the most luxurious hotel lobbies, was about fifty feet square, with a central overhead well surmounted by a glass dome etched with designs by Max Ingrand.

Surrounding this well were four murals made of polished sycamore. There was a lovely painting on one wall. The floor was covered by a lush carpet, except for a central parquet dance floor. The room was filled with handsome tables and chairs upholstered in Aubusson tapestry.

The writing room was situated on the port side of the lounge. It was a warm, pleasant, library with books and desks for writing letters. On the starboard side of the lounge, there was an attractive snack bar.

The tourist-class smoking room was located on the level above. An arc of windows extended across its full width, affording a wonderful view of the ocean behind the ship. At night, *Normandie's* wake was visible, phosphorescent in the moonlight.

For the tourist-class passenger who wanted a little exercise, there were three choices: A gymnasium, directly below the smoking room, with a stationary bicycle, a rowing machine and a bucking bronco; a tourist-class swimming pool 16 by 21 feet and almost 9 feet deep. It was outdoors, on the open promenade of the Upper Deck, a reasonably well-sheltered location, but no place to hang out on a cold and windy day; two promenades, one of which was glass-enclosed, to ward off bad weather.

In tourist-class, the children's entertainment was provided by a playroom near the gym. It boasted a good stock of toys and the obligatory Punch and Judy puppet show.

Tourist class, then, was modest but nice. Many thousands found it a memorable way to cross the Atlantic.

But there was yet another passenger class, third class. It was designed for students or tourists of modest means or impecunious immigrants traveling to join relatives or to escape the Nazi terror.

The passenger traveling third class on *Normandie* was one of a maximum of 454—23 percent of the ship's capacity. About 14,300 square feet were allotted to third-class passengers, about half the space given to tourist class. Nonetheless, they were supplied with all the basics: cabin, dining room, lounge, smoking room and promenades.

Third-class passengers entered the ship on D Deck, coming into a pleasant, modestly decorated hallway with a large stairway and wonder of wonders, an elevator, an unheard-of shipboard luxury for passengers of this class. On C Deck, a third-class information bureau helped passengers find their rooms.

Third-class cabins were near *Normandie*'s stern, on E Deck, just above engine level, or on D Deck, C Deck, or B Deck. All were simple, plain and small. On the other hand, *Normandie*'s third class was certainly much better than the dormitories of steerage days. There were plenty of "Oklahoma" rooms in third-class, and plenty of inside rooms without baths, although even the worst of them had a sink. There were also many rooms with two sets of uppers and lowers apiece.

The outside walls of most of the outside third-class cabins angled sharply inward, ceiling to floor—the reverse of the wall in an attic. That's because the hull of the ship curved sharply inward at this point, as it headed toward the bilges.

The furnishings of a third-class cabin were a little sparse: a rattan chair or bench; a folding stool, perhaps; a full-length wardrobe with a mirrored door; a coathook; some life jackets on top of the wardrobe; an overhead fixture with a bare bulb; a reading light, and a narrow bed. The week's entertainment schedule, such as it was for third-class passengers, hung on the wall.

The cabin walls and ceilings were stark white enamel. In some third-class rooms, ducts snaked in and out near the ceiling and riveted steel structural members were plainly visible. Luxurious they weren't.

The third-class dining room, situated on E Deck, deep within the ship and on the same level as most of the third-class cabins, was its most impressive public area. Unlike the cabins, it was well-furnished and well-decorated, the equal of a good shoreside restaurant. Its walls were of yellow Caramy marble. Wide mahogany columns stretched to a glass dome two decks high.

The dining room's furnishings were attractive and comfortable—large, well-upholstered chairs, tables nicely set with good linen and silver. But there was very little Art Deco to be seen.

The style was semi-institutional, a fashion which hasn't changed much since *Normandie* was built.

From the dining room, the third-class lounge was a short elevator ride to B Deck. It was a lovely, comfortable room paneled in ash and filled with green Morocco leather easy chairs. There was a small writing room at the forward end.

The third-class smoking room was located on A Deck. A handsome chamber paneled in varnished mahogany, it overflowed with red leather chairs and couches. A stage for entertainment occupied one end. Encircling the room was a covered promenade with a fine sea view.

Third-class passengers got a breath of fresh air on A Deck behind the smoking room and almost at *Normandie*'s stern, on the lowest of the tiered decks.

This was third class—all of it. No swimming pool, no dog kennels, no café grill. On the other hand, those passengers traveling third class got there just as quickly as all the celebrities in first class.

There was one more *Normandie*, however: the crew's *Normandie*.

High-ranking crew members occupied quarters at least comparable in size and decor to the average first-class cabin.

The captain had a Sun Deck suite just aft of the wheelhouse, on the starboard side, with a reception room, a dining room (the two could be joined), a bedroom and an office. The reception/dining room was 31 feet by 18, with a 9-foot ceiling. It adjoined a private terrace connected to the starboard bridge wing, which could be used for business or pleasure.

The suite's decor equaled the Deauville or the Trouville. Designed by Remon Majorelle, one of Art Deco's leading figures, it had walls of French walnut, a grand piano, a gorgeous carpet and tapestry-covered chairs.

The second captain occupied a suite almost adjacent to the captain's. Except that it had no reception room, it duplicated the captain's quarters in size, decor and luxury.

The staff captain's suite was immediately below, on the forward edge of the Boat Deck. Nearby, in cabins comparable to those in first class, were the chief wireless officer and his five assistants, the chief security officer and six ship's officers. All of these officers had access to two smoking rooms and messrooms nearby, although those of higher rank generally ate in the main dining room.

Normandie's engineering staff was housed in Sun Deck quarters surrounding the ship's third funnel (the dummy funnel). Here the chief engineer and his assistant had a bedroom and an office, both decorated in high-style Art Deco.

The three second engineers and ten engineering officers had their own cabins nearby. The four junior engineers shared a pair of cabins. A messroom and a smoking room were close by, as were two elevators leading directly to the engine rooms.

The chief purser, first class, and one of his two assistant chief pursers occupied suites suitable to their duties, which often included entertaining overflow VIPs from the captain's suite. In this case their position entitled them to three-room apartments near the embarkation ports. Tourist-class or third-class pursers had pleasant but somewhat less elaborate accommodations.

The ship's doctor occupied a suite consisting of a bedroom and consulting room adjoining the emergency room and the waiting room. The doctor's quarters were designed by Louis Sognot, another famous name in the Art Deco world.

High-ranking officers had the run of the ship in all the classes and were the only people with such freedom. As a result, their *Normandie* was all four "ships."

There remain, in this accounting, the kitchen staff, the boiler-room crew, the fire-patrol men, and the stewards. What was their *Normandie* like?

Without a doubt it was the least glamorous *Normandie* of all. Depending on the job, there were glimpses of luxury at sea, but that's all they were: glimpses.

The petty officers, seamen and fire-patrol men had cabins and a messroom forward on the upper deck. Both were functional but hardly stylish. The engine-room crew slept on E Deck, starboard. The kitchen crew slept on the same deck, to port. Bunks and messrooms for stewards were forward, on A, C, D and E Decks.

Of course, crew quarters on most earlier ships were far worse.

They were dingy dormitories, comparable at best to flea-bag hotels. On *Normandie*, there were no more than fourteen to a dorm room and everyone had his own locker, galvanized steel bed and spring mattress.

These, then, were the four *Normandies*, the ships-within-a-ship created in the midst of the depression and that were installed within *Normandie*'s unique hull beginning in the summer of 1934.

How much did all of this cost? Over the years, many different figures have been quoted. The newspapers, always looking for the largest possible number, have most often said *Normandie* cost $59 million. Other sources mention costs ranging down to $30 million.

To figure out *Normandie*'s true cost in dollars, one must consider the franc–dollar exchange rate, which fluctuated wildly between 1930 and 1940. The ship's initial cost in France, before refit costs, was 650 million francs. But this money was paid out over a five-year period, which makes it even harder to calculate *Normandie*'s cost in U.S. dollars.

When *Normandie* was planned in 1930, her projected cost, in American dollars, was about $25.5 million—almost exactly the cost of the *Queen Mary*. This figure held through her launch.

By 1933, however, the differential effects of the depression had dramatically changed the exchange rate. And by 1935, when she made her maiden voyage, *Normandie*'s total cost equaled $43 million, without any increase in her cost in francs.

In the winter of 1935–6 she underwent alterations which cost another 150 million francs—about $10 million in American money, although obviously nothing like that figure so far as the French were concerned. This would have made her total cost $53 million, assuming every dime had been spent that year. No figure higher than this really makes any sense, and even this is high, since most of the money was disbursed in the early thirties, when the franc was worth less.

On the other hand, if you calculate the value of her 800-million-franc cost when she began her last voyage, in August 1939, you'll come up with a surprisingly small figure: $19.8

million. And by the end of World War II the exchange rate had dropped so much that 800 million francs equaled only $16 million.

What does all this mean in terms of today's inflated dollars? According to the most logical calculations, it would cost about $365 million to build *Normandie* today, including refit costs. That is a huge amount indeed, but not when you consider that $400 million is being spent merely to modernize the battleship *Missouri.*

7

INAUGURATION of A QUEEN

In mid-1934, *Normandie* was rapidly heading toward a life of carefree gaiety. But the world was going in the opposite direction.

On June 14, Hitler flew to Venice for the first in a long series of talks with his fellow dictator, Benito Mussolini.

An on August 19, 95 percent of Germany's registered voters went to the polls and 90 percent—more than 38 million—voted approval of Hitler's seizure of absolute power.

In the meantime, CGT was filling the ship's major staff positions. Two of her chief officers had been chosen long ago: Jean Hazard, her chief engineer, and René Pugnet, her commanding officer. Hazard had been with the ship since her conception. As CGT's senior engineer, he'd been instrumental in the choice of turbo-electric engines and had supervised their construction at Belfort and their installation in the ship.

Early in his career Hazard had demonstrated his abilities at sea. When a steam line on the *Rochambeau* burst in mid-ocean, he managed to repair the damage and get the ship under way again, using the materials on hand. Without a doubt he was CGT's premier engineer—exactly the right man to command *Normandie*'s engineering staff.

In his own way René Pugnet was equally qualified to command *Normandie*. He's begun his career at sea on sailing ships and small steamers. He joined CGT in 1907. By 1914 he was captain of the *Espagne,* a small liner that served the France–West Indies route. During the Great War, Pugnet first served in the destroyer fleet, then in the naval aviation service, where he became a pilot of legendary skill. After the war he returned to CGT and became Le Havre's marine superintendent. Later he commanded the *Paris* and the *Ile de France.*

A ruddy-faced man with an athletic build, Pugnet was six feet tall and weighed 200 pounds. He was a man of many talents: a painter who worked in pastels, a photographer, a skilled carpenter, a builder of model ships and airplanes, a musician who composed on and played pianos, violas and violins of his own construction, a collector of boxing gloves, knives, swords and pistols (and an expert in using each) and a linguist who spoke French, English, German, Spanish, a few words of Russian and Ouloff, the native tongue of Senegal.

Pugnet settled in St. Nazaire on the day *Normandie* was launched and remained there to help oversee her construction. To the captain's suite he contributed another of his creations: a piano he'd built himself, which had been in his suites on the *Paris* and the *Ile de France.*

In the summer of 1934 CGT chose the third chief officer of *Normandie,* its purser, the man who would control her business and social affairs, a kind of combination hotel manager and social director. That man was Henri Villar.

Villar had originally been a lawyer, and an Admiralty lawyer at that. But in the early 1920s he became a CGT purser. At that time the pursers' job was mainly behind the scenes. As chief paymaster and accountant, he managed his ship's hotel services.

But, largely as the result of Villar's very considerable social skills, the job was expanded so that the purser—at least on CGT ships—also had the responsibility for keeping the passengers happy and well entertained.

Villar was handsome, charming, witty, a first-class bridge player, an extraordinary dancer and a remarkable conversationalist who was comfortable with people of any social status.

To a great extent it was Villar who'd made the *Ile de France* so popular in the late 1920s. Once they'd met him, the rich and famous of two continents adjusted their schedules so they could sail on his ship.

But there was one more man who would be crucial to *Normandie*'s success, a man who rarely set foot on her. He was Clayland Tilton Morgan—Clay to his friends, who were legion. Clay was CGT's American press agent, the man responsible for making *Normandie* famous throughout America, which, after all, would have to supply most of her passengers.

Clay Morgan rose to his job as head publicity man for CGT via the circuitous route of the stage—he was a better than average leading man, it was said—and a steamship booking desk. Almost by accident he found himself specializing in the publicity side of the business. As New York newspaperman John McClain described him, Morgan "succeeded in earning the respect of both his employers and the press."

By September, *Normandie* was so far along that CGT decided to announce the date of her maiden voyage. She would begin her career, they said, on May 29, 1935. The advertising department was duly notified and it began mentioning *Normandie* in every CGT ad. Clay Morgan was given a green light.

Morgan's aim was to make *Normandie* famous throughout the United States as quickly as possible. So he wrote a press release describing the ship, emphasizing her size, speed and glamour, mimeographed it, sent it out to 150 key newspapers all over America. He then sat back to wait for clippings.

Three days later one of his mimeographed sheets came back from an Iowa paper. Scrawled across the margin in green ink was this comment: "Fooey on this junk. Do you think that just because we live out here where the tall corn grows we are saps enough to give free advertising to your damned frog ship? Can it!"

For a moment Morgan thought disaster was upon him. But only for a moment. The clippings began to come in by the dozen. Within two weeks he'd gotten back *Normandie* stories from 149 newspapers. Most had used his release verbatim.

Encouraged, Morgan went back to the typewriter and wrote a second release which met with the same reception. So did a third and a fourth. His fifth release was picked up by two major press services and wired to their thousands of subscribing newspapers. When *Normandie* arrived in New York, Morgan was sure, she wouldn't be greeted like a stranger.

At Penhoet the tempo was picking up. Workmen were now installing *Normandie*'s four anchors: two forward, each weighing 16 tons, plus a third, a spare, in the stem, and one aft, weighing 12 tons. These were connected to anchor chains weighing a total of 180 tons.

Other workmen were installing the bridge machinery: an ultrasonic depth indicator, a device which showed the exact draft of the ship fore and aft, a wireless directional finder that gave the precise position of the ship at sea, a master compass and binnacle, an automatic helmsman unit, course recorders, rudder-angle recorders, etc.

Still others were working on the ship's exterior, building her giant funnels, putting up her railings, finishing off her davits, installing ventilator uptakes, attaching her foghorn, erecting masts and the like.

Normandie's exterior appearance was dictated both by shipbuilding considerations and by aesthetics.

For instance, the size of her funnels was the direct result of the split funnel uptakes, which rejoined each other just above the Sun Deck. Their rake was a matter of aesthetics. Likewise, the usual mast forward of the bridge was eliminated because it was an obstacle to navigation—and because of aesthetics.

To make sure *Normandie*'s exterior pleased the eye, every design feature was first tried out on a 20.5-foot scale model in Penhoet's main offices. Only when it passed inspection in miniature was it approved for *Normandie* herself.

While *Normandie* was being fitted out, another superliner raced toward completion at the John Brown shipyard on the Clyde. Having been delayed for more than two years, number 534 was finally ready to be launched.

On September 26, undaunted by the steady rain, nearly 200,000 people gathered at Clydebank to see the big British vessel take to the water. Among those present were Queen Mary, King George V, the Prince of Wales and the American Ambassador and his wife, Mr. and Mrs. Robert Bingham, all of whom occupied a special glass-enclosed platform alongside the launching berth.

At 3:00 in the afternoon, while the crowd cheered, Queen Mary herself christened the great ship, giving it her own name. After a moment's hesitation the ship slid down the ways and into the Clyde.

Now, for the first but hardly the last time, Hitler began adding territory to his nation. He began with one of the most heavily industrialized parts of Europe—the Saar.

The Saar had been taken from Germany in 1919 as a result of the Versailles Treaty. A plebiscite was scheduled for January 1935 to decide whether the Saar would become part of France or Germany. And on January 13, 90 percent of its citizens voted to join Germany.

That same day a Penhoet supervisor was walking down a *Normandie* alleyway when he noticed that some of the ship's wall panels were loose. Suspecting tampering, he quickly unscrewed them, exposing the electrical conduits that ran the length of the ship. Inside he found needles sticking out of the conduits. Removing other panels, he found more needles. Some conduits had been cut, others were missing entirely. The supervisor realized that someone had tried to sabotage *Normandie.*

It was a clever attempt. Short circuits create electrical fires that are almost impossible to put out. It had taken the saboteur, whoever he was, only a few minutes to create the short circuits. Once the power went on, there was a disturbingly good chance *Normandie* would be reduced to a burned out hulk.

Within an hour a hand-picked team of electricians was checking every conduit on the ship, making repairs, sealing up the panels. The next morning a troop of policemen surrounded the ship and took up positions on every deck.

CGT never found out who'd sabotaged *Normandie,* never learned if it had been merely one disgruntled employee or an organized conspiracy or even the act of a foreign government.

Shortly afterward the president of the International Federation of Firemen came on board *Normandie* and, without warning, turned in a fire-alarm warning from the most remote part of the vessel. In one minute and forty-five seconds a security squad, headed by the security chief himself, was on hand with all the equipment necessary to handle a major blaze.

Soon afterward *Normandie* was at last towed out of her fitting-out basin and into the adjacent Joubert dry dock. The dry dock was drained and workmen began to install the ship's enormous, three-bladed propellers.

Now Clay Morgan's American publicity effort picked up speed. Having generated a blizzard of newspaper stories, Morgan began to peddle *Normandie* news to radio commentators and newsreel people.

The publicity worked; people began to call, write and even appear in person at CGT's New York headquarters to get information about *Normandie*. Morgan answered every question—except the inquiries about her speed.

It wasn't simply that her speed was a secret. The fact was, no one was certain how fast she'd be, even after all the model-testing. Penhoet and CGT thought she'd surpass the *Bremen* and the *Europa* and even the *Rex*, but ships often turned out to be faster or slower than expected.

Anyhow, Morgan had other problems to worry about. For instance, he had to figure out which representative of France would best adorn *Normandie* on her maiden voyage to America. To help with such decisions, Morgan hired Joseph Clark Baldwin III, a former New York State Senator and a protocol expert.

Morgan had made a list of French politicians he thought might be right. He showed it to Senator Baldwin. "My God, no!" said the Senator. "Not while Congress is discussing the French war debt. Bring over the wife of the President. No one can pin anything on her."

Morgan saw the good sense to this suggestion and made the necessary arrangements.

Other New Yorkers also prepared for the arrival of the enormous new French ship. On April 10 the Army dipper dredge *Hell Gate* began deepening the North River channel along the Manhattan waterfront.

Earlier, other dredges had deepened the rocky river bottom beside Pier 88, *Normandie*'s future home-away-from-home. They'd created a reasonably flat surface with just a few rocky knobs, none of them high enough to come even close to the ship's bottom under normal circumstances. One of these, however, a small ridge about 250 yards from the pierhead, would one day play a crucial role in *Normandie*'s life. But that was a thought that occurred to absolutely no one in the spring of 1935.

While all this was going on in New York, nearly 6,200 workers were laboring on *Normandie* at St. Nazaire, desperately trying to finish every last detail in time for her rapidly approaching sea trials and the maiden voyage that would follow almost immediately afterward.

As usual in projects of this size, many of the finishing touches had not been applied, despite all the careful planning. The public rooms and the cabins were stark and undecorated. The plumbing was only half connected—and that half was full of quirks and problems. But that was about par for a major new ocean liner.

Simultaneously, *Normandie*'s three top officers—Captain René Pugnet, Chief Purser Henri Villar and Chief Engineer Jean Hazard—were busy with the difficult task of selecting her crew. Since *Normandie* would be CGT's flagship and France's ocean-going ambassador to America, her crew couldn't be just 1,350 warm bodies. They had to be France's finest.

As *Normandie* neared completion, then, her top officers and several of CGT's executives sifted through the crew lists of the company's other large liners, looking for the most skilled, most charming, most honest crew members they could find.

Out of this group Captain Pugnet hired 66 officers and 105 deck hands. Chief Engineer Hazard hand-picked 26 officers, 22 assistants, 34 electricians, 42 oilers, 17 steam machinists, 96 steam assistants and 44 water tenders.

But the greatest hiring task lay with Chief Purser Henri Villar. He had to hire 12 officers and 917 stewards, cooks and other servants, including 3 doctors, an assistant chief purser, 3 junior pursers, 6 wireless officers, 18 security patrolmen, 119 waitresses, 21 stewardesses and hundreds of miscellaneous personnel for service in the public rooms and cabins and the great variety of jobs behind the scenes.

To help, Villar assembled a panel of three elderly French

Line ex-chief pursers who knew personally the honesty, efficiency, length of service, English fluency, marital status, size of family, religion and morality of every employee in CGT's catering department.

To head the kitchen, Villar chose Gaston Magrin, ex-chief chef of the *Ile de France*, a man of legendary appetite and temper. Then he and Magrin chose an associate chef, 2 assistant chefs, a sauce chef, a roast chef, a dessert chef, a fish chef, an *hors d'oeuvres* chef, a pastry chef, a chef for frozen dishes, a jams-and-jellies chef, a food-stores chef and a menu chef.

In addition, they hired 48 assistant cooks for cabin, tourist and third classes, 12 pastry and ice makers, 2 cooks for the crew and 65 helpers.

Also selected for kitchen service were a chief accountant, 4 comptrollers, 2 chief butchers and 7 assistants, an assistant to the chief steward and 4 assistants to the said assistant, 2 chief bakers and 8 ordinary bakers, a chief wine steward and 8 assistant wine stewards for the dining rooms, plus 4 men for the wine "cellars" and 6 barmen for the three classes, not to mention their 4 assistants.

And there were more. In first class alone, one man was selected to handle the buffet, another—with 4 assistants—to supervise preparation of coffee, 13 men to attend to the silverware, 12 to the china, 2 to the knives, 4 to the glassware, 2 for toast, 2 for the butter, 2 to look after the cheeses, 3 after fruits, 2 after salads, 2 after seafood. In tourist class 21 persons were chosen for these duties. Third class had 9.

In addition Villar hired 8 telephone operators, 4 stenographers, 8 clerks, 13 elevator operators and checkroom boys, 2 baggage masters plus 2 assistants and 2 *bagagistes*, a gymnasium instructor, a children's nurse, 7 hospital nurses, 7 printers, 6 cabinetmakers, 2 photographers, 2 cinema operators, 7 barbers, 4 manicurists, 2 masseurs, a masseuse, a gardener, a florist and 22 musicians.

On April 23 the French government issued a 1.50-franc deep-blue postage stamp to commemorate *Normandie*'s upcoming maiden voyage. This, of course, was a bit premature. On the day the stamp was issued, *Normandie* had yet to move under her own power. But her moment of truth was coming. Finally, on May 5—with her maiden voyage less than a month away—she was ready for her sea trials.

Tens of thousands gathered at the St. Nazaire waterfront on that morning. Nearly everyone there had played some role in creating the giant ship, and most of them harbored hopes and dreams about what she would accomplish and how the world would perceive her.

But at least one of those who had come to see *Normandie* off had nothing whatever to do with her. He was there not to wish her well, but to report on the results of her trials. He was G. McLaren Paterson, Cunard–White Star's chief naval aviator, the man who'd rejected Yourkevitch's hull, time and time again.

In the early afternoon, smoke began to waft out of the ship's forward funnels. Finally, a 5:00 p.m., her engineers at their stations and tugs leading the way, *Normandie* slowly and majestically began to steam out of the fitting-out basin that had been her home since 1932.

At almost exactly the moment *Normandie* reached the open sea, a heavy downpour struck the St. Nazaire area. But there was no longer any reason to fear bad weather. *Normandie* was ready for anything. At least, that was the belief of the chief executives of CGT and Penhoet, all of whom were aboard the ship.

Normandie was led out of the harbor by the French destroyer *Foudroyant*. The warship, which was loaded with newsmen who had come to witness the momentous event, bobbed and pitched like a cork in the squall, while *Normandie* rode the waves as if on a pond on a calm day.

Even though the light was fading, everyone aboard wanted to get in one trial run before nightfall. Captain Pugnet brought *Normandie* out to the measured mile between Penmarch and Glenans. Some of the ship's boilers were still cold, but he decided to yield to popular demand, warning everyone not to expect too much.

"*En route libre*" (full speed ahead), he told the engine room. The throb of her engines suddenly increased and *Normandie* gathered speed, her flaring hull parting the ocean waters as they had never before been parted.

The local sardine fishermen, cynical observers of many liner trial runs, were astonished at *Normandie*'s bow waves. She had hardly any. "She rides the ocean like a seagull," one reported.

The group of CGT's top brass on the bridge watched as their beautiful new vessel gathered speed: 20 knots . . . 21 knots . . . 22 knots . . . 23 knots . . . 24 knots! *Normandie* matched the top speed of the *Ile de France* without half trying. Then she slowed, her first run over. It had been a brief but very satisfactory performance.

The next morning Pugnet once more ordered, *"En route libre!"* *Normandie* leaped forward as if she'd been whipped.

On the bridge only Captain Pugnet surveyed the ocean ahead. Everyone else stared at the gauges, calling out speed figures as though they were conducting a countdown. *Normandie* quickly reached and surpassed 24 knots . . . 25 knots . . . 26 knots . . . 27 knots . . . 28 knots.

The counting stopped. In August 1933 the Italian superliner *Rex* had covered the distance between Gibraltar and the Ambrose lightship, outside of New York harbor, at the average speed of 28.92 knots, topping the *Europa*'s fastest crossing speed by just over a knot and winning the mythical Blue Ribbon.

Now the men responsible for bringing *Normandie* to the world watched in delight as their ship accelerated past 29 knots to 30.156 knots.

Captain Pugnet spoke briefly to the engine room, then turned to the executives on the bridge, grinning broadly. "Gentlemen," he said, "there's something you should know. We still had a number of cold boilers on that last run. I think she'll do even better."

At that moment Chief Purser Villar, who had a well-deserved reputation for thinking of everything, arrived on the bridge with chilled champagne and glasses. The celebration lasted until a crew member stationed on the Sun Deck, aft, had time to hurry forward to the bridge. What he had to say cast a pall over the party.

There was, it seemed, some fairly severe vibration in the after part of the ship. It was a kind of rattle, a noisy and distinctly unpleasant pulsation. In a few moments other crew members came forward to report vibration elsewhere, particularly on the upper decks, aft.

The vibration was also present in *Normandie*'s lower decks, aft, particularly in the third class and the crew quarters. It was enough to shake the dishes and to make reading difficult, although forward of the third funnel it diminished considerably and was just barely noticeable elsewhere on the ship.

This was a problem of the first magnitude. On a great luxury liner such as *Normandie*, nothing was more important than passenger comfort, and vibration was one of its worst enemies.

Something had to be done immediately or the ship's reputation would be destroyed. But three weeks remained before *Normandie* began her maiden voyage. Pierre de Malglaive, second in command at CGT, suggested those three weeks be used to fix the vibration—if it could be done in that time.

Fernand Coqueret, manager of the Penhoet shipyard, and Paul Romano, CGT's chief engineer, were asked to take on the task. As soon as *Normandie* finished her trials and arrived at her home port of Le Havre, they were to oversee the immediate installation of new stanchions and deck stiffening in the aft third of the ship.

There were several possible causes for the vibration, a common fault in express liners: overly light construction in the ship's stern, faulty propeller-blade design or propeller-shaft bossings or— and everyone prayed this was not the cause—the hull shape itself. The first three were fixable albeit at some expense. The fourth couldn't be corrected.

For now, Captain Pugnet reminded everyone that *Normandie*'s trials had just begun. He also reminded them that they were on the bridge of the fastest liner ever built and that their immediate purpose was to see just how fast she was.

Once more Pugnet brought the ship around toward the measured mile. Again he told the engine room, *"En route libre."* Almost effortlessly *Normandie* accelerated through 29 knots . . . 30 knots . . . 31 knots . . . 32 knots! When she hit the measured mile, she was boiling through the waves at an incredible 32.125 knots. The largest liner in the world, the largest liner ever built, had reached a speed of nearly thirty-seven miles per hour.

At this moment a small chartered airplane appeared overhead. It dove toward the water and a photographer leaned out of a window and snapped a picture of *Normandie* as she flashed over the measured mile for the third time. The next day, blurry radiophotos of the ship appeared in newspapers around the world.

Of course, only those on the bridge knew how fast *Normandie* had been going at that time and they weren't talking. But that didn't stop the speculation. "The *Normandie*," opined one American editorial writer, "will capture the Blue Ribbon without half trying."

There were dissenting opinions, however. One German newspaper hinted darkly that the *Europa* and the *Bremen* had been built with untapped power reserves so they could smash any record *Normandie* might set.

But on May 6 everyone on board the great new French liner knew she would soon hold the record. And, as if to prove that the first two runs were not flukes, Pugnet now brought *Normandie* around for another try. She covered the measured mile at an average speed of 31.925 knots.

That afternoon *Normandie* headed out into the Atlantic for an eight-hour run at full power. This time her average speed was 31.2 knots—more than 2 full knots faster than *Rex*'s record run.

For the next three days Pugnet put *Normandie* through her paces. On the morning after her speed trials, without warning anyone, he suddenly executed a crash turn to starboard, an emergency maneuver meant to avoid imminent collision.

Normandie heeled over sharply, frightening everyone on board. Until that moment the ship had rolled hardly at all. The turn completed, *Normandie* righted herself swiftly.

Next Pugnet put *Normandie* through a series of jarring, disorienting maneuverability tests: sudden stops, sudden reversals, sudden turns in every direction. She was subjected to stresses that she would seldom, if ever, experience again. She shrugged them off without complaint.

Normandie arrived at Le Havre on May 11. Except for the vibration, she'd performed superbly. Not only was she faster than anticipated, she also used less fuel.

At *Normandie*'s cruising speed—29 knots—she actually consumed less fuel oil than the *Ile de France* did at 24 knots. Her performance even outdid that of the current Blue Ribbon holder, the Italian superliner *Rex*, which had burned 1,100 tons a day at just under 30 knots. At the same speed *Normandie* burned just 950 tons.

The difference was in the hull. Yourkevitch's flaring bow and semi-bulbous entry, which had never been tested outside of a model tank, now proved their stunning efficiency.

Thousands watched on the morning of May 11 as their magnificent *Normandie* entered the harbor. A small group of tugs sidled up to her and quickly turned her; then, in a burst of bravado, she steamed right up to the dock without further help and dropped anchor.

Among the welcoming throng were G. McLaren Paterson and Sir Thomas Bell, director of the John Brown Company. Soon after *Normandie* had docked, Paterson managed to collar a crew man and quiz him about her speed trials and fuel consumption. In a few minutes he got the numbers he sought. They didn't please him much, however, for he instantly realized that *Normandie* would be a formidable foe of the *Queen Mary*, possibly her superior.

Sir Thomas Bell had what might be called better luck. He, too, struck up a conversation with a *Normandie* crew member, learning about the ship's serious vibration problem. He wired Sir Percy Bates, who wrote a morale-boosting note to Cunard's top executives:

"Sir Thomas Bell gave me some particulars with regard to the *Normandie* and in particular with regard to her trials, to the effect that they did not work her up to full speed because she rattled too much," he wrote. "They are quite confident they can deal with the trouble by putting in more stiffening, but no stiffening put in afterwards is satisfactory; it is only a palliative."

In the United States an uninterrupted stream of *Normandie* stories was flowing out of Clay Morgan's office, stories about her elevators, her cuisine, her shooting gallery, her dog kennels, her shops, theater, sports deck. The press loved every word.

At this time a rash of "Normandie'" fashions also surfaced in specialty shops from coast to coast—clothes, accessories, cosmetics, even coiffures. Travelers carried *Normandie* luggage. Bartenders concocted *Normandie* cocktails.

Normandie-shaped ashtrays, inkwells, paperweights, door-stops and the like blossomed almost overnight in America's gift shops. One could hardly pick up a newspaper or a magazine without being reminded that the great vessel would shortly begin her first trip to America. Even news stories of the gold run on the Bank of France managed to mention Normandie. The New World was in the grips of the same sort of irrational frenzy that in another age and time would be called Beatlemania.

Before long, every important shopwindow in midtown Manhattan blossomed with Normandie displays. Ropes, binnacles, steering wheels, life preservers, ventilators, travel posters, Normandie models formed backgrounds for everything that might conceivably be eaten, drunk, worn, carried or used by travel-minded shoppers.

While all this hoopla was going on in midtown Manhattan, 400 Public Works Administration workers engaged in another kind of Normandie mania. They worked in round-the-clock shifts to finish Pier 88, Normandie's American home.

Another 151 men worked triple-time to finish dredging out Normandie's new berth. Two dredging machines were in constant operation. "We will provide a depth of forty-six feet at mean low water," Francis T. O'Keefe, chief engineer of the New York City Dock Department, proclaimed.

At Le Havre, carpenters, painters, carpet layers and other craftsmen frantically tried to prepare Normandie for her maiden voyage. And in the bowels of the ship, ironworkers welded additional stanchions in place, in hopes of easing the vibration.

At that moment, from shops and warehouses on shore, victualers, quartermasters, linen-goods suppliers and tradesmen from every other imaginable field loaded Normandie with everything she would need for her initial transatlantic crossings.

Among other things, they stuffed her with 38,000 bed-sheets, 91,487 tablecloths, 150,000 towels, 10,200 pillow cases, 226,000 napkins, 30,000 bath towels, 30,000 hand towels, 40,000 kitchen towels (enough linen to cover the Empire State Building completely, Clay Morgan calculated), 57,600 assorted glasses, 56,880 plates, 28,120 saucers, 28,120 cups, 15,340 knives, 600 flower vases and 1,200 silver shells for ice cream.

As for food and drink, she was loaded with 70,000 eggs, 2.5 tons of seafood, 8 tons of 17 different French vegetables, 20 tons of potatoes, 250 pounds of caviar, 175,000 pounds of ice, 9,500 bottles of mineral water, a ton of coffee, 4,000 gallons of beer, 7,000 chickens and game birds, 35,000 pounds of meat, 61,000 gallons of Burgundy, Bordeaux and Alsatian table wine, 7,000 bottles of wine and champagne, 2,600 bottles of brandy and whiskey and appropriate quantities of everything else a transatlantic passenger might desire.

Not all of these delicacies came from Europe. In the middle of May one of *Normandie*'s running mates, the *Paris*, arrived at Le Havre with a load of American foodstuffs: hominy grits, cranberry sauce, dry cereals, buckwheat pancake flour, ketchup, maple syrup, malted-milk powder and some ultra-select fruit, fish and vegetables.

The French Line also arranged for *Normandie* to bring certain gifts to America to cement Franco-American relations and call attention to *Normandie* in various American locales. The idea, which was hatched in CGT's public-relations department, of course, was for several French cities to send gifts to their U.S. counterparts.

La Rochelle, for instance, would send to New Rochelle, New York, a sculpted window keystone from her fifteenth-century city hall. Macon, a French wine center, would send to Macon, Georgia, an urn filled with soil from Burgundy, several wine growers' jars and some choice vintages. Cadillac would send to Cadillac, Michigan, two finely worked coffers, plus an album of Bordeaux photographs. Calais would send to Calais, Maine, a casket containing soil from the French city. St. Louis would send its Missouri namesake a huge copper photograph album.

And France herself provided still more gifts: a bronze bust of Champlain to be erected at Fort Niagara, handmade copies of maps showing French exploration in America and the routes of French and U.S. aviators to be distributed among Columbia, Yale, Harvard and Princeton Universities and, for President Roosevelt, a bust of Alexis de Toqueville.

Even though *Normandie* wasn't quite finished, CGT officials were confident she would begin her maiden voyage on schedule on May 29. But there was a cloud on the horizon. In recent weeks two French governments had fallen. One of the issues that had brought them down was a sailors' strike over wages.

On May 20 *Normandie*'s crew joined the strike. The government reacted with a tough communiqué. "Any attempt to interfere with *Normandie*'s maiden voyage," it said, "will be treated as a disloyal act."

Happily, the dispute was settled by negotiation.

The next day, however, *Normandie* ran into trouble of a far more serious nature, possibly related to the labor difficulties.

Just before dawn on May 21 a *Normandie* watchman on his ordinary rounds heard people running from a room near the upper bridge. Hurrying toward them, he practically ran headlong into two men. They were painters who'd been assigned to finish the officers' cabins.

The watchman shouted at the men to stop, but they ignored him. In a move that was fortunate for the ship, he rushed to the room from which they'd come. There a small pail of gasoline was ablaze and the flames were just inches from a pair of drapes.

The watchman grabbed an extinguisher and put out the fire. The whole incident had taken no more than a minute or two and the damage was virtually nil. But if the watchman had been elsewhere, *Normandie* might have burned then and there.

The watchman reported the incident to the police guarding the ship, who quickly found the two painters and arrested them. The painters claimed that one of them had accidentally tossed a cigarette into the pail, causing the fire. They were running, they said, to sound the alarm.

The French Line naturally wanted to avoid any adverse publicity about *Normandie*, especially this close to her maiden voyage. It suggested the one man be fined for "breaking smoking rules" and released. And so he was, after paying a fifty-franc fine—$3.30 at the 1935 rate of exchange.

Somehow the London *Daily Mail* got hold of the story and made it sound like barely averted sabotage. CGT labeled the *Daily Mail* story "perfectly ridiculous" and said the whole thing was a minor accident.

Perhaps it was, perhaps it wasn't. The evening after the painter was fined, a dove was seen flying over *Normandie* with a small

Nazi flag tied to its leg. The police were never able to find out anything about this.

All of this had no effect whatever on passenger bookings. By this time practically every first-class cabin was booked for the maiden voyage, and at a minimum price of $275, one way. The return maiden voyage was also heavily booked in first class. Neither the tourist nor the third-class cabins were completely filled in either direction, but that had been anticipated in light of the world's economy.

On the evening of May 23 the President of France, Albert Lebrun, formally put *Normandie* into service, an event characterized by a round of parties and other gala events. Some 2,000 VIPs were brought from Paris, 142 miles away. Among them were France's leading figures in society, politics, the arts and literature. They inspected the new ultramodern maritime station at Le Havre; and they toured *Normandie*, marveling at her well-publicized wonders.

Then everyone retired to the ship's vast first-class dining room, where they were lavishly wined and dined. At the *table d'honneur* sat President Lebrun and his wife; Marcel Olivier, CGT's president, and his wife; René Fould, Penhoet's president, and his wife; William Bertrand, *Ministre de la Marine marchande*; the ambassadors (and their wives) from Belgium, Spain, Italy and the United States; several French barons, counts and marquises—and Sir Percy Bates, president of the Cunard Line.

After dinner the guests attended one or more of the many festive events on board. This lavish binge compressed all the delights of a gala ocean crossing into one wonderful night, without the attendant hazards of *mal-de-mer*. Those attending included the press, the politicians who had voted the staggering subsidy which made the great vessel possible, the line's stockholders and directors, booking agents from all over Europe, painters, sculptors, shipyard workers—in short, practically everyone connected with designing, financing and decorating the ship, except for Vladimir Yourkevitch.

Although Penhoet and CGT had accepted his hull design, they had not accepted the man himself. His name had not been mentioned in a single *Normandie* press release. *Normandie* was intended to represent everything grand and glorious about France. Admitting that a Russian immigrant had made a major contribution to the ship—perhaps *the* major contribution—was not perceived as glorification for France.

Yourkevitch himself did not insist on public credit. After all, he wanted more work from CGT. Besides, the shipping world knew what he had accomplished, even if the public didn't. But, as *Normandie*'s maiden voyage neared, his wife, Olga, told the whole story to a reporter from a top Paris newspaper.

The story broke after the gala reception on May 23, but not too late for the embarrassed French Line to give Mr. and Mrs. Yourkevitch two free first-class round-trip passages on *Normandie*'s maiden voyage as "a token of gratitude."

The last week in May 1935 was one of those rare times in the 1930s when it seemed, briefly, that everything would be all right after all.

Pierre Laval successfully concluded negotiations with the Soviet Union for an anti-German alliance, or so he thought.

And Hitler made a grandiose "peace" speech in the Reichstag. "Germany needs peace," he screamed, "Germany wants peace. . . . No one of us means to threaten anybody."

The world economic news also seemed hopeful. Good times had not arrived, but people were at last able to remember when things had been worse.

In all, it seemed an auspicious moment for the greatest ocean liner ever built to embark upon her career.

8

RUN FOR THE RIbbON

Wednesday, May 29, 1935, dawned bright and beautiful at Le Havre. There was a distinct sense of anticipation in the air. The world's greatest ship was about to sail on her first commercial voyage, an event that had been seven years in the making.

Tied up alongside the new landing stage, *Normandie* gleamed in the sun, her black, white and red paint newly retouched for her coming out. Anyone who listened carefully could hear strange noises coming from her, the unmistakable sounds of construction: riveting, hammering, banging.

Normandie was scheduled to lift anchor at 5:00 p.m., but battalions of workmen were still aboard, installing stanchions in her rear quarter in hopes of reducing vibration, bolting porcelain *lavabos* in place in first-class cabins, laying black rubber tile on her Promenade Deck, connecting the electrical wiring of her huge public rooms.

As *Normandie*'s "hotel manager," Chief Purser Villar had to inspect every cabin personally. He was accompanied by a "flying squad" of carpenters, painters, electricians and plumbers, who handled most minor matters and referred major problems to other workmen.

Villar had little trouble with tourist and third-class cabins, since they required far less decorative work than the first-class rooms. Nor did it matter much if there were some unfinished rooms in these classes, since neither were more than a third booked for this voyage. Workmen would stay aboard during the voyage to finish them off.

First-class cabins were another story, however. These were the ship's showplaces. What's more, most of them were booked in both directions. They had to be as close to perfection as possible.

The biggest problem was plumbing, a traditional maiden-voyage headache. *Normandie*'s particular plumbing problem, Villar discovered, was an absence of sinks in most of the first-class suites.

He gathered all the plumbers he could find and told them that sinks simply *had* to be installed in every room by noon on the day of departure. Hundreds were bolted into place only hours before passengers were admitted to their cabins.

Villar didn't complete his inspection tour until May 28, the day before departure. One of the last cabins he examined was the Trouville Suite, the one chosen by Madame Lebrun.

To Villar's infinite dismay, the Trouville was a catastrophe. Nothing had been completed. The walls and ceilings were unfinished, the cabinetry was as yet unassembled and the bathtubs had no faucets at all.

Villar immediately—and wisely—put his entire flying squad to work. By the time Madame Lebrun arrived, about thirty hours later, not a nail was out of place and the paint, miraculously, was dry to the touch.

Before the sun was finally up on the morning of the 29th, *Normandie*'s crew began taking its place. This was no simple matter, since diagrams of the ship had not yet been printed. Fortunately, the door numbers were in place, but even this had been an eleventh-hour accommodation.

At noon Villar gave the signal and the passengers and their guests began to board the ship. They made their way through a mad confusion of porters staggering with heavy suitcases, red-ribboned officials trying to find out where they should be and scarlet-jacketed stewards attempting to direct this mass of human traffic.

All told, some 1,070 passengers had booked passage on this maiden voyage—about half of *Normandie*'s capacity.

The first-class passengers had paid a minimum fare of $275 and a maximum of $1,400. Tourist-class passengers had paid $138.50 each for an inside room, $2.50 more for a cabin with a porthole. Dog tickets were $20, while cats and birds in cages were carried for $5 each.

The passenger list included Martin Beck of theatrical fame, Madame Pierre Cartier, Mrs. Morgan Belmont, Madame Jeanne Lanvin, Mrs. Frank Jay Gould, Mr. and Mrs. Lowell P. Weicker (parents of today's senior Senator from Connecticut), Arthur Schwartz, Jules Stein, André Pernod, the Comte and Comtesse de Tocqueville, the Comte de la Rochefoucauld, Mademoiselle Colette and many other celebrities of stage, screen, politics and commerce—the "jet-setters" of 1935.

Perhaps the most prepossessing was the Maharajah of Kapurthala, one of the ranking princes of northern India. He was accompanied by his second son, a secretary, an attendant, a valet and his personal Hindu cook, who traveled with him wherever he went. He'd booked the suite of rooms across the hall from Madame Lebrun, the Deauville.

Normandie carried more than human cargo, however. $29 million worth of gold, in bullion, was stashed in a special vault in the hold and guarded by twenty men with rifles and pistols.

This was no gift to America. In fact, France was parting with this gold reluctantly. It was part of a massive withdrawal from French banks, spurred by a government deficit of $600 million and a general loss of confidence in France's economic stability.

Also aboard *Normandie* for this momentous trip was a corps of newsmen from practically every Western nation, there to report in excruciating detail everything that happened aboard. They constantly badgered French Line officials, Captain Pugnet and everyone else in authority about whether or not *Normandie* would make an attempt on the Blue Ribbon.

However they phrased the question, and whomever they queried, the answer was the same: No, we are not shooting for a record. We might do that on a later trip. On this trip we merely plan to maintain a normal commercial speed.

Of course the answers were a lie. All of those associated with *Normandie* desperately wanted her to win the Blue Ribbon for France, which had never held it. But no one was willing to tempt fate by announcing this intention—at least not on the record.

At 4:00 p.m., an hour before her official departure time, all visitors were ordered ashore. As 5:00 came and went, *Norman-*

die remained at her pier, delayed by the incredible crush of U.S.-bound mail that had descended upon the Le Havre post office, every piece of which had to be canceled before it was brought aboard the ship.

Finally, at 6:19 p.m., accompanied by a hysterical coterie of hooting watercraft, buzzing airplanes and shrieking crowds, the great ship was eased away from the landing stage by a covey of tugs. Her sister liners, the *Ile de France* and the *Paris*, and the U.S. Line's *Manhattan* roared out their salutes, but, in a series of blasts that set the earth vibrating, *Normandie's* deep-throated whistle drowned out all other sounds.

Then her tugs dropped away and she slowly swept out of the harbor into the twilight gathering over the Channel. *Normandie* was on her way, headed toward her first stop: Southampton.

Aboard the ship both passengers and the room-service crew tried to find their way around the ship and settle in. Each passenger was presented with a booklet full of instructions and information ranging from the obvious to the arcane.

The booklet for first class began by instructing the passenger to hand his ticket to the steward, get his stateroom key from the cabin's dressing-table drawer and read the safety notice on the stateroom door, which listed his lifeboat number and lifebelt instructions.

The booklet also advised the passenger to see the chief dining-room steward first thing to get a table reservation, and to contact the chief deck steward on the Promenade Deck, assuming it could be found, to reserve a deck chair.

It went on to say that between 7:00 a.m. and 10:00 p.m. one could ring one bell to summon a steward or another to call forth a stewardess. After 10:00 p.m., however, it was recommended that one telephone night service rather than ring.

The booklet listed in detail the ship's many activities and services, beginning with news of what many thought was the most important shipboard preoccupation: eating and drinking.

Breakfast service began at 8:00 a.m. Cabin service was available by request. Lunch service began at 12:30. And the dining room would open for dinner at 7:30.

Snack time wasn't neglected. At 11:00 a.m. stewards with red jackets and little red caps served Bovril, sandwiches and biscuits. The same stewards toured the ship with trays loaded with tea, ice cream, cakes and sandwiches at 4:00 p.m. Wines and other drinks were served almost everywhere aboard at anytime.

The information bureau handled such matters as money exchange, letters of credit and traveler's checks. It also provided safety-deposit boxes for valuables, passport service and a lost-and-found department. Secretarial service was available at $1 an hour.

Stock quotations from New York, London and Paris were posted on a bulletin board near the information bureau. (They were also printed in the ship's newspaper, which was delivered free to every stateroom each morning and which contained a schedule of the day's events.)

One could send a radiogram to New York for 5.40 francs. Wireless-telephone service was also available.

Horseracing (the shipboard variety, played with cardboard horses and dice), boxing and fencing exhibitions, bridge and backgammon tournaments and lotto games, chess and checkers were all offered for the whiling away of one's hours. Decks of playing cards could be purchased from stewards in the lounge, smoking room or café grill.

Swimming lessons were available for $1 each. A gymnasium next to the swimming pool was open from 7:00 a.m. to 1:00 p.m. and from 2:00 p.m. to 7:00 p.m. But the time slot from 10:00 a.m. to noon was reserved for ladies only.

Boxing and fencing lessons, by appointment, were another offering. There were also four deck-tennis courts on the Sun Deck between the first and second funnels, shuffleboard courts on the Sun Deck and the Promenade Deck, and Ping-Pong tables on the Promenade Deck, aft (sheltered from the wind). There was a Ping-Pong tournament on every voyage, with a trophy for the winner.

Those whose favored sport was hunting could hone their marksmanship at the shooting gallery on the portside forward Promenade Deck for the modest fee of $.35 for ten shots—pistol, rifle or revolver. Or they could shoot clay pigeons on the Boat Deck, aft—ten "birds" for $1.35. Shooting tournaments were held at both galleries, and prizes awarded on the last day of crossing.

Normandie's theater showed movies continuously from 3:00

p.m. until 6:30 p.m. (This allowed passengers an hour to change for dinner.)

Mass was celebrated daily in *Normandie*'s chapel. The chapel was also available for Protestant services, by application to the chief purser. (A small synagogue was installed the next winter.)

A small "symphony" orchestra played in the grand lounge from 4:00 to 5:00 p.m. and from 8:30 to 9:30 daily. Fifteen minutes after it ceased, a dance band took over, playing in the grand lounge until midnight and in the café grill until the last pair of dancers called it quits.

Gamblers could bet on the "horseraces" or on any of the many sporting events that took place daily. Or they could get involved in one of the card games so typical on luxury liners. Or they could join the speed pool and rush to the purser's office every day at noon to read the figures on the previous day's run.

Ladies could get their hair marcelled for fifteen francs at a branch of the Paris salon Calou, with Calou's Roger presiding; men could get haircuts for ten francs. A manicure was twelve francs for either gender, a pedicure fifteen francs.

About the only thing one *couldn't* do aboard *Normandie* was to go sightseeing in areas designated for the other classes—at least, not without an escort. "The company's regulations," read a prominently posted sign, "prohibit passengers from passing from one class to another. Passengers are therefore kindly requested to refrain from applying for this privilege and to keep within the confines of the class in which booked."

The French Line realized that human curiosity was unquenchable, so it dealt with this inconvenient urge by providing daily tours of the ship for all classes. Tourist and third-class passengers could also get a glimpse of first-class splendors by attending services in the chapel or by going to the movies.

These opportunities were naturally not enough for some tourist and third-class passengers, who took it as a personal challenge to spend as much time with first-class passengers as possible.

Petra Williams, one of those who dared, recalled that her way of getting to first class was through the engine rooms, on a metal catwalk. "When I look back," she said, "I get scared of the motion of the huge arms moving up and down and the noise. Ah, youth! All I cared about was dancing and swimming."

While *Normandie*'s passengers were learning about her glories, the newspaper reporters aboard cabled home reams of copy, most of it ecstatic. Wrote a reporter from the *New York Herald Tribune*, "The passengers were astonished tonight at the ship's perpetual sunlight, due to the brilliant, modernistic, indirect lighting. Even her amazingly wide companionways are lighted in this fashion. . . ." Cabled another, "Tonight, gay parties were going on in all parts of the ship and many passengers were still covered with the confetti and colored ticker tape thrown by the crowds on the docks just before the liner sailed."

Running smoothly across the Channel, averaging 26.67 knots— a very fast speed for any other ship—*Normandie* arrived at her first stop, Southampton, at 11:10 that same night.

While an orchestra on shore saluted the ship with a rendition of "La Marseillaise," the thousands who had waited at Southampton harbor were rewarded with a spectacular sight. As *Normandie* drew into view, they saw row upon row of portholes twinkling along her flanks. Artful indirect lighting made her enormous red-and-black funnels shimmer. And her name blazed forth in huge letters made of electric lights on the Sun Deck.

Witnessing her arrival was Frank Beken, one of the world's great marine photographers, a man who'd been taking pictures of liners in the Solent since 1885. According to his son, Beken was awed by *Normandie* and thereafter told his friends that she was the most graceful and beautiful liner he had ever seen.

As soon as *Normandie* had anchored, she was approached by the *Greetings* and the *Calshot*, two little tenders whose purpose was to deliver embarking passengers to liners anchored in the harbor and pick up those wishing to go ashore.

On this occasion the *Greetings*, a perfectly named ship if ever there was one, delivered the Mayor of Southampton, a little man with glasses, who wore his heavy gold necklace of office over a lounge suit. He'd come to welcome the ship officially. The *Calshot* brought a fresh consignment of passengers.

After a short ceremony the Mayor returned to the *Greetings*, along with his press retinue, who were heading back to shore to write stories about *Normandie*'s amazing size (bigger than Piccadilly Circus) and power (she produced more than the London Underground used at rush hour). Some 300 CGT guest passengers who'd made the first leg of the trip just for the ride departed on the *Calshot*.

At 3:07 a.m. Thursday, *Normandie* weighed anchor. Then, swept by every searchlight in the harbor, she headed for the rocky formation known as the Needles, guided gingerly by an English pilot.

Eight hours and 45 minutes later *Normandie* passed Bishop's Rock lighthouse, in the Scilly Isles off Cornwall. This was England's westernmost point, 215 miles from Southampton and the terminus from which Atlantic speed records are figured. She'd made this brief trip at an average speed of 30.17 knots—a pace more than fast enough to win the Blue Ribbon if she could keep it up.

"Her steadiness was truly remarkable," one newsman cabled back to New York. "Only when one stepped out on the open deck and faced the breeze that this speed made, or watched a fast-retreating whitecap did he convince himself that he was being borne along at the pace of a New York taxi. Picture the Empire State Building ripped from its mooring and dashing up Fifth Avenue at 34 miles per hour and you have an idea what the *Normandie* means."

Of course, no one, not even her redoubtable chief engineer, Jean Hazard, knew if *Normandie* could maintain that speed.

By the second night out, tourist and third-class passengers in *Normandie's* aft quarters knew that their voyage would be anything but ordinary. They were the chief victims of the ship's vibration, which was so bad that many passengers were moved to cabins farther forward. Those who remained had quite an experience.

Charles Colvin, returning from the Continent after a sales trip, described it this way: "Our cabin doors were hooked open. . . . There was just enough play between the hooks and the eyes so the rattle was deafening. It was impossible to sleep. But I had a ball of heavy twine in my bag, which I used to tie the doors tightly against their hooks, not only of my cabin, but of those nearby. The urgent need for noise suppression quickly made us all friends."

But the noise didn't disappear entirely. "During the first night, at intervals, there was apparently a machine gun being fired in my cabin or in the one alongside," Colvin says. "The other chap and I discussed its possible source and sat vigil in his cabin. We found it was being generated at the head of his bed, where the vertical steel parts of the bed had come adrift from the horizontal members. I wrapped them with twine. End of machine gun."

Although these impromptu alterations improved sleeping conditions, vibration popped up elsewhere. "Using the john was quite an experience," Colvin reports. "One had to sit. Standing, the stream hit the walls on each side.

"And taking a bath was an adventure which had to be experienced to be believed. During the time of a tubbing, little water spouts would appear from the surface of the water. It looked exactly as though there were a thin layer of rubber atop the water, from which small fingers stuck up in a pattern of about one every eight inches. As I knocked them off with my hand, they again appeared."

Fortunately for *Normandie*'s reputation, almost everyone who "mattered"—including the press—occupied a first-class stateroom. Reporters did hear about the vibration, of course, but few experienced it full force. Besides, everyone knew vibration was to be expected in fast, new ships.

The reporters were far more interested in *Normandie*'s speed. Vibration deserved a paragraph, perhaps, but a Blue Ribbon meant banner headlines.

Normandie started out superbly. Just after noon on Friday, May 31, in the midst of her second day at sea, Richard Reagan, the *New York Herald Tribune* correspondent, radioed the following lead to his newspaper:

"Aboard the S.S. *Normandie* (at sea), May 31. A world record was claimed by France's new superliner this noon when she completed a first day's run of 744 nautical miles. In one six-hour stretch from 10 p.m. yesterday to 4 a.m. today, she averaged 31.5 knots, despite a heavy swell and increasing wind. . . ." (This day's sailing beat the former mileage record over the same time period, 736 miles, held by the *Rex*.)

What Reagan did not know—in fact, what no one aboard except her officers knew—was that at 7:00 a.m. that very morning a tube on one of the starboard condensers had popped open and started taking on salt water.

The condenser was out until 12:15 a.m. on June 1. During this time *Normandie*'s average speed fell to 28.07 knots. The passengers knew none of this; while Hazard's engineers were sweating on repairs, *Normandie*'s record day's run was being celebrated on board with much libation and hilarity.

That afternoon Madame Lebrun formally opened the café grill (the carpenters finally having cleared out) and that night she sent a radio message to the United States, where Memorial Day was being celebrated. "I can never forget the spiritual bond of gratitude to the heroic dead, which I share with the United States," she said.

That evening Madame Lebrun was escorted by her naval attaché, Admiral Bigot, to the Trouville Suite, across the hall from her own, where the Hindu cook of the Maharajah of Kapurthala had prepared an Indian dinner for his master and for the wife of the French President.

While they ate, Hazard's crew finished repairing the condenser tube and flushed everything with distilled water. Then *Normandie* picked up speed again. During the night she averaged 30.2 knots, using only 128,000 of her rated capacity of 160,000 horsepower.

The next morning Captain Pugnet informed the press corps that he intended to speed up after crossing the Gulf Stream. "We shan't try very hard this trip," he told the newsmen, "but we will break all records easily."

Somehow correspondents for the German newspapers got it all wrong. The next day newspapers all over Germany gleefully proclaimed, in enormous front-page headlines, that *Normandie*'s master had admitted she would not be able to break the transatlantic speed record.

Germany's inclination to disparage *Normandie* came as no surprise. At that time the record transatlantic crossing speeds were held by ships from the only two fascist countries in the world: Italy, whose *Rex* held the westbound record: 4 days, 13 hours and 8 minutes, an average of 28.92 knots, and Germany, whose *Bremen* held the eastbound record, about one hour and one knot slower than the *Rex*.

At 10:00 that evening there was a *fête de bienfaisance*—a

benefit—in the ship's theater, featuring the French actress Marcelle Chantel and the French novelist Colette. Two short plays were also presented. Later there was a variety show in the grand lounge, featuring De Vito and Denny, Dorothy Stevens, Tex MacLeod, Al Nord and Jeane and Gene Dennis. The emcee was Phil Arden. And at midnight there was dancing in the café grill, to the strains of the French Tango Orchestra and Crislers' Jazz Orchestra.

The next morning, which was a Sunday, the ever-present Madame Lebrun attended the first Mass in *Normandie*'s chapel, which was celebrated by Monsignor William Quinn of New York. On this special occasion the chapel was filled to overflowing, and some worshippers were forced to stand outside in the hall. This was highly unusual, since, on average, less than 15 percent of a luxury liner's passengers attended Sunday services, the vast majority attempting to recover from their Saturday-night sins by remaining in bed as late as possible.

As for *Normandie* herself, with her engines once more in fine fettle, she set another single-day record during the twenty-five hours ending at noon on June 2, Sunday, steaming 748 miles at an average of 29.92 knots. There was nothing between her and the Blue Ribbon but a few hundred miles of open ocean.

Nonetheless, a few passengers were uneasy about what lay ahead. Even before the ship had sailed, there had been sabotage rumors. Now, as *Normandie* began her last full day at sea, the rumors intensified.

That afternoon an American novelist by the name of James Aswell dropped in on another first-class passenger, Robert Ripley, whose "Believe It or Not!" cartoon panel was a daily feature in many English-language newspapers. Ripley was to emcee an hour-long radio broadcast from the grand lounge that night, *Normandie*'s final night at sea on this trip, and he'd asked Aswell to participate. Aswell had come by to check out his piece before it went on the air. After Ripley approved it, their conversation turned to the bomb rumors that had been sweeping the ship.

"The bomb which we had been hearing about throughout the trip," Aswell later wrote, "lay concealed in the hold of the

Normandie, planted by a Nazi saboteur. It would blow us all to glory, the gabble went, in many versions.

"Nobody, of course, believed the story. Not really, except perhaps the French Deputy with the spade beard who was so sure of it that he sat on the same bar stool 14 hours a day, fortifying himself against the moment."

There was no bomb aboard *Normandie*. In fact, it seemed that nothing could threaten her or take the Blue Ribbon from her. Then, suddenly, while she was barreling across the Atlantic at more than thirty knots, she ran into something threatening indeed, something every ship's captain dreads: fog, a typical thick Grand Banks fog.

Commandant Pugnet reacted boldly. Using his radio to locate all the ships that might be anywhere near *Normandie*, he ordered the ship to proceed full speed ahead. According to his survey, no vessel was close enough to do her any harm. He was also confident that there was no threat from that other ship hazard, icebergs, because *Normandie* was holding course on the southern summer track, where no iceberg had ever been sighted this late in the year.

So the great French liner hurtled through the fog without throttling back even a fraction of a knot. She was due in New York the following morning, a Monday, and Pugnet wanted to get there as early as possible.

Before dawn the next morning CGT's Paris office radioed Pugnet telling him not to make Ambrose light before 11:30 a.m. This was the East Coast terminus from which *Normandie*'s crossing speed would be calculated, record or not. CGT wanted him to wait because it knew *Normandie*'s new New York pier would not be ready to receive her until 3:00 p.m.

Slow down the *Normandie* to meet a docking schedule? On her maiden voyage? On a Blue Ribbon run? That just wasn't in Pugnet's character. So *Normandie* kept up her pace. She was racing toward America at the fastest speed she'd yet attained on this voyage: 31.69 knots—36.44 miles an hour.

At 7:35 on the morning of June 3 a tiny plane flew over *Normandie*. Its pilot was Bill Cleveland, an aviator hired by the *New York Journal*, who later wrote:

I kept a rendezvous with the new mistress of the seas, the Normandie, *at sunrise today,* 125 *miles out in the Atlantic, just the* Normandie *and I. There weren't any other planes, so I guess you can credit us with being the first to greet the great ship and also the first to bring in the pictures of her arrival. Man, what a ship she is and how she was boiling along.*

I was flying straight out over the course the French Line had plotted for me—the Normandie's *"private" ship lane. And then all at once I saw something the like of which I've never seen before. The ocean was a silver mirror beneath me and on this mirror someone had dropped a feather plume* 10 *miles long.*

That feather was the curling wake of the ship . . . and then there was the ship herself, looking like an illustration from a futuristic poster.

I climbed down out of the sky for a little look-see at close range. Deck after deck was deserted at that hour.

But some sailors in bright blue musical comedy uniforms waved and the officers in the control room saw me and cut loose with a blast of the whistle. That sea monster's bellow cut like a buzz saw through the noise of my own motor.

I whipped around and skimmed along the port side at full gun. Then I zoomed up and got my camera into action. The first shot I got showed bare decks. But they didn't stay that way long. The whistle and my roaring motor brought out a flock of stewards in scarlet jackets.

And then the passengers began tumbling out of their cabins, some of them half dressed. And they were shouting and waving things at me—hats, handkerchiefs, scarfs, anything.

Well, I got all the pictures this paper can use and then I turned tail and started for home. On the way in, I passed a couple of other planes just starting out. I flipped my tail at them and kept right on in.

His wasn't the only plane to greet *Normandie*. At 9:00 a.m. a squadron of seven Army biplanes commanded by Major Lawrence G. Brown took off from Miller Field and flew out into the Atlantic. They arrived at Ambrose light just before 11:00 a.m., intent on accompanying the liner all the way into port.

The first man on the North American continent to spot *Normandie* was Coast Guard "surfman" Jerry Burka, who was stationed at a lookout post on Fire Island. As she approached Ambrose light, twelve miles off the Long Island shore, he saw her through his binoculars just before 11:00 a.m. and shouted to the other Coast Guardsmen. Together, the little group watched as *Normandie* thrashed toward the finishing point.

At two minutes past 11:00 *Normandie* thundered past the Ambrose lightship. She'd made the 2,907-mile trip from Bishop's Rock lighthouse, the last point off the British shore, in 4 days, 3 hours and 2 minutes, averaging 29.98 knots.

She'd done it.

The enormous French liner was now the owner of the Blue Ribbon of the Atlantic, at least in the westbound direction.

Ellie Rogard, who was a passenger on that memorable voyage, recalled her experience. "I was on deck when *Normandie* reached Ambrose light. There were a bunch of us watching, keeping time. And at the moment we passed the mark, everyone gave a cheer. An instant later *Normandie* let loose a tremendous blast on her whistle, as though she were joining us. It was an incredible moment. The ship almost seemed *alive*."

Thanks to the foresight and confidence of some unremembered employee at CGT's Paris offices, *Normandie*'s crew was able to give her passengers a memento of the occasion. Almost as soon as the ship had passed Ambrose light, stewards circulated among the passengers, distributing small *Normandie* pins. Each was decorated with a little Blue Ribbon.

9

AN AMERICAN WELCOME

At this moment *Normandie*'s officers should have been basking in the glow of success. Instead, they were occupied with a worrisome problem. A few minutes after passing Ambrose light, all four of *Normandie*'s motors had stopped.

Before Chief Engineer Hazard could tell his captain what had happened, Pugnet was on the phone to the engine room, demanding an explanation. Hazard had none. He'd run through every routine test and each one seemed to show that nothing was wrong.

Then Pugnet had an idea. He asked one of the officers on the bridge what the water depth was. "We have forty-five feet," the answer came back.

Now the captain and the chief engineer realized what the problem was. The motors' governors had been set to shut off if the load on the propellers became too light, to prevent destructive over-revving. With only forty-five feet of water depth, there was less than ten feet of water below the hull bottom. Water resistance at this depth was very low. So long as *Normandie* stayed within the channel, there was no danger of going aground, but such shallow water required engine adjustments and a slower speed.

Pugnet ordered the governors changed accordingly. The motors cut in again and *Normandie* resumed her forward motion. The scare had been brief but instructive.

By this time about 10,000 people had gathered at Coney Island, crowding the boardwalk, the beach and the buildings overlooking the ocean. Ferris-wheel rides were at a premium that morning. These spectators first saw a thin line of pale buff smoke on the horizon, then, steaming through the mists, the great ship herself—and 10,000 voices let out a roar.

In the lower bay the *Alice M. Moran*, flagship of the Moran tugboat fleet, was approaching Quarantine, with Anton "Tony" Huseby commanding a crew of seven. Huseby was going out to board *Normandie*, and act as her pilot, guiding her through the tricky channel and the shallow waters of the North River. Also aboard the tug was Morris Markey, a *New Yorker* Magazine writer who'd been assigned to do a piece on *Normandie*'s arrival.

June 3 was a typical spring day in New York harbor. As the *Alice M. Moran* chugged out toward Quarantine, she was passed by several other incoming liners—the *Sythia*, of the Cunard Line; the *Statendam*, just back from a Bermuda cruise and flying all her flags; the white-painted *Kungsholm*; and Hamburg-Amerika's *Reliance*. These were the days when liner arrivals were practically as frequent and as commonplace as Eastern Shuttle landings at La Guardia are today.

As if five liners weren't enough of a crowd, the harbor was teeming with tugs, excursion boats, sailboats and other private craft eager to glimpse the new speed queen. Flocks of airplanes buzzed and stunted overhead.

On the *Alice M. Moran*, Markey was leaning on the rail beside Captain Huseby, looking toward the mouth of the bay, with Coney Island off to port, when he said, very quietly, 'There she is."

"Yes," Markey wrote,

there she was. She was coming directly toward us, and even at such a distance, she seemed immense. The yellow smoke moved straight upward from her stacks and, within a moment or two, we could perceive the incredible sheer of her bows. Huseby turned the tug's brass wheel idly and said, "She is built with a lot of overhang. They'll have trouble getting the mail boats up to her."

We watched her come on. Now we could see that she was black and white and red, we could see the lofty masts

with their webbing of flags, we could see the superb arc
of her swept-back bridge.

As we watched, there was a little new fluttering at
the peak of her after mast and suddenly a long, long
pennant curled out over the stern, writhing like a snake
in the air. The Blue Ribbon had been broken out.

What Markey had witnessed was a historic moment—the un-
furling of a thirty-meter-long blue pennant (a meter for every
knot) that had been taken on at Le Havre to be run out if *Nor-*
mandie succeeded in setting a record.

Normandie's blue pennant, audacious as it was, was not unduly immodest; the *Rex*, running back into her home port of
Genoa after her Blue Ribbon trip in 1933, had unfurled a fifty-
foot blue pennant.

As *Normandie*'s banner fluttered out over her wake, the
spectator fleet, as if on signal, began whistling and hooting, each
in a series of three—the traditional greeting of ships at sea.

Peering toward *Normandie*, now about two miles away,
Markey saw a rushing plume of white steam appear at her forward funnel. "It took a long interval for the sound to reach us,"
he wrote.

But when it did reach us, it was a shivering thing—as
deep a tone as may be without going below the range of
human audibility. It was a sound to make a queer trem-
bling within the body and it came three times, stately
and profound.

Captain Huseby smiled a little. "She has a noble
voice," he said.

She came up with surprising speed and almost before
we had found the perfect sweep of her colossal being within
our vision, we were under her black walls, able to see only
a segment of her.

At 12:06, at the Quarantine anchorage, the big ship slowed,
stopped and dropped her stem anchor. Then she gave three
tremulous, thundering toots on her whistle, each one so vibrant
that it shook the decks of the cutters now approaching her.

The first of these was a Coast Guard boat bearing officers of the U.S. Public Health Service. Their purpose: to spot anyone aboard carrying an infectious disease.

Since *Normandie*'s boarding ports were higher than the Federal cutter's wheelhouses, the Public Health officials—and many others who boarded her that afternoon at Quarantine— had to climb a shaky ladder to enter the ship. Once aboard, they asked Captain Pugnet a few cursory questions, then departed, having given the French liner the expected clean bill of health.

Now the *Alice M. Moran* approached *Normandie*. Captain Huseby climbed aboard, finding an easier entry through her mail hatch. Within five minutes the captain's first prediction came true. The *President*, a mail boat, could not get close enough to rig the chute for the pouches. So the *Alice M.* was hailed and asked to stand alongside as a buffer between mail boat and *Normandie*. Soon the bags of mail, all 4,200 of them, were pouring down the wooden chute.

Next to arrive was the cutter *Navesink*, which offloaded the members of the Official U.S. Welcoming Committee, resplendent in silk hats and morning coats. This group included Richard Southgate, the State Department's protocol chief, the French Ambassador, the French Consul General in New York and the head of CGT in the United States, Henri Morin de Linclays.

Next came the city of New York's official greeters, brought by the city steamboat *Riverside*. This contingent included State Senator Joseph Clark Baldwin III, the chairman, and Mrs. Fiorello La Guardia.

After that came the cutters *Hudson* and *Tuckahoe*. These placed customs and immigration inspectors on board. The cutter *Calumet* was next, with more than 100 newsmen, photographers and radio broadcasters.

Once on board, the newsmen were taken to the marble-floored winter garden, with its profusion of flowers and glassed-in birdcages, where the official ceremonies were being held, presided over by Madame Lebrun, the first wife of a French President ever to visit the United States. For this occasion she wore a white straw hat, a black faille three-quarter-length coat and skirt and a 200-year-old necklace with six topazes.

Newsreel cameras cranked as Protocol Chief Southgate addressed her briefly and formally on behalf of President and Mrs. Franklin Roosevelt. Then Joseph Clark Baldwin presented the formal greetings of Mayor La Guardia. Mrs. La Guardia, who spoke next, gave Madame Lebrun a huge spray of roses.

At her side through it all was Captain Pugnet in a full-dress uniform of blue and gold, a gold-hilted dress sword trailing from his waist and his broad expanse of chest literally overflowing with glittering medals.

At about 1:30 Madame Lebrun rose from the green wicker armchair and proceeded to the Sun Deck, escorted by an impressive number of dignitaries. Against the hissing and puffing of the huge red-and-black funnels, she quickly read a prepared speech in rather good English:

"Having christened this magnificent liner myself, nothing could be more gratifying than to accompany it to New York. . . . I am happy at the thought that it will contribute to shortening the distance that separates our two continents and to strengthen the historical bonds which unite our two nations."

At 1:38 p.m. *Normandie* weighed anchor and began the last leg of her trip, majestically steaming for port.

At Fort Hamilton, at the southern tip of Brooklyn, Army officers and men lined the ramparts to watch her pass through the Narrows. Just past the fort the wide promenades of Shore Road were filled with more than 40,000 persons.

Police estimated that 75,000 to 100,000 witnessed the spectacle from other spots along the far-flung Brooklyn and Staten Island shores. At Fort Wadsworth, on Staten Island, thirty aged sea captains from Sailors' Snug Harbor, part of a throng of 5,000 who'd accepted the Army's invitation to view the scene from the fort's heights, voiced their approval of the new liner.

Another 20,000 watched *Normandie*'s arrival from Grimes Hill and Wards Hill on Staten Island, two of the highest points on the Atlantic seaboard, and from other Staten Island locales. Still another 3,000 to 5,000 watched from the terraces surrounding the Statue of Liberty.

Manhattan's Battery Park, with its wide esplanades bordering the sea, provided a grandstand for upward of 30,000 spectators. And from the Battery up to 50th Street every pier was packed and every point from which the passing ship might be visible was occupied by a spectator. The same was true of the Jersey shore on the other side of the river.

Thousands more peered out of windows along lower Broadway and West Street. In squalid tenements and roominghouses, as well as in lofty office buildings, all eyes were trained on the North River. Uptown, the roofs and setbacks of office buildings provided magnificent overviews of the spectacle.

Fortunately for those wishing a good view, housewreckers had recently demolished a row of ancient buildings on the east side of 12th Avenue, leaving behind heaps of bricks and the remains of foundations. Long before noon these vantage points were covered by teeming masses of humanity, as was the top of a gas storage tank on 11th Avenue.

Cordons of police kept all but official visitors off Pier 88 itself (although several hundred painters were still at work there, rushing to cover the structure with at least one coat of red paint before *Normandie* arrived). Still, some 25,000 people had crammed themselves into the streets and intersections nearest the pier.

Among these was Babe Ruth, "the Sultan of Swat." He had been "released" by his club, the Boston Braves, when he insisted on going to New York to "represent baseball" at the *Normandie* festivities. Braves owner Tom Yawkey did not feel that was a good enough reason to be absent from practice.

Clay Morgan could claim credit for most of this. Thanks to his efforts, New York's eight newspapers wound up competing with each other to see which could run the most column inches on the new French liner. The coverage was quite comparable to that given Neil Armstrong's arrival on the moon some thirty-four years later.

Most of New York's twenty-odd radio stations devoted a great deal of air time to *Normandie*'s maiden voyage. In fact, one of them, WABC, covered the event live, beginning in midmorning and continuing until the ship was safely docked and unloaded.

Even though he'd mobilized the media as never before, Morgan decided to try one final ploy to assure *Normandie* a tumultuous welcome, which would guarantee even more newspaper, radio and newsreel attention.

He hired an outfit called "The Voice of the Sky," consisting of a tri-motored biplane, a pilot named Boyce and a powerful loudspeaker. At about 10:30 a.m., while *Normandie* was still racing toward Ambrose light, Mr. Boyce took off, with his wife in the co-pilot's seat, and began to circle the New York area.

Speaking into his powerful loudspeaker, Boyce intoned, "go to the River. The *Normandie* is coming in." It might have been a directive from the heavens; whatever, the city hastened to obey.

Those who turned out to see *Normandie* weren't limited to shoreline bystanders, her trip up the North River also attracted a truly spectacular collection of boats, planes, blimps and even a gyroplane.

As *Normandie* weighed anchor at Quarantine in the lower bay and slowly headed toward the North River, nearly 100 tugs, steamers and private craft stood by to salute and observe. The private vessels ranged from luxurious steam yachts to the time-honored combination of a boy, a rowboat and two oars.

Also present in the lower bay were five large excursion steamers, the *Berkshire*, the *Mandalay*, the *Americana*, the *Bear Mountain* and the *City of Keansburg*, packed, for the most part, with children and their mothers.

Each of these boats greeted *Normandie* in its own way, with sirens, bells or tooting horns. Proceeding at a stately 3 knots, *Normandie* responded with three deep bass growls from her funnel-mounted whistle.

With almost theatrical effect the giant liner then swept smoothly past the four-masted schooner *Annie C. Ross*, a reminder of other days on the ocean. The schooner allowed herself to be overtaken, then, in a gesture of homage to the liner, passed eastward in her wake.

As *Normandie* reached the Battery, she was met by two city fireboats, which opened every hose line and pump they had to throw silvery jets of water in a graceful arch. Nearby, a barge displayed a huge inflated figure of Mickey Mouse, a remnant from the most recent Macy's Thanksgiving Day parade.

Meanwhile, a score of airplanes flitted around the huge vessel like moths near a flame, the staccato roar of their engines mingling with the unearthly din of ships' sirens and whistles.

While the planes roared and dove above *Normandie*'s massive red-and-black funnels, some dipping below the level of her upper decks, the Goodyear blimp hovered overhead in grandmotherly fashion. Inside its gondola was a team of motion-picture photographers recording the event for the newsreels, that age's equivalent of television.

Passing the Woolworth Building in lower Manhattan, *Normandie* received a long-distance welcome from Whitney Rogovay, a mate in the Manhattan Sea Scouts, the Boy Scouts' marine division. He wigwagged a greeting from the observation platform in the building's tower. Unfortunately, Rogovay and his fellow Scouts had been too excited to remember their binoculars, so they were unable to see *Normandie's* answer.

As *Normandie* moved up the North River, she passed the faded old *Leviathan* of the United States Line, lying in her berth at Pier 8, Hoboken, opposite West 12th Street. By some measurements she'd been the world's largest ship until *Normandie* appeared; now she looked small and shrunken beside the huge new French steamship.

Frenzied preparations for *Normandie's* arrival continued at Pier 88, at the foot of West 48th Street. At 1:00 p.m., while the ship was still anchored at Quarantine, Albert Nelson, CGT's boss stevedore who hired baggage and cargo handlers, appeared at the street entrance of the pier and tried to enter unobserved. He failed.

More than 1,000 stevedores, waiting for a crack at the *Normandie* job, made a rush for Nelson, pushing through police lines. This was, after all, the midst of the depression and unfilled jobs—especially stevedore jobs—were rare.

For a few moments it seemed as though Nelson might be trampled to death by desperate job seekers. However, a flying wedge of policemen managed to get through to him and carry him into the CGT office on the pier.

A half hour later Nelson reappeared at the pier's street entrance and flung 250 work checks into the mob. There were a few brief fistfights as the men dove to get them, but the police did not have to intervene. Nelson than admitted the lucky 250 to the pier.

Hundreds of painters and carpenters and other workmen were still hard at work on the pier. The dock was complete, but the building on it was only half finished. Even while *Normandie* was proceeding upriver, these workmen were trying to make the structure presentable and functional.

Out in the river *Normandie* and her escorts proceeded upstream slowly and with great dignity until finally, at 2:45 in the afternoon, the giant liner pulled even with Pier 88, slowed and stopped. So far as most spectators were concerned, she'd ended her epochal first voyage. But Captain Pugnet and the docking pilot, Anton Huseby, knew the voyage's hazards were by no means over.

Now the working tugboats chugged out of the pack of spectator watercraft and took up their positions. Five lined up on *Normandie*'s port quarter, took the offered hawsers and began their struggle to hold her stern in position against the downstream rush of the tide.

Six other tugs pressed against her starboard bow and side, easing her gently toward the landing floats that had been set up at the northwest corner of the new pier to protect the pilings. Three others exerted a southward push against the port bow.

These fourteen tugs were attempting to turn the ship like the hour hand on a clock, from a nine-o'clock–three-o'clock position perpendicular to the dock to a twelve-o'clock–six-o'clock position parallel with it and beside it. *Normandie* thus would be "warped" into position.

The tugboat captains chosen for this delicate task were the finest New York harbor had to offer—Anton Huseby, generally regarded as the best tugboat man in America, Al Howell, former docking pilot of the *Leviathan*, and Herbert Miller, docking pilot of the *Bremen* and the *Europa*.

Coordinating their actions and ready to cast the leads were two uniformed members of *Normandie*'s crew, who had taken up positions on roosts just below her bows.

Almost as soon as the giant vessel came to a stop, the tugs began their work. Slowly the bow came in and the stern swung out. As *Normandie* touched the landing floats, a steel cable two inches thick was cast down from the ship and made fast to a bollard on the pier.

But then the tide caught the ship and pulled her stern away from the pier. The cable stretched taut, then broke, snapping with the sound of a cannon shot. *Normandie*'s stem began to slide toward the next pier upriver, the *Queen Mary*'s future home. From high up on the bridge Captain Huseby blew his police whistle urgently, commanding the tugs to take hold of her once more.

On the pier a little boy in a blue sailor suit blew sharply on his own police whistle, unknowingly giving conflicting commands and adding to the confusion.

Huseby had Captain Pugnet back *Normandie* out of the slip under her own power, a trick the turbo-electric power plant could handle with ease, since the propellers could be reversed simply by throwing a switch. The water turned black around the ship, which showed that she was "smelling bottom," as the old salts put it.

Now she came on again. This time her bowline was made fast to a dockside winch. This was turned laboriously, and the ship edged nearer, inch by inch. Then, with a sound like the crack of thunder, the thick rope parted, whipped through the air and splashed into the water.

A little launch that had been stationed in the slip darted for just this spot. As soon as it got there, a man in a bathing suit jumped out of it, into the murky, muddy water and, on the second attempt, fished out the hawser.

Soon it and 100 more lines fastened *Normandie* securely to the pier. At 3:55 she gave one long and two short blasts on her powerful whistle, signaling the tugs that their jobs were done and giving notice to the world that the first voyage of the greatest ship ever built had come to a successful end.

The new French liner was, however, slightly the worse for the experience. The straining tugs in New York harbor and also at Le Havre and Southampton had scraped quite a bit of black paint off her hull, leaving nothing in some places but raw metal and tufts of hemp from the tugs' bumpers.

Now began the job of unloading passengers, baggage and cargo. The former exited via the gangways. The last two were handled by a conveyor belt reaching from cargo ports to street level and were presided over by teams of grunting longshoremen pushing rubber-wheeled dollies.

Despite the mass confusion, all the baggage was ashore by 4:45 and the last of the cargo came out of the hold just after 6:00 p.m. The passengers departed simultaneously.

They walked into an incredible crush of friends, relatives, well-wishers, newspapermen, sightseers—and pickpockets. According to Mrs. Martha Levin, who was there, thieves were stealing passengers' cameras wholesale, despite a forty-man squad of plainclothes cops on hand to thwart the pickpockets.

Almost as soon as the first-class gangway was in place, five passengers, among them Mr. and Mrs. William Goetz, rushed ashore and grabbed a cab for New York's Municipal Airport (now La Guardia). They were making connections with a TWA Sky Chief flight to Los Angeles. Their purpose: to set a record for the trip from Le Havre to Los Angeles. To *Normandie*'s crossing would be added another seventeen hours, for that was how long the flight took aboard the fastest intercontinental transport then available.

Soon the famous novelist Colette came down the gangway. Even though pandemonium reigned on the pier's lower level, the celebrity-spotters recognized her instantly.

Reporters soon took up the scent. "Dressed in a sports costume," one newspaperman later wrote, "Mme. Colette wore no hose and her feet, encased in roman sandals, were tinted [!] and her toenails colored a vivid red. She told reporters that she liked to wear sandals and believed there would be less sickness in the world if more persons would abandon stockings."

Other reporters located the Maharajah of Kapurthala. "A slender, grave-faced man," according to one paper, "the Maharajah was highly amused when he was asked about a report that he was the third wealthiest man in the world. He said that there were about 999 men in the world wealthier than he, but that he had enough to 'live comfortably and get along.'

"He declined to discuss Indian affairs, but he did say that Gandhi's retirement soon was inevitable, as all political movements reached an apex and then were destined for oblivion."

Reporters also had a few moments to interview Mme. Lebrun, France's first lady. According to the *New York Times*, "She made no attempt to conceal her enthusiasm at seeing the celebrated skyline for the first time," expressing a desire to visit the Empire State Building as soon as she could.

Then Captain Pugnet himself came down the gangplank. Responding to newsmen's questions, he said *Normandie* had done "very well for a young ship."

Questioned about *Normandie's* vibration, Pugnet disingenuously said that constant adjustments on the voyage had gradually reduced it. He predicted that in two or three months, "as little kinks work out of the machinery, it will disappear almost entirely."

Every one of New York's eight newspapers made *Normandie's* maiden arrival front-page news. The tabloids dealt with it in headlines worthy of the Second Coming. The *New York Journal* put out eight editions, the major changes being *Normandie's* progress toward port.

The next morning the papers were filled with opinions from "impartial shipping men" and other technical observers. All pronounced *Normandie* a great marine achievement, "despite certain faults," such as the vibration in the aft quarter.

The *Times* devoted three pages to *Normandie's* arrival in New York. One of the inside pages also carried a large display ad from the *Bremen* and the *Europa*, which reminded readers that the German ships held records for "punctuality," whatever that meant.

The Germans were not gracious about *Normandie's* achievements. When the German papers had gotten the mistaken impression that she'd failed to set a record, they had headlined the news on the front page.

By contrast, Commander Francesco Tarabotto, master of the *Rex*, sent the following cable to Captain Pugnet: "Our sincere admiration for a splendid ship and a remarkable performance on her maiden voyage enables us to relinquish with a smile our possession of the Blue Ribbon of the North Atlantic won two years ago."

The British press gave *Normandie's* accomplishment good play, but when Cunard's Sir Percy Bates was informed that *Normandie* had broken the record, he said mildly, "She seems to have done very well." When asked if he thought the *Queen Mary* would do better, he replied, "I am not doing any speculating."

Madame Lebrun left the ship at 3:40, got into a long green limousine and was taken directly to the Waldorf-Astoria. But, true to her word, she soon left her hotel and headed for the Empire State Building, where she was met by the former Governor of New York and onetime presidential candidate Al Smith. He took her to the top and showed her the sights.

That night Madame Lebrun and others of the French delegation were guests of honor at a dinner given by the City of New York at the Waldorf-Astoria Hotel. About 850 guests attended.

The next night there was an enormous reception on board the ship at which Madame Lebrun presented Mayor La Guardia with a $500 check "for the poor of New York."

One of those attending was Robert Chesebrough Kennedy, whose father's and grandfather's construction company had built the new pier. He was fourteen at the time, but remembers the experience well: "Being aged fourteen, I was in my white starched collar and blue serge suit (a terrible collector of lint). I still vividly recall the beauty of the ship and of the occasion: for example, Miss Anne Morgan, the daughter of J. Pierpont the Elder, progressing through the salons like a frigate under full canvas, with the ribbon of the *Légion d'honneur* stretched across her ample bosom. A brave sight indeed."

Louis Sobol, who wrote a newspaper column for the *Journal-American* called "The New York Cavalcade," recalled it all in a June 27, 1945, item entitled "Down Memory Lane":

"The luxury liner *Normandie* was thrown open for a public inspection—that is to say invitations were extended to a few thousand people to come to a party—and what a party it was.

"Among those we spotted were Beatrice Lillie, the William Gaxtons, Ethel Merman, Victor Moore, Rudy Vallee (in colored glasses), Fannie Hurst, Grover Whalen, Sophie Tucker and the Ponselle sisters, Rosa and Carmela."

On the following day there was yet another party. The Meyer Davis orchestra began playing in the grand salon at 10:00 a.m., and at 12:30 there was a presentation of the latest French fashions, modeled by Paris' most famous "mannequins." That afternoon, partygoers saw the superb dancers Georges and Jalna, of the Waldorf-Astoria's Starlight Roof, and the stars of *Anything Goes*, Ethel Merman, William Gaxton and Victor Moore. They were followed by the De Marcos, "America's Foremost Dancers," then appearing in the Persian Room of the Hotel Plaza, who took the stage and danced to the music of Eddie Duchin. Later, Xavier Cugat and his orchestra played tangos and rhumbas for dancing.

Eleven p.m., found the café grill alive with dancing to Crislers' Jazz Orchestra. At midnight more French fashions were presented. Then Beauvel and Tova danced to the music of Meyer Davis, Tito and Coral sang songs and Raul and Eva Reyes of the Starlight Roof danced to Cugat's music.

The next day *Normandie* was thrown open to the public. Though it was raining, crowds began to gather at Pier 88 at 8:00 a.m. for the 10:30 a.m. opening.

At 10:30, as promised, the ship was opened and visitors streamed up the gangplank 100 at a time, paying fifty cents each for the privilege (the money was split between French and American seamen's charities).

Despite all precautions, the ship was virtually stripped bare by sticky-fingered souvenir seekers. Reported one New York newspaper, "The three perpendicular tunnels that are the funnels of the *Normandie*, France's floating answer to Radio City, by some oversight were not removed by the 15,000 or so souvenir-crazed New Yorkers who inspected the super-super-liner on June 5."

Interviewed by reporters, Chief Purser Henri Villar said that sightseers had also failed to escape with the grand organ and the children's merry-go-round.

But many smaller items were missing: hundreds of fountain pens (taken from the writing rooms); dozens of ashtrays and flower vases; about 400 initialed bar glasses and a wide assortment of tableware and china. The souvenir hunters, an unusually skilled lot, even managed to lift seven little round red hats from the very heads of as many bellboys.

Not every visitor attempted to make off with a tangible reminder of the occasion, of course. Most were satisfied to leave with only their impressions of the great ship. But at least one of those who paid half a dollar to visit *Normandie* was after more. He wanted information—as much of it as he could get.

William Francis Gibbs, America's foremost naval architect, and an assistant began the tour like everyone else, but soon vanished through a "CREW ONLY" doorway and found their way to the engine room. Once there, according to John Maxtone-Graham in *The Only Way to Cross*, Gibbs and his assistant spent two hours studying the ship's propulsion system. Then they retired to the smoking room, where Gibbs dictated a detailed description of what he'd just seen.

Why was Gibbs so interested? He was contemplating an ocean-liner design of his own, a ship that would one day be known as the *America*. This liner, though considerably smaller and slower than *Normandie*, nonetheless would be the largest, most important passenger ship ever built in the U.S. until Gibbs' own *United States* came into being after World War II.

Finally, on June 7, *Normandie* departed on the return trip, this time with nearly 1,600 passengers, just a few hundred short of capacity.

Her passenger list was even more distinguished this time. Naturally, Madame Lebrun was there, back from a whirlwind tour of Washington, D.C., and Hyde Park, and many visits with President Roosevelt and Eleanor. And so were such leading lights as Charles Boyer and his wife; Walt Disney, Roy Disney and their families; Richard Dix; Jules Bache (the stockbroker); Princess Alexandra Kropotkin; Carl M. Loeb (another noted stockbroker); Baron Philippe de Rothschild; and a man named Peter Belin, who two years later would survive the *Hindenburg* disaster.

Once more *Normandie* was running for the ribbon, this time quite openly. Now she wanted the eastbound record so that her supremacy would be uncontested.

Four days, 3 hours and 28 minutes after passing the Ambrose lightship off Long Island, *Normandie* steamed past Bishop's Rock lighthouse, off the English coast, winning the Blue Ribbon in that direction, too.

Normandie's average speed over the 3,015-mile distance was 30.31 knots. It was the first time in history that any passenger ship had crossed the North Atlantic at a better than 30-knot average. It was the steamship equivalent of breaking the sound barrier.

Naturally, an enormous crowd was on hand to welcome *Normandie* home and to exult in her triumph. Elliot Paul characterized the French attitude toward their superliner this way in his famous book *The Last Time I Saw Paris*: "The *Normandie* was the pride, not only of the French marine, but of all the French, from the poorest to the most influential and prosperous. Shop girls, delivery boys, sisters of charity, and clerks . . .

would pore over columns in the newspapers and cheap magazines or listen to descriptions on the radio whenever the *Normandie* was mentioned. They saved folders and pamphlets and clippings about the great ship that was to rule the ocean not with force, but with elegance, and put the British and the Germans to shame."

For *Normandie*'s masters, her maiden voyage had been a spectacular success. Rarely, if ever, had a ship gotten so much attention and so much praise. And rarely had a ship so completely met everyone's expectations of her.

But there were at least three clouds on the horizon. First, despite the unceasing work of carpenters, painters and decorators, the ship was still unfinished. As soon as she docked and the passengers disembarked, some 2,000 workmen hurried up her gangways.

Second, there was the vibration. Maiden-voyage passengers might forgive it, aware that there were still kinks to be worked out. But if the ship was to attract passengers of the quality and quantity she needed, this problem had to be cured as quickly as possible—if it could be cured at all.

Third, there was the matter of the *Queen Mary*, now being completed on the Clyde. At the moment *Normandie* was both the world's largest and the world's fastest passenger liner. But when the *Queen Mary* began her career the next spring, she might snatch both honors from the French ship.

10

THE PERFECT SHIP

Normandie's successes were grimly received in Britain, where the Cunard–White Star liner *Queen Mary* was being readied for her own maiden voyage in spring 1936.

By beginning service a year before the British superliner, *Normandie* had certainly stolen much of her thunder. And on her maiden voyage she seemed also to have stolen every honor to which the British liner might aspire.

When *Normandie* docked briefly at Plymouth, England, on her way home from New York, three Cunard–White Star engineers boarded her for the last leg of her journey. They did not identify themselves.

During their five hours or so on board, this British espionage team swept through almost every corner of the French ship. Their report told the Cunard–White Star board pretty much what it wanted to hear, denigrating *Normandie* whenever possible.

However, the Cunard–White Star board almost simultaneously got another evaluation, this one from a more objective source: a Royal Mail Lines passenger-department executive, a Mr. D. MacKinnon. It was not so comforting.

- Public rooms: The scheme of decoration throughout all the public rooms is of the most luxurious kind.
- Swimming pool: This is the best I have ever seen.
- Grand lounge: This is a magnificent room, the most lofty I have seen on any ship. It is beautifully fitted in every way.

- Winter garden: Much more elaborate than on other ships afloat. It is really beautifully fitted out with palms, tropical plants, etc. It is really a delightful place to visit.
- Vibration: Amidships and in the dining saloon in particular, it is not noticeable.

  To sum up, I think it is safe to say that the *Normandie* is the most luxurious vessel afloat.

Given its natural prejudices, though, Cunard not surprisingly chose to believe its own agents. The next batch of *Queen Mary* press releases, therefore, harped on *Normandie*'s vibration problem. "Cunard–White Star," the releases pronounced gravely, "is building a vibrationless vessel, which must be done from the start, in its initial design."

However Cunard–White Star's spies felt, *Normandie*'s passengers loved her and forgave her flaws, which they were convinced were temporary. Her passenger lists continued to be studded with stars and celebrities.

Among those who sailed on her on her first voyages were Allen Dulles, Kay Francis, Donald Ogden Stewart, Mr. and Mrs. Percy Uris, Joseph Schenck, Ruth Draper, Dwight Fiske, Natalie Kalmus (of Technicolor fame), Joseph P. Kennedy (then U.S. Ambassador to England) and his wife, Rose, Mrs. Ogden Mills and Mrs. Orme Wilson, both members of "the 400," the cream of New York society.

Many of *Normandie*'s first-class passengers tended to know one another. For that reason voyages sometimes seemed like four-day parties or events in private clubs. Even those who didn't know each other had much in common: social standing, power, fame, sophistication, culture and, of course, money, usually old money. But there were always "intruders"—the *nouveaux riches* and the celebrities.

The 1930s were a class-conscious age and nowhere was this consciousness more acute than on board the great liners. Yet there *was* contact between the classes, despite the physical separation and the long list of rules designed to prevent it.

The experience of Mrs. Kitty Lee, a passenger on one of *Normandie*'s early trips, is instructive:

I was 16 years old, given my first trip aboard by a real-life fairy godmother. We shared a tiny, sparkling, hospital-white cabin with double-deck berths, in tourist class.

Below us, in third class, was Dennis McGlinchey, Aunt Emma's Irish chauffeur. And below Dennis—I assume far below Dennis—was Aunt Emma's block-long Packard car, which would, luxuriously, see us travel France.

We breakfasted and lunched with others of our caste, but due to some sort of monetary considerations to the powers that were, we dined first class. I don't know how Aunt Emma managed it, but I have a pretty good idea. The Captain was or became a personal friend of hers.

Another early *Normandie* passenger was Mrs. Edna Cohee. When her husband, a doctor, received a fellowship to study in London, they decided to cross on *Normandie* and make it a second honeymoon.

Tourist class was the best we could afford, but our state-room was large and most satisfactory. However, to my dismay, I found salt water in the shower. There was apparently soap made to lather in sea water, but we didn't find out about that until later.

A Reader's Digest was given to each passenger. And continental breakfast was served to us in our cabin. At the elevators, the operators were young French children dressed in little red monkey suits.

The food was all varied, abundant and typically French. I think with nostalgia of all the wonderful meals I skipped. The waiter was most insistent and he didn't seem to understand my bird-like appetite. He would smile and say, "C'est bon" and heap food on my plate. It has been said that a French waiter doesn't care if he kills you, as long as you die well fed.

Not everyone had such a happy trip, however. In fact, one of *Normandie's* early passengers, Madame Nastia Poliakova, sued the French Line as a result of her voyage. She claimed that "the violent and excessive and unseaworthy vibration" loosened a stone in her left kidney and sent it careening around inside her body, causing damage and suffering worth, she figured, $100,000.

CGT, which liked the bad publicity even less than the amount named, settled out of court with the stipulation that Madame Poliakova never again utter a word in public about *Normandie's* vibration.

On Wednesday, July 3, and right on schedule, *Normandie* steamed out of Le Havre for her third trip to New York. That night, as usual, she stopped briefly at Southampton to pick up British passengers bound for the United States. Among them was Harold Nicolson, the British diplomat and writer. He was traveling with his twenty-one-year-old son, Ben. The next day he began a diary of his trip, addressed to his wife, Vita Sackville-West.

> It was hours before they got the luggage on board and at last the tender trembled and began to move. We swung round and out into the fair way and from my wicker chair, I observed yachts at anchor sliding past the port-hole. . . .
>
> Miles away, a huge white shape could be discerned and a red funnel. This was the Normandie. . . . In ten minutes I went out again. She was now quite close, looking dangerously top heavy. And in a few minutes we stopped dancing up and down and crept motionlessly into the lee of that huge black precipice.
>
> I looked up the precipice wondering if I should see a familiar face. But it was like trying to pick out a friend on the top of Gibraltar. And eventually when I crossed the gangway, there was Ben waiting all pleased.
>
> We went straight to our cabins. Mine is Maritime with satinwood cupboards and every form of gadget conceivable, including a telephone. Ben's is prettier but smaller, being light blue shiny stuff with a faint pattern of Chinese effect in gold. . . .
>
> It is just like the very best hotel one can conceive. . . . You know how the big rooms on the Bremen were all on one floor? Here they are on different floors, com-

municating by vast decorative staircases. Thus one has a series of vistas seen from above.

The decks are also arranged on the same system and there is a really superb deck at the back, rising in slight terraces and lit by lampposts, like an exhibition. Out of this opens a circular grill room with modern steel chairs and glass all round. Very Le Corbusier. But the rest is Lalique at his most extravagant. . . . The whole ship gives one exactly, but exactly the impression of an exposition des arts décoratifs. Even now we have not explored it thoroughly. . . .

Friday, July 5. Now that we are in full Atlantic, I can see what is meant by the vibration. At the stern, where the Le Corbusier circular grill room is—the nicest part of the ship—the flowers on the little tables wobble something dreadful and it would be difficult to read for long. . . . It must be even worse in the tourist class and I can well imagine that in some cabins it is really intolerable.

But where we are, one does not notice the vibration in the least and I have never known such luxury as that in which Ben and I live. The food is really delicious and although I am still careful, Ben eats a lot. Caviar and pâté for dinner yesterday. . . .

As he observes, the whole place is like the setting for a ballet. Choruses of stewards, sailors, firemen, stewardesses, engineers and passengers. There are also some fifty liftiers in bright scarlet who look like the petals of salvias flying about these golden corridors. That is the essential effect—gold, Lalique glass and scarlet. It is very gay, but would drive me mad after a week.

There was a good film and then Ben and I went and bicycled in the gymnasium. After dinner, there was an auction pool. I had taken a ticket. When my name was called out there was some turning of heads and a ghastly German woman rose and came towards me.

'You are not really Harold Nicolson?'

I did the look-down-my-nose face. She is obviously a bore. She implied that T. E. Lawrence had been murdered. Now people who regard Lawrence as a mystery and

a romance are obviously bores. . . . So I see this Ger-
man woman is going to be hell.

Saturday, July 6. We are now more than half way
across. All this speed fuss is rather nonsense. An extra
day makes very little difference and going at this pace
has very definite disadvantages. In the first place, there
is the vibration and in the second place, the wind. For
unless the wind is strong behind one, the rush of air on
the sun deck is really terrible. It is like being on an aero-
plane. One is thus mainly confined to the promenade deck,
which is enclosed in glass and thus protected and a trifle
airless. . . .

Ben is well so far, but I think a trifle livery. . . .
He finds it difficult to work or to read serious books. So
do I. There is something about a boat which upsets one's
brain.

In general, *Normandie* did not attract the British upper crust, of
which Nicolson was a card-carrying member. This particular
group preferred to travel on British ships, which naturally reflected its tastes and attitudes.

Normandie, by contrast, attracted the American upper crust—
both the landed gentry and new money: top-ranking merchants,
stockbrokers and film stars. It was very much a New York and
Hollywood crowd.

Despite hopeful public statements from Captain Pugnet and
various CGT officials about breaking in the engines, CGT knew
the vibration problem was serious and that it wasn't going to go
away by itself. Unfortunately, little could be done while *Normandie* remained in service.

While *Normandie* crossed and recrossed the Atlantic that first
summer, Fernand Coqueret and Paul Romano assembled a team
of scientists and designers to suggest solutions and sent engineers
on every trip to determine the exact extent and character of the
trembling.

Before *Normandie*'s first season was over, Coqueret and Romano were back at the Hamburg model tank, testing alternate
propeller designs, rotation schemes and shaft bossing shapes.

Normandie, however, continued on her travels as though all were well.

When *Normandie* arrived in New York on July 8 (with Nicolson and son aboard), the *Rex*, moored at Pier 59, was preparing to depart. As the French liner glided upstream toward her pier, the *Rex*'s orchestra struck up "La Marseillaise." Her officers stood at attention. Her ensign was dipped in salute to her rival. In response, *Normandie* let loose with three blasts on her whistle and her own crew members gave a cheer. It was the summer of 1935, and France and Italy still thought they might be friends.

Normandie was off again on July 10 with 1,631 passengers on board, the largest number she'd ever carried. The summer had just begun and Americans were going abroad in droves.

British travelers, on the other hand, were as usual scarce aboard *Normandie*. It came as no surprise. From the start the French Line had known British travelers would be suspicious of *Normandie*. There was really only one possible counter: to let the British see the ship so they could judge her for themselves.

For this reason CGT had left a gap in *Normandie*'s transatlantic schedule during which she could take a cruise to Britain, attract British interest and approval and pick up as much British trade as possible before the *Queen Mary* entered service the next spring.

On Thursday, July 19, *Normandie* steamed out of Le Havre for a long-weekend cruise around the British Isles. There were more than 1,700 French tourists aboard. On Saturday, July 21, having completed her circle, she steamed into Southampton harbor and dropped anchor in Cowes Roads.

It was not unlike her reception in New York. Thousands of Britons filed through the great ship, having paid five shillings for the privilege.

An impressive number of VIPs came by special Pullman train from Waterloo Station, among them Sir Thomas Bell and S. J. Piggott of the John Brown Company, which was building the *Queen Mary*, and Walter Runciman, a high official in the Minstry of Foreign Trade. They were welcomed by CGT's Henri Cangardel and Pierre de Malglaive.

Runciman, one of the speakers at the obligatory ceremonial

luncheon, talked about the competition between *Normandie* and the *Queen Mary*.

> *When I had an opportunity of discussing the matter with representatives of the CGT, we parted with the assurance that the* Normandie *and the* Queen Mary *would not be competitive in the widest sense of the term, but would be cooperators.*
>
> *It is most essential that in the sailing schedule, we should find alternate weeks to be shared by these two great companies.*
>
> *If that is fully attained, we can be sure of a few striking and simple facts. The first is that the* Queen Mary *and the* Normandie *will never be in the same port at the same time.*
>
> *The second is that . . . they will never meet on the high seas and will always be running in the opposite direction and well clear of each other.*

This was true, unfortunately for posterity and for those who would have liked to see a real race between the two vessels.

Having done everything possible to attract British travelers, *Normandie* resumed her regular transatlantic schedule.

On one of these trips a crew from Universal Pictures came aboard to film a movie, a feature-length musical called *Sweet Surrender*. It starred Frank Parker and featured Abe Lyman and his orchestra and Jack Dempsey. But if the producers were hoping to capitalize on *Normandie*'s popularity, they were disappointed. The film never opened in New York, earned no reviews from the film journals of the day and simply disappeared into Universal's film vaults. Still, it had made the voyage memorable for *Normandie*'s passengers and crew members.

Another memorable voyage began on July 31 from New York. It was *Normandie*'s fourth eastbound trip. There were 1,335 aboard, tourist traffic to Europe having begun to slack off for the season.

The first day out, *Normandie*'s fiddler, fencer and marksman captain, René Pugnet, brought his expensive twenty-gauge shotgun to the bridge, hoping to get in some target practice on what had turned out to be a beautiful, calm day.

Normandie was off the Nantucket lightship when Pugnet spotted what he'd been looking for—a huge bird circling over the vessel. He raised his shotgun, took aim and fired.

The bird stopped flapping its wings, then tumbled out of the sky, landing on *Normandie*'s Sun Deck. It was, reported the newspapers, "killed but not shattered." The bird turned out to be an eagle with a wingspread of five feet.

Pugnet, who had hunted big game in Africa, proudly displayed his trophy in the grand salon—before sending it to a taxidermist.

That same trip was marked by another incident involving an animal. It seems that a certain blue-haired lady, traveling first-class, had managed to convince Chief Purser Villar to let her keep her Pekingese in her cabin. Villar was known to bend the rules when the dog was very small or the passenger obviously inseparable from her canine or feline companion. Such cases almost always involved women.

Anyhow, this particular canine, seeing the cabin door slightly ajar in the middle of the night, sneaked out of Madame's stateroom, which happened to be on a lower deck.

That night was rather rough. The steward should have closed all the cabin portholes, but for some reason had left Madame's open. At any rate, a sizable wave hit the ship and drenched the room.

Madame, rudely awakened, began screaming for help, which arrived almost instantly. A bevy of stewards and stewardesses mopped up, changed the bedclothes and dried everything out as best they could.

Suddenly the woman realized her dog was missing. She broke down and began sobbing, certain the animal had been swept overboard to a watery death. A few minutes later, however, her steward appeared, carrying a dry Pekingese. He'd found the dog hanging around *Normandie*'s butcher shop, salivating.

The steward tried to tell the woman what had happened, but she would have none of it. Instead, she was convinced that the gallant Frenchman had jumped overboard in midstorm and rescued her beloved pet.

To his credit, the steward tried to refuse the enormous tip Madame proffered; but then he realized how much pleasure the woman would get from repeating the story and he took the money without further hesitation.

During the summer of 1935, while *Normandie* shuttled back and forth between new world and old, engineers Coqueret and Romano and their team pondered the vibration and what to do about it.

Traveling aboard the ship during her regular voyages, they went about their study largely unnoticed. Their instruments revealed that the vibration had a *periodic* quality. The number of oscillations in any given time period, they found, was always equal to the number of propeller revolutions multiplied by three—which happened to be the number of blades on each propeller.

The engineers also discovered the vibrations had nothing to do with *Normandie*'s speed. Once the throbbing began, at about 25 knots, it didn't get worse as the ship reached higher speeds. In fact, after about 29 knots the trembling began to ease slightly.

The cause of *Normandie*'s vibration, evidently, lay with the motion of her propellers. Water rushing through their blades at high speed was bouncing off the propellers, then off the hull, then back onto itself. The result was tremendously powerful turbulence.

Every time the propellers turned, this turbulence smashed into them three times—at least so the theory went. This whipped the propellers back and forth on their shafts. The movement wasn't great—just two to three millimeters on each oscillation. But it happened about 120 times a minute.

This whipping action, Coqueret and Romano thought, was transmitted directly to the giant shafts on which *Normandie*'s propellers were mounted, and then to the bossings which held the shafts in place where they protruded from the hull, then to the huge thrust blocks inside the hull, against which the propellers pushed, then to the engine beds themselves. That, in turn, caused the entire ship to vibrate.

If this were the case, the motion would be worst near *Normandie*'s stern, where the propellers were mounted, and least noticeable forward. That appeared to fit the observed facts. But all of this was still only theory. More careful tests had to be made aboard the ship—tests impossible to conduct with a full load of passengers.

For this reason CGT decided to take *Normandie* out of service after her eighteenth transatlantic crossing, which was scheduled to end in Le Havre on October 28. That meant canceling four voyages in November and December 1935 and several others in the early months of 1936. Transatlantic travel being at an ebb in those months, it was not a cataclysmic move.

After she was taken out of service, CGT planned to put *Normandie* through a series of new trial runs to prove the vibration theory was correct and to test some possible solutions.

CGT's engineering team, scouring the technical literature regarding ship vibration, came up with five possible cures for the problem:

1. To design, build and install new four-bladed propellers;
2. To keep the three-bladed propellers, but change the rotational direction of the outside pair;
3. To keep the three-bladed propellers, but to *synchronize* them so the blades were always in the same position at the same time;
4. To install "friction stanchions"—shock absorbers—throughout the ship;
5. To cut an expansion joint into the superstructure above the Promenade Deck, between the café grill and the open first-class terrace just behind it.

CGT's chief engineer, Arthur Merot du Barre, took on the task of designing the new propellers. Unfortunately, designing and casting propellers couldn't be done quickly. The new set would not be ready until early spring of 1936—just in time for *Normandie*'s second season on the Atlantic.

The other potential solutions were simpler. All could be tested on the trial runs now scheduled for November.

CGT was naturally ambivalent about publicizing all of this. In the end, however, the publicity decision was taken out of CGT's hands. In midsummer the London *Times*, of all papers, reported that during her winter lay-up *Normandie* would get a new set of propellers.

These propellers, the *Times* said, would have four blades instead of the three blades of the original sets. The *Mauretania's* vibration had been greatly reduced by exactly such a change, it noted.

While one set of engineers was working overtime to fix *Normandie's* vibration problem, another was working on a revolutionary device which promised to make the great French liner the safest ship at sea.

This device was nothing less than the first radar warning system to be installed on a passenger ship. It worked by sending out a beam of shortwave impulses which swept the horizon at a 45-degree arc, with the ship at the center of the arc. When these impulses struck an obstacle in the distance within that arc, they were reflected back into a delicate receiving device.

The waves were then amplified and made audible on ordinary telephone receivers on the control panel where officers were standing watch and listening. According to Captain Pugnet, the device could detect ships, floating wrecks and icebergs at a distance of up to four miles, depending on their size. "We've even picked up channel markers at a distance of two miles," he said.

At the very moment radar was being installed on *Normandie*, the British were setting up their first coastal early-warning radar stations. They were nervous about the Germans, and with good reason. Germany was quickly rearming. And in Italy, Benito Mussolini was preparing to extend his power to North Africa by conquering Ethiopia (then known as Abyssinia).

After provoking a skirmish at an oasis, Mussolini demanded that Ethiopian Emperor Haile Selassie pay a huge indemnity and cede territory to Italy. Selassie refused. And so, at dawn on October 3, *Il Duce's* forces—a 300,000-man army—moved into Ethiopia, striking southward from Eritrea. Meeting hardly any opposition, their entry was more like a parade than an attack.

After much debate the League of Nations voted a week later to brand Italy an aggressor—the first such action in League history. Then it voted anti-Italian sanctions, prohibiting member nations from trading with the aggressor.

But the sanctions were ludicrously weak. They did not include closing the Suez Canal to Italy, which would have stopped the war in a moment. (It was the only way Italy could get arms to Ethiopia.) They did not restrict sales of coal, iron and steel, the chief commodities of war, nor did they stop the sale to Italy of oil, on which *Il Duce's* motorized legions depended.

All of this delighted the Germans. If Mussolini stumbled and got himself mired in Africa, Hitler could seize Austria, which Mussolini had formerly protected. If Mussolini won, in defiance of the League, he would be a natural German ally against the Western democracies.

While Mussolini's legions, equipped with every modern weapon, were making mincemeat of Ethiopia's barefoot brigades, *Normandie* was making the last voyage of her first season on the Atlantic, fighting her way through her first real storm. Slowed by the high winds and rough waters, the giant liner made just 613 miles in one twenty-five-hour period, averaging a very slow— for her—24.52 knots.

Frank Bishopp, who was aboard at the time, recalls that there were only five people in the tourist dining room all the way and that all the doors to the decks were locked.

Later Pierre de Malglaive wrote about this trip, pointing out that *Normandie* actually covered more than the indicated mileage, since she'd zigzagged according to the direction of the wind and sea. "She rode very easily," de Malglaive said, "without slamming and without shipping any great amount of water on her foredeck." But this was not to say that she did not roll. She did roll—and quickly came up again, only to roll once more.

Some ships roll lazily from one side to the other, like an underpowered windshield wiper. Their slow return to vertical frightens some passengers, but the discomfort is more psychological than physical.

Other ships roll, then right themselves quickly, then roll again. This is somewhat less frightening, but it's very hard on the stomach.

Normandie, it's said by those who knew her well, was a "snappy" roller. The *Queen Mary* rolled slowly.

But *Normandie*'s rolling never bothered her officers. According to Dr. Pierre Thoreux, the son of *Normandie*'s second commanding officer, Commandant Pierre Thoreux, "My father often told me that he was most relaxed during storms. The ship was marvelously seaworthy, many of the passengers were seasick and dinners and lunches with the Commandant were canceled!"

Toward the end of the season the Duke of Sutherland presented *Normandie* with the greatest honor to which a transatlantic liner could aspire: the Hales Trophy, a tangible award that represented the mythical Blue Ribbon.

A British M.P., Harold Keates Hales, designed and had executed at Sheffield the "Hales Trophy," as it became known, a gold-and-silver concoction three feet six inches high, complete with Neptunes, mermaids and other denizens of the deep.

On October 23, while *Normandie* was tied up at Pier 88 in New York, preparing to depart for France for that last time in 1935, a small ceremony was held in the grand salon. The Duke of Sutherland, who was chairman of the Hales Trophy committee, presided.

Said Pugnet, "Now it is my job to see if *Normandie* can hold on to this prize. Let me assure you that we will do our utmost." Everyone knew the French captain was referring to the coming competition with the *Queen Mary*, which would join *Normandie* on the Atlantic the following spring.

CGT was delighted to have the Hales Trophy and hoped to hang on to it, whatever the *Queen Mary* did. But its first order of business was to end *Normandie*'s vibration. So when the ship arrived back in France, workmen once more boarded her to try to eliminate her vibration.

First, they transposed her two outside propellers and reversed the poles of the motors driving them. Studies in the Hamburg test tank seemed to show vibration could be substantially reduced this way.

Second, they fitted "brake stanchions" or shock absorbers throughout the aft quarter of the ship, from top to bottom.

Third, they added differential gear to the turbines' speed governors so *Normandie*'s propellers could be synchronized.

Fourth, they cut a temporary expansion joint into the superstructure just behind the café grill. A similar cut had successfully reduced superstructure vibration in the *Bremen*.

To see how well these solutions worked, they mounted vibration gauges throughout the ship.

Unfortunately, the fifth and perhaps the most promising solution—Du Barre's four-bladed propellers—could not be tried, as they were still being fabricated.

Normandie left Le Havre again on November 15, carrying only engineers, mechanics and workmen, all of whom were supervised by the anti-vibration team leaders, Paul Romano and Fernand Coqueret. After stopping at St. Nazaire to pick up more technicians, the ship steamed out into the Bay of Biscay for three days of trials. The weather was terrible, which pleased CGT, since it wanted to test these ideas in the most trying conditions possible.

Early on the 16th Captain Pugnet again ordered full speed ahead and *Normandie* leaped forward on possibly the most important voyage of her career.

As the huge ship built up speed, a team of engineers monitored the vibration gauges, which revealed that reversing the rotation of the outside propellers did indeed cut their vibration, but only by about 20 percent.

The engineers next studied the effects of the "brake stanchions" or shock absorbers—sort of glorified springs. These were installed around the shaft bossings and thrust bearings and throughout the aft quarter of the ship on every deck. Vibration gauges were stationed nearby.

But, no matter how the engineers fooled with the springs, they couldn't stop the vibration. All they could do was transfer it from one deck to another.

At this point, attention turned to propeller synchronization. Unfortunately, true synchronization turned out to be nearly impossible. What's more, the closer the engineers got to it, the more the ship vibrated.

All of this left just one more potential solution to be tried: cutting an expansion joint in the superstructure, just aft of the café grill. This was quickly and easily accomplished.

This solution worked, at least for the upper decks. Forward of the cut, on both the Sun and Boat Decks, vibration was reduced by 60 percent. This meant, at the minimum, that the occupants of *Normandie*'s finest suites, which were located on the Sun Deck, need no longer spend their voyages involuntarily quivering.

Now *Normandie* returned to Le Havre, where Du Barre had finished designing the new four-bladed propellers. At least in the model tank the new propellers eliminated practically every trace of vibration and also proved more efficient than the original three-bladed propellers.

On December 6 Henri Cangardel, CGT's managing director, announced the results of all this work. "With the knowledge and means we now possess," he said, *"Normandie*'s vibration troubles may be regarded as a thing of the past."

Not everyone was convinced. Three days later "Stainless Stephen," a featured performer on the BBC, told his audience, "The vibration on the *Normandie* is so great that when a passenger asked for a poached egg, it was scrambled by the time the steward served it."

Cangardel immediately protested to the BBC, which apologized half-heartedly—and immediately aired another *Normandie* vibration joke, this one a bit on the bawdy side. "If the *Queen Mary* vibrates as much as the *Normandie*," it went, "God help the King."

While *Normandie* was undergoing trials in the Bay of Biscay, the European political scene was getting grimmer.

In Germany, Jews were officially excluded from citizenship by the Nuremberg Laws, which had been announced on September 15.

In Ethiopia, Mussolini's army, which had started off so well, was beginning to bog down. To cross the mountainous terrain, the Italians had to build their own roads, a laborious, time-consuming process. By the time the roads were ready, Mussolini might have to pull back, hurt by the costs of the campaign and by the League's sanctions, weak as they were.

But the League itself solved Mussolini's problems. Hoping to appease the dictator, Samuel Hoare, the British Foreign Secretary, and Pierre Laval, his opposite number in France, secretly agreed to offer Mussolini Ethiopia's fertile plains. The Emperor, Haile Selassie, would retain his mountain kingdom and get a long-desired corridor to the Red Sea. All this would be imposed on the two warring countries by the League of Nations. And Mussolini would remain in the British-and-French camp.

The offer was never made. Somehow the secret deal became public knowledge two days after Hoare and Laval agreed on it. The rest of the League, which had seen Britain and France as the most energetic supporters of joint action against aggression, were devastated. If they didn't oppose Mussolini, who would?

The result: Both Hoare and Laval were forced out of office. No compromise was ever offered. Mussolini ordered his army to build the roads it needed in Ethiopia. And Hitler, who'd once feared that a militant League might stand in Germany's way, now realized he had nothing to worry about.

Late that year Compagnie Générale Transatlantique released the financial results of *Normandie*'s first season.

During this period, the French Line announced, *Normandie* brought in 50 million francs, covering her operating and general costs almost exactly, but leaving nothing to repay the government loan that had made her possible in the first place. Still, considering the fact that 1935 was the second worst year for transatlantic liners since the Great War, *Normandie* had done fairly well.

On her nine westbound trips *Normandie* averaged 1,059 paying passengers. Eastbound, the average was 926. By contrast, her main rival at the time, the *Bremen*, which stopped in Britain, France *and* Germany, averaged 991 passengers westbound in 1935 and 859 passengers eastbound.

This seems a slim difference until you break down the averages by passenger class. *Normandie* averaged 385 first-class passengers a trip, while the *Bremen* averaged just under 200. On the other hand, *Normandie* averaged only 230 third-class passengers per voyage, while the *Bremen* carried an average of 421.

These comparative statistics may reveal more about the times than about the drawing power of the two ships. The exodus from Nazi Germany had already started—and it wasn't traveling first-class. That's one reason every major liner carried more people westbound than eastbound, on average, during the last half of the 1930s.

There were portents in the air, not only for the people of Europe but also for transatlantic liners in general. On November 22, for instance, a huge flying boat—Pan Am's "China Clipper"—departed San Francisco for the first commercial flight to the Orient, arriving at Manila on November 29 after an 8,210-mile trip with stops at Honolulu, Midway, Wake and Guam. Could transatlantic air travel be far behind?

Early in 1936, while Mussolini's troops marched toward Addis Ababa, CGT finalized and made permanent the measures intended to cure *Normandie's* vibration problems.

And since it was exquisitely aware that the *Queen Mary* would soon be joining the fray, the company also decided to improve *Normandie* in a dozen other ways.

Some of these changes were minor—the sort one might expect in any liner before the beginning of a new season:

- □ Six of the main dining room's twelve floor-mounted lighting towers were removed, to increase floor space and make room for a few more tables;
- □ A longitudinal glass partition was put in between the first and second funnels, on the sun deck;
- □ The bridge wings—the small catwalks on each side of the bridge, from which officers commanded the docking process—were enlarged and extended forward about three feet.

But CGT also undertook some major revisions, changes that went far beyond the usual off-season alterations:

A room on a lower deck was converted into a small but architecturally beautiful synagogue which seated forty-eight people. Its doors and ceilings were marked with Jewish stars, its Torah covered in silver and ivory. The installation was supervised by Simon Langer, chief rabbi of the Paris Orthodox Jewish community.

In addition CGT tore out the double-decked tourist-class salon and redivided the space into two decks. Twenty new tourist-class cabins were installed on the lower one and a dozen more were put in on the Promenade Deck, in the space once occupied by the dome of the tourist-class lounge.

To replace this retreat, CGT now built a spectacular new tourist lounge on the Boat Deck, directly aft of the café grill, with a tourist-class sports deck on its roof. The addition was served by the new tourist grand stairway in the center of the room.

This dramatically improved *Normandie*'s tourist accommodations, but it also eliminated the beautiful first-class Art Deco outdoor terrace, with its vast expanse of teak deckwork, its zigzag benches and its street lamps.

It also added a large new on-deck structure where none had been before and, in the opinion of most observers, none belonged.

Worst of all, the new tourist lounge partially blocked the formerly unimpeded sternward ocean view from the café grill. The blocked windows were removed and a wall was installed in their place. As for the once magnificent view of *Normandie*'s wake, that was now the exclusive property of the tourist-class passengers.

Why did *Normandie*'s designers ignore the original plan, which had been so carefully conceived?

It wasn't because the tourists had demanded the changes. It was because of the vibration. All of these changes were intended to help stiffen the ship. The improvements to tourist-class facilities were just a bonus—and the harm done to the ship's appearance and to the café grill an unhappy necessity.

While all of these changes were being made in the passenger accommodations, other alterations were being made deep within the ship, along the lines of Coqueret's and Romano's recommendations.

In all, eighty tons of steel were added to *Normandie*'s stern to combat vibration, most of it used to stiffen the decks and to reinforce the shaft bossings. And 200 tons of pig iron were added to the ship's forward ballast tanks to keep her in trim.

The cost of all these extensive alterations was enormous— 150 million French francs, or just under $10 million at 1935 exchange rates. By this time, however, the French government was thoroughly commited to *Normandie*. As her builders and owners had hoped all along, she'd become the symbol of France, both to the world and within the country itself.

While French shipbuilders were busy perfecting *Normandie* at Le Havre, British shipbuilders were racing to finish their own superliner in time for her maiden voyage, scheduled for May 27.

Amazingly, Vladimir Yourkevitch popped up once again. Somehow he managed to have his case stated—and rather persuasively at that—to Lord Essendon, one of Cunard–White Star's directors.

In February 1936 Essendon wrote Percy Bates and asked him to look into Yourkevitch's ideas. Bates responded with noticeable exasperation: "Yourkevitch has moved around so much during these last few years that I cannot believe any builder of fast ships in this country can be ignorant of his theories."

Then Bates changed the subject—and revealed, at least by implication, that *Normandie* and her accomplishments were definitely on his mind.

"In this connection," he went on, "it is worth remembering that the *Normandie* when she comes out next will not be quite the same ship as she was last year. There is a good deal of additional weight going into the hull, and I anticipate that her loaded draft will be decidedly greater. It will be very interesting to see what she does this year."

True, there would be no direct competition between *Normandie* and the *Queen Mary*. The two great liners would never race across the Atlantic side by side to determine which was *really* the faster. Nevertheless, there was no way their owners could prevent them from vying with each other for honors both tangible and intangible, for as long as they shared the same ocean.

On March 7, 35,000 German soldiers crossed the Rhine and reoccupied the Rhineland, that part of Germany west of the river. This was distinctly forbidden by the Versailles Treaty.

The Versailles Treaty, which had ended World War I in favor of the Allies, was dead. So was the Locarno Pact, which had "guaranteed" peace in Europe. The League of Nations was an empty shell. Britain and France had both demonstrated their reluctance to oppose aggression. Nothing stood in the way of German rearmament and Nazi aggression.

On March 19, 1936, the British Board of Trade's Surveyor's Office officially notified the John Brown Company that the *Queen Mary* had been measured and that her gross tonnage had been calculated.

That figure, according to the official records, was 80,773.59 gross tons.

Cunard–White Star officials, who'd previously estimated the size of their new superliner at anywhere from 72,000 to 77,000 tons, were ecstatic. The *Queen Mary* was now the largest ship in the world—1,493 gross tons larger than *Normandie* (which was registered at 79,280 gross tons).

Normandie might be slightly longer, overall, but the *Queen Mary* had already wrested the size title from her, Percy Bates told Sir Ashley Sparks, his American representative. With a little luck she might also steal away the title of the world's fastest liner.

Cunard–White Star was preparing to proclaim this triumphant news to the world when, on March 24, a French announcement took the wind from its sails. Because of her extensive alterations, CGT said, *Normandie* had been remeasured. And as a result of the changes in tourist class and the addition of the new tourist-class lounge, she was a larger ship than before.

According to the French Line, *Normandie* now measured 82,799.45 gross tons. So instead of being some 1,400 tons smaller than the *Queen Mary*, she was more than 2,000 tons larger!

The executives at Cunard–White Star were so disturbed by this unexpected turn of events that several of them broadly hinted to the press that *Normandie*'s new measurement was inaccurate and inflated.

The French Line answered these objections with aplomb. Actually, it said, the surveyors had first come in with a figure of 86,496 gross tons. But the company had felt this figure was too large and had asked that the ship be remeasured as conservatively as possible.

We don't really care which ship is larger, the French Line said coyly. As a matter of fact, it's to our advantage to keep gross tonnage as low as possible, since dock fees and taxes are calculated on that basis.

Since there was some disagreement over this figure, CGT asked the surveyors to measure *Normandie* once more. This they did—and came up with yet another figure: 83,423 gross tons. CGT "reluctantly" accepted this measurement, to the undisguised consternation of Cunard–White Star.

Still hoping to be able to call the *Queen Mary* "the world's largest ship," Cunard–White Star now tried changing the rules in midgame. Their superliner's displacement was 77,482 tons, while *Normandie*'s was just 66,400. Surely that made *Queen Mary* the larger of the two.

It did not. Displacement tonnage is a measure of *weight*. And it had long been known that the *Queen Mary* was heavier than *Normandie*, largely because the French ship was built with a much greater proportion of high-tensile steel.

Traditionally, the comparative size of liners is determined by their relative gross tonnage, which has nothing whatsoever to do with weight. It is simply a measure of the interior capacity of the hull and its superstructure. Each "ton" equals 100 cubic feet.

Cunard–White Star eventually regained its equilibrium and stopped insisting that the *Queen Mary* was larger than *Normandie* if the criteria were changed. Instead, it took the more modest but entirely accurate tack of referring to its great new ship as "Britain's largest liner."

On the very day *Normandie*'s staggering new measurement was announced, the *Queen Mary* left Clydebank under her own power for the very first time, to undergo a series of "unofficial trials." Very soon Cunard–White Star officials would know whether or not their new ship had a chance to wrest away from *Normandie* the honor of being the world's fastest liner.

On April 17 the *Queen Mary* began her speed trials—seven double runs with and against the tide, over the measured course off the Isle of Arran, including runs at overload power and maximum power.

On the last run the *Queen Mary*'s engines were run out to

208,000 horsepower—50,000 above their normal service power. With this output she hit a maximum speed of 31.2 knots. *Normandie*'s top trial speed had been superior, however—32.125 knots. But no one knew which ship would be faster in actual service.

Nonetheless, after the news of the *Queen Mary*'s trials Vladimir Yourkevitch issued a press release on the relative merits of the two ships, naturally favoring the vessel he'd designed.

He pointed out that although *Normandie* was the longer of the two when measured from the front of her upturning bow to her taffrail, the *Queen Mary*, with less overhang at either end, had a waterline forty-two feet longer than *Normandie*'s. Since waterline length is directly related to potential speed, from the pure physics point of view the *Queen Mary* should be faster than her French rival, everything else being equal.

The British ship's designers, of course, were well aware of this fact. It was one reason they'd chosen to break with Cunard tradition and build its huge new ship with a cruiser stern, rather than one of the "counter" variety. (Cruiser sterns have no overhang.)

Four other factors played a major role in the speed of the two ships, however. The first was hull shape. Here, *Normandie* had a distinct edge. There was no question that she cut through the water more easily and with less resistance than the British superliner.

"It is interesting to compare photographs of the *Queen Mary* and *Normandie* steaming at full speed," Yourkevitch wrote. "The former rises a great swell at the bow and carries voluminous transverse waves all along the hull, while *Normandie*'s bow wave is smooth and flat and small transverse waves are very sharply slanted to the vessel's direction, setting into motion only a very small amount of water."

The second factor was engine power. Standard reference books say that *Normandie*'s engines produced 160,000 shaft horsepower and that the *Queen Mary*'s produced 200,000, a 25-percent difference. The truth is considerably more complex.

In actual fact, both ships produced a wide range of horsepower, depending on demand. To reach a normal service speed of about 29.5 knots, *Normandie* needed about 130,000 horsepower and the *Queen Mary* about 158,000. For their Blue Ribbon attempts (or to make up time lost during storms) the engines of both ships could put out considerably more than that, however.

Normandie's engines were eventually coaxed to a maximum of about 193,000 horsepower during record runs in 1937 and 1938, for instance. And the *Queen Mary*'s engines probably put out a maximum of 220,000 horsepower when she made her fastest trips. Thus, the British ship's engines were only 14 percent more powerful than *Normandie*'s.

Another factor in the liners' relative speeds: their propeller efficiency. It's impossible now to say which ship had more efficient propellers. However, it should be noted that both changed their propeller designs several times, in the search for greater efficiency and speed.

The final factor was hull weight. *Normandie*'s displacement was 66,400 tons, the *Queen Mary*'s 77,482 tons. In other words, the British ship was about 14 percent heavier than the French ship, so more power was required to drive her at the same speed.

Here's how all this totaled up:

1. Waterline length—edge to the *Queen Mary*;
2. Hull design—edge to *Normandie*;
3. Engine power—edge to the *Queen Mary*, by 14 percent;
4. Propeller efficiency—probably a toss-up;
5. Hull weight—edge to *Normandie*, by 14 percent

On paper, then, it was practically a dead heat. The final determination would come on the Atlantic—assuming Sir Percy gave the *Queen Mary* her head.

By April 1936 the suspense at Le Havre was palpable. The alterations had been completed, and all that remained was to put on *Normandie*'s new four-bladed propellers, then take her out to see if her vibration was truly cured and find out if she'd kept her speed.

When the new propellers finally arrived in late April, *Normandie* was already dry-docked and waiting for them. On April 29 a new and very different *Normandie* steamed out of Le Havre for her third set of trials.

At sea Captain Pugnet once more put his ship through her paces. Groups of engineers were stationed on every deck, fore and aft, their vibration gauges in place. Commandant Thoreux stood on the Deauville's terrace, alert to the slightest quiver. And Henri Cangardel, CGT's general manager, sat at a table in the café grill, where on previous trips water glasses had been kept half empty to keep the tablecloths dry.

Normandie picked up speed. In the past her vibration had shown itself when she reached 25 knots. This time there was nothing. She continued to accelerate. There was no noticeable vibration at 26 knots, and nothing to speak of at 27 knots. She was still steady at 28 knots. Smooth at 29 knots. Whatever effect her new propellers had on her vibration, they had not diminished her speed.

When *Normandie* hit 30 knots, Pugnet held her there. Cangardel walked forward from the café grill. In the smoking room he stood an unsharpened pencil on end, on a table. It stayed put. On the Deauville terrace Commandant Thoreux felt nothing.

Now the engineers began to report in. In most areas of the ship the vibration had simply vanished. Motion at the thrust blocks and shaft bossings was hardly large enough to measure. Even directly over the propellers, on the lowest deck, vibration had been reduced by 80 percent.

When all the engineers' reports were in, Cangardel solemnly embraced Romano, then Coqueret. "We all cried with joy," Maurice Coquin, one of the chief engineers, later related.

Approaching the landing stage, *Normandie* cut her engines and let the tugs take her in. And then, without anyone noticing, something strange occurred. Somehow, the inboard port propeller came loose. As the ship glided toward the landing stage, it slipped off its shaft and fell to the bottom.

Satisfied that the vibration problem was at an end, Cangardel told the French Line's public-relations and advertising department to spread the word. They outdid themselves.

One typical full-page magazine ad, decorated with two *Normandie* silhouettes, was headlined "The vibrationless *Normandie* in 1936."

"During the winter lay-up the ship was fitted with propellers of a new type and the shape of the tail shaft bossings was changed," the copy read. "The result has far exceeded all expectations and *Normandie* is now THE PERFECT SHIP."

A banner across the ad emphasized the message to the point of overkill. "NO VIBRATION FROM PROPELLERS," it said, "NO VIBRATION FROM TRANSMISSION, NO VIBRATION FROM GEARS, NO VIBRATION FROM ENGINES."

In Ethiopia, Mussolini's invasion was reaching its successful conclusion. On May 2, as the Italian armies approached Addis Ababa, meeting little resistance, Emperor Haile Selassie fled to exile in Great Britain.

In Great Britain, however, attention was focused on the upcoming maiden voyage of "Britain's largest ship." Cunard–White Star was doing its best to alert the world to the event, and British royalty cooperated fully in this effort.

During the *Queen Mary's* last few weeks in port, as workmen rushed to complete her cabins and public accommodations (repeating the scene at Le Havre the previous year), practically all of titled Britain dropped by to pay its respects.

While Mussolini's troops were marching into the Ethiopian capital, Commandant Pierre Thoreux, soon to take over from the retiring Captain Pugnet, told reporters that "*Normandie* now vibrated no more at 30 knots than the *Ile de France* had vibrated at 23." She would prove that when she departed for America the next day on her first voyage of the new season.

No sooner had the newsmen departed than a grim-faced Chief Engineer Hazard appeared at Thoreux's door. A diver sent to inspect the hull had discovered that a propeller was missing. Thoreux was incredulous. A half-hour later a second diver had confirmed the report.

Now *Normandie* had a problem. In fact, she had two problems. First, the missing propeller had to be replaced somehow with one of the old ones. The other inboard propeller also had to be replaced with an old model, to maintain balance. This change had to be accomplished practically overnight, since *Normandie* was due to depart at noon the next day. Second, how would the ship behave with a mixture of old and new propellers? Would she start vibrating again?

That night a double shift of workers managed to put two of

the old-model three-bladed propellers back on her inboard tail shafts. The next day, May 6, she left for New York with 629 passengers aboard.

As soon as *Normandie* was out at sea, it became obvious that some of the vibration had returned. Many of the passengers were disappointed or angry, but the story of the lost propeller mollified most of them.

On the very day *Normandie* departed from Le Havre, the 803-foot-long, hydrogen-filled *Hindenburg* zeppelin lifted off from Friedrichshafen, Germany, on her maiden voyage to America, the first of ten trips scheduled for the year. She carried fifty-one passengers, who afterward said that traveling on a zeppelin was just like traveling on a ship "without the roll."

On May 8 the *Hindenburg* floated over *Normandie*, almost 2,000 feet below. "She was," Dr. Hugo Eckener, the airship's developer and captain, reported later, "a very beautiful sight."

Fortunately for *Normandie* and the *Queen Mary*, the *Hindenburg* was not competing for the Blue Ribbon. If she had been, she would have won easily, since she completed the trip to Lakehurst, New Jersey, in three days, at an average speed of seventy-two knots. She arrived on May 9.

On that same day Mussolini announced the annexation of Ethiopia. "Civilization," he proclaimed, "has triumphed over barbarism."

Normandie returned to Le Havre on May 16, by which time a replacement four-bladed propeller had been cast and made ready in record time. It was installed before she departed for New York again four days later. This time it was made fast.

From that moment on, *Normandie*'s vibration was essentially a thing of the past. Newsmen traveling aboard the ship reported that this time the French Line's claims were true.

Three well-known *de grand luxe* passengers—Joseph Schenck, Frederick Coudert and Alexander Laughlin, the Pittsburgh steel magnate—all of whom had experienced terrible vibration when they crossed in 1935—decided to try again.

After the voyage they wired CGT, "Happy to congratulate French Line on entire disappearance of vibration on *Normandie*." Clay Morgan circulated the telegram to the press.

By now the *Queen Mary*'s maiden-voyage departure, set for May 27, was only weeks away. Using Clay Morgan's techniques, Cunard–White Star filled the newspapers, airwaves and newsreels with *Queen Mary* stories. But there was a difference: they all compared the British ship to *Normandie*.

One effect was to rekindle public interest in *Normandie*. As a result, some 10,000 New Yorkers visited her in three hours when she was thrown open to the public at Pier 88 on May 26, the day before the *Queen Mary* began her career.

That noon *Normandie* departed with 1,077 passengers on board, an average load. It included such luminaries as Dr. Alexis Carrel, Edward Johnson (general manager of the Metropolitan Opera) and Ginette Marboeuf-Joyet, the French Shirley Temple.

A day earlier the *Queen Mary*'s maiden-voyage jubilation reached its peak when the royal family once again descended on the ship— King Edward VIII, his mother, Queen Mary, and a host of other regal visitors.

On May 27, 1936, amid celebrations and crowds remarkably reminiscent of Le Havre the year before, the *Queen Mary*, "the stateliest ship in being," as King Edward had properly described her, majestically steamed out of The Solent and into the English Channel on her way to America.

No news of the *Queen Mary* or her maiden voyage appeared in Italian newspapers, however. Mussolini had ordered silence on the subject, in partial retaliation for British sanctions against Italy because of the Ethiopian affair.

But in the United States, in Britain, in France—everywhere where such things seemed to matter—people forgot their cares and turned their attention to the great new transatlantic vessel steaming toward New York.

11

CHALLENGE FROM A QUEEN

While the world's newest superliner, the *Queen Mary*, plowed through the Atlantic, *Normandie* was steaming in the opposite direction, proudly flying her Blue Ribbon. But the eyes of the world were on the British ship.

Like the World Series or a championship boxing match, *Normandie* and the *Queen Mary* were business enterprises. Nonetheless, their rivalry was one of the greatest sporting events of the 1930s.

The primary question was: Would the big British ship be able to duplicate *Normandie*'s feat, winning the Blue Ribbon her first time out? Whatever Sir Percy Bates said about that, it soon became clear that the *Mary* would try her best.

The first day out, the *Mary* matched *Normandie*'s record-breaking pace of the previous year. She did equally well on her second day. And on her third day at sea, May 31, she broke *Normandie*'s one-day mark, covering 766 nautical miles in twenty-five hours, averaging 30.64 knots. Britons began to anticipate victory.

Then the fog hit. Commander Britten slowed his ship to 22 knots, hoping to break through the fog momentarily. But the hours passed and visibility remained poor. Finally, ten hours and fifteen minutes after the *Mary* had steamed into the fog, she was back in the sunlight.

By that time she was eighty miles behind schedule. There was no way the deficit could be made up in the time remaining.

At 7:40 a.m. on June 1 the *Queen Mary* churned past a red lightship on her starboard quarter, to the cheers of the early birds on deck, who were certain that she'd won the Blue Ribbon. Unfortunately, this was not the Ambrose light, the western end of the "course," but the Fire Island lightship.

At 9:03 a.m. the giant British vessel glided past Ambrose light, having made the crossing from Bishop's Rock in 4 days, 5 hours and 46 minutes—2 hours and 44 minutes slower than *Normandie's* trip the year before. The French vessel had averaged 29.98 knots, the *Queen Mary* 29.133 knots.

This was a difference of .97 miles an hour—pretty trivial in the grand scheme of things. By such small differences, however, champions often emerge victorious and challengers come in second. When *Normandie* docked at Le Havre that afternoon, she was still proudly flying her thirty-meter Blue Ribbon.

Despite the *Queen Mary's* failure to win the Blue Ribbon, "it is hard to imagine," one reporter reflected, "how the greeting could have been more ecstatic had she shattered every record."

In most ways the welcome given the *Queen Mary* was fully the equal of that given *Normandie*. And that seemed fair enough, for in terms of size the British ship was very nearly the equal of the French vessel and in terms of speed she just might prove superior. (Later figures showed, however, that the Yourkevitch hull was more efficient than the British design. At 30 knots the *Queen Mary* consumed 1,196 tons of fuel oil a day, while *Normandie* burned just 950.)

What kind of ship was the *Queen Mary?*

In many of her essentials she was like *Normandie*. They were approximately equal in size, speed, power and fuel economy. But in style, mood, concept and execution they were quite different.

One writer put it this way: "*Normandie* is racier, more chic, a Parisienne—graceful, youthful, confident that no one in the world is clad more smartly than she. The English ship has the smartness of conservatism, the temperament of Bond Street rather than of the boulevards."

In general, *Normandie* had the look of motion. Her lines

were streamlined, rounded and raked. Her profile was strikingly similar to two ships of the future, the *France* (III), built in 1961 (now known as the *Norway*), and the *Queen Elizabeth 2*, built in 1968.

The *Queen Mary*, on the other hand, clearly sprang from the *Mauretania/Lusitania* line. Friends and critics alike said she looked like a larger *Aquitania*. She was solid, foursquare and a little fussy, stately rather than racy, impressive rather than graceful.

Each ship represented the temperament of the nation that had created her. This was even more true inside than out.

The *Queen Mary*'s interior had touches of Art Deco and Bauhaus design, but the overall impression was *institutional*; she simply didn't have *Normandie*'s panache.

In *The Sway of the Grand Saloon*, John Malcolm Brinnin describes the *Mary*'s interior: "Miles of linoleum that glistened like a low-grade fever, acres of laminated surfaces—flooded with 'indirect' lighting and machine-waxed to the glow of a subaltern's shoes—gave the ship the atmosphere of an enormous sanitarium."

Publicists called the *Mary* "the ship of wood." They might more accurately have called her the ship of plastic, since her decorators had used plastic—specifically, Formica—to cover the top of every piece of furniture in every cabin and public room and on the bathroom walls of all the luxury suites. Plastic, of course, was new, interesting and easily maintained. Still, *Normandie*'s designers managed to avoid using even a single square foot of it.

To a degree *Normandie* was built mainly for her first-class passengers, while the *Queen Mary* was designed primarily with tourist class in mind. The respective passenger capacities of the two ships, broken down by classes, is indicative:

	Normandie	Queen Mary
1st Class	864	776
Tourist	654	784
3rd Class	454	579
Total:	1,972	2,139

This wasn't simply a difference in design; it was a philosophical one. The French ship sought the elite; the British ship catered to the masses.

This difference was also evident in the number of staff on the two ships. *Normandie* carried a crew of 1,345; the *Queen Mary*, 1,101. *Normandie* had one crew member for every 1.47 passengers. In the Cunarder it was one for every 1.94 passengers.

While the two ships had essentially equal complements of officers, engineers and ordinary seamen, *Normandie* had some 240 more stewards, stewardesses, porters, bartenders, bellhops, busboys, waiters, hairdressers, pursers, attendants. As a result, her service was legendary.

In practice, the difference favored *Normandie* even more than the figures indicate, since the Cunarder was usually more nearly filled to capacity than was the French Line ship. Traditionally, there was more tourist and commercial traffic between Britain and America than between France and America.

Normandie carried the largest crew ever found on any passenger ship. And her 1.47-to-one passenger-to-crew ratio was the highest of all time. The *Empress of Britain*, a Canadian Pacific ship renowned for her luxury, was next, with one crew member for every 1.61 passengers. The only other major liners with a less than two-to-one ratio were the *Queen Mary*, the *Queen Elizabeth* and *L'Atlantique* (a ship of Cie. Sudatlantique, Bordeaux, which burned in 1933).

From a passenger viewpoint, *Normandie* was also more spacious than any other ship. Not only was she larger than the *Queen Mary*, she was also designed to carry fewer passengers. But how much roomier was she?

It's not easy to quantify roominess, but one reasonable approach is to divide a ship's passenger capacity into her gross tonnage, then multiply by 100. The result is the number of cubic feet per passenger. This calculation doesn't take into account differences in engine-room size, or differences between classes, but these are fairly similar on ships of similar gross tonnage.

Figured this way, the per-passenger space on *Normandie* was 4,330 cubic feet of space, while the per-passenger space on the

Mary was just 3,780 cubic feet. And since *Normandie* was rarely as packed as the *Queen Mary*, the effective difference was even greater.

These two calculations—passenger-crew ratio and per-passenger roominess—can be combined into what might be called a "luxury index." This single number is an interesting way to quantify shipboard luxury, although many other factors also mattered: food quality, crew courtesy, furniture comfort, the ship's riding qualities. At any rate, here's how some of the major ships of the 1920s and 1930s measure up.

Ship	Luxury Index
1. *Normandie*	2,945
2. *Empress of Britain*	2,211
3. *Queen Mary*	1,918
4. *Europa*	1,240
5. *Majestic*	1,226
6. *Bremen*	1,172
7. *Ile de France*	1,083
8. *Berengaria*	834
9. *Conte di Savoia*	825
10. *Leviathan*	774
11. *Rex*	755

Most pre-World War I ships had even fewer crew members per passenger and much less room. For instance, the *Titanic*, which was intended to be positively sybaritic, had a luxury index of 665. The legendary *Mauretania* had a lowly luxury index of 292. This was partly because of the thousands these ships carried in steerage.

Ships as different as *Normandie* and the *Queen Mary* naturally attracted very different types of passenger, at least in first class. The British ship generally drew a very rich, and quintessentially *Burke's Peerage* type of crowd, the sort of people who—until the war—were said to prefer Hitler to Stalin.

Even on the maiden voyage they were a fairly staid group. Writing in the London *Daily Mail*, star British foreign correspondent Sir Percival Phillips said, "Ours has been a singularly quiet ship . . . very few people are about after midnight. There are no late or over-lively parties."

Normandie's passengers were cut from different cloth. They were an ebullient, even noisy bunch who kept late hours and often danced till dawn. They were the *nouveaux riches* as opposed to the landed gentry. Politically, *Normandie*'s clientele was as left of center as the *Mary*'s crowd was right.

The *Queen Mary*'s debut was a smashing success, but she was not without problems. She vibrated badly, despite the claims from Cunard–White Star that she'd been built from the start as a "vibration-free" ship.

She also suffered from smokestack difficulties. During her first season Cunard–White Star paid a pretty penny to passengers whose clothing had been dirtied or damaged by funnel smut.

Then there was the matter of rolling. The *Queen Mary*, it was said, would roll in wet grass. This would become a very troublesome and stubborn problem for the British ship.

Commercially speaking, the advent of the *Queen Mary* had very little effect on *Normandie*. The British ship carried many passengers, but *Normandie*'s bookings did not suffer.

On June 17 *Normandie* departed from New York on her third eastbound voyage of the season. Among her 1,487 passengers: Edward G. Robinson, Feodor Chaliapin, Edna Ferber, Ely Culbertson and Virginia Gildersleeve, dean of Barnard College. In the hold was a record number of passengers' automobiles—fifty-two.

Normandie crossed the Atlantic without incident, stopping first at Southampton. But just as she was about to depart, a small Royal Air Force seaplane buzzed the ship, circling lower and lower until it was at the Sun Deck level. At this moment one of *Normandie*'s deck cranes was lifting an automobile out of the hold. One of the plane's wingtips caught the crane, causing the crane to quiver and crumple. The car dropped back onto the ship, half on and half off the deck, and barely missed the fifty-man detail which had been unloading it.

Meanwhile, the little biplane spun toward the forward funnel like a tossed boomerang. Over the funnel, the pilot desperately tried to regain control, but the funnel's hot exhaust gases robbed him of his lift. His plane was sucked down toward the ship.

So frantically did the pilot pull back on the stick that the plane somersaulted, then dropped on the forward tip of the whaleback at *Normandie*'s bow and smashed.

"The landing was one of the most extraordinary sights I have ever seen," commented *Normandie*'s sophisticated and well-traveled commander, Captain Pugnet.

The unloading detail rushed to the rescue, but before they could get to the plane, out stepped Lieutenant G. K. Horsey, the pilot, who was unhurt. "I am terribly sorry about this," he said to a bosun's mate.

Captain Pugnet met Lieutenant Horsey on deck. After a moment's hesitation—there was no protocol for such an occasion—they shook hands.

"Sir," said Lieutenant Horsey, "could we offload the plane before you depart?"

Pugnet checked his watch. "We're already running late. We'll drop off the wreckage next week on our way back to New York."

"Well, then, could I go with you to France and come back with the wreckage?" Lieutenant Horsey asked.

Pugnet laughed. "That will just make matters worse at headquarters, don't you think?"

Lieutenant Horsey ruefully agreed. He boarded a tender and reported back to the Royal Air Force station at Gosport, not far from Southampton. The newspapers did not record his punishment, if any.

Shortly after the *Queen Mary*'s maiden voyage, the French political picture changed dramatically. The Communists joined forces with the Socialists and the Radicals and swept into power. Léon Blum, the Socialist leader and a onetime literary critic, became Premier. The Nazis and the extreme rightists in France promptly dubbed him "the Jew Blum."

Blum immediately instituted a forty-hour work week, a

minimum wage and collective bargaining. France's workers rejoiced, but her businessmen were horrified.

To thwart the changes, the Right Wing tried to slip huge armament increases past the Chamber of Deputies, hoping to take the money away from social programs. The Left, recognizing the ploy, killed the arms increases. France needed to re-arm to match the Germans, but politics had prevented it.

On July 11, 1936, Austria and Germany concluded a "gentlemen's agreement" concerning Austrian sovereignty. In the agreement Austria's independence was "assured." At the same time her Chancellor, Kurt von Schuschnigg, acknowledged that Austria was a "German state," and agreed to admit members of the "so-called National Opposition" (the Austrian Nazis) into his government.

Hitler, who had long coveted Austria, now sat back, content in the thought that Austrian Nazis would gradually take control of the government and seek union with Germany.

On the very same day a small British chartered plane left the Canary Islands on a secret flight, carrying a very important passenger. The Spanish general Francisco Franco, who'd been exiled for his role in an attempted coup, was flying to the Spanish colony of Morocco, where he intended to seize control of the Army of Africa and use it to depose the duly elected Spanish government.

On *Normandie*, Captain René Pugnet was ready to retire at the age of fifty-five, to take up duck hunting and to seek big game in Africa. His successor would be his longtime assistant, Commandant Pierre Thoreux.

On July 15 *Normandie* departed from New York on Captain Pugnet's last voyage in command. Aboard were some 1,610 passengers, among whom was perhaps the largest group of celebrities ever to travel on a single ocean voyage.

These included Edward G. Robinson (his second *Normandie* trip of the year), George Raft, Ruth Etting, Marlene Dietrich, Bert Wheeler, Ham Fisher (creator of the "Joe Palooka" comic strip), Edward Everett Horton, Tommy Manville, Irving

Berlin, Edna Ferber (also on her second *Normandie* trip of the year), the former Mayor of New York and his wife, Mr. and Mrs. Jimmy Walker, and newspaper columnist Leonard Lyons.

The next four days at sea were a madhouse of parties, celebrations, musical events and other festivities, most marked by celebrity participation.

On the second night out, the featured performers at the ship's concert were Edward G. Robinson and George Raft. The host introduced the men as "the cinema's toughest guys." Robinson and Raft rose from their seats, exchanged murderous glances, reached for their imaginary "gats," then embraced and began to rhumba.

At a later party Ruth Etting dedicated a number to Captain Pugnet and sang the touching French song, "Is It True What They Say About Dixie?" Then Bert Wheeler rose to do one of his vaudeville routines, a charming bit of whimsy concerning "the yidoo mousie who was so dam dwunk." He was followed by Ham Fisher, who, in Captain Pugnet's honor, took the stage to draw a picture of Joe Palooka—upside down.

Between the parties the stars continued to provide considerable entertainment for *Normandie*'s passengers, sometimes inadvertently.

For instance, Marlene Dietrich made a big issue of privacy—even though her movie studio had been publicizing her trip for weeks. Once aboard and safely ensconced in one of the Sun Deck's enormous suites, she walked out on her "private" verandah. To her surprise, she was now face-to-face with tourist-class passengers playing deck games on top of the new tourist-class lounge. When Miss Dietrich realized that many passengers were pointing their cameras her way, she rushed back into her suite, only to re-emerge in white slacks and swathed in purple veils, her makeup freshened and her false eyelashes firmly in place.

The oft-married playboy Tommy Manville also gave passengers a thrill by parading around the decks with a fetching blonde he insisted was his secretary. Bert Wheeler enjoyed following them and loudly asking the girl to "take a letter."

Manville had been forced to change rooms when he discovered that his cabin adjoined one occupied by Avonne Taylor, one of his ex-wives. He told Leonard Lyons that he had once assembled all of his ex-wives in his office for a business discussion and "even at such a necessarily cramped vantage point, was unable to suffer any sentiments of remorse."

Passengers who visited *Normandie's* theater were almost certain to run across composer Irving Berlin, who tried to escape his seasickness by watching over and over again the new hit movie *San Francisco* with Clark Gable, Jeanette MacDonald and Spencer Tracy.

On July 20 *Normandie* docked at Le Havre. Her huge whistle let loose three blasts as Captain Pugnet left the ship for the last time. He transferred to his own eighteen-foot pleasure boat, which he had named the *Super-Normandie.*

In the few days *Normandie* had been at sea, much had happened in the world. Despite an impassioned plea from Haile Selassie, the League of Nations had voted to lift all sanctions on Italy on June 15.

Two days later General Franco arrived in Morocco, took command of the Spanish army there and proclaimed a revolt against Spain's republican government. The Spanish Civil War had begun.

That summer, while *Normandie* and the *Queen Mary* vied on the Atlantic and the republicans and the Nationalists vied in Spain, athletes from fifty-one countries tested their mettle at the Olympic Games in Berlin.

The Nazis made the games a huge propaganda event, running them on a lavish scale never seen before and doing their best to portray Nazi Germany as a twentieth-century paradise.

On August 19 the *Queen Mary* successfully dethroned her French rival. She was carrying 1,720 passengers at the time, among them Jesse Owens, who was returning home with his Olympic gold medals. She'd steamed from Bishop's Rock to the Ambrose light in just 4 days and 27 minutes, at an average speed of 30.14 knots (*Normandie* had made the trip at an average speed of 29.93 knots).

But CGT wasn't about to surrender the Blue Ribbon without a whimper. The French steamship line noted that while the *Queen Mary* had indeed gained the westbound record, *Nor-*

mandie still held the eastbound record—and at the fastest average speed at which any liner had ever crossed the Atlantic: 30.31 knots.

The captain changed his mind about claiming victory. He wanted to silence all doubt by besting *Normandie's* eastbound time, too.

On August 31 the *Queen Mary* steamed past Bishop's Rock at 8:12 p.m., having started out from Ambrose light 3 days, 23 hours and 57 minutes before. For the first time in history a passenger ship had crossed the Atlantic in less than four days!

The *Mary's* average speed for the voyage was 30.63 knots. *Normandie's* best time was 3 hours and 31 minutes longer, and .32 knots slower. This time there was no denying the British vessel's triumph.

But Commodore Britten was gracious about it. "The French will beat our mark and we theirs, and all in the best of spirit," he said.

The members of the Hales Trophy committee now notified Sir Percy Bates that the French Line would deliver this symbol of transatlantic speed supremacy within three months. They were shocked by his response.

"Cunard doesn't want the Hales Trophy and would feel obliged to refuse it if offered," he said. "I regret, for myself, that a Blue Ribbon cup was ever brought into existence. We aren't racing and don't go in for racing."

Why, then, asked reporters, had the *Queen Mary* made two record-breaking runs, back to back?

"We did let the ship out on this voyage," said Sir Percy. "But our only purpose was to get experience that would be useful in building her sister ship."

This was nonsense. During the twenty-two years when the *Mauretania* had held the record, this fact had been grandly proclaimed on every Cunard passenger list and menu. Why now, suddenly, had Cunard turned coy?

"Remember our company regulation number seven," said Sir Percy. "It says, 'Masters of ships should run no risk for the sake of a speedy voyage, nor endanger the lives of passengers or property in sailing expeditiously.' "

Every shipping line had such a regulation, however, and

Cunard's had been in full effect when the *Mauretania* threw all caution to the winds to win the Blue Ribbon.

By denigrating the Blue Ribbon, Bates was ignoring the history of speed competition on the Atlantic, a competition that had steadily lowered crossing times from 12 days and 10 hours in 1840, when the first Cunard steamship, *Britannia*, made the trip, to 7 days and 15 hours in 1876 (by the *Germanic*), to the *Mary*'s 3 days, 23 hours and 57 minutes.

The Blue Ribbon competition also helped New World and Old grow closer together, increasing commerce, making possible the largest population shift in world history and forever changing the political and economic complexion of the world.

Bates' attitude toward the Blue Ribbon was so transparently silly that Robert Wilder, the *New York Sun*'s ship columnist, devoted an entire column to making fun of it. "In a spirit of pure charity," he wrote, "we suggest to the French Line that it get down to 25 Broadway [the Cunard–White Star office] posthaste, leave the trophy on the door and run away like all getout, calling back over your shoulder to Cunard, 'You're it!' "

But Sir Percy had the last word. The question of steamship speed wasn't important at all in the larger scheme of things, he said. "The crux of the matter lies in whether twenty-five years from now it will be the universal desire of mankind to travel like rockets at supersonic speeds in a closed metal container or whether many will still prefer a more leisurely progression."

While the *Queen Mary* was breaking records, the Spanish Civil War was heating up. Hitler had decided to help Franco, feeling that a fascist power on France's western border would weaken her resolve. Hitler also knew that if he aided Franco, Mussolini would have to do the same. And that would create friction between Italy and France.

In August and September, German transport planes ferried Franco's army to Algeciras and other Nationalist coastal enclaves. On October 1 some army officers proclaimed Franco head of the Nationalist state. Soon afterward he and his army began the march to Madrid.

By late October, Nationalist forces had reached the southern fringes of Madrid. The republicans, although they had armed the workers as best they could, seemed doomed. But in the first week of November thousands of soldiers of the International Brigade joined the republicans. They were bearing Russian arms.

But the Spanish Civil War wasn't the only headline event of fall 1936. In the United States, Franklin Delano Roosevelt ran for re-election against Republican Alf Landon, winning every state but Maine and Vermont.

And in Great Britain a certain Mrs. E. A. Simpson had filed for divorce from Mr. E. A. Simpson at the Ipswich Assizes. The case inspired a storm of gossip because the woman in question was the constant companion of none other than Edward, King of England.

At sea the *Queen Mary* had also run into her first storm. She'd rolled horribly, like a 5,000-ton tramp steamer. Her designers, who apparently never envisaged such a possibility, hadn't installed handrails on her splendid broad alleyways. As a result, her passengers, screaming in terror, careened around the ship like bowling pins.

A stewardess described the ship's motion: "It was in the middle of the night and she suddenly started to go and she went, so slowly, down and down and down and down. I was thrown out of my bunk and thought that she was never coming back. I remember thinking to myself, even as she went down: This is the end. She can never come back from this angle.

"Slowly she righted herself and then began a horrible corkscrew motion that went on and on even after the sea had become calm. She just didn't seem to be able to stop it."

The *Queen Mary* arrived at Southampton three and a half hours late, with eight passengers and four crew members injured. One passenger had to be taken to a hospital.

These troubles caused quite a stir in the British press. And, to Sir Percy's distinct annoyance, they again raised the subject of Yourkevitch's hull.

On November 10 Lord Strabolgi, a Yourkevitch partisan and an acquaintance of Sir Percy's, suggested that Cunard–White Star reconsider the design of number 552—the future *Queen Elizabeth*.

"I feel I must revert to our former correspondence about the hull design of the *Queen Mary* and especially of the second Cunarder and the comparison I made with the hull design of the *Normandie*," he wrote. "My information, which of course you can check, is that in recent gales, the *Queen Mary* rolled badly . . . while the *Normandie* behaved well."

Strabolgi enclosed a photograph of each ship at 28 knots. "I, as a seaman, can see that there is far less friction at the bow of the *Normandie* than in the *Queen Mary* and you can see it too.

"If the facts that I have been given are correct, there is something worth study in the Yourkevitch hull design. . . . Yourkevitch is ready to work quite anonymously if it would hurt the feelings of our fellow patriots if a Russian naval architect was known to have assisted."

To make sure his letter got the proper attention from Bates, Strabolgi sent a carbon to Lord Essendon, a senior Cunard–White Star director.

Bates replied first to Essendon. "We have known right from the start that the *Normandie* is an easier model to propel, but only in smooth water with waves not exceeding three feet in height.

"As regards 552, a complete study has been made of the *Normandie* and her performance and partly as a result of this, the shape of the 552 will differ from that of the 534, but will still not be of such an extreme type as the *Normandie*.

"As you know, we expect to get another half knot out of this change."

Obviously, *Normandie*'s innovations had had their effect on Cunard, despite public protestations to the contrary. Even Sir Percy was concerned with his ships' speed capabilities.

Essendon also wrote Strabolgi, pointing out that it was impossible to compare the performance of the British and French ships in the recent storm because they were headed in opposite directions.

But the issue didn't rest there. Questions were soon raised in the House of Commons about the "inconvenience" suffered by the passengers in the "recent rough weather."

Bates finally notified the Parliamentary Secretary that steps would be taken to "prevent recurrence of the difficulties."

On the *Queen Mary*'s next voyage a group of carpenters fit handrails to the ship's alleyways and anchored the furniture. Bates also ordered Commodore Britten to slow the ship down to a crawl in any future storm, to minimize passenger discomfort. Consequently, the *Queen Mary* was thirteen hours late after one big storm.

While Bates dealt with the *Mary*'s rolling problem, a series of momentous events was taking place in quick succession.

On November 13 King Edward told his Prime Minister, Stanley Baldwin, that he wanted to marry Mrs. Simpson.

Five days later the German and Italian governments, acting in concert, recognized the regime of Francisco Franco.

A week after that, Germany and Japan signed an anti-Comintern pact. Joachim von Ribbentrop, Hitler's Foreign Minister, said, with a straight face, that the two nations had joined together to "defend Western civilization."

Shortly after, Germany and Italy proclaimed the "Rome-Berlin Axis."

And, finally, the Belgians said they were withdrawing from their alliance with France. This left a huge gap in the Maginot Line, which ended at the French-Belgian border. This frontier was simply too long to fortify. French generals reacted to this unsolvable problem by pretending it did not exist.

In December, Cunard–White Star decided to bring the *Queen Mary*'s season to a close a few voyages early. The problems with smokestack grit and vibration had to be resolved.

Concurrently, a major change was made in number 552. A stem anchor like *Normandie*'s was added to the plans. This required a raked bow so the anchor could fall freely into the sea. The result: a cross between the graceful swoop of *Normandie*'s stem and the nearly straight knife-edge entry of the *Queen Mary*.

This alteration, which was made just before the ship's first keel plates were laid, added 11 feet 6 inches to 552's overall length. Otherwise, in all of her most important dimensions she was essentially a twin to the *Queen Mary*.

As a result of this change, the *Elizabeth* would be 1,031 feet long overall—exactly sixteen inches longer than *Normandie*. When she entered service (Cunard was aiming for a 1940 maiden voyage), she would be the longest and probably the largest ship in the world.

Soon after the *Queen Elizabeth*'s first keel plates were laid, and just after her sister ship's refit had gotten under way, *Normandie* encountered what turned out to be the worst storm of her career.

She'd left Le Havre on December 18 with 928 passengers and 5,000 bags of holiday mail. No sooner was she at sea than she ran into hurricane-force winds and waves high enough to drench her funnel tops.

Said Captain Thoreux, "We had westerly gales for two-and-a-half days. The worst of it was last Saturday night and Sunday, when the wind sometimes reached a velocity of 85 miles an hour—hurricane force. I slowed the ship down to 25 knots and then had to slow her to 18 knots for three hours.

"It was the worst storm that this ship has ever been through and one of the worst I have ever seen. But the ship behaved better than any other big ship I have ever been on."

According to her officers, *Normandie* was so stable that there wasn't even any need to close down the swimming pool. But this was something of an exaggeration, as Ronald Dendievel, a *Normandie* passenger, recalled. "During the hurricane they drained half of the water from the swimming pool and took my photograph while I was swimming in the other half, supposedly denoting the 'great stability' of the ship. But most of the passengers were testing the great stability in their beds. Great savings must have been made in the food department on that trip."

Among the seasick passengers were a host of celebrities: Jo Davidson (the sculptor), Robert Frost, Countess Furstenberg, Arnold Gingrich (publisher of *Esquire*), Dorothy Thompson (Mrs. Sinclair Lewis, and a well-known writer in her own right), Basil Rathbone, Igor Stravinsky, Mlle. Bethsabée de Rothschild, Lupe Velez, Sophie Tucker and Mr. and Mrs. Edward G. Robinson and their three-year-old son.

Mr. Robinson, a newspaper reported, brought back a collection of paintings by Corot, Picasso, Gauguin and Cézanne said to be worth "about $120,000." Lupe Velez, who was married to Johnny Weissmuller, came off the ship with an armload of bulldog puppies. She'd been given their mother in England

and hadn't known the dog was pregnant. "I was double-crossed," she complained.

All of this was public-relations fluff, typical of the dockside material with which editors filled their shipping pages on slow news days. But *Normandie* was about to participate in a considerably more serious venture.

The Spanish Civil War had now reached a bloody stalemate. Hoping to help the republican side, the American Communist Party had begun recruiting soldiers for what would be known as the Abraham Lincoln Brigade.

By the middle of December more than 100 men were drilling every evening at the Ukrainian Hall in New York City. They slept at Sloan House, the 34th Street YMCA. The party gave them $1.50 a day for food and transportation.

Just before Christmas seventy-six of the best recruits were told, to their great delight, that they'd soon be sailing to Europe aboard *Normandie*.

It was a varied group—a junior-high-school principal from Alabama, a black county-fair wrestler from Provincetown, a Japanese-American cook from California, a onetime gunnery instructor from West Point, a *Daily Worker* columnist, an Armenian carpet salesman, a City College soccer star, a U.S. Army deserter, a Texas redneck and a nihilist from Greenwich Village who looked forward to death.

Early on December 26 a modest *bon voyage* celebration was held in a movie house near Communist Party headquarters. Each man was given a carton of Lucky Strikes, a Gillette razor, two cakes of Palmolive soap, a tin of coffee and a third-class ticket.

Finally, every man was given $10 to cover all shipboard expenses, including tipping. They were told to tell anyone who asked that they were tourists headed for the Paris Exposition.

One man among them carried a .45-caliber automatic. He also brought $15 for every one of the recruits. They would carry this money on their persons when they disembarked, to prove they weren't vagrants. Once ashore, however, they were to return it promptly.

It was an unusually warm day—62 degrees—in December when they boarded *Normandie*. As usual, the ship cast off at noon.

As soon as the recruits learned that tourist class was filled with girls from the *Folies Bergères,* they undertook their first invasion. Evidently the girls were equally happy to see the recruits. As one writer said, "If their tales contain even a grain or two of truth, they broke records and made history."

When not chasing girls, the recruits pored over out-of-date ROTC manuals, which were circulated secretly like "choice bits of pornography." Their leader, who had a conspirator's paranoia, forbade the men to assemble in groups larger than five.

On the second day at sea the third-class purser, who'd quickly divined the true character of this odd collection of passengers, posted a notice on the bulletin board for their benefit: Representative McReynolds, chairman of the House Foreign Affairs Committee, said he would urge the Justice Department to apply the section of the Criminal Code providing a penalty of $3,000 or a year in jail for any U.S. citizen convicted of enlisting in a foreign war.

That night a few portholes were opened and the highly valued ROTC manuals jettisoned.

When *Normandie* landed at Le Havre on the last day of the year, the customs agents winked at the Communist recruits and waved them through the line without even a glance inside their identical suitcases.

liFE ON THE ATLANTIC

Normandie had spent the winter of 1935–6 having her vibration problems attended to. Now, in the winter of 1936–7, it was the *Queen Mary's* turn to undergo corrective surgery. It was time for the vibration, severe rolling and smokestack-grit problems to be addressed.

To reduce vibration, eighteen-inch steel stanchions were installed within the ship from the Sun Deck to the double bottom, even though the staterooms and public rooms had to be stripped to the steelwork to do the job. Existing stanchions were reinforced by twelve-by-fourteen-inch steel channel beams joined to nine-by-three-inch steel beams running across the ship. Similar beams were run the full length of the liner on both sides of the Promenade Deck. The engineers' accommodations were shifted from the lower decks to the Sun Deck, and steel beams were installed in part of the vacated space. Finally, the *Mary's* propellers were replaced by propellers of a different design. These added a half-knot to the *Mary's* top speed.

To reduce the ship's rolling, her bilge keels—the projecting strips of metalwork that ran along most of her length underwater—were widened by several inches, and immense "rolling chocks" were fitted on both sides of the hull above the bilge keels. (These measures may have seemed heroic at the time, but they did not solve the problem. In 1958 Cunard spent half a million pounds sterling to install four hydraulic stabilizer fins on the hull. This was considered money well spent; the *Mary's* rolling smashed an average of 25,000 dinner plates every year.)

Lastly, to keep passengers' clothing as clean as possible, specially designed soot-extractors were installed on each of the *Mary*'s three funnels.

Meanwhile, CGT was taking advantage of the winter layoff to tune up *Normandie*. Having been forced to surrender the Blue Ribbon the previous summer, the French Line intended to win it back.

Sixteen extra steam nozzles were installed in *Normandie*'s boiler room to boost her power output, the size of the pipes that supplied steam to her turbines was increased, and her propellers were replaced once more. The new ones had the same basic design as those which had corrected her vibration problems, but they were smaller and were built to revolve faster, allowing the engines to develop more horsepower.

While the British and the French were getting their flagships ready for the summer's transatlantic *duel à deux*, the newspapers were filled with ominous stories.

On January 23 the Moscow "show trials" began as Josef Stalin purged the Communist Party, liquidating ten generals and hundreds of other officers and sending thousands more to Siberia.

A couple of weeks later Málaga fell to Franco's Nationalist armies—a major defeat for the Loyalists.

In America, Congress passed the Neutrality Act of 1937, forbidding loans or arms sales to belligerents. The measure helped the Nationalists more than it did the Loyalists, since the Loyalists were short of cash and were getting much less military equipment from the Soviet Union than the Nationalists were getting from Germany and Italy.

In England, Sir Percy Bates continued to insist that even though the new propellers made the *Mary* faster, his main aim was economy. And, indeed, there was some truth to this stance. More efficient than the old propellers, the new ones promised to save Cunard 15,000 pounds a year at the *Mary*'s customary cruising speed.

But Bates may not have been completely innocent in the

matter of the *Mary*'s top speed, as demonstrated by an amusing exchange of letters between him and Stephen Pigott (president of the John Brown Company, the *Mary*'s builder and refitter).

Pigott led off in March 1937. Most of his letter discussed a technical paper on the *Queen Mary* which he intended to deliver to the Institute of Naval Architects. But he closed with this revealing remark:

"In our conversation on Friday of last week, you mentioned your intention to have a 'tilt' at the Blue Ribbon business, but were not quite sure whether the occasion which you then had in mind would be sufficiently early to forestall a further effort which might be made by another vessel.

"I take the liberty of suggesting for your consideration that the meeting of the Naval Architects on the 17th March would give early opportunity for such a tilt should you regard the occasion as suitable and of giving the desirable wide publicity. I am confident that you will not regard this suggestion on my part as remiss."

Unfortunately, Bates' reply is missing from the files, but its tenor can be easily gathered from Pigott's second letter.

"I am a bit disturbed by your letter received this morning," Pigott wrote to Bates (who was, after all, his most important customer). "With reference to [my comments] concerning the 'Blue Riband,' I fear I did not make myself clear. . . . I had absolutely no intention of myself making reference to the 'Blue Riband.' I had taken the liberty of suggesting that you might wish to avail yourself of such opportunity as the Naval Architects' meeting to make your 'tilt' at this controversy. I am sorry that I raised the matter with you."

On March 10—less than a week after Pigott's second letter to Bates—the *Queen Mary* arrived in New York on her first round trip of 1937. On board was Sir Thomas Brocklebank, a senior Cunard director and a man whose family had been involved with that shipping line since long before Sir Percy was born. "If the *Normandie* tries to recapture the Blue Ribbon," he told reporters, "our ship will attempt to lower her present speed record this summer."

One can only imagine how Bates reacted to that.

Normandie's first arrival in New York in 1937 was a spectacular one, not because it broke any records—it didn't—but because her captain managed to dock the ship *without* help from the usual tugboats, whose crews were on strike.

"At about 10:05, we reached the Pier," Captain Thoreux wrote.

> As foreseen, not a tugboat around. I observe by the drift that there is still a light current. So much the better. It will help the turn. I swerve the ship to the right and with wheel of the helm and the propellers, it turns satisfactorily.
>
> At about 10:20, we are heading east. I engage the bow between the two piers and majestically, the ship moves forward toward its post. One third of the ship is now safe from the current, but there are still about 200 meters outside and any drifting could throw the ship dangerously against the dock.
>
> Instead of tugboats to correct the drifting, I incessantly maneuver the propellers and manage to maintain the ship's axis in the right direction. The forward lines are ready and thrown to the mooring crew on the quay. Then, as easily as a tugboat, the Normandie moves slowly toward its post.
>
> At 10:40, the ship is in its place. . . . Not only has the maneuver been particularly successful, but the docking has been the fastest of all the ones achieved by Normandie.

John McClain, the ship columnist for the *New York World-Telegram*, was on hand to witness Normandie's arrival and there to check on the effects of the new propellers,

> It's taken almost two years to do it, but apparently the French engineers have finally developed a set of propellers of the proper weight, pitch and size to cure the jitters that afflicted Normandie during her first days afloat [he wrote].

We recall one unhappy moment during the maiden voyage . . . two springs ago when a guide undertook to show us through some of the ship's finest suites. The vessel was making something in the neighborhood of 30 knots at the time and the guide took us to the palatial Deauville apartment, aft on the Sun Deck, flung open the door and said, "This is the greatest thing of its kind in any ship."

We stepped in ahead of him and for a moment, we thought we were in a cross-town street car. The floor was bobbing up and down like a Coney Island crazy-house and the woodwork gave out hideous groans and creaks and a sink in the kitchen was threatening to tear itself out of the wall and spring at the first passerby. It would have been impossible for anybody to live in the place.

Yesterday, we talked to Mr. and Mrs. Howard Weintraub, who occupied the suite on the way over. He's publisher of Esquire *and according to friends is not accustomed to put up with discomfort. We were amazed to find him leaving the suite as the ship docked, clean-shaven and apparently unwounded. "You mean . . ." we said, indicating the apartment. He said, "Not a tremor. Just like a hotel." All of which goes to show you what four new propellers can do."*

As *Normandie* lay docked at Pier 88, she was joined on the North River by a unique convocation of big liners, one after another: Cunard–White Star's *Berengaria*, formerly the *Imperator*, which was the world's largest ship in 1913 and 1914; the *Europa*, holder of the Blue Ribbon from 1930 to 1933; the *Rex*, which captured the Blue Ribbon from the *Europa* in 1933. Also in port was the *Georgic*, a large British diesel liner.

This gathering, which took place on the morning of March 19, lasted only an hour before it began to disperse, the liners leaving for Europe loaded with American tourists. *Normandie* was the first to depart.

After two days at sea it became clear that Pugnet was ready for *his* "tilt" at the Blue Ribbon. Evidently he was eager to test out *Normandie's* alterations.

On March 21 *Normandie* recaptured the record for a single day's average speed: 31.65 knots. The previous mark—31 knots even—had been set the summer before by the *Queen Mary*.

And on March 22 *Normandie* passed Bishop's Rock and recaptured the eastbound transatlantic speed mark. The trip had taken her 4 days and 6 minutes, despite storms and headwinds. This was actually nine minutes more than the *Mary*'s record trip, but it was over a route that was thirty-nine miles longer.

The next day CGT officials revealed that *Normandie* had several times hit and maintained the totally unprecedented speed of 33 knots—three quarters of a knot faster than she'd managed, full out, in her original trials.

On April 20 Hitler celebrated his birthday. A public holiday was declared in Germany and there was a great military parade. Hitler stood on the viewing stand "as happy as a child with tin soldiers . . . saluting every tank and gun," according to William Shirer. "The military attachés of France, Britain and Russia, I hear, were impressed. So were ours."

Six days later the Germans staged an even more impressive event: the annihilation of Guernica. For three hours waves of Junker and Heinkel bombers from the Condor Squadron dropped thousands of aluminum incendiary projectiles while Heinkel fighters strafed townsfolk fleeing into the fields. For the first time the world witnessed the total terror of aerial warfare.

There was no way the lives of the people of Guernica could be restored, but the Germans did suffer a sort of divine retribution shortly afterward. On May 3 the zeppelin *Hindenburg* floated up from Frankfurt on what was to be the first of eighteen scheduled transatlantic flights. She carried thirty-six passengers, a crew of sixty-one, including many trainees, and giant swastikas painted on her tail.

Three days later the pride of the Nazis burst into flame as it came in for a landing at Lakehurst, New Jersey. Thirty-five people died. Once again, for a time, liners were the only way to cross.

They were also making their bid as the best place for a vacation. Toward the end of April CGT announced that *Normandie* would take a twenty-one day, 11,000-mile cruise to South America the following winter.

In May, on the twentieth anniversary of America's involvement in the Great War, thousands of American Legionnaires departed from the United States to see the Marne and Argonne battlefields once more. They crowded aboard practically every liner on the Atlantic, including—ironically—the *Bremen* and the *Europa*.

Normandie, one of the symbols of the Allied triumph, took more than her share of Legionnaires to see the Paris Exposition.

Among the attractions they visited was the *Petit Normandie*, a floating restaurant stationed on the Seine, within view of the Eiffel Tower. *Petit Normandie* was a forty-year-old river steamer that had been rebuilt to look more or less like her namesake. It had three squat funnels, tiered aft decks and a bow that resembled Yourkevitch's design. It contained two restaurants.

In the Spanish pavilion a less amusing exhibit was on view: Picasso's *Guernica*—a twenty-six-foot-long artistic representation of the decimated Spanish village, painted from start to finish in just six weeks.

In England one era was ending and another beginning. King Edward abdicated to marry Wallis Simpson and King George VI was enthroned. The British Prime Minister, Stanley Baldwin, also stepped down. He was replaced by his Chancellor of the Exchequer, Neville Chamberlain.

A new era was beginning on the Atlantic, too, On May 25, ten years after Lindbergh flew to Paris, a Pan Am S-42 and an Imperial Airways flying boat took off simultaneously, one from England, the other from America, on the first of four survey flights.

Commercial air service began just three weeks later, at the rate of one round trip per week per company. From that moment on and forever more, liners were no longer the only way to cross.

In America patriotism was running at high tide. On June 15— Flag Day—New York Assemblyman Phelps Phelps gave a speech at the base of the Statue of Liberty. He condemned the European nations for failing to pay their war debts and called for the seizure of *Normandie* and the *Queen Mary* as part payment. "They'd be a fine nucleus for an American merchant marine," he noted.

In Germany the Nazis opened the first concentration camp, Buchenwald. At the same time Jews were ousted from German trade and industry, ordered to wear a yellow Star of David and barred from parks, theaters, health resorts and other public institutions.

As if the troubles in Europe weren't enough, fighting now broke out between Chinese and Japanese troops at the Marco Polo Bridge on the outskirts of Peking. Soon after, Japanese warplanes bombed and strafed large parts of northern China. The Japanese infantry, led by tanks, followed shortly afterward, and, one by one, major Chinese cities began to fall—Peking, Tientsin, Shanghai, Nanking, Hanchow.

Meanwhile, the rivalry on the Atlantic continued. But the ships were not entirely insulated from contemporary political realities.

Everett E. Viez sailed on *Normandie* on June 30. An agent with Thos. Cook & Son, the travel company, he was escorting more than 100 tourists. "There was not too much anti-Nazi feeling in evidence among passengers or crew," Viez recalls, "but nevertheless the strain was there and noticeable if you were looking for it. Example: We passed the *Bremen* in the English Channel, and under other circumstances both ships would have exchanged the traditional three-blast salute. Not this time, however."

But most passengers weren't thinking about Nazis. For instance, Leonard Lyons, the *New York Post* columnist, mainly remembered the voyage by this incident: "At the charity dance on the third night out, the vessel lurched and one haughty couple collided with my wife and her dance partner. 'People who can't rhumba shouldn't be allowed on the dance floor,' said the haughty lady. We've seen her many times since then, but avoided introductions. And we still see my wife's dance partner of that evening, Mr. Arthur Murray."

As if to thumb her nose at her British rival, *Normandie* now showed the world just how fast she was. On August 2 she arrived in New York harbor, flying the Blue Ribbon once more, after the fastest westbound steamship voyage in history: 3 days, 23 hours and 2 minutes; average speed, 30.58 knots.

On shore Captain Thoreux told reporters that his ship would have shaved another half-hour from the record if it hadn't been for 70-mph headwinds. Actually, Thoreux understated the matter. Samuel E. Silvernail, a passenger on that voyage, said, "The last day we encountered a very bad storm. In spite of its size, the ship was tossed about like a cork. Decks were roped off, doors slammed shut and the tables and chairs slid across the floors. There were many seasick people, including myself."

The passenger list, according to Silvernail, included Ilona Massey, the Hungarian actress, and Simone Simon, the French actress. It also included Ed Sullivan, the *New York Daily News* columnist, and Floyd Gibbons, the radio news announcer. "Gibbons and I took turns watching the vain effort of the SS *Bremen* to overhaul the big French liner," Sullivan wrote later.

Normandie already held the record for the eastbound passage, having set it that March. She now proceeded to set a new record, making the passage from New York harbor to Bishop's Rock in 3 days, 22 hours and 7 minutes. Her average speed was 31.2 knots—the first time the Atlantic had ever been crossed at an average faster than 31 knots.

Newspaper reporters, mischievous as usual, asked the *Queen Mary's* captain if he intended to accept *Normandie's* challenge. The captain mustered his dignity. "We've been warned by Sir Percy against the needless use of fuel," he said.

That season, while the *Queen Mary* economized on fuel, *Normandie* capitalized on her own pre-eminent speed, carrying an average of 2,101 passengers on each round trip, against 1,819 the previous year. All told, she carried some 10,000 more passengers in 1937 than she had in 1936.

Among these passengers were some of the day's most famous figures: Vladimir Golschmann, Rouben Mamoulian, David Sarnoff, King Vidor, Harry Winston, Madeleine Carroll, Walter P. Chrysler, Max Factor, John Hay Whitney, William S. Paley, the Duchess of Leeds, Jack Buchanan, Pierre Cartier, Danielle Darrieux, Douglas Fairbanks, Jr., Sonja Henie, Ezio

Pinza, Cole Porter, Ramon Novarro, Mischa Auer, Noel Coward, Jed Harris, Alfred Lunt and Lynn Fontanne, Eddie Cantor, Theodore Dreiser, Leopold Stokowski, Gloria Vanderbilt, Monsignor Fulton J. Sheen and Marlene Dietrich—to mention just a few.

Once more *Normandie* was the most glamorous vessel on the Atlantic, and American advertisers associated themselves with her elegance and prestige whenever possible. The Packard automobile ads, for instance, showed a Packard at dockside with *Normandie* in the background. A Camel ad in *Life* Magazine, featuring Mrs. Anthony J. Drexel III, pictured her in *Normandie*'s main dining room and mentioned that her favorite food was mushrooms under glass and her favorite liner, *Normandie*.

Meanwhile, the designer of *Normandie*'s hull, Vladimir Yourkevitch, was still trying to find another customer for his talents.

He'd given up on the British. Now he turned to the Germans. They were a much more likely prospect, he thought, since they'd worked with him while models of *Normandie*'s hull were being run through the Blohm & Voss test tanks in Hamburg.

The Hamburg-Amerika Line had decided to build *three* new liners—not superliners or Blue Ribbon contenders, but large, solid, reasonably swift vessels that could bring many tourists to Germany and make a lot of money for the Reich. They thought Yourkevitch was just the man to design them.

The Hamburg-Amerika Line now gave Yourkevitch a contract to design the prototype of the class, a ship it intended to call the *Vaterland*, after the great ship Albert Ballin had built in 1914, the ship later known as the *Leviathan*.

The Russian emigrant drew up the plans for a vessel that in many ways resembled *Normandie*. She would have a flaring bow, a whaleback forecastle essentially identical to *Normandie*'s and turbo-electric engines.

On the other hand, she'd be much smaller than *Normandie*—41,000 gross tons, 824 feet long and 98.4 feet wide, with a cruising speed of 25.5 knots.

After he submitted his design to Blohm & Voss, Yourkevitch was delighted to get a call from CGT's sister steamship line, Compagnie Sud-Atlantique. It wanted him to design a new medium-sized passenger liner for the Bordeaux–Buenos Aires run, the *Pasteur*.

Looking to parlay this success, Yourkevitch decided to try to sell his services to the United States. And so in the middle of 1937 Vladimir Yourkevitch sailed to New York (aboard *Normandie*, of course) and set up a branch of his Paris office at 17 State Street in Manhattan, under the name of Yourkevitch Shipbuilding Designs.

Yourkevitch had heard that the U.S. Maritime Commission was about to award the contract for what would be the largest passenger liner ever built in the United States. He hoped he could convince the Americans to let him design it.

In the midst of her most successful season yet, *Normandie* lost a propeller for the second time in her career.

For two voyages—while a new propeller was being cast—*Normandie* limped along at a couple of knots below her normal cruising speed. Few noticed, however, until the ship was laid up briefly in late September to have her missing propeller replaced.

"The flagship of the French Line was three days late due to the fact that a new propeller had to be fitted at Le Havre to replace the one she lost two or three weeks ago," wrote Robert Wilder, the *New York Sun* columnist, in his "On the Sun Deck" maritime column. "The vessel sailed today, however, making a quick turn around in order to pick up the lost days."

Actually, Wilder was at least as interested in *Normandie*'s passengers as he was in the ship. "Sonja Henie," he wrote,

> whose arrival or departure would get us up any morning at 5 o'clock, was inclined to be a little put out that the late arrival of the ship made it necessary for her to take the next plane to California. She is to make another picture, tentatively titled "Bread, Butter and Rhythm." . . .
>
> Douglas Fairbanks Jr., looking more and more like his pappy every day and filling us with the uneasy feeling that he is going to shout "Hola!" any minute and vault over the rail, will appear in Hollywood's version of "Having A Wonderful Time." . . .

Mrs. William Paley, who was leading two Scotties around the deck, had a bad minute or so when the terriers decided that a St. Bernard about the size of a large calf was just their dish and started after him with considerable fury. The St. Bernard eyed the frantic puppies for a moment in a quizzical fashion and then opened his mouth and let out a roar which sounded like Normandie's fog siren. It didn't seem to frighten the Scotties, but gave their owner quite a turn. . . .

It was a great temptation to sit right down and gawk at Danielle Darrieux when we saw her in the winter garden and let the rest of the ship go. She is under contract to Universal and her first film will be "Rage of Paris."

Wilder's column was fairly typical of the New York press at that time—half news, half gossip, an early ancestor of *People* Magazine. At about the same time another ship reporter, John McClain, took the occasion to discuss one of the better-known entertainers on the Atlantic, Gaston Brossard, *Normandie's* puppeteer:

Among seafaring men who have developed curious niches for themselves is Gaston Brossard, chief guignologist of the Normandie. He is the smiling little gray-haired man dressed in modest steward's garb, who operates the children's Punch and Judy theater inside the rearmost of Normandie's giant funnels.

Brossard learned the art of puppetry many years ago in the French countryside, never realizing that he would one day take his art to sea. But somebody in the French Line, considering the best method of keeping children occupied during an ocean trip, hit upon the idea of installing a grand guignol theater. A temporary puppet show was tried aboard the old liner France, with Brossard in charge, and it was discovered that not only the children but many of the adult passengers gave it big play.

From that point forward, it has become an institution aboard all the ships of the line. Brossard, the dean

*of all the puppeteers, was moved from one ship to the next
as each new one was put into service. His theater aboard
the* Ile de France *seemed sumptuous compared to the one
in the* Paris, *but the* Normandie's *is a midget music hall.
Apart from the slapstick Punch and Judy shows, Brossard has a repertoire of almost 70 plays and sketches.*

While the children of the rich and famous watched Monsieur
Brossard manipulate the comic-opera battles of Punch and Judy,
Adolf Hitler and Benito Mussolini began to consider how they
might jointly manipulate the world. Feeling that their interests
now coincided sufficiently, Hitler invited his Italian counterpart
to Germany. No firm agreements were made between the dictators during their historic meeting, but *Il Duce* was definitely
drifting away from France and Britain.

Even in the mid-Atlantic, travelers could not entirely avoid these
political rumblings. The October 5 issue of *L'Atlantique*, the
newspaper which was distributed to *Normandie* passengers, noted
that the official Austrian newspaper *Wiener Zeitung* claimed that
the Hitler-Mussolini meetings "did not endanger the independence of Austria," but merely "provided for the peaceful collaboration which has been the strong basis for the prosperous de-
velopment of our small country."

Arriving in France, *Normandie* passengers picking up the
October 8 issue of the *Herald Tribune*, European edition, read
that the Japanese had warned other nations against interfering
in China and refused to take part in any conference.

Back in the United States, President Roosevelt called for a
"quarantine" against aggressor nations. Warning that the world
was moving toward disaster, he said that America could not hope,
simply by shutting its mind, to remain immune to the coming
catastrophe.

Now Mussolini joined Germany and Japan in the anti-
Comintern pact and, on December 11, withdrew from the League
of Nations. A day later the Japanese bombed and strafed the U.S.
gunboat *Panay* in the Yangtze River, then unctuously apologized.

In the United States the Maritime Commission let the contract for the new American passenger liner. It awarded the job not to Vladimir Yourkevitch but to William Francis Gibbs, the redoubtable reconstructor of the *Leviathan*.

Yourkevitch's disappointment didn't last long. A new opportunity suddenly appeared, perhaps his greatest yet. In a paper read to Britain's Institute of Marine Engineers on December 14, 1937, Pierre de Malglaive—*Normandie*'s godfather—and A. C. Hardy, an expert on transatlantic shipping—proposed a giant new ship, their vision of the transatlantic liner of the future.

This fantastic vessel would be 1,350 feet long—not counting the soaring overhang of the bow—with 400,000 horsepower, six screws and a cruising speed of 36 knots. As Malglaive and Hardy saw it, the deck of this incredible ship would be completely enclosed with glass, her funnels would be retractable and most of her interior would be air-conditioned.

CGT needed such a ship to compete with the *Queen Elizabeth*. And Yourkevitch was determined that he would design her hull. He returned to Paris and once more sat down at his drawing board, this time to produce a detailed design of what he confidently believed would be his masterpiece.

13

ONE LAST YEAR OF "PEACE"

While CGT was dreaming of a fantastic, futuristic companion to *Normandie*, Cunard–White Star's second supership, the *Queen Elizabeth*, was rapidly nearing completion. At the beginning of 1938 her launching was only eight months away. The *Elizabeth*, Bates thought, would completely eclipse her French rival. She would be larger, newer and, her builders assured him, faster.

The future success of the *Elizabeth* was not enough for Sir Percy, however. Despite his protestations, he was determined that the *Queen Mary* regain the Blue Ribbon. Toward that end he now directed that the preservative paint covering the *Mary*'s bottom be removed to help ease friction and, he hoped, to add a fraction of a knot to her top speed.

Meanwhile, in Germany, on February 14, Hitler demanded that Austrian Chancellor Kurt von Schuschnigg appoint several Nazis to his cabinet, free all Nazi prisoners and restore the rights of the Nazi Party or face invasion by the German Army.

After only two days the Austrian Chancellor gave in to Hitler's demands. But Schuschnigg, hoping to save Austria's independence, announced a plebiscite for March 13 to let the Austrian people vote on the question of Nazism. Hitler was infuriated by his "treachery."

The mood on *Normandie* could hardly have been more gay and lighthearted. She was embarked on a kind of winter vacation, a glorious, gala South American cruise.

Although the primary purpose of ships such as *Normandie* was to carry tourists, business people and diplomats between Europe and America, shipping lines eager to gain revenue from their vessels in the off-season had long ago invented the winter cruise. William Makepeace Thackeray undertook a cruise aboard the P&O liner *Lady Mary Wood* in 1844, taking along eighteen shirts and a "sea stock of Russian ducks." He visited Malta, Athens, Smyrna, Constantinople, Jerusalem and Cairo.

Normandie's southern trip had been months in the making. Marcel Castienau, CGT's assistant marine superintendent, had traveled more than 10,000 miles by air, scouting the route. He'd even arranged with Standard Oil to dispatch three special tankers to refuel the giant ship at various stops along the way.

Normandie was scheduled to sail from New York on February 5. On February 7 she'd arrive in Nassau, on February 9 in Trinidad. From there she'd sail on to Rio, where she'd remain anchored for five days while passengers went on automobile excursions, took the electric cog railway to the summit of Corcovado and the aerial railway to the top of Sugar Loaf. On February 24 she'd stop at Martinique, and would arrive at Quarantine off New York on February 27.

This grand tour was being conducted under the auspices of the Raymond-Whitcomb Travel Agency, which had chartered the ship for the sum of $750,000. It took Henry S. Woodbridge, the director of the travel agency, and Henri Morin de Linclays of CGT just fifteen minutes to agree on that figure, but they argued for six weeks about how to divide revenues from deck-chair rentals. In the end they decided on a fifty-fifty split—$3,000 apiece, as it turned out.

Raymond-Whitcomb and CGT also agreed that no more than 1,000 passengers would be carried on this cruise—the largest number a liner had ever taken on a junket to South America.

It was an unbeatable combination—*Normandie*'s glamour, the novelty of the trip (in that era) and CGT's flair for publicity. The cruise was sold out a couple of weeks after it was announced. Since the fare wasn't exactly pocket change, this was not unremarkable.

The Trouville and Deauville Suites, for instance, each cost $9,970 if occupied by eight persons. Average outside first-class rooms cost $2,700, while the least expensive room in tourist class was $790 for two.

The passenger list for this festive occasion included Mary Roberts Rinehart (and maid), Jack Barricini, Mary Duke Biddle, Mrs. Louis B. Mayer, George McManus (the cartoonist), Mrs. Arnold Gingrich, William F. Raskob, William Lybrand (of the giant accounting firm), John Ford (the movie director) and Mr. and Mrs. J. M. Studebaker.

Normandie's cruise was marked by more superlatives than any of its predecessors. She was the largest and fastest ship ever to cross the equator. She was stocked with more food than any other ship had ever carried: 2 tons of caviar, 150 quarts of French champagne, 269 tons of food taken on at New York, tons of fresh vegetables, fish and fruits taken on at each port and 15 tons of butter.

Normandie also carried—quite by accident—more lobsters, perhaps, than had ever been assembled in any single place. By some mistake, the original order was garbled. "Dozens" became "gross." As John Maxtone-Graham tells it in *The Only Way to Cross*, "every fish purveyor in sight was alerted by the French Line commissariat to fill a monumental order." The cooks attempted to refuse the overage. Alas, having procured the enormous quantity with great difficulty, the seafood suppliers were not inclined to take the lobsters back. Consequently, while *Normandie* cruised the Caribbean and along the South American coast, her passengers were served enough lobster, no doubt, to last them for the rest of their lives. Even so, a great deal of cooked lobster meat had to be jettisoned.

Cruising had become a way of life for a certain class of people, so much so that books on shipboard etiquette had been published. While playing deck games, one such publication advised, male passengers must wear a single- or double-breasted flannel, tweed or gabardine jacket, a four-in-hand, bow tie or silk bandanna, canvas or buckskin shoes with rubber soles and heels, a tweed cap and "only such jewelry as is essential."

In the evening, however, the men were advised to wear a dinner jacket of black, midnight blue, white or tan. If a hat was in order, it should be made of sennit straw, while the coat should be of camel's hair and the shoes patent-leather oxfords or pumps.

Jewelry should be limited to shirt studs and links of gold or semi-precious stones and a pocket watch.

"It is quite permissible to go to the bathroom or men's room or swimming pool attired in your pajamas, robe and slippers, but don't walk around the deck this way. We suggest that you wear a jacket when entering the dining room although today a collar and necktie are not necessary as they may be replaced by a silk foulard handkerchief or muffler," one booklet advised.

Normandie's passengers, however, included few who were in need of such advice. Most were experienced ocean travelers taking the cruise in order to bask in the ship's unprecedented luxury.

"Every evening after dinner, around ten o'clock, we would change from our dinner coats to casual wear and commandeer the bar at the stern of the ship," one *Normandie* cruise passenger recalled. "We would invite twelve or fifteen people to join us, mostly girls, and carry on until the early morning hours. The staff catered to our every whim. If we wanted steak at one a.m. or chile con carne or whatever, it was prepared accordingly," Edwin Fisher remembers.

Normandie didn't dock once during the cruise. Instead, it dropped anchor a mile or so off port. Tenders brought passengers ashore, where they shopped, ate, drank, saw the sights and immersed themselves in the romance of the tropics. And *Normandie* was as great a spectacle for the island natives as their customs were for the liner's passengers. Said Edwin Fisher, "Wherever we anchored, crowds of natives would travel by foot, donkey or broken-down jalopy to see this great liner."

On board, it was like living in a fairy tale. "One glorious moonlit night, just as we were raising the Southern Cross," recalled Katherine Wharton, another cruise passenger, "the crew got out on the bow and sang both French songs and American songs—with a French accent. It was a great thrill homeward bound, to have the most beautiful ship and the fastest in the world racing northward past the Windward Islands, with the spotlights on the funnels saluting each French island, the islands responding with a wild fireworks display."

For the passengers the cruise had been a splendid way to forget their troubles—and the world's. But the latter's were not

(Upper left) One of the first performances in Normandie's theater, the first full-size, fully-equipped theater installed on an ocean liner. (Upper right) The kennels. On board Normandie, *even pooches had elegant accommodations.* (Above) The first-class swimming pool, the most elaborate ever installed on a ship. The black objects are rubber bumpers indicating changes in depth levels.

(Top) The grand lounge. The rolling doors are opening, showing the smoking room and, beyond that, the grand stairway. (Bottom) The main first class dining room, circa 1936. Note that there are three lighting towers on each side. Originally, there were six (see jacket photograph). (Facing page) The grand stairway, showing a view through the smoking room, the grand lounge and into the lounge vestibule. This unique vista was made possible by the split funnel uptakes that went up the sides of the ship rather than through her center.

*One of many publicist's
fantasies, each designed
to awe the public with
Normandie's size*

*Normandie tied up
at quarantine, outside
of New York City*

Maiden voyage arrival in New York

Pier 88, as she received Normandie *for the first time in June 1935*

(Clockwise from upper left) Normandie's *radar installation.*
FDR's Treasury Secretary Henry Morgenthau chats with movie star
Madeleine Carroll. The freak plane crash on Normandie's prow.

Normandie *after refit. Note room at top of uppermost aft tiered stairways which eliminated the open terrace behind the cafe grill, but added a tourist lounge and sports deck.*

The Queen Mary. Normandie's near equal in size and speed, but a dowdy lady compared to her streamlined French rival. Note the visible deck machinery and ventilators.

A unique convocation:
*the world's three largest ships.
From top,* Normandie, Queen
Mary, Queen Elizabeth.
Note how the Elizabeth's *decks,
like* Normandie's *are free of
most obstructions. Cunard
learned from CGT.*

*When the United States
government seized* Normandie,
*President Roosevelt ordered
her name changed to* Lafayette.
*The letters of her name were
removed from her hull in
January 1942, but they were
never replaced with new letters.*

so easy to block out. As Mrs. Wharton remembered it, "There had been a radio blackout while we were in Rio and no one got any mail. The French were very worried about their loved ones at home due to the uncertain conditions even then."

There was reason to worry. Hitler made it clear he would not permit Schuschnigg to hold the announced plebiscite. On March 12 German troops crossed into Austria at dawn and met no resistance.

There were protests from France and Britain and mutterings from the United States, but, except for a single voice, they were feeble indeed. The exception was Winston Churchill.

"If a number of states were assembled around Great Britain and France in a solemn treaty of mutual defense," he said, ". . . and if it were done in the year 1938—and believe me, it may be the last chance there will be for doing it—then perhaps . . . mankind would be spared the deadly ordeal towards which we have been sagging and sliding month by month. . . ."

Swallowing up Austria merely whetted Hitler's appetite. He now cast hungry eyes toward Czechoslovakia.

On the face of it, few countries were in a better position to resist the Nazi embrace than Czechoslovakia. She was allied with France and Russia; she was home to the vast Skoda arms works, which had fabricated *Normandie*'s massive rudder; she had a well-regarded army of forty-four divisions; and she had a strongly fortified frontier with Germany.

But Czechoslovakia was a patchwork of nationalities. There were 7.5 million Czechs, 3 million Germans and 2.5 million Slovaks, Ruthenians, Poles and Hungarians. And the Germans among them, most of whom lived in the Sudetenland, were eager to join the legions of the Reich.

It soon became obvious that this little country was Hitler's next target, his next meal. His Czech stooge, Konrad Henlein, demanded that Prague create a German state within the republic. Czechoslovakia, aware whose demand this really was, now asked France if she would keep her treaty obligations.

France and Britain told Prague to give the Sudeten Germans as much as possible. At the same time they warned Hitler very mildly that they supported Czechoslovakian sovereignty.

Hitler did nothing. But during the spring of 1938 Nazi thugs stirred up as much trouble in Czechoslovakia as they could, forcing that country's police to come down hard on them. The Sudeten German party protested Czechoslovakia's brutality with violent demonstrations of its own.

Meanwhile, on the Atlantic, violent storms battered the *Queen Mary*. On April 12, for nearly twenty-four hours gale-force winds sent enormous waves crashing against her funnels. When the ship docked at Plymouth, she was met by ambulances. Forty passengers were given on-shore medical attention and many more limped down the gangplank, delighted to be back on *terra firma*.

Normandie did not steam through such weather totally unscathed either. "If you have never seen the North Atlantic in a winter storm, you have missed a magnificent, stupendous explosion of nature. Sixty- to seventy-foot waves are common, with winds varying from calm at the trough of the waves to fifty-five or sixty-five miles per hour at their crests," remembered Oscar Williams, who witnessed one such event. "Sleep was impossible because you were always waiting for the starboard list to correct itself, and then just as you gave a sigh of relief, back she would go for a quick swing to port."

In such seas no ship could remain on an even keel. "She would roll to port, then rapidly roll to starboard and stay there sometimes for ten minutes at a time," Williams recalled. "Even I began to worry whether she would be able to right herself, but she did."

On April 22 *Normandie* remained at Le Havre for a few extra days to have installed her fourth and, as it happened, her final set of propellers. These were simply a larger version of the screws with which she'd recently recaptured the Blue Ribbon.

CGT didn't even bother to publicize this latest change, but Sir Percy Bates got wind of it anyway. He then dispatched a spy to sail on *Normandie*'s next voyage and find out if the new propellers had changed anything. The report can still be found in the Cunard archives.

"No vibration noticeable outside Grill Restaurant (a good deal of steel work has gone in here since she came out)," the report began.

All large furniture arranged to fasten down. In foyers, wide staircases and open spaces, brass plugs in floor show where stanchions and ropes can be fitted. Doubt whether we should put any fixed rails into the Queen Mary. *It would look bad in comparison with* Normandie. *Think* Normandie *can roll as much as the* Queen Mary, *but have detected no difference in* Normandie's *behavior today, as compared with what I would expect of the* Queen Mary. *Easy motion, hardly a roll.*

April 30: Went down to engine room. Think it at least as quiet as Queen Mary *and probably cooler. Boiler rooms definitely cooler. Outer propellers running at 230 rpm, inner at 220, all turning outwards. All said to be same weight. Engine room very clean.*

Tourist lounge and balcony aft most charming place with good view of the sea.

Undoubtedly to Sir Percy's annoyance, the report cited no weakness he could take advantage of in any way.

Normandie remained the glamour ship, the speed queen of the Atlantic, with the *Queen Mary* only a runner-up. True, their Blue Ribbon rivalry had caught the public's imagination, but when it came time to fictionalize this event for the screen, in *The Big Broadcast of 1938*, starring Bob Hope, Dorothy Lamour and W. C. Fields, the producers decided to pit a *Normandie*-like ship against a liner streamlined in the Raymond Loewy fashion, complete with airplane propellers.

In the movie, *Normandie*—called the *Colossal*—lost the transatlantic race to the modernistic *Gigantic*, although the *Gigantic* had to hit 60 knots to defeat her!

The real *Normandie* continued to draw the celebrities, perhaps because there was no *Gigantic* to run against her. In her third season she carried such luminaries as Eddie Foy, Leopold Stokowski, Leslie Howard, Noel Coward, Kitty Carlisle, Pierre Cartier, Nadia Boulanger, Mr. and Mrs. Ogden Phipps, Mrs. Paul Robeson, David Sarnoff, Simone Simon, Arturo Toscanini, Rudolf Serkin, Elsa Lanchester and Herbert Hoover.

One of the passengers who boarded for the return trip was the young Olivia de Havilland. "I was a British subject twenty-one years of age and soon to be twenty-two, having been born in Japan and brought up in the States. I had never seen my own country," she recalls.

> *I saved the money for first-class passage for my mother and me, and with her boarded* Normandie *for Southampton.*
>
> *I was exhausted from overwork, extremely thin and needed a respite from anything to do with my career. The ship's program, however, listed* Robin Hood *as a film to be featured in the cinema during the crossing and one of the officers put considerable pressure on me to attend one of the showings.* [The Adventures of Robin Hood *starred Errol Flynn, Basil Rathbone and Claude Rains, in addition to Miss de Havilland.*]
>
> *The film had only recently been completed and was soon to go into worldwide release and to be an enormous success. But I was too depleted and too shy to go to those shipboard viewings and did not see the film until twenty years later.*

Miss de Havilland did accept an invitation to a party in the captain's quarters, where she was joined by Claudette Colbert, "a great star and gracious lady." The conversation soon turned to international politics. "Miss Colbert had just had an unnerving experience while traveling in Austria, as her husband was Jewish," Miss de Havilland remembers. It seems that they had arrived almost on the eve of the *Anschluss* and had barely escaped.

By now the distant drums of war could be heard even in the middle of the Atlantic, in one of the most peaceful and most protected locations imaginable—the quarters of *Normandie's* captain.

For Vladimir Yourkevitch, however, times had hardly ever been better. In France he was hired to design three fast cargo motor ships, *Malgache, Indochinois* and *Caledonien*, not to mention a 113-foot fishing trawler called the *Tatiana*.

And in February the keel was laid for his new passenger liner, *Pasteur*. A few months later the Germans began building the *Vaterland*, yet another Yourkevitch-designed vessel.

At about this time the leader of the Sudeten German party broke off negotiations with the Czech government, claiming it would not meet his "reasonable" demands. Hitler then ordered German troops to assemble secretly at Czechoslovakia's borders. But word leaked out before everything was in place and practically all of Europe mobilized—Czechoslovakia, France, Russia and England.

For a moment full-scale war seemed imminent. Hitler was not quite ready for that, however. On May 23 he ordered his troops to stand down and he loudly proclaimed his innocence. "I have no aggressive intent whatever toward Czechoslovakia," Hitler said.

The rest of the world, which was paying millions of dollars a day to keep its troops in the field, accepted Hitler's words at face value. By May 28 the crisis was over. But on that same day the Nazi leader ordered his generals to prepare to invade Czechoslovakia on October 2.

Meanwhile, these same German generals were demonstrating and perfecting the tactics of the *Wehrmacht* in Spain, to the dismay of the Loyalists, who were gradually losing ground.

On May 31 *Normandie* arrived in New York, bringing Ernest Hemingway back from Spain, along with four stowaways, all deserters from the Loyalist army. Hemingway, a Loyalist sympathizer, tried his best to make the Loyalist side look good.

"Government forces are well-organized, well-equipped and they have a good chance of winning," he told reporters. "On the other hand, Franco is handicapped by lack of troops and considerable friction among the foreign elements in his army." As for his writing, Hemingway said, he wanted to write some short stories and a novel—the novel that would become *For Whom the Bell Tolls*.

On July 14 *Normandie* began her 100th crossing of the Atlantic. She'd carried nearly 100,000 passengers, traveled 330,000 miles at an average speed of 28.54 knots, been at sea 559 days, dispensed 572,512 bottles of wine and champagne and played host to about 375,000 visitors.

Among her famous passengers on the 100th voyage were Irene Dunne, Gloria Swanson, Ruth Etting, Charles Boyer, Johnny Weissmuller, David Niven, Fred Astaire, Harold Ickes, Sophie Tucker, José Iturbi, André Maurois, Bill Tilden and Joseph P. Kennedy with his sons Joe, Jr., and John Fitzgerald Kennedy.

Also on board was a Kennedy friend, financier Bernard M. Baruch. He told everyone he was on his annual vacation when in fact he was undertaking a confidential mission for President Roosevelt, who'd asked him to verify reports of growing Nazi military strength.

Celebrities sailing on *Normandie* frequently made the news. On August 3 the French actress Simone Simon managed to win herself a few inches in the New York newspapers by tussling with the Internal Revenue Service just before departure. Miss Simon, whose contract with Twentieth Century–Fox had just expired, was stopped on the pier by an IRS man who wanted to make sure she'd paid some $4,000 in taxes. He demanded that she produce her re-entry permit, a document that can't be secured without proof that all U.S. taxes have been paid in full.

At first Miss Simon could not find the paper. Finally, she located it in what one newspaper saw as "one of her numerous handbags." The altercation delayed *Normandie*'s departure by twenty-five minutes and apparently left Miss Simon in a snit. According to Gerald J. Burke, one of her fellow passengers, Miss Simon never left her cabin after that. Nor did she entertain. Kitty Carlisle did, though. Wearing a pink satin gown with a short train, she sang "Les Filles de Cadiz" in both cabin and tourist class on behalf of the Seamen's Fund.

Three weeks after *Normandie*'s 100th voyage the *Queen Mary* finally took revenge on her French rival. On August 7 she won the one-day speed record, steaming 790 miles at an average of 31.6 knots. *Normandie*'s best one-day run was 781 miles at 31.24 knots. The next day the *Queen Mary* arrived off the New York coast, having completed the trip in 3 days, 21 hours and 48 minutes, at an average of 30.99 knots. This was an hour and 14 minutes faster than *Normandie*'s best time.

On the return trip to England the *Mary* made the voyage in 3 days, 2 hours and 42 minutes, at an average speed of 31.69 knots, once more eclipsing *Normandie*'s mark, and this time by about an hour and a half and half a knot.

CGT talked bravely of making further alterations in its flagship and winning back the speed record during the next season, but this was not to be. *Normandie* had already made her fastest voyage across the Atlantic. The British ship was now the fastest liner afloat.

Normandie did manage to find her way into the headlines again, however. On August 22 she arrived at Le Havre with fourteen stowaways, the largest number ever discovered on an Atlantic crossing!

Eleven were Americans, evidently hoping to join the International Brigade of the Spanish republican army. They had among them $17.85, 3 Spanish pesetas, 30 French centimes and 5 Estonian kroons. All were arrested.

The other three were French citizens who'd boarded the ship in hopes of getting a free ride to America on the next voyage. They were kicked off without ceremony.

In the United States on that same day the keel of the *America* was laid. This was the ship Yourkevitch had wanted to design, but had been beaten out by William Francis Gibbs.

At almost the same time Gibbs signed a contract to design the *Fire Fighter*, the most powerful fireboat ever conceived. It was capable of pumping 29,500 gallons of water a minute. By a strange coincidence, its path would one day cross *Normandie*'s.

As the summer of 1938 drew to a close, Hitler announced that he was no longer prepared to see Germans persecuted in Czechoslovakia. At the same time he manufactured rumors of Czech troop movements along the Czech-German border.

Once again England and France mobilized their armies. Once again Europe felt itself sliding toward the brink.

Americans and others anxious to get out of Europe before

armed conflict began found cabins on any ocean liner that had room. Among them was Wanda de Muth Hellpen, the *première danseuse* at the Théâtre du Châtelet in Paris, an American dancer who'd found fame in Europe. At this moment fortune smiled on her. "The threats of war were so great," recalls Mrs. Hellpen, "that my father wired me to please come back to America. I heeded my father's plea and bought a third-class ticket for the States aboard the *Normandie*—the best accommodations I could get. Once I was aboard ship, I called the chief purser, whom I knew from a previous trip. After several hours of waiting a bellhop called me to come up to the upper deck. They had a *deluxe* cabin for me."

Also on board *Normandie* were Harry and Jeannette Whitebook. "I remember the grand salon, smothered in orchids, where we danced the newly created Lambeth Walk, to the music of the George Thurand orchestra," Mrs. Whitebook recalled.

Among the passengers on the trip were Secretary of the Treasury Henry Morgenthau, Jr., and his family, Francis Warren Pershing—the general's son—and his bride, returning from their honeymoon, and George Jessel. Jessel, always joking around, said, "Crossing the ocean is delightful. Can't imagine why Columbus's sailors complained."

We docked in New York on August 29. Harry and I were so engrossed with the view of Manhattan that we didn't realize we were in an enclosed section guarded by Secret Service men. Suddenly, Eleanor Roosevelt appeared. She'd come out on the pilot boat to welcome the Morgenthaus.

When the Secret Service started to escort Mrs. Roosevelt to the special gangplank, Harry whispered, "What do we do now?" I whispered back, "Just follow along. Each will think—I hope—that we belong to the other party."

And so that's how we disembarked from the Normandie *that day. First went Mrs. Roosevelt, then Mrs. Morgenthau, then Secretary Morgenthau, then Harry and I, two secretaries, some newspaper reporters, the Secret Service men and the Morgenthau children.*

In Europe the Czech crisis was intensifying.

On September 14 the French announced that the Maginot Line was at last complete. And Britain ordered her fleet to go on alert. On that day William Shirer made this entry in his diary: "War very near and since midnight we've been waiting for the German bombers. A few Sudeteners and Czechs killed and the Germans have been plundering Czech and Jewish shops. Jews excitedly trying to book on last plane or train."

Then there was a second entry: "Sept. 14, evening. Newspaper headlines say Chamberlain to fly to Berchtesgaden tomorrow to see Hitler! The Czechs are dumbfounded. They suspect a sell out and I'm afraid they're right."

Hitler told Chamberlain that if the British agreed to self-determination for the Sudetenland, he would consider the Czech matter settled. Britain and France then recommended to Czechoslovakia that she cede to Germany all areas in which Germans were at least half the population.

Eduard Beneš, the President of Czechoslovakia, agreed to these demands, but Hitler still seemed unsatisfied. Once more Chamberlain flew to visit Hitler, only to be told Czechoslovakia must evacuate the Sudetenland by September 28, just five days from then. The Beneš government fell and a Czech government of "national defense" rejected Germany's demands.

Hitler, reacting with an emotional promise to invade Czechoslovakia by October 1 if his demands were not granted, screamed, "German patience has come to an end!"

On September 27 the British Foreign Office said France was obliged to aid Czechoslovakia if she were invaded by Germany and in that case Britain and Russia would stand by France.

On that same day Britain was engaged in a most unwarlike ceremony: the launching of the *Queen Elizabeth*, the ship that, when fitted out, would take from *Normandie* the title of the world's largest passenger ship, just as her running companion, the *Queen Mary*, had taken from the French ship the honor of being the world's fastest ocean liner.

It was a very strange ceremony, a stark contrast to the tumultuous celebrations which had characterized the *Mary's* launch. The crowds were thin and nervous. The King, consumed by the Czech crisis, decided not to attend. Neville Chamberlain was packing his bags to fly to Munich to see Hitler one last time. And so the ship was launched by the lady from whom her name had been taken, Queen Elizabeth.

That evening Chamberlain addressed the British people by radio, taking no note of the launching. "How horrible, fantastic, incredible it is that we should be digging trenches and trying on gas masks here because of a quarrel in a far away country between people of whom we know nothing."

The next morning, just before leaving for Germany, Chamberlain repudiated his Foreign Office's firm stand of the day before. "We cannot in all circumstances undertake to involve the whole British Empire in war simply on [Czechoslovakia's] account."

On that day *Normandie* left New York with only 408 passengers aboard (786 had originally booked passage). Among those who had canceled were Jack Warner, Lily Damita, Arthur M. Loew and Ben Levy (of Coty Perfumes).

According to the *New York Post*, "There were tears bitterer than the tears of mere tourist partings, there was laughter tinged with just a touch of hysteria, there were farewells so morbidly flippant that those who shouted them and those who heard couldn't keep their memories from leaping back to World War days."

But among those who, undismayed by wars and rumors of war, went boldly up the gangplank were Mr. and Mrs. C. L. Preisker of Santa Maria, California, and their two daughters, Patricia and Katherine. They'd left California on an around-the-world tour. Originally, they'd booked passage on the Hamburg-Amerika liner *Hansa*, but it departed without any passengers aboard. Preisker said he was going on a world cruise and most certainly into Germany. "After all, I have a good German name and that ought to get me by in Berlin," he said.

Equally determined to make the crossing, crisis or no crisis, was Miss Polly Ward, a London musical-comedy star who'd been visiting America on a shopping trip. Just before boarding *Normandie*, she told reporters that everything was going to be all right "because the stock market is going up."

Another optimist was Mrs. Martin Hood, bound for London, her home. After boarding the ship she evidently heard a radio announcement of the Munich meeting scheduled for the next day. She hurried back to the rail and called to an elderly gentleman on the pier, "Don't worry, Pop. There's wonderful news. Everything's going to be all right."

Some American celebrities were also aboard, among them Bennett Cerf, of Random House, and Irving Berlin, who was going to England for the London premiere of the movie *Alexander's Ragtime Band*.

At least six newspapermen were also on the ship, all of them on assignment to cover the war if and when it was declared. And *Normandie* herself sailed under sealed orders, not to be opened until and unless a telegram was sent by the French government.

Robert Wilder, in his "On the Sun Deck" column in the *New York Sun*, said *Normandie*'s sailing was "far different from what you usually see at a French Line pier. Ordinarily, there is a great deal of well-bred roistering, the clink of champagne glasses sounds well out into West Street, flags fly, banners snap in the breeze and there is an atmosphere of gaiety." But on this occasion, he continued, the mood "was one of quiet apprehension. The impending war in Europe was very close to home. Travelers made their adieus with restraint and there were more tears to the square yard than we would have believed possible."

Another New York newspaper saw *Normandie*'s departure this way:

> *The crowd on the pier was small, but it tried to be gay. "Goodbye, troop ship," somebody shouted. "Don't forget to duck those bullets," another called. But many burst into tears as they turned away.*
>
> *Pierre Olagnier, the ship's chief receptionist, listened gravely at the rail. "We'll see you again in 12 days!" he yelled defiantly, as the vessel moved out toward the channel.*

Jittery and nervous, Cerf and Berlin were sitting together when Berlin was suddenly summoned to the transatlantic telephone. "He turned white," Cerf said. " 'This is it,' he predicted, 'the world is at war. We may be torpedoed at any minute.' The rest of us fidgeted in the smoking lounge while he was gone. But one look at him reassured us when he returned. 'That vital call,' he reported, 'was from the editor of a London tabloid. He called me up in mid-ocean at a time like this to ask which I considered more important: classical music or jazz.' "

While *Normandie* steamed toward Europe, Thoreux was waiting for a telegram from France, and Neville Chamberlain, umbrella in hand, was meeting with Hitler, Mussolini and French Premier Édouard Daladier.

Just after midnight on September 30 the four men signed the Munich Pact, dismembering Czechoslovakia. By the terms of this agreement German occupation of the Sudetenland began the very next day. Approximately 10 million more Germans had joined the Reich. The Czech government was not consulted.

On October 1, while German troops were crossing the Czech border, London welcomed Chamberlain back with great acclaim. Said *The Times*, "No conqueror returning from a victory on the battlefield has come home adorned with nobler laurels than Mr. Chamberlain from Munich. . . . The terms of settlement . . . deliver the world from a menace of extreme horror, while doing rough and ready justice between the conflicting claims."

Despite *The Times*' praise, many in Europe—Americans, European Jews and other refugees—thought they'd better depart. As a result, when the *Queen Mary* arrived in New York on October 4, she offloaded 2,112 passengers, the largest number she'd ever carried. Some of these were originally booked on the *Europa*, the German superliner, which had canceled her voyage.

Normandie left Le Havre on October 5. The crisis, apparently, was over. Still, 1,465 people booked passage on her—several hundred more than was usual for this time of year, among them, Alexander Kerensky, Clare Boothe Luce and Arturo Toscanini.

In New York, according to *Normandie*'s newspaper, the stock market—with the Munich crisis behind it—reached a new high for the year, the gains ranging up to twelve points in very brisk trading.

But there were signs that the crisis was not really over. One passenger, G. W. Dean, recalled that on this trip *Normandie* was carrying part of Britain's gold reserve, which was being sent to America for safekeeping.

William L. Shirer was among those who weren't fooled by the Munich Pact. Back in Paris, he jotted down his reaction on October 8: "Paris is a frightful place, completely surrendered to defeatism, with no inkling of what has happened. . . . Ed Murrow is as gloomy as I. We agree on these things: that war is now more probable than ever, that it is likely to come after the next harvest, that Poland is obviously next on Hitler's list."

However, optimism was the word of the day as far as most people were concerned, in Germany no less than the rest of Europe. Therefore, on October 29 the Hamburg-Amerika Line decided to go ahead with the keel-laying of its new ocean liner, the *Vaterland*, the first of three sister ships, all with hulls designed by Vladimir Yourkevitch.

French shipping authorities were also optimistic about the future and were eager to surpass the forthcoming *Queen Elizabeth*. So now they announced that they had definitely decided to provide *Normandie* with a running mate.

This liner, according to CGT, would closely resemble the vision discussed the previous year by Pierre de Malglaive and A. C. Hardy at the Institute of Marine Engineers. It would cost $60 million and take four years to build.

In Europe troubles began again on November 7, 1938. An unemployed seventeen-year-old Polish Jew, Herschel Grynszpan, killed the third secretary of the German embassy in Paris. He did it, he said, to avenge Nazi treatment of his fellow Jews.

On hearing of this, Hitler flew into a fury; within sixty hours of Grynszpan's confession German thugs were rampaging through Jewish synagogues, homes and stores. In the course of their orgy of vandalism, called *Kristallnacht*, thirty-five Jews were killed, thousands were arrested and fines totaling a billion marks were levied against the Jewish population.

Normandie continued to be affected by world politics. Her November 26 departure from New York was delayed a half-hour while two fast pursuit planes built by the Seversky Aircraft Corporation of Farmingdale, Long Island, were loaded on board.

Major Alexander de Seversky, who also sailed on the ship, intended to use these planes as demonstrators in Europe. "Both are capable of a top speed of 330 miles," Seversky told reporters. He said he intended to show them to the governments of France, England, Holland, Belgium and possibly Turkey and Rumania—but not Germany or Italy.

On the return trip from Europe, *Normandie* was involved in a political incident, centering on some 148 Abraham Lincoln Brigade volunteers who had booked passage on her, eager to get home to America after serving with the Loyalist side—the losing side—in the Spanish Civil War.

When these men arrived at Le Havre, it looked as though they'd be stranded because of a seamen's strike. They were taken to the Le Havre equivalent of Ellis Island, a dingy compound six miles outside of town.

At the time CGT was putting together a scab crew so *Normandie* could depart on schedule. But the Lincoln Brigade veterans, unionists to the core, decided they wouldn't sail on a ship crewed by scabs.

A Seamen's Union representative offered to have his men crew *Normandie* so that the Lincoln Brigade veterans could get home—but only if all other passengers were excluded. This proposal, of course, was unacceptable to the French Line.

Eventually the volunteers sailed for America aboard the *Paris*, which was manned by a crew from the French Navy.

14

THE END of OPTIMISM

As 1939 began, thousands were fleeing Europe. There were refugees aboard *Normandie*'s every voyage. In fact, beginning with the Munich agreement, refugees filled at least half of the ship's third-class accommodations, westbound.

Not every refugee who sailed aboard *Normandie* was a paying passenger, however, There were as many as a dozen stowaways on each voyage.

Certain *Normandie* crewmen made it known at Le Havre that they were willing to find a place aboard the ship for any stowaway who would pay $25. Not only would sleeping quarters be provided, but food would be served in a secret, makeshift dining room on C Deck.

Once docked at New York, these stowaways would be kept on board for an extra twenty-four hours to evade immigration checks and customs officials. Then, while *Normandie* was being refueled and reprovisioned, they'd be hustled off the ship in crew uniforms, hidden amid groups of ordinary seamen going on liberty.

After some investigation CGT uncovered the stowaway ring. In January of 1939 a number of *Normandie* seamen were arrested, but stowaways continued to find passage to America on *Normandie* until war broke out in Europe.

On one voyage, however, *Normandie* carried not a single stowaway. This was its second South American cruise, which began on February 4. It arrived off Nassau in the Bahamas on

February 6, made Trinidad on February 9, anchored off Rio from February 15 to 19, reached Barbados on February 24, Martinique on February 25 and docked at Pier 88 in New York at noon on February 28. Among the 1,000 passengers on this cruise: I. J. Fox, Wilfred Funk, David Lilienthal, Grand Duchess Marie, and J. J. and Lee Shubert, the New York theatrical impresario.

In most ways *Normandie*'s 1939 cruise duplicated the previous year's voyage. But one noteworthy event occurred in Rio, involving Lee Shubert.

Shubert had heard that a sensational singer was performing nightly at one of Rio's premiere night spots, the Casino Urca. Eager to sign her up if she was any good, he visited the nightclub on his first night in Brazil. What he found was a Latin American beauty with a radiant smile, an insinuating set of wiggles and a repertoire of suggestive songs that got their message across without translation.

Her name was Maria do Carmo Miranda da Conha. Shubert signed her, brought her to New York, changed her name to Carmen Miranda and created a star.

In Europe the dictatorships were ascendant. Franco's victory in Spain was sufficiently complete by February 27 for his Nationalist government to earn recognition from France and Great Britain. The last Loyalist holdout—Madrid—surrendered a month later, ending the Civil War.

That same month Germany completed the dismemberment of Czechoslovakia. And a few days later Hitler sent a registered letter (!) to the President of Lithuania, informing him that the city of Memel—once a part of East Prussia—had been reclaimed by the Reich.

Shortly afterward Hitler rode into Prague, every last inch the conqueror. Neither France nor England was willing to go to war yet, but neither were they willing to allow Hitler any more bloodless conquests. As a result Britain and France jointly announced that they would defend the independence of Poland, Greece, Rumania, the Netherlands, Denmark and Switzerland.

Hitler reacted by renouncing the 1935 Anglo-German agreement to limit naval forces and by abrogating the German-Polish non-aggression pact of 1934.

Even in America, Europe's problems were beginning to encroach on everyday life. When the 1939 World's Fair opened in New York, to great public and critical acclaim, the Czechoslovak pavilion lay unfinished. Germany built no pavilion at all.

In France the Nazis—many thought—created another sort of incident altogether, involving one of *Normandie*'s sister ships, the 34,000-ton *Paris*.

On the morning of April 19 the *Paris* was tied up at Le Havre, getting ready for a return trip to New York. On board were ten crates of art treasures bound for the World's Fair.

Suddenly fire broke out aboard ship—not in one place, but in several. The worst outbreak was in the bakery. Ship's firemen rushed to the scene, but could not open the door. The lock had been purposely jammed.

Fireboats flocked to the scene and started inundating the ship with water . . . too much water. The water put out the fire, sure enough, but it also unbalanced the ship. A day after the fire started, the *Paris* slowly rolled over on her side.

Vladimir Yourkevitch, surveying the scene, offered to oversee the raising of the ship, which he felt could be easily repaired and restored. But the French were more concerned with rearmament, and when war broke out, they lost all interest in the capsized *Paris*. She lay in the harbor, rotting, for eight long years.

During the *Paris* fire *Normandie* was being serviced in the Le Havre dry dock. The masts of the *Paris* had to be cut off so that she could get out.

The *Paris* fire, which was clearly sabotage, made CGT exceedingly nervous about the safety of its great superliner.

From then on, the shore guard was increased whenever *Normandie* was in port, and on-board firefighters were drilled to the peak of efficiency. Furthermore, visitors to the ship were increasingly restricted and carefully watched.

The *Paris* fire may even have prevented *Normandie* from attempting to regain the Blue Ribbon. Evidently she was to have been fitted with new propellers late in April for a run at the record on May 3. But she wasn't able to get in and out of dry dock and still keep her schedule, so the new propellers were never installed. When the Germans invaded France in 1940, they captured the giant bronze screws and took them home with them. Not until 1951 were they returned to France.

The *Paris* fire left CGT seriously short of ships. So, despite the war portents, the company decided to announce that it intended to build a sister ship to *Normandie*, the long-rumored *Bretagne*.

This ship, according to France's Minister of Merchant Marine, Louis de Chappedelaine, would not be the giant described earlier by A. C. Hardy and Pierre de Malglaive. Instead, it would be built from *Normandie*'s blueprints, with minor modifications that would make it just slightly larger than the forthcoming *Queen Elizabeth*.

Bretagne's engines, it was said, would develop a nominal 250,000 horsepower, 90,000 more than the original *Normandie* design. This would give her a potential top speed of about 35 knots and a cruising speed of about 33 knots, more than enough to win and hold the Blue Ribbon against any competitor in sight.

Vladimir Yourkevitch was furious. It appeared as if CGT intended to leave him out of the new project entirely. To get himself involved, he held a press conference and described his own plan for the ship.

His vessel, he said, would be totally new. She would have an overall length of 1,148 feet (outranking the *Elizabeth* by 117 feet) and a cruising speed of 34 knots. With a gross tonnage of 100,000, she'd be able to carry 5,000 passengers.

Yourkevitch's ship would also have a revolutionary physical appearance. There would be no projections from the superstructure, not even the captain's bridge. She would have two short funnels abreast of each other, one on each side of the hull. And between them there would be a broad, sloping platform—a flight deck.

Yourkevitch now sat back and waited for CGT to approach him. Now that he'd tantalized the public with his vision of the new ship, he was sure the French Line would hire him to design it.

In May, Hitler began to pick fights with Poland. What interested Hitler now was Danzig, the former German seaport. This city, along with a corridor leading through Germany, had been given to Poland by the Versailles Treaty. Hitler also wanted the corridor. In fact, he wanted all of Poland.

He had a problem, however: What would Russia do if Germany seized Poland? Maxim Litvinov, the Soviet Foreign Secretary, favored some kind of alliance with Britain and France. And, foolhardy as he may have been, Hitler was wary of a two-front war.

Hitler hated and feared the Soviet system and its leader. The Russians felt likewise. As Ribbentrop had said earlier that year, "We will never come to an understanding with Bolshevist Russia."

But on May 3, 1939, Stalin fired the pro-Western Litvinov and appointed Vyacheslav Molotov in his place. Hitler decided to find out exactly what this meant.

Meanwhile, *Normandie* continued on her festive way. On June 3 the French liner celebrated her fourth anniversary. She'd spent 841 days at sea, covering 443,918 nautical miles at an average speed of 28.52 knots. She'd carried approximately 125,000 passengers and played host to 850,000 people in New York, Le Havre and Southampton.

In this year her passengers had included such notables as Alfred A. Knopf, Winthrop W. Aldrich (chairman of the Chase National Bank), Charles M. Schwab (chairman of Bethlehem Steel), Ignace Paderewski, Mary Pickford and Buddy Rogers, Robert Morley, Dimitri Mitropoulos, Clare Boothe Luce, Harry Anslinger (the government's former chief Prohibition enforcer) and Ludwig Bemelmans, the famous author of *Madeleine*.

"I have always given more affection to the *Normandie* than to any other ship," Bemelmans later wrote, in a piece he called "Souvenir." "I loved her for her gaiety, for her color, for that familiarity with all the world that was her passenger list. . . . I think she was more female than all the other ships that I have known."

In "Souvenir," Bemelmans described one of his *Normandie* voyages.

I had booked passage on her and was ready to sail when an eager young man with an extensive vocabulary came to see me. He told me that the French Line was delighted to have us cross on the Normandie, *and that in-*

stead of giving us just an ordinary cabin, they were glad to be able to offer us a suite de luxe. *I am not one to sleep on a hard mattress when I can have a soft one, so the young man and I bowed to each other and had three martinis each.*

It seemed that at the last moment, all the ordinary cabins de luxe *had been taken and the only thing left to do with us was to put us into one of the* Suites de Grand Luxe. *We went into a palace called Trouville—private terrace, servants' dining-room, feudal furniture. Everybody was satisfied, particularly with the Lalique ashtrays.*

What a wonderful day was the day after sailing. The great hall, crowded the night before with good-by sayers, messenger boys, pickpockets and weeping relatives, was swept clean. The runners had been taken up, the furniture put back in place. The room of silver, gold and glass, large as a theater, floated through the ever clean, endless ocean outside the high windows.

There was a dark fortress of a woman on board that voyage, an old countess with a face made of Roquefort and eyes like marbles, the kind of marbles that boys call "aggies." She sat wrapped in her sables in the front row of three lines of deck chairs outside the main salon.

On her lap, covered by a small hound's-tooth blanket, asthmatic and dribbly, sat a Pekinese with thyroid trouble; his eyes were completely outside of his head. Whenever my daughter Barbara passed by her chair, the old countess lifted the blanket, gave the dog, whose name was Piche, a little push, and said to him, "Piche, regardez donc la petite fille qu'elle est mignonne!" One day she reached out her hand, but Barbara ducked and ran all the way to the Trouville suite nursery, where she burst into tears.

The other outstanding figure on that trip was a young widow. She was dressed in long, glamour-girl blonde hair and black satin. I think she rubbed herself with a lotion every morning, and then pasted her clothes on her body;

*there wasn't a wrinkle on them. A doctor could have ex-
amined her as she was. Her arms were weighed down with
bracelets, all of them genuine, and of course she had a
silver fox jacket. An icebox full of orchids helped her bear
up throughout the voyage. She appeared with fresh flowers at every meal, and she had with her a sad pale little
girl, who was not allowed to play with other children.
She wore a little mink coat on deck—the only junior mink
I have ever seen.*

*The way the young widow managed her entrances
into the dining-room reminded me of Easter at the Music Hall. She waited until the orchestra played Ravel's
Bolero and then she came, surrounded by expensive va-
pors, heavy-lidded, the play of every muscle visible as a
python's. At the first landing of the long stairs, she bent
down, while everyone held their breath, until she succeeded in picking up the train of her dress.*

*Then a faultless ten inches of calf and ankle came
into view and, with industrious little steps, she climbed
down the rest of the stairs to the restaurant. Once seated,
she smeared caviar on pieces of toast and garnished them
with whites of eggs until they looked like cards one sends
to the bereaved; with this she drank champagne and looked
out over the ocean. The sad little girl said nothing the
whole day long.*

After John Maxtone-Graham published his liner history, *The Only
Way to Cross*, which quoted a bit of the Bemelmans piece, he
received a letter from none other than Bemelmans' "sad little
girl," who turned out to be a certain Patti Hall.

"Mother had, indeed, wonderful legs and, in the days of the
Normandie, wonderful everything else!" Mrs. Hall wrote.

*A dear friend, staring at my mother, once said that her
resemblance to the popular Garbo was startling, but
wasn't it a shame that Garbo had such large feet and
coarse hands. You get the picture.*

Mother was 28 when we sailed on the Normandie.

She was 5'8", a natural ash blonde, and a free-wheel-ing, free spirit. Divorced, with one child, me, she and I had "done" a grand tour.

From the first day out, Mother decided to play a role. She would be a widow, mysterious, remote, but not too remote. She had told no one the same story, said her life had been "so tragic" she could never "love again" etc. The poor fellows never had a chance. She met a number of interested gentlemen, including a young English phy-sician with a neat sandy mustache who wore tweeds and came to our stateroom for drinks while I was relegated to the children's dining room.

The nursemaid assumed "the worst" and as the door was still closed when we came back from dinner, would not even let me knock.

Later, when Bemelmans' passage was read to Mother, she laughed so hard she cried. You see, the role played out on that voyage had stood Mother in good stead for the rest of her life. Discovering the ridiculous power of good looks, she did lop off a few more heads before she grew too old. However, 'til the last, she had a way of making males subservient without them minding at all.

"My own good fortune," said Mrs. Hall, "is that I am very much like her, and not at all!"

In 1939 *Normandie* was celebrated not only in print but in the movies. In *Made for Each Other*, a comedy-drama, James Stewart and Carole Lombard—newlyweds—board *Normandie* and almost sail off on their honeymoon. Instead, business changes their plans and they content themselves with waving goodbye to the ship as she pulls away from the pier.

While beautiful "widows" were cavorting on *Normandie*, William L. Shirer, the foreign correspondent, was headed back to America aboard the *Mauretania* for a brief vacation, a lull before the storm. On board he encountered Sir Percy Bates, who assured Shirer that there would be no war.

A few weeks later, returning on the *Queen Mary*, Shirer found himself sitting with Paul Robeson and Constantine Oumansky, the Soviet Ambassador to the United States. Oumansky, Shirer noted, thought Russia would link up with Britain and France *if* those two nations showed that they meant business and weren't merely trying to maneuver the Soviet Union into a war alone against Germany.

But, unbeknownst to them, Russian and *German* representatives were then meeting in the private dining room of a Berlin restaurant. The German representatives hinted that they might be willing to pay for Soviet neutrality in the event of a German-Polish war. How much? Well, said the Germans coyly, we may not want *all* of Poland.

Meanwhile, Germany intensified its pressure on Poland. When Danzig voted to rejoin Germany, Poland instituted economic reprisals. Hitler protested. The Polish government rejected his protest. It was, so far, a war of words.

On July 11 *Normandie* got her third captain, Etienne Payen de la Garanderie, fifty years old, the former master of the *Ile de France* and the *Paris*, a man with thirty-three years of service in the French merchant marine.

Despite tightened security, *Normandie* continued to lead a normal life. On August 3 she sailed for France with 1,397 passengers, a record number for an August voyage.

On board was Mrs. James Mills, the former Alice du Pont, of Wilmington, Delaware. Her husband, James Mills, departed at the same moment by Pan Am's "Clipper America." It was his intention, he announced, to beat *Normandie* to Southampton. "I'll meet her at the pier when the *Normandie* docks," Mills predicted. And he did.

On August 9 *Normandie* departed once more for New York. On board were Erich von Stroheim, Gaby Morlay, Michel Simon, twenty-seven other French actors and actresses and a complete crew of moviemakers. They were making a film called *Paris to New York*, a story of crime at sea and its detection.

Neither the film crew nor the passengers knew it, but this was a very unusual voyage, a voyage made to test *Normandie's* emergency steaming abilities, a voyage made with the conviction that war was near.

CGT wanted to find out if *Normandie* could carry enough

oil to make the round trip without refueling. To determine the answer, some of *Normandie*'s ballast tanks—normally filled with water—were loaded with oil. Four additional tanks in the propeller-shaft tunnels, which were usually kept empty, were also filled with oil.

Normandie took on 1,500 additional tons of fuel oil, for a total of 8,930 tons. To keep her in trim, 1,500 tons of pig iron were added to the forward holds. On the trip, De la Garanderie limited *Normandie*'s speed to 24 knots; she burned just twenty-nine tons of fuel an hour, about 42 percent less than her normal rate.

It took *Normandie* five full days to reach New York. But she burned only 3,480 tons of fuel. At that rate she could make a round trip on 6,960 tons—leaving almost 2,000 tons in reserve.

At Le Havre, CGT officials grimly considered the figures and pronounced the experiment a success.

In Moscow lower-level British and French military representatives were meeting with their opposite numbers on the Soviet side. These meetings, however, were marked by a curious lack of urgency. Germany was obviously gearing up for an attempt to conquer Poland; yet Britain, France and Russia seemed unable to agree on the terms of an alliance.

Much as the British and the French hated and feared Hitler, they also hated and feared Stalin and felt that making a bargain with him was tantamount to selling their souls to the devil.

But Stalin was dragging his feet because he'd begun to believe Germany was stronger than Britain and France combined and that Hitler might give him better terms.

On August 17, 1939, Russia broke off her talks with Britain and France. On that same day Hitler secretly asked the *Wehrmacht* to supply the SS with 150 Polish Army uniforms. These were to be used as "evidence" of Polish aggression in a faked border incident.

The Poles knew trouble was coming, but they didn't know how to deal with it. Should they ask Russia's help? Should they appease Germany? Said one Polish official, "With the Germans, we risk losing our freedom. With the Russians, we shall lose our soul."

In England a government spokesman told Parliament, "War today is not only not inevitable, but it is unlikely." One of the few to disagree was Winston Churchill.

Somehow an illusion of normality prevailed in the world of transatlantic liners. On August 19, for instance, more than 700 Americans boarded the *Columbus*, a German liner and a running companion to the *Bremen* and the *Europa*, and sailed out of New York on a twelve-day cruise to the West Indies.

A few days later Vladimir Yourkevitch's latest creation, the *Pasteur*, successfully passed her sea trials. Her maiden voyage was set for September 10. She would ply a route between Bordeaux and South America.

On August 23 CGT announced that the *Bretagne*'s construction would begin late in 1940. The *Bretagne*, it affirmed, would be built largely from *Normandie*'s plans, thus saving time and money. The name of Vladimir Yourkevitch was not mentioned.

Marcel Olivier, CGT's president, added that the company was looking forward to a profitable season. "If affairs in Central Europe clear," he said, "France can expect a record travel season, since the exchange is now in the tourist's favor."

But on that very day Ribbentrop and Molotov astonished the world by committing their countries to a mutual non-aggression pact. The bitterest of enemies had suddenly and inexplicably become the best of friends.

Their pact had two sets of provisions. The public part simply said that neither nation would attack the other or join with any other nations in order to attack the other. The secret part gave both dictators the freedom to invade or conquer any third country, and it called for the division of Poland between the two of them.

News of the pact threw the French and British governments into bewildered consternation and created utter chaos among foreign Communist parties, which for six years had been violently denouncing Hitler or anyone who gave him even the slightest benefit of a doubt.

In France the event was summed up in the streets in one classic French phrase, "*Nous sommes cocus*"—we've been cuckolded. Some people realized Germany must now be preparing to invade Poland and share the spoils with the Soviet Union.

On the day the ominous agreement was announced, France mobilized, expecting war at any moment; Britain gathered her warships in the Skagerrak, evidently preparing to blockade Germany; and in Berlin rumors freely circulated that the German Army would march into Poland by 6:00 p.m.

This was the situation as *Normandie* began her 139th transatlantic voyage. She was bound for New York on what would be her final crossing, with 1,417 passengers aboard.

It was an unusually distinguished list. Among those on board were Sonja Henie, Lee Shubert, Thomas J. Watson, Lily Daché, Hattie Carnegie, Constance Bennett, Mrs. William Randolph Hearst, Roland Young, George Raft, Josef von Sternberg, Mrs. Henry du Pont de Nemours and James Stewart.

This time, however, the usual festive atmosphere was missing. "It was not a pleasant voyage," said Sir John Wheeler-Bennett, Britain's political-warfare expert, who was traveling to America to take up his duties in New York, at a British intelligence office.

> *War was now accepted as inevitable and there were those, both British and French, who were leaving their countries "while the going was good," in order to escape the massive bombing which everyone expected would immediately follow the opening of hostilities.*
>
> *There were some embusques of military age who were deliberately avoiding their "call-up" into the armed services when mobilization was declared. There were refugees, German and Czech and others, who were very understandably anxious to put as great a distance between themselves and Europe as possible.*

A new element was in the air on this trip, an element of fear. It had infected the passengers and it had affected the officers and the crew as well.

Normandie stopped at Southampton at 6:50 p.m. on August 23 after a slow trip across the Channel. She left for New York at 8:00 p.m., holding two boilers in reserve and anticipating a leisurely voyage to America.

Early the next morning, however, Captain de la Garanderie spotted the *Bremen* off *Normandie*'s port side, apparently following the French ship as she steamed westward. Afraid that the *Bremen* might be playing bird dog for some German submarines, Captain de la Garanderie ordered Georges Cusset, his chief engineer, to bring the reserve boilers on line and increase *Normandie*'s speed. At the same time the commandant adjutant told the radio operators that they were to cease all transmissions, since German submarines could use them as a beacon.

In Europe, Poland called up its reserves and began to prepare for war. CGT telegraphed the news to *Normandie*, describing the situation as "grave."

De la Garanderie again assembled his officers. When the sun went down, he told them, they were to cover the grand-salon windows and instruct passengers to turn off their overhead cabin lights and draw curtains over their portholes.

According to passenger George McCullagh, publisher of the *Toronto Globe and Mail*, "At dark the stewards went through the ship drawing curtains. I finally asked a steward what all the activity was about. He threw his hands in the air and exploded. 'Hitler!' he said."

"We were all very tense," says Suzanne Braud, another passenger on that voyage. "All the passengers received a bulletin telling us that the *Bremen* was following us. And that night, when we dined with some officers, they told us they were sure there was a spy aboard the ship. They told me not to use my camera."

During the night, steaming at almost 30 knots, *Normandie* left the *Bremen* behind, to everyone's relief. But the next day brought more ominous news: Britain and Poland had signed a five-year mutual-assistance treaty.

Since Captain de la Garanderie had no intention of letting *Normandie* become the *Lusitania* of a new European conflict, he ordered his helmsman to begin following a zigzag pattern—the classic tactic for avoiding torpedoes. Also hoping to lose the submarines altogether, if there were any, he set a new course that took *Normandie* more than 100 miles farther north than she had ever gone before.

Normandie's passengers bombarded De la Garanderie and his staff with questions. No answers were provided, however.

"The atmosphere was one of near hysteria," said John Wheeler-Bennett. "More than once it was bruited that war had actually been declared, and on several occasions, there were moments of panic when rumors ran through the ship like wildfire that a U-boat had been sighted on one bow or the other, passengers jostling each other in their rush for life-jackets."

On Saturday, August 26, France urged Hitler to negotiate directly with Poland, in the hope of somehow avoiding war. Nonetheless, according to Janet Flanner, the lights of Paris were blacked out that night—and from then on.

The next day Britain ordered all able-bodied men twenty and twenty-one years old to report for military induction.

At sea Captain de la Garanderie sent a notice to his crew:

"If, on the arrival, the representatives of the press or any person questions you about current events, your ship, your family, your role in the case of hostilities, don't say anything. If you say anything, you will be subject to severe penalties reserved for those who commit ESPIONAGE."

That afternoon the captain called Chief Engineer Cusset and several other key officers to his quarters. He asked Cusset about *Normandie*'s vulnerability in the event of attack.

Cusset said *Normandie*'s #4 boiler room contained much essential equipment. If she took a torpedo there, she'd be crippled. Even worse, that area contained the diesel motors that powered the lifeboat davits and opened dropped watertight doors. If she was struck there, her passengers would be trapped aboard the ship.

De la Garanderie asked the engineer to tell the crew what they should do in the event of an alert. Then he called in the radio operators, telling them that they must not answer any telegrams from New York because American communications were being monitored by the Nazis.

Cusset asked De la Garanderie when *Normandie* would arrive in New York, but the captain, possibly afraid that one of the men in the room was a spy, refused to answer. "Will we be delayed?" Cusset asked. The captain just looked away.

After the meeting broke up, the officers were nearly swamped by passengers. "Has war broken out?" they asked. "When are we getting to New York?" "Are we heading back to France?" "Will we be safe?" "When can I send a telegram?" All of the questions were met with a smile and a shrug.

At 1:07 a.m. on Monday, August 28, *Normandie* picked up the Ambrose pilot. She was in Quarantine at 2:41 a.m., and at 10:45 the giant French liner tied up at Pier 88, to the vast relief of everyone on board.

Despite her odd course and her zigzagging, she'd made the trip at the brisk average speed of 29.71 knots, leaving submarines, if any, far behind.

Scores of reporters were waiting for *Normandie*, hoping to get eyewitness accounts of conditions in Europe. Swarming off the gangways, the passengers grabbed newspapers right out of the hands of the newsmen, and the pier resounded with whoops of delight when they read that hostilities had not started.

Despite the hysteria, it seemed that many had bet on whether war had broken out during the radio blackout. As soon as the news swept through the crowd that it had not—at least not yet— wagers were paid off by the dozen.

Robert Wilder, the ship reporter, took note of the unusual atmosphere among the departing passengers. "Whatever else it may have done," he wrote in his "On the Sun Deck" column, "this latest European crisis certainly had a humanizing effect on the *Normandie*'s passengers. The liner is a big ship—so big that a voyage on her is likely to have an impersonal quality. [But on this voyage] it seemed to us that almost everyone knew everyone else. They shouted back and forth at each other, clustered at the rails to gaze affectionately at the skyline or trotted about the deck grinning openly at acquaintance and stranger alike."

Other reporters buttonholed passengers to find out about Europe's mood. Lily Daché told one newsman that "the women of France were using their most potent weapon—clothes—to prevent war." Hattie Carnegie remarked that "everyone in Europe was talking about corsets, but though I've bought some, they aren't here to stay."

Thomas J. Watson, president of IBM, had no opinion as to whether or not there would be war. But if there was a war, he said, it would "destroy civilization as we know it."

Sonja Henie, the ice-skating champion and movie star, said, "Paris this year was far worse than last. Things were at a standstill and mobilization was much faster."

Constance Bennett, standing by Henie's side, added that "Half the Ritz Hotel in Paris was mobilized the day before I left."

James Stewart told reporters that he planned to fly to Hollywood later that day. "I will be starring with Marlene Dietrich in a picture called *Destry Rides Again*," he said.

Thomas Rouston, president of a Brooklyn grocery chain, and his wife, the former Marjorie Hillis, author of *Live Alone and Like It*, were also interviewed by a reporter. Miss Hillis admitted sales of her book had fallen off since her marriage.

What really intrigued the reporters was the talk of the radio silence, the blackout and the zigzag voyage across the Atlantic. They boarded the ship in search of any officer who could confirm any of this. None would. Finally, the newsmen cornered Captain de la Garanderie.

"The passengers are saying *Normandie* zigzagged during her voyage. Is that true?" one reporter asked.

Captain de la Garanderie smiled. "If there was any zigzagging," he said, grinning, "it was due to too much attendance at the ship's bar."

"The Radio Marine Corporation told us *Normandie* didn't answer any messages," another reporter tried. "Why did you do that?"

"Well," the captain said, "we cut outgoing messages because we didn't want to tie up the radio. We thought we might receive orders from the government at any moment."

"How about guns, Captain?" queried another newsman. "Tell us the truth—does *Normandie* carry any hidden artillery?"

The captain could scarcely restrain his merriment. "I don't know about guns," he said. "I only carry my handkerchief."

"The Commandant is what is known to the cracker barrel brigade as something of a card," Wilder wrote the next day. "He didn't want to answer any of the questions put to him and to this end he pretended that the whole business was quite a joke and that the reporters had only come down the bay to have a good laugh."

No one was laughing when the *Bremen* tied up at her pier the next day. Her captain, keenly aware of the international situation, had her refueled and reprovisioned in near-record time. But just as he was preparing to depart, *sans* all passengers and cargo, the ship was boarded by a swarm of U.S. customs inspectors and other Federal agents.

At the same time President Roosevelt announced that all ships of potentially belligerent nations would be searched to prevent them from being converted at sea into raiders.

To show that America was playing fair, inspectors also descended on other German, British and French liners in United States ports. But it was the *Bremen* that got the royal treatment. Many thought the U.S. was purposely delaying the German ship until British cruisers could arrive outside of New York harbor.

Once the weapons inspection was complete, nothing else seemed to stand in the way of the *Bremen*'s departure—until officials of the Steamboat Inspection Service arrived. They proceeded to order a lifeboat drill. With cold anger her crew lowered a lifeboat. That was not enough for the inspectors. The crew lowered another, then another, until all of the twelve lifeboats on her starboard side had been tested.

Normandie had been scheduled to depart even earlier than the *Bremen*—at 10:00 that morning—but her departure was postponed. Instead, Captain de la Garanderie held a full-scale wartime alert, on wireless orders from Paris. Crewmen were led through a drill that assumed the ship had been shelled by naval guns, that a fire had broken out in the tourist smoking lounge and that a torpedo had struck boiler room #2.

By 7:40 a.m. on the 30th, Chief Engineer Cusset had twenty-six boilers on line and everything else was ready for the return trip. Then the phone rang at his station. "We're postponing our departure," the captain told him. "We've also received orders from Paris to disembark all passengers and cargo. We'll be going back home empty. Maintain maneuvering power. We may be leaving very soon, and without notice." Cusset acknowledged his orders.

At 9:55 a.m. De la Garanderie phoned down to the engine room again. "Bank the fire and start shutting down the boilers," he told Cusset. "We won't need power until 6:30 a.m. on the 31st."

At 7:00 p.m. *Normandie*'s passengers (only 350 had reserved space) and her cargo left for Europe aboard the Cunard–White Star *Aquitania*, which itself had been in port for less than forty-eight hours.

A couple of hours later Cusset phoned the captain. "I am sorry, Mr. Cusset," De la Garanderie said. "Our departure has been indefinitely deferred."

On the Atlantic the normally orderly flow of passenger liners between Europe and America had deteriorated into chaos. The *Manhattan*, a passenger ship of the United States Line, skipped its normal stop at Hamburg and returned to America carrying 500 cots for extra passengers.

The Holland-Amerika Line chartered a Royal Mail liner for a special voyage to New York to bring home approximately 800 Americans.

By the time the *Bremen* pulled away from her Hudson River pier on the night of August 30, the British cruiser *Exeter* was on station in the Atlantic, just beyond the three-mile limit, waiting for her.

The *Exeter* could not cover all of the approaches to New York, however, and the captain of the *Bremen* knew that. He took his ship inside the Nantucket lightship, guiding her through the shoals himself, into thick fog.

As day broke, *Bremen* crewmen were lowered over the side of the ship in lifeboats, given buckets of paint and long-handled brushes and ordered to paint the ship's hull a dull gray while she maintained full speed. Soon she disappeared into the light mist.

At Southampton a record 2,332 passengers jammed into the *Queen Mary*, finding sleeping room wherever they could. Still following the agreement Cunard–White Star had made with CGT, she departed for New York on August 30, at almost the same moment *Normandie* had been scheduled to begin the return trip. But this time the two liners would not pass each other in mid-ocean. They would meet in the same port for the first time.

On August 31, with the *Queen Mary* still at sea, Germany cut off all communication with Warsaw. In Britain three million people—children, invalids, women and elderly men—were evacuated from London, Birmingham, Manchester, Liverpool, Edinburgh, Glasgow and twenty-three other cities, all of which British authorities expected to be bombed the moment war started.

In the United States the mood was decidedly different, at least at Newport News, Virginia. For this was the day on which the United States Line passenger vessel *America* was launched.

This day, as it happened, was the final day of the peace that had ended the Great War in 1918. There would not be another one for nearly six years. For in the early hours of the next morning German panzer brigades swept into Poland.

15

AT THE MERCY Of STRANGERS

The day after German troops marched into its territory, Poland called on Britain and France to attack the Nazi nation immediately. France said she would. Britain sent ten bomber squadrons to France.

The next day France, Britain, India, Australia and New Zealand declared war on Germany. The British Navy blockaded the German coast. French soldiers occupied a token three square miles of German territory.

Only in Poland, however, were guns being fired in anger. And in that unlucky land the *Wehrmacht* was sweeping through the countryside with unprecedented speed, its panzer divisions brushing aside antiquated Polish armies, which were often mounted on horseback.

On September 3 the last ocean liner left Europe—or, at least, the last from the belligerent nations. It was the *Ile de France, Normandie's* smaller and older sister.

Over 3,000 passengers packed the ship, far above her usual capacity. Almost all of them were American. To accommodate them, temporary bunks had been set up everywhere, even in the dining room.

The *Ile* crossed safely, but the *Athenia* did not. She'd departed from Liverpool on the 2nd bound for Canada with 1,400 passengers, including 292 Americans. Two hundred miles west of the Hebrides Islands she was torpedoed and sunk. Almost all of the passengers were rescued, but the incident made it very clear that the Atlantic was no longer safe for passenger traffic.

While all of this was happening, the German superliner *Bremen* pounded across the ocean on an arc far north of the Great Circle route, confounding Allied search parties. She reached Murmansk, on Russia's northern coast, on September 6. The Nazis taunted the British by broadcasting the news.

In New York the crews from *Normandie* and the *Queen Mary* were preparing to go home. On the night of September 8 more than 750 of them met in Meyer Oppenheim's Anchor Tavern at 12th Avenue and 49th Street for one last goodbye.

"The Anchor was a house of all nations before the war," Oppenheim later said. "Cole Porter would come in as the *Normandie* was about to sail and say to me, 'If so and so shows up, tell him I'll see him in Nice.' This was a post office for all of the crews."

There was much celebrating, much back-slapping, much bittersweet reminiscing. And in the small hours of the morning the crews linked arms and marched up and down the West Side Highway, laughing and shouting and singing. They were comrades with shared experiences and shared values.

Evidently some Nazi sympathizers were also on hand; a few days later Berlin radio reported a "great fight" between the *Normandie* and *Queen Mary* crews. "It seems that the French crew recognized that, as in the past, Britain is willing to fight to the last Frenchman," the Nazi announcer observed.

The next morning 900 *Normandie* crewmen straggled down the gangplank, tears in their eyes, seabags on their shoulders. They were sent by train to Nova Scotia and later taken back to France by military transport.

Their places were taken, in part, by sixty special detectives and uniformed guards of the Oceanic Patrol Service, a private agency. CGT was determined that *Normandie* not suffer the fate of the *Paris*.

In Europe, Germans continued to advance across Poland at lightning speed, practically ignoring Polish resistance. On September 17 Russian troops crossed Poland's eastern border. Two days later the two armies met, dividing the country between them. A week later Warsaw surrendered.

The French Line, realizing that *Normandie* might be trapped in New York for two or three years, ordered the ship's officers to pack her up and put her in mothballs.

Fourteen barrels of crushed mothballs were brought in and spread over the enormous Aubusson carpets in the saloon, dining room and smoking room. Crew members tracked it into the staterooms on their shoes, leaving white footprints. The pungent odor pervaded the ship from stem to stern.

In the public rooms the wooden dance floors were covered with tarpaulins. Rich blue and red chairs, jacketed in drab olive-green covers, were stacked one on top of the other. Hundreds of mattresses were piled in large heaps. The silverware was wrapped in flannel and put into boxes.

The ship's bright metal parts were coated with grease. The plants in the winter garden were regularly watered and pruned and the birds were lovingly tended.

The engines, however, were not shut down. Instead, they were run in rotation, each for a month at a time, so they would be in top running condition in case the situation changed.

"As a result of several weeks of packing and crating, the *Normandie*'s present condition is reminiscent of a summer resort hotel that has been closed down for the winter," said the *New York Times*. "At night, especially, the *Normandie*, moored at Pier 88 alongside the *Queen Mary*, deserves the title of 'ghost ship.'"

By now only 559 crew members remained aboard *Normandie*. Morale, it was reported, was excellent. "The only trouble the ship's officers have had with the men," said Henri Villar, "was in making them see that their duty is to remain on board the ship instead of returning to France to fight."

"The ship was interned," Roger Marneffe, a former crewman, recalled. "But the crew was marooned."

In the middle of October the Germans sneaked a submarine into the British fleet's home port, Scapa Flow, where it torpedoed and sank the battleship *Royal Oak*. The Allies could hardly have been more shocked. If Scapa Flow wasn't safe, what port was?

Far across the Atlantic even New York's harbor seemed unsafe. On October 23 an informant approached the American embassy in Mexico and told Ambassador Josephus Daniels that members of the German-American Bund intended to blow up both *Normandie* and the *Queen Mary* at their North River piers.

According to the informant, the saboteurs were already in New York, and five of them were aboard the *Queen Mary*, having made several crossings on her while pretending to be crewmen.

This information was passed on to J. Edgar Hoover at the FBI.

Hoover decided to test the ships' security for himself. He asked Naval Intelligence to sneak someone aboard the two ships if it could. A Lieutenant Commander Coddington made the attempt. He had no difficulty getting on board either vessel without a pass of any kind.

Next Hoover had P. E. "Sam" Foxworth, the Special Agent in Charge of the New York District, summon officials of the French Line and Cunard–White Star to tell them what Daniels had learned, so they could step up their own security on board their ships.

Hoover also asked Foxworth to inform the New York City police. They doubled the police guard in the area from fifteen patrolmen to thirty. Autos were not permitted to stop in front of the ships, and pedestrians were kept on the east side of 12th Avenue. Also, a small police launch was permanently stationed at the far end of Pier 88 to watch nearby waters for debris that might actually consist of floating mines or bombs.

FBI informants continued to supply information about a coming sabotage attempt. The saboteurs were planning to destroy the bearings in *Normandie's* and the *Queen Mary's* engines, one informant said.

Then another warning came from Mexico. This one said that men had been placed with the wholesale vegetable dealers who furnished supplies to *Normandie* and the *Queen Mary*. It alleged that they were going to plant bombs in crates of vegetables being delivered to the two ships, and if that failed, the truck drivers delivering these supplies would bring the bombs on board themselves.

Once more Agent Foxworth called in the shipping-line officials. Each told him that the ships took on new vegetable supplies once a week. They promised to check out the crates thoroughly from then on.

In Paris, Vladimir Yourkevitch decided that Europe no longer offered him any opportunities to practice his trade. So, just before 1939 came to an end, while the "phoney war" still prevailed, he and his family boarded one of the few small ships still plying the Atlantic—the *De Grasse*—and headed for the United States.

At about this time four famous gangsters—Lucky Luciano, Frank Costello, Meyer Lansky and Moe Polakoff—were hatching a plot in Dannemora Prison in upstate New York that ended up involving *Normandie.*

Luciano, the only one of the four in jail, told his three guests that he wanted out and that he thought he knew how to accomplish that. The first step, he said, was to help elect his old enemy Thomas Dewey, the prosecutor who'd put him in prison, Governor of New York. The second was to perform some kind of public service that would give Dewey an excuse to release him from jail.

Costello, Lansky and Polakoff apparently conveyed this message of support to one of Dewey's lieutenants, who received it non-committally. It lacked a key element, they all knew: the noble deed which would transform public opinion enough for Dewey to act in Luciano's favor.

World War II seemed to be suspended. Some thought that France and Britain would not attack Germany, and that Germany would be satisfied with her booty.

But the Germans were using these quiet months to train their entire army in the type of rapid, mechanized warfare which had enabled elite *Wehrmacht* units to conquer Poland so quickly.

The Allied powers knew all-out war would almost certainly begin in the spring. As a result Britain extended conscription to all men between the ages of nineteen and forty-one, Belgium ordered full-scale mobilization and Holland canceled all army leaves.

Many of the smaller European nations did nothing, however, but stand behind their oft-proclaimed neutrality. "Each one hopes that if he feeds the crocodile enough," said Winston Churchill, "the crocodile will eat him last. All of them hope that the storm will pass before their turn comes to be devoured."

By February 1940 only 115 *Normandie* crew members remained on board ship—just enough to keep the ship and her engines properly maintained and to conduct a formal fire watch.

"The *Normandie* stands in the water as motionless as if she were set in concrete, huge and a little tattered where the weather has chewed up her paint," wrote Morris Markey in the *New Yorker*.

> *It was a weird place we entered, I can tell you that: corridors of silence and of gloomy half-light, swatches of grey-white cloth covering the walls and lengths of taut canvas covering the floors.*
>
> *On a tour with the purser, we walked up and down haunted stairways, with their dim bulbs casting deep shadows. We walked through hushed corridors, lit by half-shuttered portholes. We looked into the magnificent public rooms, abandoned and futile.*
>
> *The atmosphere of loneliness hung heaviest of all, I think, in the great dining room. Ghost chairs stood at ghost tables. The purser smiled. "Did you ever read the books of Rider Haggard?" he asked. "Well, this is like one of those queer rooms in his jungle palaces." The description was not perfect, but it was on the right track.*

At about this time the film star Ramon Novarro, a frequent *Normandie* passenger, called the captain and asked if he could obtain one of the birds from the winter garden, a particular favorite of his. As it happened, *Normandie* had just transferred its winter garden birds—there were several dozen of them—to a pet shop on 14th Street. The Captain gave Novarro the name of the shop, and a few days later the actor phoned to say that the bird was his.

In England the only ship in the world larger than *Normandie*—the *Queen Elizabeth*—was still unfinished, but her engines were in and ready. Because her berth was needed to refit the *Duke of York*, a British warship, and because Churchill was afraid the Germans would bomb her if she remained in her berth, it was decided to send her on a secret voyage to America.

On February 26 the *Queen Elizabeth* was successfully brought down the Clyde. From there she was scheduled to go to Southampton, where technicians were to check out her engines and various supplies were to be loaded aboard.

German bombers were hovering over Southampton at the appointed time, but the *Queen Elizabeth* did not appear. Instead, on the morning of March 2 she sailed out into the Atlantic, escorted by four destroyers and a squadron of seaplanes. When she was 200 miles west of Rathlin Island, they left her on her own.

Steaming with all of her might and constantly zigzagging to avoid German submarines, the *Queen Elizabeth* made for New York, relying on speed and secrecy for safety.

Five days and 19 hours after departing from England, the giant ship appeared in the Narrows of New York harbor, "like an empress incognito, grey-veiled for her desperate exploit," as one paper described it.

At a quarter to five in the evening of March 7, her secret a secret no longer, the *Queen Elizabeth* eased into her berth, watched by 10,000 cheering New Yorkers and 100 extra police patrolmen.

Now, for the first and last time, the world's three largest ships were tied up together, side by side. This unique assembly was not destined to last, however.

A week after the *Elizabeth*'s arrival her lifeboats were carefully tested and 500 crewmen from the *Aquitania* came aboard. On March 21 the *Queen Mary* quietly eased out of her berth, steamed down the North River, out into the bay . . . and disappeared. She was headed toward Sydney, Australia, to be converted into a troopship.

Normandie's crew watched all of this with mixed emotions. On April 1 a *New York Post* reporter interviewed some *Norman-*

die crew members. "What would you say if the United States seized the *Normandie?*" the reporter asked.

"I would say the crew is indifferent about it," a crew member answered. "Certainly we would prefer giving it to America to letting the Germans have it."

"Would anyone in the crew harm the ship?" the reporter asked.

"We'd never sabotage THAT boat," said the crew member. "Don't worry."

That month the other shoe finally dropped. Nazi troops marched through Western Europe, crushing the antiquated armies that vainly attempted to stop them.

The first to fall was Denmark, which surrendered to the Nazi troops in just four hours. Then Norway; British and Norwegian forces offered spirited opposition, but Germany emerged victorious.

On May 10 seven German armored divisions swept into Belgium, the Netherlands and Luxembourg while other German forces invaded France. They marched not through central Belgium, as expected, nor did they attack the Maginot Line head on; instead, they threaded their way through the supposedly impenetrable Ardennes Forest region and Luxembourg.

Moving rapidly, German armored columns headed toward the French ports on the English Channel, cutting off Allied forces in Belgium and threatening to surround the entire British army in France.

At this point Neville Chamberlain stepped down as British Prime Minister and Winston Churchill took his place. It was a grim situation and Churchill did not try to disguise that. Britain would prosecute the war at all costs, he said, "for without victory, there is no survival." But, he added, "I have nothing to offer but blood, toil, tears and sweat."

A week after Churchill took office, the Germans reached the Channel. And a week after that, 861 ships of all descriptions began to evacuate more than 350,000 British, French and Belgian troops from France. Most of their heavy equipment—tanks, trucks, artillery—had to be abandoned.

There were also Nazis in New York harbor, watching the ships there, *Normandie* in particular. On June 3, 1940, two weeks before France fell, the FBI intercepted a coded short-wave radio message from German secret-service headquarters in Hamburg to the secret Nazi radio station at Centerport, Long Island.

"Thanks for reports," it read. "Observe *Normandie.*"

So far as *Normandie*'s crew was concerned, however, nothing was happening on the ship, nothing at all. The crew did its best to stay occupied. Many studied English. There was a movie on board almost every night. Practically every deck of cards on the ship was worn out. The crew played soccer, bocci and basketball on the pier.

New York worked hard at entertaining the Frenchmen. The crew members were given passes to the World's Fair, the Broadway movie houses, the Metropolitan Opera and some of the legitimate theaters. They were also given full privileges at the Seaman's YMCA in Manhattan. And every so often they were taken on bus trips to upstate New York, where the countryside reminded many of them of home.

But *Normandie*'s crew was homesick, painfully homesick, and nothing short of returning to France to see its families and fight for its country could have helped.

In France it was time for the maiden voyage of the Yourkevitch-designed liner, the *Pasteur*, and it would be almost as strange as the *Queen Elizabeth*'s. Instead of carrying rich passengers, the *Pasteur* transported most of France's gold reserves to safety in Halifax, Canada.

Later that week the Allies completed their evacuation at Dunkirk. With the rest of the French forces fleeing in disorder, nothing stood between the Germans and Paris.

"The inhabitants are bitter at their government, which in the last days, from all I hear, completely collapsed," William Shirer wrote. "It even forgot to tell the people until too late that Paris would not be defended."

Less than six weeks after the Germans had invaded, France surrendered. Germany occupied the northern half, including Paris, and put the rest under the control of the old soldier of World War I, Marshal Pétain.

The next day General Charles de Gaulle, broadcasting from London, asked Frenchmen all over the world to join him in continuing the fight. "France has lost a battle," he said, "but France has not lost the war."

His nation now alone in the battle against Hitler, Winston Churchill also broadcast an appeal to his people. "Let us brace ourselves to our duties and so bear ourselves that if the British Empire and its Commonwealth last for a thousand years, men will say, 'this was their finest hour.' "

In New York, *Normandie* crew members heard De Gaulle's call and heeded it; all but a handful got permission to leave the ship and make their way to England to join the "Free French."

On June 26 the French Shipping Commission in New York asked the Vichy government if *Normandie* should try to run the British blockade and return to France. The French-Nazi armistice called for all French ships to return to their home ports. At the same time a Vichy official in Washington said that all French ships would be handed over to Germany.

Germany clearly wanted *Normandie*, to prevent her from someday being requisitioned by the Allies for troop-carrying duty or as a cargo ship to transport arms.

The British consulate in New York was not pleased with this thought. "*Normandie* might leave New York," said one British official, "but she might never get to France." The American government, also anxious to keep *Normandie* out of German hands, vetoed the move. *Normandie* stayed put.

The summer of 1940 was marked by two events that, if there had been no war, would have gotten headlines on newspaper shipping pages.

On August 10 the largest passenger ship ever built in the United States—the *America*—undertook her maiden voyage. She'd originally been intended to travel across the Atlantic, but, under the circumstances, all that was possible was a cruise to the West Indies.

A couple of weeks later Yourkevitch's German liner, *Vaterland II*, his last major ship, was launched in Hamburg. She was beautiful, a kind of three-quarter-sized version of *Normandie*.

With France conquered, Hitler began to look at the only countries that prevented him from totally dominating Europe: Britain
and—despite the non-aggression pact Ribbentrop and Molotov
had signed the previous year—the Soviet Union.

Even the mighty German Army could not hope to tackle
both of these enemies simultaneously. However, Hitler thought,
it should be a fairly simple matter to first conquer Britain, then
defeat Russia.

The German dictator now ordered *Luftwaffe* chief Her-
mann Goering to destroy the British air force and seize control
of the skies over the English Channel, clearing the way for an
invasion. At the same time he ordered his General Staff to work
out a plan to invade the Soviet Union.

Thus began the Battle of Britain, the Messerschmitts vs. the
Spitfires. For a month they fought it out over southern England. Germany had more planes, but Britain had radar stations
to warn of their approach. She also had the desperation of a nation that knew her very survival depended on the outcome of
this one contest.

Toward the end of August RAF bombers attacked Berlin for
the first time. Infuriated, Hitler ordered the *Luftwaffe* to switch
its efforts from RAF airfields to London. It was an enormous
strategic blunder. London suffered, but the RAF got a little
breathing room.

From that moment on, the RAF had the upper hand. By
the middle of September it had defeated the *Luftwaffe*, not vice
versa. Hitler postponed his invasion, first for a few days, then
indefinitely.

Slowly but surely the United States was drawn into the conflict.
With the very survival of Great Britain at stake, the two nations
concluded a lend-lease agreement whereby America would loan
the British fifty old but desperately needed destroyers in exchange for leases on British bases in the Caribbean and Canada.

At the same time America began the largest naval build-up
in its history; Congress approved America's first peacetime conscription plan; and the government began to cast a worried eye

toward Japan, whose aggression in the Far East seemed likely to spread.

By this time more than 90 percent of *Normandie's* original 130-man maintenance crew had volunteered to fight with General de Gaulle, many defying threatened reprisals against their families by the Pétain government *and* the Nazi government of occupied France.

These *Normandie* crewmen made their way by ship or train to Canada, where they were given the choice of joining De Gaulle's forces, then training in Britain, or serving on British ships. Most chose De Gaulle.

To make up for the defections, the French Line transferred to *Normandie* crew members of the *Winnipeg*, once a passenger liner, later a freighter, and now interned at New Orleans.

Trying to bolster the morale of this small group, Vichy's Ambassador to the United States, Gaston Henry-Haye, visited the crew one October morning. He came, he said, "to express the solicitude of the French government and to tell the men about their families." More likely, his purpose was to try to win their loyalty and to prevent further defections to General de Gaulle.

Normandie, still lying in her berth at Pier 88 and painted in her civilian colors, continued to attract the interest of her host city. A story by Inez Robb in the *New York Journal-American* captured that feeling. "Ever since the beginning of the Second World War," Miss Robb wrote, "*Normandie* has rested like a sleeping beauty at her pier in the North River. Once she was queen of the seas. Today she is a silent, echoing refugee from the war that vanquished the proud nation that built and launched her."

That fall Roosevelt was elected President for an unprecedented third term. Not long afterward Roosevelt called for direct aid to Britain. The United States, he said, must become "the great arsenal of democracy." Public-opinion polls showed that two out of every three Americans agreed with him. Early in 1941 Congress approved a $7 billion lend-lease program.

In Europe, the Vichy government, led by Marshal Pétain and his Prime Minister, Pierre Laval, drew closer and closer to Berlin. What had begun as a frosty, correct relationship had become a collaboration.

In Washington, President Roosevelt and Secretary of State Cordell Hull realized that this friendship could endanger the great French liner tied up in New York. The Vichy French and the Germans knew they could not force *Normandie*'s return through diplomacy. But she could be sabotaged.

Roosevelt wanted to put Coast Guardsmen aboard *Normandie* to protect her from any of her crew members who might sympathize with the Vichy government. Hull thought an appeal to Vichy itself might be enough. He told Ambassador Leahy, America's envoy to France, to tell Pétain that the U.S. might be forced to put guards on board the French vessels in American ports unless the Vichy leader forbade any sabotage.

Pétain and his naval commander insisted they'd sent no sabotage instructions and agreed to prohibit sabotage if the U.S. guaranteed that the ships wouldn't be used to help Britain. Soon afterward they did indeed send a "no sabotage" order.

Word of these talks leaked to the New York newspapers, which promptly printed a number of inaccurate reports about *Normandie*. The *Daily News* claimed *Normandie* was already under guard and that U.S. authorities had hinted they might seize her.

The *World-Telegram* said that *Normandie* was primed for a dash to freedom. It also reported (inaccurately) that Captain Hervé Le Huede—De la Garanderie had returned to France months earlier—was being paid only $29 a month, while crew members were receiving an average of only $5 a month.

Actually, the crew was receiving normal salaries, but these were being paid directly to their families in France since French funds in America were blocked. The money mentioned was in fact spending money.

De Gaulle also heard about the *Normandie* negotiations, and he instructed his American agents to tell the press the Free French were ready to place trained crews loyal to the Allied cause aboard any French ships seized by the United States.

While this was going on, Germany attacked Yugoslavia and Greece. Yugoslavia surrendered after eight days of resistance. Greece lasted a week longer.

In Vichy, Pétain responded to the Nazi successes by announcing a policy of even closer cooperation with Germany in Europe and Africa.

About this time the *New York Daily News* published another inaccurate *Normandie* story. It claimed her French crew had bollixed up her wiring, making it impossible for her to go to sea without major repairs.

The real danger to *Normandie*, however, was from Germany. On April 15, 1941, the FBI picked up another reference to her, this one from Nazi spy Kurt Ludwig. "At Pier 88 north is still *Normandie*," he informed his superiors in a report written in invisible ink.

Just what the Nazis had in mind for *Normandie* the FBI had no way of knowing. But Roosevelt and Hull took this as one more piece of evidence that *Normandie* could not be left unguarded very much longer.

When several small German and Italian ships tied up at Central and South American ports were scuttled by their crews to avoid seizure, Roosevelt decided he could wait no longer. He ordered a detachment of Coast Guardsmen put aboard *Normandie*.

On the evening of May 15, 1941, with no advance warning, a detail of armed Coast Guardsmen appeared on Pier 88 and a Coast Guard cutter, the *Icarus*, tied up at *Normandie*'s stern.

Shortly afterward John Baylis, Captain of the Port of New York and second in command of the New York District Coast Guard, walked on board *Normandie* with a party of about 100 Coast Guardsmen. This was the same man who'd led a boarding party onto the enormous German liner *Vaterland* in April 1917 when the United States entered the Great War.

The Coast Guardsmen were commanded by Lieutenant Commander Earl G. Brooks, aged forty-eight. Their mission: to take *Normandie* into "protective custody," to keep unauthorized persons off the ship and to make sure *Normandie* crew members did nothing to harm her.

Normandie's French crew greeted the Coast Guardsmen without hostility, but without any great affection either. "If any champagne was opened, I didn't know about it," Baylis said later. "We weren't even offered a cup of coffee."

Despite the presence of the Coast Guardsmen, *Normandie's* crew retained technical custody of the ship. Crewmen were allowed to remain on board and were permitted to come and go as they pleased.

At first the Coast Guardsmen were quartered and messed on the *Icarus*. But when the *Icarus* went off to patrol the Atlantic, the Coast Guardsmen were moved into the crew's quarters in *Normandie's* bow. *Normandie's* French crew was moved into some staterooms. The two groups kept a separate mess for bookkeeping reasons—and because they couldn't agree on a single menu.

According to Conrad Trahan, a Coast Guard cook who served with this detail, "American and French sailors got along very well. Those of the French crew that we suspected had no love for us, we kept away from.

"I do recall one incident where some of our boys raided the French captain's quarters and took some of his personal champagne," Trahan said. "One simply does not barge into a captain's stateroom and steal his liquor. He complained bitterly to Commander Brooks about it, but I don't ever recall the champagne being returned."

After that the ship's liquor and wines were kept under lock and key in the main storeroom, guarded by a Coast Guardsman twenty-four hours a day. "To my knowledge," Trahan said, "no one ever gained entrance to the liquor supply."

As Trahan remembers it,

The French had a cat aboard, mostly black with a white face. An outstanding feature of this animal was its small mustache under its nose that closely resembled Hitler's. One day the poor cat happened to cross the path of a loyal Frenchman. He was given a sound kick and went reeling.

I thought this was rather cruel and mentioned the incident to my friend Jean, the steward. He replied, "Don't let it disturb you. Did you ever notice the mustache on that cat? It resembles the mustache of Pierre Laval, the

*traitor, and every true Frenchman on this ship feels com-
pelled to vent his wrath on the poor cat."*

Seaman 1st Class R. M. Epstein, another Coast Guardsman
aboard *Normandie*, recalled that "the French crew were friendly
enough. Their officers were quite social, as a matter of fact. They
entertained a great many guests, mostly ladies."

The Coast Guard detail not only stood watch, it studied
Normandie's engines. Tutored by the French crew, the Coast
Guardsmen learned enough to take *Normandie* to sea in an
emergency.

As for the French crew, protective custody brought few real
changes. Boredom and frustration still reigned supreme. "Many
Normandie crew members are from Brittany and some had farms
there," one newspaper article noted.

> *The sweep of Nazi conquest engulfed their holdings and
> none know with certainty what is happening to their
> families.*
>
> *Nazi censors in the occupied area do not permit out-
> going letters, but instead furnish printed cards on which
> families are allowed to check such statements as "re-
> ceived your letter," and "we are all well." The seamen
> find this sort of correspondence tantalizing, both because
> it tells so little and because there is no proof that the an-
> swer is from the person addressed.*

Meanwhile, according to recently declassified government documents, the United States was trying to decide what it might do
with *Normandie* in the event of war. On May 27, 1941, Admiral Harold Stark, then Chief of Naval Operations, directed
the Bureau of Ships to see if *Normandie* could be converted into
an airplane transport complete with a flying-off deck and a crane
to hoist planes aboard. A month later the Bureau of Ships reported that *Normandie* could transport a total of 131 fully assembled planes.

The Bureau wasn't at all happy with Admiral Stark's idea.
Its engineers pointed out that *Normandie*, with its thin, unar-

mored skin and its few watertight bulkheads—few in comparison to the normal warship—would be a very vulnerable combat carrier. The engineers proposed instead that *Normandie* be turned into a troop transport with a flight deck. Admiral Stark decided to do nothing—for the time being anyway.

Normandie remained at her pier, a kind of ghost ship. "As gloomy a spectacle as you are likely to encounter these days along the West Side water front is the *Normandie*, a-mouldering at her slip in 'protective custody,' " wrote Robert Wilder in the *New York Sun*.

> *The sight of the* Normandie, *stained and fettered, is all the more depressing if you can recall her in the days of her glory. Everything which France once represented— gaiety, color and vitality—were embodied in this ship and her sailings from New York, usually at noon, were unrivaled.*
>
> *They were events with scarlet-coated page boys flitting up and down her magnificent staircases or through the paneled corridors, the famous from a dozen walks of life crowding her lounges and cabins. She was France and the line's assertion that the passengers were in France when they crossed the gangplank was no mere playing with words.*
>
> *In any event, the* Normandie *still holds at her pier at the foot of 48th Street for those who want a quick and distant look at her. She is the last remaining link between the present and those days when four great lines, the North German Lloyd, French, Cunard and Italian, made of the dozen blocks along the West Side a district without counterpart on any waterfront.*

According to the *New York Daily News*, however, some thought *Normandie* should be more than a monument to bygone days. "In the urgent search for more electric power for defense industries," it reported, "government experts are considering plans to utilize the power plants of large ships. One report was that the Government was studying the plans of the power plant on the

$80 million [!] liner *Normandie* for possible use in augmenting New York's power supply."

Normandie could have provided an enormous amount of power—146,800 kilowatts' worth, enough to light all the homes in Pittsburgh. But in the end America did without the power she might have generated.

Not only did *Normandie* attract the attention of dreamers and schemers, she continued to attract the attention of known Nazi spies. On June 18 Kurt Ludwig walked down 12th Avenue from 59th Street, followed by an FBI agent. He stopped at Pier 88 and examined it closely.

Finally, he walked on, stopping again and again and looking back at *Normandie*. At 42nd Street he took the Weehawken ferry. As soon as it left its dock, he climbed to the upper deck, with its good view of the New York waterfront. He studied *Normandie* with great care. When he landed in Weehawken, he spent twenty minutes writing in a small black notebook. What was he planning? The FBI had no idea.

In Europe, Hitler decided to attack Russia instead of Britain. On June 22 he hurtled some 3 million troops, 600,000 vehicles, 3,500 tanks and 1,800 airplanes against the Russians. The Soviet Union had 4.5 million troops stationed along their 1,800-mile frontier, but they were caught totally unprepared, despite warnings from Britain, the United States and their own spies.

Churchill promptly offered British help. FDR sent Harry Hopkins to assess the situation. Most Westerners felt that Russia could not survive. Hopkins disagreed and he convinced Roosevelt he was right.

After conferring with the Russians, Britain and the United States agreed to send each *month* to the Soviet Union 400 airplanes, 500 tanks, 200 gun carriers and a great deal of other materiel, including food.

Nonetheless, German advances soon forced the Soviet government—except for Stalin himself—to leave Moscow. A day later the Germans torpedoed their first American vessel, the *Kearney*, a destroyer. And in Japan an unabashed warhawk named Tojo became Prime Minister.

Tojo promptly ordered the Japanese fleet to prepare to attack Pearl Harbor.

As trouble approached, *Normandie*, sitting idle in New York harbor, drew more and more interest. James Duffy, the *World-Telegram*'s marine editor, led the speculation:

> *If the United States should enter the war and the government seizes the* Normandie, *it is believed she would be converted into an aircraft carrier without delay. It is even possible the Navy has already prepared plans for this change, as naval men have gone over the big vessel on several occasions in recent months.*
>
> *One of the startling discoveries made in this survey was that the* Normandie *undoubtedly was designed for quick conversion into an aircraft carrier.*
>
> *As proof of this fact, an outstanding feature is that her three giant funnels split at their base, directly over the boilers and run up the sides, a design in construction followed on all naval aircraft carriers, leaving a sweep of the deck the length of the ship for landings.*

This was all nonsense. In two specific ways *Normandie* did resemble an aircraft carrier: She had a carrier's turbo-electric engines and she had a hull that looked more like a warship than a passenger liner.

But she was unlike a carrier in any other way. Carriers have armor—as much as fifteen inches of it. *Normandie* had a steel skin less than an inch thick. She had only a fifth as many watertight compartments as a carrier. She had no gun mounts. As for the split funnel uptakes, she was built that way to give her a series of huge and magnificent public rooms—not to make room for a landing deck.

Most American naval experts thought *Normandie* would make a better transatlantic airplane ferry than a combat aircraft carrier.

Unfortunately, so long as the French remained in technical custody of the ship, there was no unobtrusive way for U.S. naval engineers to survey her accurately. So the dreams were held in abeyance.

But the Secretary of the Navy, Frank Knox, realized *Normandie* could not long remain in French hands, whatever the United States eventually decided to do with her. He suggested to FDR that the U.S. seize the ship and deposit payment in a bank for France to collect after the war.·

Roosevelt checked out the idea with his Secretary of State, Cordell Hull. Hull suggested the U.S. first try to buy the ship. With FDR's approval, he had Ambassador Leahy try to do just that.

But now events overtook the negotiations. On November 20 Japan offered its "final" proposal to the United States—an ultimatum demanding that America agree to stay out of Asia.

On November 24 U.S. Navy commanders in the Pacific were warned that talks with the Japanese weren't going well and that Tokyo's military forces might be preparing some kind of attack. It came on December 7. The United States had joined the conflict.

In France the Vichy government told Ambassador Leahy on December 10 that it was willing to sell *Normandie* to America if the Germans okayed the deal and if the Americans paid immediately in fuel oil, food and cotton goods.

A year earlier the deal might have worked. But on December 11 the United States declared war on Germany, making a purchase "impractical," as Secretary of State Hull delicately put it. The United States decided to seize *Normandie* instead.

There were many precedents for such an act. Several small Italian ships had been taken over a few months before. And when the United States entered World War I in April 1917, it had seized many German ships that had been interned in U.S. ports. Some were used to carry troops or munitions to Europe.

At noon on December 12 Captain Baylis once more led a party of armed Coast Guardsmen aboard *Normandie*, this time to take possession of the ship in the name of the government of the United States.

Soon after they boarded, a number of U.S. sailors arrived at Pier 88 by taxi. Some took over pier services, including the telephone switchboard, while others took over *Normandie*'s engine room.

When the pier's longshoremen returned from lunch, they found their way barred by two Coast Guard sentries carrying loaded rifles with fixed bayonets. Reporters who went to the pier were stopped by a steel cable stretched across the pier entrance.

On board, Captain Baylis took the French crew members into custody on the technical charge of having overstayed their leaves in port. He told them they would be taken to Ellis Island for routine questioning, then released.

Captain Hervé Le Huede asked Baylis' permission to haul down the French flag. Through an oversight, however, this deed was actually performed by a Coast Guard officer, who also raised an American flag in its place.

Shortly afterward Baylis noticed Captain Le Huede sulking on the bridge. "I asked him the trouble," Baylis said, "and he told me about the flag. So I ordered the U.S. colors down, the French tricolor was hauled up the truck again and, in the glare of a spotlight, the captain ceremoniously hauled it down. The crew sent up a cheer and went off to Ellis Island in good spirits."

Conrad Trahan, who was there, remembers the scene vividly. "For some of the French crew it was a traumatic experience. This was home to them and they were being evicted.

"Later that afternoon," Trahan recalled, "I stood by the gangway and sadly watched each of these poor souls leave the ship. As each walked by, there were tears, laughter, curses and some wistful smiles from those I had made friends with."

Sea bags over their shoulders, valises in their hands, the French crewmen trooped down *Normandie*'s gangplank and boarded two Coast Guard cutters, which took them to Ellis Island, where they were briefly questioned, issued ID cards and told to report every thirty days. Captain Le Huede and his staff received permission to stay aboard the ship for one last night.

Meanwhile, the Coast Guard assumed the task of maintaining steam, the duties of the fire watch and all the other minor maintenance jobs aboard the ship. "There was now a definite change in the mood of the Coast Guard detail on the *Normandie*," Trahan recalled. "For the time being, we were the sole occupants. That evening was spent in small groups of us roaming the corridors and making new discoveries. Most of us felt like a bunch of peasants turned loose in the king's palace."

In France, Ambassador Leahy informed the Vichy government what had been done, at Hull's request. The French already knew; the Germans had seen to that.

On December 16, at 2:00 p.m., Captain Granville Conway, North Atlantic District Director of the Maritime Commission, accompanied by Carl Farback of the Commission's legal staff, boarded the ship and posted a legal notice saying the government had taken title and would compensate the owners.

The French government protested mildly. And the French official who delivered the protest told Leahy that "*Normandie* is a symbol of the days of France's power and greatness. For this reason, the French government hopes that the American government would consider *Normandie* still owned by France and only requisitioned by the American government 'for the duration of the emergency.' "

The *Normandie* seizure was a sensation in the United States, especially in New York. Everyone began to speculate on what America would do with her. Newspapers revived the talk of converting the liner to an aircraft carrier or a fast destroyer or a troop transport. Government officials merely said *Normandie* would become an "auxiliary vessel."

In its December 22 issue *Life* Magazine printed an artist's conception of *Normandie* as a combination aircraft carrier and troop transport. "Thus reconditioned," ran the caption, "her 40 planes can act as a self-sufficient convoy to the ship and to the 10,000 soldiers aboard her. Because she is 1,029 feet overall, her entire length is not required for a flight deck. Some 125 feet of the after-deck space on four different levels can be used for troop recreation. In addition," *Life* noted naïvely, "the flight deck (longest of any ship in the world) is perfect as a drill and parade ground for infantrymen and machine gunners."

Although the government wasn't saying just how *Normandie* would be used in the war effort, it was obviously in a hurry to carry out whatever plans it had in mind.

On the day before Chistmas the U.S. Maritime Commission transferred custody of the ship to the U.S Navy. The Commandant, Third Naval District—Rear Admiral Adolphus Andrews—accepted "delivery" at 10:00 a.m. Conversion to a military vessel was to start immediately.

The *New York Times* thought the occasion worthy of an editorial:

> The Normandie *ought to be glad. Now she is free again. Since late in August, 1939, she has been lying in a dock in midtown Manhattan, a great, dispirited bulk of steel, looking seedier week by week, deserted by the admirers that used to stare up at her tall bows, bridge and funnels.*
>
> *But on Friday, the United States took her over, probably for a transport or airplane carrier, and in due course, one of the most brilliant liners of the world will be cutting salt water again.*

Meanwhile, Lucky Luciano's old enemy Thomas Dewey had been elected Governor of New York. Now all Luciano had to do, he thought, was to dream up some sort of extraordinary public service he could perform that would convince Dewey to pardon him.

After the Pearl Harbor attack it came to him. Late in December 1941 Luciano summoned his gangster pals. "I had this newspaper with me," he later wrote. "And I showed them how the Navy Department was worried about German subs sinking our ships or some spies blowing up ships in the harbor. It looked like the whole Eastern waterfront, especially in New York, was a mess of sabotage."

Luciano then asked his friends to create some kind of sabotage incident on the New York waterfront—"front-page stuff"—that would force the Navy to ask the mob for help. Luciano would see that the help was delivered—and Dewey would pardon him.

It was a crazy idea, perhaps, but the four men felt it might work.

16

GETTING READY FOR WAR

Now America owned a new ship, and what a ship she was: two-time holder of the Blue Ribbon, the second-largest and second-fastest passenger liner afloat, a vessel far ahead of her time technically, an Art Deco palace.

There was only one problem with her. She was totally worthless as she was. The Atlantic was infested with German U-boats. No rich and famous passengers were booking trips from America to Europe. And the battle for the Blue Ribbon had been suspended.

The war made passenger liners and ocean travel seem trivial indeed. In her present state *Normandie* could provide no help. As a weapon of war, however, she just might play a vital role.

When the United States seized *Normandie*, the Navy wasn't sure what sort of weapon, since it had never had the chance to survey her adequately. Despite her vulnerability, some Navy officers thought she'd make a perfect combat aircraft carrier. Others felt she was totally unsuited to combat, but that she'd be a fine troop transport and airplane ferry. Eventually even President Roosevelt got involved in the debate.

In those first days after *Normandie* was seized, the Coast Guard detail remained on board and continued to take care of the ship's upkeep, security, fire watch and overall operation. Until January 23 Captain Le Huede, Chief Engineer Leborgne, Chief Electrician (propulsion) Guillou, Chief Electrician (hull) Fontaine and Engineer Cariou came to the ship at 10:00 a.m. to teach Coast Guard engineers how to run the ship's complicated machinery.

Thirty-six Coast Guardsmen were assigned to the fire brigade. They were divided into four watches of nine men each. Boatswain Oliver Rahle was in charge, with Chief Carpenter's Mate Morris Bach as his assistant.

One Coast Guardsman was stationed at *Normandie*'s central fire-control station on B Deck at all times. The other eight made continual rounds of the ship. Each time they passed one of the eighty-four fire-watch substations, they pushed a button which lit up a light on the central control board. When all the lights were lit, the board was cleared and a new watch began.

While one group of nine Coast Guardsmen patrolled the ship, the other twenty-seven remained in their special quarters on the main deck. If a fire broke out, the man at the central control board could summon them immediately by telephone or by ringing an alarm.

Normandie had 224 individual fire alarms and a Klaxon general fire-alarm system. She was also connected directly to the New York Fire Department via a telegraph line on her bridge.

If fire did break out, *Normandie* was well equipped to deal with it. She had 32 main fire cupboards and 211 general fire cupboards—all filled with such fire-fighting equipment as extinguishers, gas masks, asbestos suits, oxygen, extra hose, special nozzles. In addition, she had 504 hose connections—two at every fire cupboard. There were seventy-four city-water hose outlets on the north side of Pier 88, to which two-inch hoses could be attached.

To handle all of these duties, the little Coast Guard detail was eventually expanded to 275 men and 6 officers.

While the Coast Guard mastered the ship, the United States set about finding out what its new possession was worth. On December 17 it began an inventory of the ship. Forty-eight Maritime Commission employees were assigned to the job, along with fifty former *Normandie* crewmen and representatives of the French Line. The inventory took three weeks.

"You've never seen so many nooks and crannies," one of the inventory checkers remembered. "When we opened a door, we never knew what would be behind it. We would expect to spend ten minutes counting a few pieces of furniture. Then the door would be unlocked and we would find rooms lined with shelves and on the shelves would be small boxes containing needles, thread, girls' hair ribbons, party favors, powder boxes and God knows what."

Shortly after *Normandie* was seized, President Roosevelt authorized the Maritime Commission to resell her to the French Line after the war. That required a totally different study of the ship—a careful appraisal to determine her worth as of December 1941 so that there'd be a basis for negotiations with CGT when the war was over.

Three different ship surveyors were sent aboard *Normandie* to estimate her value—Robert S. Haight, Frank S. Martin and H. A. Bagger. Normally, they appraised a ship by comparing her to similar vessels, then factoring in age, condition, etc. But in the case of *Normandie* they had no basis of comparison.

Still, they tried. Frank Martin's evaluation technique was typical. First, he compared French and American ship-construction costs in 1932, and discovered that American ships cost about 13 percent more to build at that time.

Martin then added 13 percent to what he was told was the original cost of *Normandie*: $56,985,694. Forgotten was the fact that *Normandie* actually cost much less than this (at the true 1932 franc/dollar exchange rate).

The 13-percent addition brought the figure to $64,393,834. To this Martin added 40 percent for inflation and reached a total of $90,151,367. From this he deducted an estimated scrap value of $834,230. Then, figuring *Normandie*'s normal life at twenty years—a CGT estimate—he depreciated his total by 5 percent a year and arrived at a final evaluation of $61,123,297. The other two appraisers, working with the same information and the same numbers, produced almost exactly the same total.

While all these technical matters were being taken care of, a new party entered the debate about what to do with *Normandie*: William Francis Gibbs. Gibbs saw the upcoming *Normandie* conversion as an opportunity to repeat his spectacular *Vaterland/Leviathan* success and get work for his design firm, Gibbs and Cox.

Oddly enough, one man who might have had something to

say about *Normandie's* fate was not consulted. Vladimir Yourkevitch had reopened his ship-design office in Manhattan and
had become chairman of Navcot, a shipping firm. He also served
as a consultant to Veritas, a French shipbuilding company.

On December 20 the Auxiliary Vessels Board of the Bureau
of Ships—which was officially entrusted with such matters—made
the decision. It recommended that *Normandie* be converted into
a "convoy loaded transport." This kind of ship carried troops (and
a minimal amount of battle gear) from rear staging areas to offshore anchorages near the war zone.

On the same day Rear Admiral Alexander van Keuren, chief
of the Bureau of Ships, received a letter from Gibbs outlining a
plan to convert *Normandie* to an aircraft carrier. Gibbs pointed
out that the bottlenecks in shipbuilding were (a) steel and (b)
machinery, and that *Normandie*, with her "excellent hull" and
engines, eliminated both.

Van Keuren wasn't moved. He and Admiral Stark had already agreed with the Auxiliary Vessels Board recommendation.
They knew American troops were needed in England to bolster
the exhausted British forces so recently withdrawn at Dunkirk.
They were also needed in Australia to fend off the expected Japanese invasion, and in Burma to reinforce Chinese troops trying
to keep the Burma Road open, and in North Africa, where the
British hoped to strike their first offensive blow against Hitler.

America also needed aircraft carriers. The Japanese were
advancing throughout the Pacific, and carriers were an excellent
way to project American military might into the area. But,
Washington decided, America needed troop transports even more.
A single *Normandie*-sized troop transport could deliver enough
American troops around the world to alter the balance of power
in four different parts of the world, and it could do so faster than
any other American ship afloat, fast enough to outrun the German and Japanese submarines that were wreaking havoc in both
oceans.

On December 22 and 23 the Bureau of Ships and the Navy
worked out the main details of *Normandie's* conversion. They
decided to install bunks and mess facilities for some 10,000 soldiers, but to leave *Normandie's* structure as it was. They also

agreed to install enough guns to fend off enemy raiders and aircraft.

Aware that the ship's watertight subdivisions did not meet combat standards, they decided to remove all the doors in the main transverse bulkhead below the main deck and permanently seal the openings. They also decided to install degaussing equipment to protect *Normandie* against magnetic mines of the sort that had recently sunk several British ships in the English Channel.

These and other necessary changes, the Bureau of Ships estimated, would cost about $3 million and take only a month to complete, so long as the work was performed according to the Bureau's "General Specifications for the Conversion of Merchant Vessels to Navy Auxiliaries" and no time was wasted drawing up formal plans.

Knox and Stark approved these recommendations on December 23, ordered a $3 million account set up at the Brooklyn Navy Yard for the job and directed that work start immediately.

Gibbs, however, was not yet beaten. On December 26, with workmen already aboard the ship, he sent a memo from the renowned naval architect Dr. William Hovgaard to Van Keuren and to Captain J. M. Irish, the Navy's Superintendent of Shipbuilding.

Dr. Hovgaard pointed out that all of *Normandie*'s motors were in a single compartment aft, all of her alternators in the next compartment forward and all of her boilers in the compartment after that. "Therefore, a single bomb, torpedo or mine striking any one of these compartments will prevent the ship from moving, making her an even more inviting target than a normal vessel, due to her size," Hovgaard said.

A warship of *Normandie*'s size, of course, would have had thirty or forty transverse bulkheads, allowing her to survive all kinds of damage. The giant French liner had only eleven, and because of the way her main propulsion machinery was distributed, she had *no* effective longitudinal bulkheads.

Hovgaard also felt *Normandie* had a stability problem. In his memo he noted that she had a "low metacentric height," which meant she was quite likely to capsize if more than two underwater compartments were flooded when she was carrying a full load of passengers and cargo.

Captain Irish was evidently not willing to risk 18,000 troops in such a vessel. He thought *Normandie* should become a carrier instead. "I am very much convinced of the validity of the argument in favor of making this ship an aircraft carrier and not a troop ship," he wrote the chief of the Bureau of Ships.

"This ship offers an opportunity for an aircraft carrier to augment the fleet that is comparable in every way to the carriers CV9-12 [the *Enterprise*, the *Yorktown* and the *Hornet*]," Irish told his boss. He also mentioned that *Normandie* could be converted to a carrier far more quickly than a new carrier could be built and without tying up dockyard space.

Van Keuren told him that Chief of Naval Operations Harold Stark had made a final decision: *Normandie* would become a troopship. The matter was settled.

Now everything changed at Pier 88, where *Normandie* lay quietly bobbing with the tide, still dressed in her civilian colors and tended by Lieutenant Commander Brooks' Coast Guard detail.

The Robins Dry Dock & Repair Co., a subsidiary of the Todd Shipyards, was hired to do the conversion work. Navy Captain Clayton Simmers, the District Materiel Officer of the Third Naval District, a man with considerable naval engineering experience, made the decision, which wasn't difficult, for Robins was the only obvious candidate.

Robins had been converting civilian vessels to warships for more than thirty years. It had converted most of the Hamburg-Amerika liners caught in New York at the outbreak of World War I. And just before the *Normandie* job presented itself, Robins finished converting the U.S.S. *Kent*, formerly the S.S. *Santa Teresa*, so it had a large work force ready for a new job.

Robins agreed to do the job for a maximum sum of $3,890,005 under an open-ended contract it had with the Navy.

For security reasons Simmers asked Robins to provide him with a list of all of its foreign employees. As it turned out, these included one enemy alien. He was checked out by Naval Intelligence and given a clean bill of health.

For some reason, though, Simmers didn't ask any of the job's thirty-five subcontractors for a similar list.

The contract Robins signed required it to "exercise the highest possible degree of care to protect the vessel from fire. To this end, the contractor shall maintain an adequate system of inspection over the activities of welders, burners, etc."

Since *Normandie* was too large for any New York dry dock or shipyard, Simmers decided that Pier 88 should be the work site. For legal—and security—purposes, Simmers ordered that Pier 88 be considered an extension of the Todd/Robins shipyard in Brooklyn.

He next chose Lieutenant Commander Lester G. Scott, forty-seven, a reserve officer with only a few months' regular service, to oversee the job. Scott was officially designated Naval Inspector and was given nine assistants.

Before the war Scott had supervised a number of New York street-paving projects for the WPA. After joining the Navy he was put in charge of converting several small ships to wartime use. When Simmers chose him for the *Normandie* job, he had a half-dozen other ship-conversion jobs on his hands, at docks ranging from Erie Basin in Brooklyn to Bethlehem's shipyard in Hoboken.

While New York was gearing up to convert *Normandie*, the war news from the Pacific was bad. The Japanese captured Wake Island and landed troops on the Philippine Islands. MacArthur decided to evacuate most of Luzon and make a last stand on the peninsula of Bataan.

The European news was only slightly brighter. The German invasion of Russia was slowly grinding to a halt. Nazi troops seemed unable to capture Moscow.

In the Atlantic, however, wolf packs of German U-boats roamed the seas, sinking Allied shipping practically at will, destroying ships far faster than the Allies could build them.

At Pier 88 *Normandie* was in no way ready for hordes of workmen to swarm over her and begin installing tiers of Army bunks, anti-aircraft guns and military mess facilities. She was, after all, still the queen of the seas, a showplace of paintings, sculptures, lacquered and etched-glass wall panels, hand-made carpeting, tapestry-covered chairs and fine silver and glassware. All of these masterworks had to be removed and disposed of before the conversion could go into high gear. Roosevelt ordered the Bureau of Ships to put everything of value into storage so the ship might someday be restored to her prewar splendor.

Simmers hired the Chelsea Warehouse Company to strip *Normandie* of her treasures. Chelsea brought in four other huge storage warehouses, the Lincoln, the Manhattan, the Metropolitan and Morgan Brothers.

Now, in the closing days of December, the moving trucks began shuttling back and forth between Pier 88 and New York's five largest storage warehouses. All told, expert workmen removed some 2,400 vanloads of valuables from *Normandie*, with an estimated total value of between $6 and $8 million.

Whenever possible, workmen removed the decor of a room as a unit and carefully numbered and labeled everything so that it could be easily restored after the war. All rugs and draperies were thoroughly cleaned before being put into storage, to prevent damage by moths or other infestations. Some forty-five tons of glass were removed from the main dining room—all of the hammered and etched wall panels and the fluted glass lighting standards. Not a piece was broken.

Chelsea also removed and stored some $150,000 worth of silverware, $20,000 in wines, Leleu cabinets, Laboret panels, the six-ton, twenty-foot-high bronze dining-room doors, and the forty-by-twenty-seven-foot Aubusson carpet from the grand lounge that had eight million hand-knitted stitches.

The firm also tried to remove the four huge floor-mounted, glass-covered light fixtures in the grand lounge. It did strip away the ornamental glass, uncovering tall iron stanchions, but removing the stanchions would have involved using an acetylene torch. Scott vetoed that operation on fire-safety grounds.

Despite the stripping, some of *Normandie* was left intact. For example, the Deauville and Trouville Suites were not touched. The excuse given was that their costly wooden wall panels could not be removed without damage. Actually, these suites were being saved for the commanding generals of the troops that would be bunked below.

Also untouched were the synagogue, the chapel and the theater. In fact, additional projectors were installed in the theater so it could show movies twenty-four hours a day, giving every soldier aboard a chance to see a new film about once every three days.

Chelsea Warehouse had posted a $100,000 bond guaranteeing that it and its four partner storage warehouses would finish the job in thirty days. Twenty-nine days after the job began, the last vanload of fine fittings was removed.

Detaching and putting into storage Normandie's sumptuous furnishings cost the U.S government $115,227. The monthly storage charges ran to $12,000.

Of course, the Navy could not wait until Normandie was completely stripped before beginning the conversion process. So, on the day before Christmas 1941, 1,759 Robins workmen trooped aboard the French liner, accompanied by some 675 other workmen employed by subcontractors.

Speed was the watchword. The Chief of Naval Operations, Admiral Stark, wanted Normandie converted, equipped, manned, tested, fueled, provisioned and ready to take on troops no later than January 31—less than five weeks away.

Suddenly, Normandie was alive again, with regiments of joiners, pipe fitters, steam fitters, ironworkers, welders and tradesmen of every other type, there to transform her into a war machine, a troop transport capable of totally altering the strategic balance of power in a single, high-speed voyage.

These workmen labored twenty-four hours a day in three shifts, their work scene illuminated at night by huge lights strung along Normandie's decks and hung from her hull.

For those watching from the West Side Highway or from one of New York's skyscrapers, Normandie now underwent a startling transformation. Her civilian colors, which had faded somewhat during her twenty-seven months in port, were quickly replaced by a camouflage paint job that actually seemed to change her shape.

Workmen climbing over her hull like acrobats welded steel

plates over her lower three rows of portholes. Other workmen began to remove from *Normandie*'s hull the yellow-gold letters that spelled out her name, for, just as President Wilson had decided to rename the *Vaterland* the *Leviathan*, President Roosevelt now decided to rename *Normandie*.

Seeking to honor her French origins and to remind Vichy France of its historical friendship with the United States, FDR chose to call her *Lafayette*. As the *Lafayette*, *Normandie* was entered on the list of Navy vessels as vessel AP 53.

Keen-eyed observers might also have spotted another startling change aboard *Normandie*: the weapons that were being added to her upper decks. Fourteen three-inch 50-mm. anti-aircraft guns were installed on newly built gun platforms on the Promenade Deck, A Deck, Upper Deck and Boat Deck; and twenty-four 20-mm. machine guns bolted onto the deck house, the Sun Deck, and the first-class Promenade Deck.

But the greatest changes were taking place inside the huge passenger liner. Bunks for 14,800 troops were installed wherever there was space—2,000 in the glassed-in Promenade Deck, the rest squeezed into cabins on decks A through E.

These were "standee" bunks—collapsible iron-pipe frames arranged in tiers. There were two kinds: two-high with wire bottoms (for lower-ranking officers and for the ship's crew) and four-high with canvas bottoms (for the fighting men).

Victor Scrivens, who was a Coast Guardsman aboard *Normandie* during her conversion, remembered the bunking changes. "When I first went on board," he said, "we were quartered in the crew's quarters, forward. Each room held twelve—six upper and lower berths. After the passenger cabins were converted for troop use, we were moved aft. The cabins, which formerly had two twin beds, now held twenty-two men in four-high bunks."

Normandie's best accommodations, quite naturally, were reserved for the highest officers. Her spacious officers' quarters were earmarked for the ship's new officers. A number of first-class cabins on the Promenade and Main Decks were reserved for high-ranking troop officers.

Workmen also converted most of the major public rooms to wartime use. They made the dog kennel into an armory and cartridge-clipping room, the children's playroom into a radar room, the café grill into a wardroom and the winter garden into a troop washroom (its twenty-eight plate-glass windows, which followed the curve of *Normandie*'s streamlined superstructure, were covered over with galvanized sheet iron).

The main dining room, stripped of its glass walls and lighting fixtures, became a mess hall equipped with machines for sterilizing GI trays and pipes to run hot coffee up from the galley below at the rate of 2,500 gallons a day.

The open-air second-class swimming pool was covered over and became a gun platform. A distilling plant capable of producing 240,000 gallons of fresh water daily from salt water was installed in the swimming pool. "I remember the day the desalination plant was hoisted aboard with *Normandie*'s own cranes," Scrivens recalled. "She really listed then."

Most of the ship's bars were converted to troop canteens.

A trash incinerator was installed in the first-class gym and the ship's print shop was turned into a brig. Where the Bon Marché shop had been, a soda fountain was installed. The refrigerated cargo room in the forward hold became an ammunition magazine.

As for the huge windows in the grand saloon and the other public rooms, which had given *Normandie*'s first-class passengers an unprecedented view of the sea, all were covered with at least two coats of black paint.

Other kinds of military equipment were added to the ship: paravans to fend off floating mines, a battle telephone system, lights, blinkers, laundry equipment, icemaking machinery, gangway ladders, boat booms, life rafts, damage-control lockers, splinter shielding around the wheelhouse and landing nets for disembarking troops over the side.

Normandie's engine rooms, which were the equal of any in the U.S. Navy, were left as they were, except for their French labels. A group of Navy translators exchanged these for labels in plain old Navy English.

Steel blanks were fabricated to close off permanently the many cargo ports, gangway openings and holes in *Normandie*'s huge slab sides, but Robins delayed installing them time and time again because these openings were useful for bringing supplies and stores into the ship.

Before conversion began, security around the ship had been extremely tight. "Coast Guard Commander Baylis and his staff tried to sneak aboard one night," recalled Jim Kane, a Coast Guardsman who served on *Normandie* during that period. "They were stopped cold by the guards."

But now, despite Roosevelt's specific orders, the security system was a shambles, strained to the breaking point by the comings and goings of nearly 2,500 workmen amid incredible noise, confusion and disorder.

"When the companies started to send their workers aboard, it was ludicrous," Coast Guardsman R. M. Epstein recalled. "A handful of us were supposed to check thousands of workers. They wore buttons—Todd, Robins, etc. Christ, you could have worn a Mickey Mouse button and walked aboard."

At the time there was widespread talk that New York harbor was wide open to sabotage. And toward the end of December the newspaper *PM* assigned reporter Edmund Scott to find out if the rumors were true. "See if you can get on board *Normandie*," he was told by *PM* editor Ralph Ingersoll.

On January 3 Scott turned in his story. "We didn't print it then," Ingersoll later wrote, "because it was a blueprint for sabotage." It was published later, however.

"For the last two days," Scott's story read, "I have been wandering all over the *Normandie*. I have been lighting imaginary fires, I have been planting imaginary bombs. I have succeeded in 'destroying' a dozen times over the second biggest ship in the world."

Scott began his mock sabotage attempt by joining Local 824 of the International Longshoremen's Association. A friendly union business agent helped him by knocking off four fifths of the initiation fee. This same agent got him onto the gang removing *Normandie*'s expensive Art Deco furniture and loading it onto moving vans.

Once on the ship, Scott found he could wander about as he pleased. Any genuine saboteur could have done the same, he wrote. "He could lock himself in a restroom on the ship for 15 minutes, as I did. He could carry matches and cigarettes and smoke on the ship, as I did. He could fool around with barrels of excelsior, as I did."

Instead of publishing Scott's story, *PM* editor Ingersoll told Captain Charles H. Zeerfoos, chief of the Antisabotage Division of the U.S. Maritime Commission, what Scott had found on the waterfront. "Zeerfoos didn't even ask the name of the ship," the editor later wrote. "He just said, 'Better get your reporter out of there before he gets shot.' He told us he didn't think we had accurate information and that there wasn't any point in continuing the conversation."

Other newspaper reporters also watched what was happening to *Normandie*. They weren't pleased. "Of all the transatlantic liners we can think of, none is seemingly so ill-suited, from a romantic point of view, to transport labor as this *Normandie*," wrote Robert Wilder in the *New York Sun*.

> *This* Normandie *was more than a bottom. In a fashion, she was France, colorful, bright and temperamental. There will probably be nothing like her again.*
>
> *On Friday, we talked with several Naval officers and a Marine engineer about* Normandie. *From the Navy, we could draw little information. The Marine engineer, however, told us some things which will probably interest you.*
>
> *Eventually, if the war lasts longer than Washington now thinks it will,* Normandie *(now the* Lafayette*) will be converted into a raider. So, if you hear of her again, during this war, it will probably be in the name of destruction.*

This was simple misinformation, a wartime necessity.

As a troop transport (and not a raider, as Navy men had evidently hinted to Wilder) *Normandie* would certainly be a valuable addition to America's troop-lifting capacity. By mid-January 1942 the Navy could transport 25,000 troops, using a half-dozen ships built or converted to that purpose. None of them, however, was even two thirds as fast as *Normandie*. By February 1, it was hoped, that capacity would be expanded by 18,000, more than half provided by *Normandie*.

In mid-January the United States began sending GIs to Northern Ireland to relieve British divisions for service elsewhere: North Africa, the Middle East and the Far East. The first loads—4,000 GIs—went out on the veteran Army transport *Chateau Thierry* and the British troopship *Straithaird*, formerly a passenger liner. A second convoy, nine vessels carrying a total of 8,555, sailed from New York for Belfast on February 19.

Normandie may have been scheduled to carry the next load, probably including the 37th Ohio Infantry Division, according to Dick Cull, who was part of that outfit. As it was, no further American troops were sent to Northern Ireland until April 30, when eight ships transported some 13,924 men.

Other evidence indicates *Normandie* might have been used elsewhere. After the war General George Marshall, America's Chief of Staff, wrote that the lack of available shipping and assault craft in early 1942 forced the Allies to delay attacking North Africa and to concentrate on preparations for the Normandy invasion that would not take place for more than two years.

But, according to still other evidence, President Roosevelt seriously considered using her to transport troops to the Far East, or so Harry Hopkins informed General Joseph W. Stilwell, commander of the joint American and Chinese forces operating in that theater.

As fate would have it, however, *Normandie* would never carry a single GI to any battle zone.

In the Pacific the war continued to go badly. On Christmas Day, Hong Kong surrendered to the Japanese. On December 29 the Japanese attacked Corregidor Island in Manila Bay. Two days later Manila was evacuated as Japanese troops approached.

But there were bright spots elsewhere. On January 5, with the Nazi armies bogged down in Russia, Stalin ordered his army to go on the offensive. In Libya, British forces handed Rommel's panzer division a resounding defeat—the first British victory over German troops in World War II.

At about this time Frank Costello visited Lucky Luciano in Dannemora Prison to discuss a scheme Albert Anastasia had worked out with his brother, Tough Tony (a major power in the International Longshoremen's Association).

"His idea was to give the Navy a real big hunk of sabotage, something so big that it would scare the shit out of the whole fuckin' Navy," Luciano said later. "Albert figures that if something could happen to the *Normandie*, that would really make everybody crap in their pants.

"It was a great idea and I didn't figure it was really gonna hurt the war effort because the ship was nowhere near ready and besides, no American soldiers or sailors would be involved because they wasn't sending them no place yet.

"So I sent back word to Albert to handle it."

At Pier 88 the *Normandie* conversion continued at a frantic pace. And gradually, unnoticed by Lieutenant Commander Scott and Lieutenant Commander Brooks, the changes began to affect the integrity of *Normandie*'s fire-fighting system.

For instance, on *Normandie*'s bridge both of the fire-alarm switches were disconnected by a contractor who was rearranging bridge controls and instruments. When his work was finished, he forgot to reconnect them.

Then there was *Normandie*'s ship-to-shore fire-alarm box, which linked the bridge to the New York Fire Department. The French Line had leased this line from the American District Telegraph Company, but on January 7 it canceled that arrangement because it was no longer responsible for the ship. When Lieutenant Commander Brooks found out, he posted a notice at the gangway that the nearest city fire-alarm box was on the pier.

It wasn't as though no one cared about *Normandie*'s fire protection. In fact, Captain Simmers, the District Materiel Officer, ordered Walter Kidde & Co. to inventory *Normandie*'s fire-fighting equipment. Walter Kidde discovered that only 50 percent of *Normandie*'s 660 fire extinguishers were in working order, and that only 10 percent met American specifications. Furthermore, the company found, the hose-line and hydrant couplings and valves were of a French gauge and design. They couldn't couple with any American hoses.

Simmers held back on replacing the fire extinguishers, but he ordered Kidde to systematically change the couplings and valves to the American type so that there would always be either a French coupling to fit on a French valve or an American coupling to fit on an American valve.

The District Materiel Officer wasn't too concerned with the switchover because he knew he had a backstop—the two-inch hoses that connected *Normandie* with the hydrants on Pier 88.

What Simmers may not have known is that these were not standard fire hoses with nozzles. They simply connected city water mains to *Normandie*'s pumping system, supplementing the ship's water supply with city water and pressure.

Simmers may also not have known that Robins fire watchers—who stood by during every burning or welding operation—had almost no idea what they were doing. Each had been given a single sheet of instructions and a ten-minute explanation of his duties. None had any fire-fighting experience.

As if what was happening on board *Normandie* wasn't confusing enough, a new element of disorder now made itself felt. It involved just which service should be responsible for the ship.

When conversion began, this was a closed issue. *Normandie* was to be a Navy ship. But the Navy was desperately short of men. With hundreds of new ships coming down the ways, it was hard-pressed to crew them. *Normandie* needed a crew of 1,000 men, maybe more, and she needed them immediately.

Admiral Stark and General Marshall discussed the problem at length. Stark suggested that it might be best to give the Army control of *Normandie*, since it didn't have such a severe manpower shortage and since the ship would be used to transport Army troops anyhow.

Marshall accepted, with the proviso that the Navy finish the conversion job itself, altering specifications to suit the Army's marine engineers and naval architects. Stark agreed.

The switch was made in mid-January. Army technical experts showed up almost immediately. Not surprisingly, they found several flaws in what the Navy had so far accomplished. They demanded, for instance, that non-coms be given quarters that were physically separated from privates. They also required that the four-tier bunks be exchanged for the five-tier variety.

For more than a week almost all of the conversion work was suspended while the Army experts figured out what changes they wanted.

Meanwhile, back in Washington, Stark reconsidered his decision. True, he was short of men, but the more he thought about it, the more he realized that he didn't really want to relinquish control of *Normandie*. She was simply too big a fish to let off the hook that easily.

Toward the end of January, Stark again met with Marshall. The Navy wanted *Normandie* back. In effect, Marshall shrugged and said okay.

Aboard *Normandie*, work ground to a halt again. Almost all of the Army's suggested changes were canceled. And the five-tier standee bunks were removed and replaced by the original four-tier models.

It was now January 26, five days from *Normandie*'s originally scheduled departure date. Obviously, that would not be met.

Admiral Adolphus Andrews, commandant of the Third Naval District, wrote Rear Admiral Alexander van Keuren, chief of the Bureau of Ships, that, because of the dilly-dallying between the Army and the Navy, *Normandie* wouldn't be able to leave New York until February 14. She'd arrive in South Boston for docking and underwater alterations on February 15, depart on February 22, return to New York a day later and be ready to load troops on February 25.

Two conversion items, the ship's side ladders and military-standard fathometer, would not be ready by departure time. Other equipment was doubtful—the degaussing apparatus, the paravans, the evaporation plant. Once more, it seemed, *Normandie* would depart on a maiden voyage with hundreds of workmen still aboard.

While *Normandie* was changing hands, the war in the Pacific was going from bad to worse. The Japanese invaded New Britain, Borneo and the Solomon Islands and managed to force the British out of Malaya. At the same time Japanese bombs began falling on Singapore and Rangoon.

In the European theater the Russians were beginning to make progress. And, closer to home, German U-boats were now attacking ships off the American east coast.

Between January 27 and January 30 the Navy supply depot in Brooklyn began delivering to Pier 88 1,413 bales of Navy-standard life jackets, or Mae Wests. Each thirty-five-pound bale, which was wrapped in waterproof tarpaper and covered with burlap, contained ten life jackets. These consisted of canvas covers stuffed with kapok, an oily, cottonlike vegetable fiber from Java.

The life jackets were delivered to the pier to be stenciled U.S.S. LAFAYETTE before being distributed around the ship. But the pier was jammed with standee bunks, etc., so the bales were brought aboard *Normandie* and neatly stacked in the grand lounge.

Coast Guard Commander Brooks realized that these bundled life preservers presented a fire hazard. He told his men not to smoke in the area (and, in fact, Coast Guardsmen, Navy personnel and civilian workers were prohibited from smoking anywhere on the ship).

Brooks also asked Herman Minikine, the Robins supervisor, if any welding or burning was contemplated in the grand lounge. Minikine assured him no such action was planned.

On January 31 *Normandie*'s prospective commanding officer reported aboard. He was Captain Robert C. "Plug" Coman, a thirty-three-year veteran. His most recent command had been the 624-foot battleship *New Mexico*, a 21-knot vessel of 32,000-tons displacement which had escaped the attack on Pearl Harbor.

The Navy had given *Normandie* to a battleship captain because the *New Mexico*, like *Normandie*, had turbo-electric propulsion. Coman's knowledge of the *New Mexico*, the Navy hoped, would help him run his new command.

When Coman arrived at Pier 88, he was dismayed to learn that less than 500 members of *Normandie*'s prospective crew had arrived, most of them only a few days before.

All in all, the Navy had assigned 1,652 men to *Normandie*, almost 300 more than she'd needed as a passenger liner. These included 653 seamen, 180 artificers (including 125 electricians), 97 yeomen, storekeepers, pharmacists and buglers, 81 commissary people (including 58 cooks), 180 messmen and an engine-room force of 461.

Most of those on board by the end of January were engineering ratings. The Coast Guard detail was attempting to teach them how to run *Normandie* machinery, a task complicated by the fact that the translators hadn't gotten very far with the French labels.

The new crew's unfamiliarity with the ship was a serious problem. Normally, green crews are given weeks—even months—to familiarize themselves with an ordinary ship, not to mention one as large, complicated and different from American standards as *Normandie*. But America was at war and standard practice couldn't always be followed.

The arrival of *Normandie*'s prospective captain on board did not make the chaos vanish and the vessel soon become shipshape. Captain Coman was only *Normandie*'s *prospective* commanding officer. Not until the ship was commissioned would he have any real power. This was strict Navy policy.

During the conversion, it seemed, authority was split between Lieutenant Commander Scott, who represented Captain Simmers, District Materiel Officer of the Third Naval District, and Lieutenant Commander Brooks, commander of the Coast Guard detail.

There was a higher authority, however: Admiral Adolphus Andrews, commandant of the Third Naval District. But, according to Navy regulations, "The commandant shall not direct, nor shall he be responsible for the technical work [being carried on in his district], but will transact the necessary business with the officer [in charge]."

The day after Coman arrived, workers began installing standee bunks in the quarters of the Coast Guard fire brigade on the Main Deck. To make room for them, the fire brigade was moved to temporary quarters below on A Deck.

These temporary quarters had no direct telephone link with the central fire-control station. So members of the fire brigade stood watch at all times at the old quarters to receive messages from the control station and transmit them in person to the fire brigade below.

Commander Scott was told about this, but he didn't think

it was necessary to tell his superior, Captain Simmers, the District Materiel Officer.

Simmers was occupied with another element of *Normandie*'s safety: the danger of capsizing. Several times during the course of conversion Coast Guard engineers had noticed that minor ballast shifts dramatically affected the ship's stability. On one occasion, moving twenty tons of water from port to starboard was enough to relieve a 2-degree list.

During this period *Normandie* usually listed in her slip—slightly. There were two reasons:

1. The tons of bunks, supplies and other material being brought aboard her were stowed without regard to the effect on her trim;
2. There had been a huge, uneven silt build-up on the slip's bottom.

Back in the early 1930s, when Pier 88 was built, the bottom was dredged out to a depth of 46 feet below mean low water—average low tide. When fully loaded, *Normandie* drew 34 feet at her bow and 37 feet at her stern. A bottom 46 feet deep provided sufficient clearance, as long as the depth was maintained by occasional dredging. But dredging had been impossible ever since *Normandie* had been idled in New York in August 1939. The silt and mud had slowly built up, inch by inch, until the bottom was only 34 feet down, maximum, at mean low tide (37 feet at high tide). That meant, quite simply, that *Normandie* was completely grounded at low tide and partially grounded at high tide. By itself, that wasn't dangerous—although the silt would have to be cleared away before *Normandie* could pull out of her slip. Because this silt had built up unevenly, it contributed to *Normandie*'s slight list at low tide.

Simmers' office was in downtown Manhattan and he spent little time aboard *Normandie*, but, aware of this problem, he ordered Scott and Brooks to keep *Normandie* in trim and to reduce her tendency to list by keeping her ballast and fuel tanks topped off at all times.

His orders would have kept the ship as "bottom heavy" and as stable as possible. Unfortunately, they were not followed.

Washington was also concerned with *Normandie*'s stability, especially at sea. Apparently, Secretary of the Navy Knox was worried about the potential effect on American morale if *Normandie*, fully loaded with servicemen, were lost at sea.

And so, on February 1, a high-level decision was made to remove a large part of *Normandie*'s superstructure, including practically everything above the Promenade Deck: the Deauville and Trouville Suites, the tennis courts, the dog promenade and most of the large major public rooms—the café grill, the first-class smoking room, the grand lounge, etc.

This meant slicing off some 24,000 pounds of structural steel and decorative plaster. It also meant that *Normandie*'s profile and character would be permanently and catastrophically altered. Whatever happened to her after the war, she would no longer be the beautiful, graceful Art Deco palace of prewar days. Navy officials estimated it would take a month or two to do the job.

For some reason the Navy Department didn't tell anyone in New York about this important decision. As a result, work continued at a frantic pace, in some cases on the very decks that were now scheduled for removal.

On *Normandie*, Coman realized there was just no way that this enormous ship could be ready to sail by February 14, just two weeks away. Two thirds of her crew hadn't arrived. The conversion was still incomplete. The new engineering staff had yet to put her machinery through a trial run.

On February 5 Captain Coman visited Captain Simmers and asked for a delay of at least two weeks. Simmers was sympathetic, but he didn't have the power to postpone the sailing date. So he took Coman to see his commanding officer, Admiral Andrews.

Andrews told the two junior officers that, while he was inclined to agree with their arguments, he couldn't do anything either. "Call Admiral Stark in Washington," he suggested. "If you can convince the Chief of Naval Operations, you'll get your delay."

Simmers called and got Stark's assistant, who flatly refused to allow the delay, not knowing that the superstructure removal had been approved and would delay sailing even beyond Simmers' request. Simmers and Coman then got Andrews' permission to go to Washington to state their case.

The next day Coman and Simmers took a train to Washington and managed to get an audience with Admiral Stark and Bureau of Ships chief Admiral van Keuren. Now they finally learned about the decision to remove *Normandie's* superstructure. They were delighted and relieved to realize they'd gotten the delay they wanted.

As soon as the meeting broke up, Simmers called Herman Minikine, the Robins supervisor of the *Normandie* job, and told him to lay off all Robins employees working in the affected areas of the ship. Minikine immediately dismissed 1,000 workers.

Late that afternoon Simmers and Coman returned to New York.

And later that day President Roosevelt heard about the plan to remove *Normandie's* top decks and postpone her sailing. His reaction was immediate: He would brook no delay.

Stark argued with FDR, but the best he could do was to get the President to agree that the superstructure would be removed as soon as the ship could be taken out of transport service for a couple of months.

Late Friday evening, February 6, Stark phoned Simmers at home and told him of Roosevelt's decision. Frustrated and angry, Simmers called Minikine and told him they'd have to meet the original schedule, so he'd better get his men back to work. Minikine and the Robins office made hundreds of telephone calls and sent out hundreds of telegrams recalling Robins' workers.

Simmers next called Coman to tell him the bad news. But Coman wouldn't take no for an answer, even though it had come from the President himself. He finally persuaded Simmers that they should try once more. The two officers made an appointment with Admiral Andrews for Monday, February 9, at 3:00 p.m. They hoped he would accompany them to Washington to persuade Admiral Stark to see Roosevelt and state their case once more.

With that, Coman returned to *Normandie*, his mind buzzing with what he'd say to Andrews. He wandered through the giant ship, trying to imagine the moment—exactly one week away—when he would guide *Normandie* out of her slip and take her to Boston.

Coman walked into the grand lounge, where the bales of life preservers had been stacked. As an officers' lounge it was now a far cry from the spectacular room in which first-class passengers had listened every afternoon to *un orchestre symphonique de 6 musiciens*, danced every evening to a ten-piece band and often come to snack, play cards or just talk.

There were still some decorative elements in the room, however—the four eight-foot lighting standards. These had once been covered with fluted glass, but this glass was now in storage. Only four naked steel structures remained.

Coman imagined the room overflowing with as many as 800 Army officers. He thought about the ship rolling and pitching in heavy seas. In that situation, he realized, these steel structures could be a hazard. He decided to have them cut down to their twenty-inch-high bases, which could be used as seats.

The prospective captain didn't himself have the authority to order this work done. So that afternoon he cornered Lieutenant Commander Scott, the immediate supervisor of the conversion work, and suggested the idea. He also proposed laying Navy-grade linoleum in the room. Scott agreed to both ideas.

The next day, February 8, the linoleum-layers showed up at the ship: several employees of the Tri-Boro Carpet Company under the supervision of Edward J. Sullivan, a former alderman from Greenwich Village.

While laying the linoleum over the original parquet floor, Sullivan and his men had to shift the bales of life jackets again and again. By the time they finished, the life jackets were scattered all over the grand lounge.

That night, according to Barbara Smith, her cousin Larry Trick—a workman on *Normandie*—had dinner at her home. He was extremely upset by the "who cares?" attitude of his supervisors. Trick had told them that the welders' oxygen tanks were improperly stored and often left open when not in use. His supervisors shrugged and told him to stop bothering them.

Joseph Curiale, one of the workmen who'd helped to strip *Normandie* of her marblework, was also disturbed. He'd noticed that the passageways and Main Deck had been covered by a wooden flooring, supported by two-by-fours laid down along the length of the vessel. He and his brother Anthony, who worked with him, thought that the floor and the two-by-fours formed "wind chutes" nearly 1,000 feet long. If fire broke out on the ship, he thought, these structures would quickly carry it from one end of the vessel to the other.

The next morning, Monday, February 9, Captain Coman and Captain Simmers once more called Washington. This time they talked at length to Captain N. L. Rawlings, one of Admiral Stark's chief assistants. He said he agreed with them, but that the President had spoken.

They had one last opportunity to win the delay they thought so important. It would come that afternoon at 3:00 when they met with Admiral Andrews, commandant of the Third Naval District, in his Manhattan office at 90 Church Street.

Unknown to Simmers and Coman, Admiral van Keuren, chief of the Bureau of Ships, had also become convinced that a delay was vital. He called Admiral Stark and made an appointment to see him at about the same time Coman and Simmers were talking with Admiral Andrews.

While all these people were considering delaying *Normandie*'s departure, momentous events were taking place elsewhere.

In Norway the Nazi puppet Vidkun Quisling took office as Minister President. In the Malay Peninsula the Japanese began to tighten their stranglehold on Singapore.

In the United States, troops were being trained by the hundreds of thousands. The biggest problem was transporting them to the battle zones where they were needed most.

The United States needed the troopship it called *Lafayette*, and it needed her as soon as humanly possible.

17

fate decides

At 6:58 a.m., February 9, 1942, the sun rose on a typical winter day in New York—clear, crisp and breezy, the temperature ranging between 24° and 31° F., the winds averaging about twenty-five miles an hour.

All over the city, thousands of workers ate their breakfasts, kissed their wives goodbye and headed toward the huge passenger ship at the foot of 48th Street in Manhattan to continue transforming her into a weapon of war.

Frank Trentacosta was such a worker. A tall, strong, gentle man with a fine sense of humor, Trentacosta was thirty-six. He and Gemma, his wife of less than two years, lived in Brooklyn.

Trentacosta, a licensed physiotherapist with several private patients, was also the trainer of the St. Francis College basketball team. Gemma worked to supplement their income, but she'd been hoping to quit so they could have a family.

She'd gotten her wish. A few weeks earlier her brother, Albert de Marco, a driver for some high officials at Todd Shipyards—parent company of Robins Dry Dock—had managed to get his brother-in-law a job on the *Normandie* as a fire watcher at the princely weekly salary of $80. As a result Gemma was planning to give notice at her job at local #89 of the International Ladies Garment Workers' Union.

Frank hadn't told Gemma much about his new job, but what he'd told her she didn't like. The ship was a disorganized mess, he'd said. Many workers didn't seem to have any idea what they were doing. A lot of them spent most of their time loafing. "Is it dangerous?" Gemma had asked more than once. "Nah, not really," he'd told her. She'd remained apprehensive.

About 7:30 on the morning of February 9, Trentacosta finished his breakfast, put on his coat and headed for work.

At the ship the night shift was coming off and the day shift was taking its place. These included:

- ☐ 1,759 Robins employees, including Frank Trentacosta and 49 other fire watchers, under Robins Vice President Herman Minikine and his assistant, Robert Krause;
- ☐ 675 employees working for some 35 different subcontractors, each of whom controlled his own men;
- ☐ 456 prospective Navy crew members, including Captain Robert Coman; Commander F. M. Adams, the prospective damage-control officer; Lieutenant Commander Clay McLaughlin, the prospective fire-security officer; and Commander Philip Lohmann, the prospective engineering officer;
- ☐ 282 Coast Guard officers and men, commanded by Lieutenant Commander Earl Brooks, including Lieutenant John German, who was serving as chief engineer, Boatswain Oliver Rahle, who was in charge of the fire watch, and Morris Bach, Rahle's assistant;
- ☐ 10 representatives of the District Materiel Officer of the Third Naval District, who were supervising the conversion. These men were commanded by Lieutenant Commander Lester G. Scott and they included Lieutenant Henry Wood and Lieutenant Commander McCloskey.

All told, there were 3,182 people aboard *Normandie*, more than at any other time in her history. (The greatest number who'd ever sailed on her was 3,176, in the summer of 1937, 1,831 passengers plus a crew of 1,345.)

As usual, Pier 88 was the scene of frantic activity. Barges pushed through the thin Hudson River ice and nosed up to open cargo ports on *Normandie*'s port side to deliver stores and supplies. High up on the ship, painters suspended from the ship's funnels covered her civilian colors with camouflage paint. Below them, welders closed *Normandie*'s portholes with steel blanks.

Inside the ship, workers continued the complicated installation of the water-distilling plant, in the space formerly occupied by *Normandie*'s swimming pool. In the bowels of the ship Navy engineers had emptied the double-bottom fuel tanks and the water ballast tanks that extended up the sides of the ship—contrary to Captain Simmers' orders—and were cleaning them. The tanks' manhole covers were stacked on one side of the main engine room.

Other Navy engineers, having uncoupled *Normandie*'s propellers, were testing her machinery. Elsewhere, workers were walking from fire hose to fire hose, removing the snap-on French couplings and fitting screw swivel couplings of the standard American variety.

Meanwhile, thirty-two members of the prospective Navy crew, having been assigned to fire-patrol duty two days before, were meeting with the Coast Guard fire brigade, dividing up the watch and learning what was expected of them.

In his office, formerly occupied by one of *Normandie*'s chief engineers, Commander Philip Lohmann, prospective chief engineering officer of the Navy crew, was on the telephone with Standard Oil, ordering 26,000 barrels of fuel oil, enough to top off *Normandie*'s practically dry fuel tanks.

Lieutenant Henry Wood, one of Scott's assistant naval inspectors, was talking with Herman Minikine, supervisor of all the Robins workers. He asked him to see that the four lighting stanchions in the grand lounge were cut down. Minikine agreed.

Minikine summoned his welding supervisor, Alphonsus Gately, and told him about the job. At that moment Gately was overseeing more than 110 welders working on eighty different jobs around the ship, most of them crucial, top-priority tasks. The stanchion job was nothing more than a nuisance, but it had to be done.

After checking out the lounge work scene, Gately headed down to the swimming pool on D Deck, where a group of welders was working on the water-distilling plant, to find someone to do the cutting. He chose Clement Derrick, a Wall Street clerk turned welder.

Together, the two men went back to survey the work scene. There were five objects to be cut down: a small steel structure behind the bandstand and four stanchions 15 feet high and about

15 inches in diameter, resting on a base that was about 20 inches from the deck. Ventilating ducts were concealed in the base of each stanchion. The burning was to be done at the top of the base.

In *Normandie*'s days of glory this base had been the foundation for a circle of red, tapestry-covered seats and the tower had been covered with fluted Lalique glass lighted from within. Now only the naked steel remained—about 500 pounds of it.

Each of the four main stanchions was a short distance from one of the room's four corners. Since they play such an important role in the story that follows, let's give them reference numbers. The stanchion at the forward starboard corner will be called #1, the stanchion at the aft starboard corner will be called #2, the stanchion at the forward port side will be called #3 and the stanchion at the aft port side will be designated #4.

Elias Nadel, the supervisor of Robins' fire watchers, soon joined Gately and Derrick in the lounge. Together, they assembled a "chain gang"—a work crew consisting of nine men in addition to Derrick: Fred McGraw and John Venuto, fire watchers; Melvin Title, Charles Collins, Anthony Zagami and John Panuzzo, ironworkers; Martin Collins, clean-up man; Leroy Rose, helper, and another helper named Pristora.

Together, Gately and Derrick figured out how to remove the heavy stanchions. Using his acetylene torch, Derrick would cut through two of the three steel members supporting the stanchion tower, at a point just above the base. Then, holding three guide ropes, the chain gang would slowly ease down the stanchion tower, preventing it from crashing into the floor, until it rested at a 90-degree angle. Derrick would burn through the last steel member, and the tower, now severed from the base, would be lowered to the deck for removal.

Meanwhile, Nadel reviewed fire-safety procedures with fire watchers McGraw and Venuto. He told them to start by wetting down the area around the base of the stanchion with a few cups of water to prevent sparks from igniting the parquet floor.

Once the burning operations began, Nadel said, one fire watcher should place a semi-circular metal shield around the stanchion base to prevent sparks and drops of molten metal from splattering the area. The other should hold an asbestos board above the metal shield as a further precaution against ricochet-ing sparks. Two three-gallon buckets of water were to be kept within reach at all times, in case of fire.

A fire extinguisher and a hose connected to a standpipe and ready for immediate use were also supposed to be present, but on this occasion these items were forgotten. As it happened, there *was* a fire hose in the grand lounge—buried under the bales of life preservers that had been stored there ever since the end of January.

Gately and Derrick sent Rose to tell the "bottle gang" to bring a tank of acetylene and a tank of oxygen to the lounge. Gately walked out onto the Promenade Deck beside the lounge and grabbed a piece of scrap sheet metal for Derrick to use as a spark shield.

While the welding crew was preparing to cut down the stan-chions, other workers were busy in the grand lounge, rolling up carpeting, tearing up wooden parquet flooring and laying Navy-grade linoleum.

At the same time four linoleum workers were unrolling lin-oleum and glueing it to the deck. To make sure it didn't crack as it was being unrolled, the room temperature had been raised to about 75°. Most of the men were working in their shirt-sleeves.

The workers were but part of what filled the lounge. Piled there were the 1,413 burlap-wrapped bales of kapok life jackets, some practically touching the lighting stanchions on the port side of the room. Near the port stanchions lay several rolls of carpet and linoleum, two five-gallon cans of linoleum cement, several upholstered chairs and some piles of ripped-up parquet flooring. A grand piano stood at the forward end of the room.

Just outside the lounge, 2,250 canvas-bottomed bunks were stacked on the Promenade Deck, waiting to be distributed to various parts of the ship.

At about 10:30 Derrick and his crew began to cut down stanchion #1. They finished a little after 11:00, then started on stanchion #2. At about 11:20 a spark from Derrick's torch fell on a little piece of paper, which caught fire. Leroy Rose, the helper, stamped it out with his foot.

A few minutes later Lieutenant Commander Scott strolled

through the lounge, glanced at the linoleum work, took a look at the welders and walked on.

Just before noon stanchion #2 came down and the men went to lunch. They expected to be back by 1:00 p.m. Soon afterward Nadel told fire watchers McGraw and Venuto, who'd been at work since 7:00 a.m., to knock off until 2:00 p.m. Then Nadel himself went up to the Boat Deck.

There, he asked Minikine's assistant, Robert Krause, to send a couple of fire watchers down to the lounge to work with Derrick's crew from 1:00 p.m. till 2:00 p.m., when McGraw and Venuto would return.

Krause looked around the Boat Deck, where *Normandie*'s lifeboat davits were being removed, and found two extra fire watchers—John Fennelly and William Salomone. A bit confused, he told them to go to the "main dining room" on the Promenade Deck and watch the burning operation there until McGraw and Venuto got back.

Fennelly and Salomone couldn't find the "main dining room" on the Promenade Deck (no surprise, since the dining room was actually on C Deck, four decks below). Since they didn't see anyone with an acetylene torch in any of the Promenade Deck rooms, they thought Krause had made some kind of mistake. They decided to go to lunch.

Some of the chain gang went in Jack Panuzzo's car to a French restaurant on 48th Street, near Sixth Avenue, where some of *Normandie*'s old crew hung out. "How's our baby?" they asked Panuzzo and his friends. "You fixing our baby up nice?"

Derrick returned just before 1:00 p.m. and went immediately to the small stanchion near the bandstand and did his best to remove it; because of the way it was fixed to the floor, however, he couldn't really finish the job.

By then the rest of the chain gang had returned, taken off their coats and begun moving life-jacket bales away from stanchion #3, on the port side of the room, forward. By piling up some of the bales, they'd cleared an area large enough to walk around in.

A few minutes after 1:00 Boatswain Oliver Rahle, the Coast Guard security officer, walked through the lounge. He saw nothing out of the ordinary and walked on.

Now Derrick brought his acetylene torch over to stanchion #3 and started to work, cutting through the steel members while the chain gang held up the stanchion with their ropes. The metal shield at the stanchion base partly protected the floor from the droplets of molten metal. Charles Collins held the asbestos sheet above the metal shield to help contain the sparks.

Derrick cut through two of the three steel members connecting the stanchion tower to its base and the chain gang began to lower it toward the deck. It was nearly there when a rope slipped and the tower suddenly fell. It crushed the metal spark shield, but did no other damage.

Gately, who was supervising the job, went back out onto the Promenade Deck and found another piece of sheet metal to use as a spark shield. He bent it slightly so it could stand alone. Meanwhile, Derrick's crew began clearing the life-jacket bales away from stanchion #4, on the port side of the room, aft. It was about 2:00 p.m.

About then Captain Coman walked through the lounge. He noticed Alderman Sullivan and his linoleum workers, but he didn't see the welding crew, which by that time was almost entirely surrounded by life jackets. Coman's mind was on his upcoming meeting with Rear Admiral Andrews, now about an hour away.

Moments later fire watchers McGraw and Venuto returned from their prolonged lunch hour and sauntered into the lounge. But, like Coman, they didn't see Derrick and his crew. They went back to the swimming pool to resume the duties from which they'd been taken earlier that day.

Just about that time, two sailors wandered into the lounge, sat down at the piano and started to play.

Shortly after 2:00 Derrick turned on his acetylene torch once more and began to cut through the steel members of stanchion #4. There were no fire watchers in attendance. Nonetheless, Derrick made sure that the metal shield was in place, Collins held the asbestos board above it and Leroy Rose wet down the stanchion's base, taking a little water from the two nearly full buckets nearby.

Leaning against some bales of life preservers, Derrick burned through the first leg of the stanchion tower, then the second.

His crew slowly lowered the structure toward the deck until its tip rested on a roll of carpeting.

At that moment Lieutenant Henry Wood walked into the lounge, on his way to another part of the ship. He glanced over at stanchion #4, where Derrick was igniting his torch for the final cutting operation. "Well, boys," said Wood, "down with the old apple tree." Then he proceeded on his way.

Meanwhile, on A Deck, Captain Coman ran into Commander Adams, his prospective damage-control officer, and Ensign Hemby, who was talking to Adams. Coman asked the men to direct him to the C Deck gangway, where his chauffeur was waiting for him. Adams pointed out the way.

A few moments later Coman got into the waiting car. It was now a few minutes after 2:30. "Take me to the Third Naval District Headquarters at 90 Church Street," he told his driver.

Up in the lounge Derrick ignited his torch once more and began cutting through the last "clip" of metal connecting the stanchion tower to its base. His crew stood by, holding the ropes, waiting to lower the tower to the deck, most of them perched on piles of life-preserver bales.

It was during the final seconds of the job that Charles Collins, an eighteen-year-old Brooklyn boy, the youngest member of the chain gang, noticed a small flame darting upward from one of the bales nearest the base of the stanchion, the bale closest to Derrick's torch. "Fire!" he shouted. "Fire!" It was about 2:37.

Before the words were out of Collins' mouth, the flames had swept across the fuzzy surface of several nearby burlap-covered life-jacket bales, fed by warm air coming out of the ventilating ducts at the stanchion's base. All the men in the chain gang leaped down from their perches and started beating at the fire with coats, sweaters, pieces of carpet, asbestos boards—even their bare hands. Derrick shut off his torch and joined the effort. The carpenters and linoleum workers hurried over to help.

Meanwhile, the flames raced from bale to bale, "like fire in dry grass," one of the men later said. The burlap fuzz needed no heating up. The merest touch of flame set it instantly ablaze.

Leroy Rose finally remembered the two buckets of water that were standing by for just such an emergency. He ran toward them and promptly tripped over one of them, spilling it. Cursing, Rose picked up the other bucket and looked around to see where the water would do the most good. A man was standing between Rose and the main body of the fire, his legs spread, beating away at the flames with a jacket. Rose flung the water between the man's legs. He succeeded mainly in getting his colleague's trousers wet.

Then one of the chain-gang members moved to fling away from the fire the life-jacket bales that hadn't already burst into flame. Several bales were thrown clear of the blaze this way, but one, given only a weak toss, broke open at the very heart of the fire, sending burning life jackets tumbling into practically every part of the room.

Seeing that the fire was getting ahead of them, Gately and a helper pulled out the hose that had been buried under the bales, connected it to a standpipe on the port promenade, and began playing it on the fire. The nozzle emitted only a thin dribble of water.

Other workers brought out a hose from the starboard promenade. It disgorged a bucketful of water, then ran dry. Still others brought a hose through the smoking room, forward of the lounge. But it had a French fitting and every standpipe they could locate had already been converted to American-type fittings.

A sailor found a fire extinguisher in a nearby fire cabinet and brought it in, but couldn't figure out how to get it working. Eventually he threw it onto the deck in disgust.

By this time Lieutenant Wood, having heard the commotion, had run back into the lounge and begun shouting out a series of orders. "Don't be a God-damned fool," Alderman Sullivan told him. "You can't put this out. Hell, get the New York Fire Department!"

After directing Coman to the C Deck gangway, Commander Adams and Ensign Hemby had proceeded up two flights of stairs to the Promenade Deck, then headed aft toward the engineers' quarters. They entered the lounge through a starboard door and were amazed to find it burning furiously.

"Go back down forward to A Deck and give the alarm," Adams told Hemby. Then Adams himself started looking for fire extinguishers and for a fire-alarm box.

About this time a member of the Coast Guard fire watch, a young and inexperienced recruit, heard the Robins employees in the lounge yelling "Fire, fire!" He went to *Normandie*'s theater nearby, picked up a telephone, called the ship's central fire station and told the man who answered—a Coast Guardsman named Martin—that there was a fire in the grand lounge.

Martin tried, unsuccessfully, to contact his immediate superior, Morris Bach, the assistant Coast Guard security officer. Instead, he sent a messenger to the fire-brigade headquarters to tell them to go to the fire.

Then Martin called *Normandie*'s bridge and asked the Coast Guardsman who answered to turn in the alarm. A few moments later the Coast Guardsman called back. "Where is the alarm switch?" he asked. "I can't find it." It was now about 2:42. The fire had been burning for nearly five minutes.

Lieutenant Commander Scott was in his office when a Robins employee burst in on him. "There's a fire in the grand lounge," he told the naval inspector. "A bad one?" Scott asked. "I think it's out of control," the Robins worker said. Scott dashed out of his office to see the situation for himself.

In the meantime Ensign Hemby, following Adams' order, ran through the ship, alerting everyone he saw. Lieutenant Commander McCloskey, one of Scott's three assistants, ran down to D Deck to turn off the ventilator blowers. Then he hurried up to the lounge to turn off the power to prevent short circuits and electrical fires.

Lieutenant John German, the Coast Guard's chief engineer, reacted to the fire news by heading for the engine room. When he got there, he turned on the fire pumps and ordered the water pressure raised from 60 to 120 pounds per square inch.

By this time everything in the lounge was afire. Flames and thick, acrid smoke filled most of the room. Fortunately, someone had thought to close the doors at both ends of the grand lounge—at least as much as the assorted debris, linoleum rolls and carpeting would permit. Both sets of doors were intended to be fireproof, so there was at least a chance that they'd confine the fire to the immediate vicinity.

When Scott saw the fire, he ordered one of his men to sound the city fire alarm from the dock. He then found Herman Minikine and ordered him to get all of the workmen off the ship.

On the way to Minikine, Scott ran into Lieutenant Commander Brooks, who raced up to the lounge and tried to take charge of his men, but was driven back by the dense smoke.

Oliver Rahle, the Coast Guard security officer, also arrived at the lounge at about this time. Seeing the flames, he ran all the way to the bridge. He didn't remember or didn't know that the general fire alarm had been disconnected, so he threw the switch, intending to sound a warning throughout the ship. Nothing happened. He tried again and again to sound the alarm. Still nothing.

Seething with frustration, Rahle ran to the main fire locker on the Main Deck and started handing out fire extinguishers to anyone who would take one. At that moment Rahle's assistant, Morris Bach, came by, and Rahle put Bach in charge of distributing extinguishers. Rahle then dashed to a gangway and yelled to a policeman on the pier to turn in the city fire alarm.

Back in the lounge the doors between it and the smoking room burned through and the fire swept aft, through the smoking room, toward the café grill. The doors between the lounge and the great hallway, however, held.

On the pier a policeman noticed a sailor shouting at him from a gangway. "There's a fire on the ship!" the sailor cried. "Could you turn in the alarm?"

"I'll do it," the policeman replied. He ran to the private fire-alarm box located at the center of the pier and pulled the handle. At almost exactly the same moment Seaman Curran, a Coast Guardsman, called the New York Fire Department from a telephone in the CGT offices on Pier 88 and reported the fire.

It was now 2:49 in the afternoon. The fire had been ablaze for about twelve minutes.

The moment the New York Fire Department got the alarm, four engine companies—two trucks and two hook-and-ladder units—one fireboat and two battalion chiefs headed for the ship.

Commander Scott now gathered some men and led them out onto the pier to clear away piles of lumber, scaffolding and other obstacles so the fire trucks could get close to the ship.

At 2:51 the first fire trucks arrived, their bells clanging, firemen hopping off the vehicles even before they'd come to a complete stop, playing out their hoses and connecting them to standpipes on 12th Avenue.

"Where's the fire?" one of the battalion chiefs asked Scott.

"Come on," the naval inspector told him, "I'll take you to it."

The firemen followed Scott aboard *Normandie*, dragging their hoses with them.

At about the same time someone finally thought to call the headquarters of the Third Naval District and tell Rear Admiral Andrews about the fire. Andrews was waiting for Captain Coman and Captain Simmers.

"How bad is it?" he asked the caller.

"I'd say it's out of control."

"What happened? What started it? Was it sabotage?"

"No one knows for sure, sir. It may have been sabotage, it may have been a welding accident."

"I'll be there in a few minutes," Andrews said. He asked his assistant to inform Admiral Stark in Washington. Then he rushed out of the building and told his driver to take him to Pier 88. It would be the very first time he had seen *Normandie* close up.

Andrews had been in charge of the Third Naval District for less than a year. A close friend of Mrs. Cornelius Vanderbilt and the Duchesse de Talleyrand, he was known as a "social admiral." As Drew Pearson put it, "Admiral Andrews is famous in Washington for his beautifully tailored clothes and for having served as an aide to Teddy Roosevelt, to President Harding, to Calvin Coolidge and as commander of the Presidential yacht *Mayflower*."

A tall, slow-speaking man, Andrews had had absolutely nothing whatever to do with *Normandie*. While he was Captain Simmers' superior, Simmers actually took his orders from the Bureau of Ships in Washington and had never even discussed the ship with Andrews.

On the other hand, *Normandie was* under the jurisdiction of the Third Naval District and, as such, she was Andrews' responsibility—especially if something went wrong, which is why he'd dropped everything to go to the scene.

While Andrews was heading toward Pier 88, Herman Minikine was on the bridge speaking through the same loudspeaker system that had once ordered "all visitors ashore."

"Everybody off the ship," Minikine announced. "There's a

fire on the ship and we want everyone off. Walk, do not run, to the nearest gangway."

It is possible that this announcement saved lives, since on a ship the size of *Normandie* many workers hadn't had the faintest idea that anything was wrong. But it is a certainty that the announcement bred confusion. Everybody aboard—including the fire-patrol teams—thought it applied to them. For that reason many of the very men needed to fight the fire now began to disembark.

There was mass confusion. The thousands of civilian workers, Coast Guardsmen and members of the prospective crew surged across the very gangways by which the firemen were boarding. It was instant gridlock.

Elsewhere on the ship, in the quarters of the prospective Navy crew, Minikine's announcement caused near-panic. Some seventy-five sailors were sound asleep at the time, all except for a young master-at-arms who was more or less standing guard. When he heard the announcement, he immediately began waking his fellow sailors and telling them to leave the ship. By this time smoke had begun wafting into the room. Some of the men— most were little more than boys—started yelling and running around, thoroughly frightened. But they eventually calmed down and, holding each other's hands, stumbled through the smoke, up the stairways and over the gangways to safety.

At about 2:55 the first city fireboat arrived. It was the *James Duane*. She'd chugged upriver from her 35th Street berth in six minutes flat. Her nozzles began spraying *Normandie*'s port side with water even before she'd pulled up to her, even before the land-based engine companies could begin pumping.

At 90 Church Street, Captain Coman picked up Captain Simmers and they headed for Admiral Andrews' office, determined to convince their superior to join them in the campaign to delay *Normandie*'s departure. They were flabbergasted to learn he'd just hurried out of the building to a serious fire aboard *Normandie*. They went after him in Coman's car.

On *Normandie* the fire was totally out of control. It ignited the beautiful lacquered wooden paneling in the smoking room, then ran up the grand stairway to the café grill. At the same time its heat broke the huge windows of the grand lounge, giving the flames access to the 2,250 canvas-bottomed bunks stored on the Promenade Deck, port, starboard and forward.

Before the fire the engine room had been busy and crowded. Robins employees, Coast Guardsmen and members of the prospective Navy crew had been cleaning the fuel and ballast tanks, testing the motors and running the boilers, dynamos and auxiliary motors.

Then Minikine's voice boomed out over the loudspeakers, instructing that "everybody get off the ship." Elsewhere in the vessel, workers just dropped whatever they were doing and ran to the nearest gangways.

In the engine rooms, however, departure wasn't so simple. The boilers, dynamos and motors were alive and operating, providing power for the ship's lights, heating plant, pumps, automatic watertight doors, etc. This equipment couldn't simply be abandoned and left running but had to be carefully closed down. Otherwise, it would destroy itself.

As soon as the Robins employees heard Minikine's announcement, they turned off some of the auxiliary equipment and began to leave the ship. But they left the boilers burning, making sure the Coast Guard was attending to them. By then some of the fire's acrid smoke had been drawn down into *Normandie's* engine rooms through the boiler uptakes.

Commander Philip Lohmann, the prospective Navy engineering officer, and Lieutenant John German, the chief Coast Guard engineering officer, both got to the Engine Deck a couple of minutes before 3:00. They were joined by Lieutenant Commander McCloskey, one of the assistant naval inspectors.

With the Robins employees hurrying off the ship and smoke beginning to billow into the engine rooms, Lohmann, German and McCloskey felt they had no choice but to order the fires banked and the motors shut down. They gave the order, thinking the fire would be under control shortly and that they'd return to the engine rooms and get everything running again.

There was steam enough in the boilers to keep *Normandie's* generators and pumps running for fifteen to twenty minutes. After that, everything would come to a stop and the ship would go dark.

By now a thick plume of dense black smoke was pouring out of the ship and drifting over Manhattan, driven by a twenty-five-mph northwest wind. Starkly visible on this clear, cold Monday afternoon in February, the smoke began to attract the attention of the millions who lived and worked in New York City.

In Washington the Chief of Naval Operations, Admiral Stark, got a telephone call from Admiral Andrews' office in New York telling him about the *Normandie* fire. Stark canceled his meeting with Admiral van Keuren. The question of delay was now moot.

At about 3:00 the canvas-bottomed bunks on the Promenade Deck ignited. The fire swept forward through the officers' quarters, roaring over the tennis courts, the dogs' promenade, the shooting gallery, the solarium, the radio room, the captain's quarters and the bridge. Heated by the flames, Derrick's oxygen tank exploded. A few minutes later a couple of oxygen tanks stored on the Boat Deck did likewise.

The land fire companies were having a very difficult time rigging their hoses, which had to be stretched for long distances from the street, the pier or the fireboats, At the gangways the firemen had to struggle through the exiting Robins workers to get onto *Normandie* and then had to grope through the unfamiliar ship to the scene of the fire.

The fireboats had no such problems. This is why more water—thousands of gallons more water—was poured onto *Normandie*'s port side than onto her starboard or pier side, at least at the beginning of the fire. Already resting on the bottom of the silt-filled slip, the *Normandie* began to list away from the pier, slightly but perceptibly.

Flames now covered most of the ship's Promenade Deck and were quickly spreading upward to the Boat Deck and the Sun Deck. The battalion chief realized that if the fire weren't put out quickly, it could easily spread to the pier, then down the entire Manhattan waterfront. He told a fireman to sound a second alarm.

The fireman dashed back through the ship, back over the pier, to the city alarm box 852 at 48th and 12th and, at 3:01, banged out a second alarm—2–2–852, as it was received by the

Fire Department. Four more engine companies, another fire-boat, a rescue company, a water tower and a deputy chief began to move to the fire.

At 3:02, on the battalion chief's instructions, another fireman hit the box again and the Fire Department got a third alarm—3–3–852. Five additional companies, a third fireboat, a hook-and-ladder company, another battalion chief and Assistant Chief John McCarthy responded.

Meanwhile, engine companies all over the borough of Manhattan relocated, on the alert, so the rest of Manhattan Island would be protected.

About this time Admiral Andrews arrived at Pier 88. What he saw confirmed his worst fears. *Normandie*'s entire superstructure seemed to be ablaze. The pier was in a state of total confusion. It appeared that no one was in command.

Immediately after Andrews arrived, a police car pulled up to the pier, its siren screaming. Out hopped New York City Police Commissioner Lewis Valentine, Chief Inspector Louis Costuma and Deputy Chief Inspector John Conway. Coast Guard Captain John Baylis, the man who'd led the first Coast Guard detail aboard *Normandie*, arrived shortly afterward.

These officials were almost immediately followed by four more fire engines, tires squealing and bells clanging, plus a rescue truck, a water tower and Fire Marshal Thomas Brophy—all summoned by the second alarm.

Elsewhere in Manhattan the few *Normandie* officers who'd remained in America heard about the disaster and rushed to the scene to help in any way they could. These included Captain Hervé Le Huede and Second Captain Raymond Agnieray.

Fiorello La Guardia, the Mayor of New York City and its most famous fire buff, was giving a radio speech, assuring his constituents there would be no increase in the subway fare. But when someone passed him a note about the fire, he cut short his speech and headed for Pier 88.

Hundreds of less exalted New Yorkers, attracted by the enormous clouds of smoke and the clanging fire engines, were also making their way to the fire scene.

The fuss was escalating. Five more fire engines and another hook-and-ladder (responding to the third alarm) came screech-

ing up to the pierhead, their sirens and bells multiplying the cacophony. Accompanying them was Assistant New York Fire Chief
John McCarthy.

The scene inside the huge vessel was at least as confused as
the scene in and around the pier, as hundreds of civilian employees, Coast Guardsmen and Navy personnel, all half blinded
from the smoke, felt their way through the ship's unfamiliar
corridors, each clutching the belt of the man in front of him.

"I looked out a porthole to see what was happening," remembered Arnold Christofferson, a civilian worker on board.
"Two fellows were on the pier. They hollered, 'The ship's burning.' I smiled. I thought it was sort of a gag. Then one of the
men on the pier crosses his heart and I see he isn't kidding." To
escape, Christofferson had to fight fire, smoke and terrific heat
through *Normandie*'s maze of corridors. At several points he was
almost overcome by the dense smoke. "How I got out, I don't
know."

As the *Normandie* workers came off the ship, coughing, their
faces blackened by smoke, some of them singed, they were taken
to the temporary command post inside Pier 88, in the CGT offices, and questioned by Admiral Andrews, Police Commissioner Valentine and two recent arrivals on the scene, P. E.
Foxworth, the FBI agent in charge of the New York office, and
District Attorney Frank Hogan.

"When did you first hear about the fire?" they asked. "Did
you see it start? How did it start? Who was involved? What efforts were made to put it out? Did you see anyone with gasoline
or anything else inflammable? Were there any strangers in your
work area? Did you see anyone doing anything suspicious?"

What everyone feared, what everyone strongly suspected, was
sabotage. Most of the officials on the scene knew of Germany's
interest in *Normandie* and how important she was to America's
war effort. Several feared *they* might be blamed for the disaster.

Within a few minutes Gately, Derrick, most of the chain
gang that had been working on the stanchions and many of the
linoleum layers and carpenters who'd been working in the grand
lounge when the fire broke out were being questioned at the
command post. All of them told a similar story.

Those who hadn't been near the fire scene were questioned

briefly, then sent on their way. Many of them gathered at neighborhood bars to talk about the fire or call relatives.

Not all of those coming down *Normandie*'s gangways could be questioned, however. Scores had been burned or overcome by smoke. Some were dazed, their wet clothing frozen to their skin. Some, unconscious, were carried off the ship by their companions and taken to the shore end of the pier, where a first-aid room had been set up.

At Bellevue the hospital gong sounded its dreaded seven strokes: The city had been struck by a catastrophe. Soon ambulances were on their way to Pier 88, not only from Bellevue but also from New York Hospital, Roosevelt Hospital, French Hospital, Metropolitan Hospital, the Naval Hospital at the New York Navy Yard, St. Vincent's Hospital and Lenox Hill Hospital. There were twenty-four ambulances in all, manned by seventy-five doctors and eighty-five nurses and orderlies.

Eventually, Pier 92, the American home of the *Queen Mary* and the *Queen Elizabeth*, was converted into an emergency hospital. Many of the less seriously injured, including those who were suffering only from the effects of smoke inhalation, were led or driven here, covered with blankets and put to bed on cots delivered by the Red Cross.

Red-eyed doctors and nurses, crying from the acrid smoke, treated for exposure the more than fifty men who'd jumped from the ship into the icy Hudson River. They gave artificial respiration to those suffering from smoke inhalation and bandaged those who'd been burned, sending the more seriously injured to various city hospitals by ambulance.

At the fire scene the sound of wailing ambulance sirens was now added to the bells and sirens of the fire engines. The dense smoke, the milling, disorganized crowd, the miles of fire lines stretched out along the street, the freezing spray from the hoses, and the noise combined to create a nightmarish spectacle.

Ambulance after ambulance drove over the tangled fire-hose lines to the pierhead, picked up an injured worker and drove off, to the shouts of policemen trying to clear a way through other workers and spectators.

Assistant Chief John McCarthy, the highest-ranking Fire Department official on the scene, now banged out a fourth alarm:

4–4–852. This one triggered a response from five more engine companies, another hook-and-ladder and New York City Fire Commissioner Patrick Walsh himself. It was 3:12. The fire had been raging for about thirty-five minutes.

At this point the fireboat *John J. Harvey* chugged into *Normandie's* slip, having come up the Hudson from her berth at Bloomfield Street. She took up a position amidships on *Normandie's* port side and began deluging the ship with water.

These streams of water were a welcome addition to the overall fire-fighting effort, but they increased the imbalance between water being pumped onto *Normandie's* port side—the water side— and water going aboard her starboard side, which was flush against the pier. In the contest between the fireboats and the fire engines, the fireboats were ahead and pulling away.

Inside the ship, one of the men from Derrick's crew was fast becoming a hero. He was Jack Panuzzo, an ironworker. Along with the others in the grand lounge, he'd done his best to fight the fire. As it roared out of control, however, he ran to the Deauville Suite on the Sun Deck, where he knew some of the civilian employees were goofing off, sleeping. He awakened them and sent them scurrying off the ship.

Then Panuzzo returned to the lounge, just in time to see Charles Collins collapse from smoke inhalation. He carried the young man off the ship on his back, then re-entered the inferno.

"I went back three times," he later recalled. "Each time I found somebody—Roy, Chick, Jim. When I got there the fourth time, the fire had reached the boys. I beat out the fire in Sandy's clothes and I dragged him out."

On his fifth trip into the burning *Normandie*, Panuzzo was himself overcome by smoke. He was unconscious when Joe Reardon, another ironworker, tripped over him, picked him up and carried him out to the pier. He was taken to Polyclinic Hospital, treated and ordered home. Instead, he went back to the pier and made four more trips into the ship, bringing out another sailor or worker each time.

Panuzzo's wife, who was shopping in Macy's when she heard the ship was burning, immediately took the subway home and, like hundreds of other wives that day, hung over the radio and repeatedly phoned the Robins office and the Navy. "I won't ever believe the radio again," she said later. "They kept announcing 'Flash! Hundreds of workmen trapped inside the ship! It's a furnace. All are lost!' I couldn't find out a thing from anyone I phoned. I never knew whether Jack was burned up or what till he walked in at eleven o'clock that night."

By 3:15 the fire had pretty much gutted *Normandie's* super-structure, her top three decks. The great public rooms that had made her famous were destroyed, all except the theater, which was miraculously untouched.

At about this time the ship's generators used up the last of the steam and whined to a halt. Throughout the vessel the lights flickered, then went off, leaving everyone still on the ship, fire-men included, in total darkness. The elevators also ground to a halt. The clocks stopped, as did the pumps that were providing water pressure for the fire hoses.

The power failure also shut down *Normandie's* Horowitz-type drainage system. This was a plumbing network used to carry off all of the ship's excess water: water from soil drains, toilets, bathtubs and showers, even the water from the waves that broke against the ship at sea during storms.

The Horowitz system was a modernized replacement for, among other things, the old-fashioned scuppers. Unlike scup-pers, though, it functioned on air pressure supplied by the ship's auxiliary boilers.

At 3:15 these boilers ran out of steam. And the Horowitz system, which had been trying to dispose of the thousands of gallons of water being sprayed onto the ship by the fireboats in the slip and the fire engines on the pier, suddenly ceased work-ing.

At the moment the lights went out, John Pyle, an electri-cian, was working with a colleague "in the ship's foremost com-partment, at the lowest possible level, right over a sea valve." They knew nothing whatever of the fire.

"Suddenly, the lights went out," Pyle recalled. "Shipyard employees had been told that if the lights ever went out, they were to stay where they were.

"We kept calling up to attract someone's attention. After about maybe fifteen minutes, someone called from above, 'Anybody down there?' and we answered in the affirmative. A voice told us that we should get out of there and leave the ship. We managed to clamber up and found our way to the Main Deck by way of many detours. It was then that we first saw the smoke and learned that there was a fire aboard," Pyle recalled.

On the pier *Normandie* workers were still pouring down the gangways, three of which exited to the lower level of the pier, three to the middle level.

More than 200 men were unable to reach any one of these gangways, however. They were trapped on *Normandie*'s whaleback, near her bow, the fire cutting them off from the rest of the ship. To rescue them, firemen raised two eighty-five-foot ladders, their lower ends resting on the pier side of 12th Avenue, their tops leaning against the tip of Vladimir Yourkevitch's famous prow. The workers who'd been trapped on the forepeak slowly descended these ladders. Some, those who'd been badly burned or overcome by smoke, were carried down by their colleagues.

At the same time five police emergency squads, about 100 men in all, ranged through the inner darkness of the ship, flashlights in hand, searching for the hundreds of men rumored to be trapped below. They didn't find hundreds, but they did locate several dozen, many overcome by smoke. These were laboriously carried to the deck, lowered to the pier and taken to hospitals by ambulance.

Around 3:20 two railroad fire tugs pulled into the *Normandie* slip and turned their nozzles on her port side, adding their streams to those of the *James Duane* and the *John J. Harvey*.

By now the enormous quantity of water coming from the fireboats was beginning to have an effect. *Normandie*'s list to port had increased noticeably. As she slowly tilted, *Normandie*'s gangways were pulled away from the pier, inch by inch, until they finally swung loose and crashed against her slablike black hull, nearly dumping a number of firemen into the water.

The gangways were soon refastened to the dock, but the accident alerted everyone to *Normandie*'s list. At that point Scott checked her mooring lines. They'd been slackly strung that morning. They were now as tight as piano wires.

Normandie's list was still slight, but just as a precaution Scott had a few more hawsers strung, wrapping them around the huge steel bollards which were set, like enormous molars, in Pier 88's cement floor.

By now crowds of curiosity seekers were flocking to 12th Avenue, straining the police's ability to keep them off the pier. Commissioner Valentine called for reinforcements.

One group of spectators had come to help, not to gawk. These were former *Normandie* crew members, common seamen who'd come to the scene from the Hotel Bristol, on West 48th Street, where they lived. They were not able to get through police lines.

Among those who did manage to get through were Graham McNamee, the famous NBC announcer, and Clay Morgan, the French Line publicity man who'd done more than anyone else to make *Normandie* a household word. He was now an assistant to NBC's president.

McNamee and his crew set up a microphone right at the head of the pier and the honey-voiced announcer began broadcasting the story to all of America, interrupting afternoon soap operas to describe the tragedy in a manner reminiscent of the famous Hindenburg disaster broadcast.

Overhead, Navy and Coast Guard planes circled the great burning vessel, making a photographic record of the catastrophe. Below, five more clanging fire engines and a hook-and-ladder unit arrived at the scene, accompanied by New York's highest-ranking fireman, Fire Commissioner Patrick Walsh.

Three other high officials reached the pier almost immediately afterward: Mayor Fiorello La Guardia, wearing his familiar corduroy-collared black raincoat and black homburg; Captain Robert Coman, prospective master of the giant ship; and Captain Clayton Simmers, the District Materiel Officer of the Third Naval District and the man nominally in charge of *Normandie's* conversion to a troopship.

Simmers and Coman peered through the smoke, looked at the ship, then at the fireboats next to her. Four fireboats, each with several nozzles, were now drenching *Normandie* with great torrents of water. But, high up on the ship, only a few small streams of water dribbled over the sills of the Promenade windows and fell back into the slip.

Simmers, who had closely studied *Normandie*'s stability characteristics, was worried about the effect of all that heavy, free-flowing water so high up in the ship. He recalled two other ship fires—the *Europa* fire of the late 1920s, when that great liner had been saved from capsizing only by scuttling her at her pier, and the *Paris* fire of 1937, which had ended with that beautiful ship lying on her side in the harbor, a worthless wreck. Was *Normandie* now threatened with a similar fate?

The two men joined the other high officials in the command post. Their only problem: No one felt entitled to take overall responsibility. To be sure, Commissioner Walsh considered himself in charge of fighting the fire. And Commissioner Valentine felt he was responsible for maintaining law and order. But no one seemed to want responsibility for *Normandie*. Everyone on the scene, from Admiral Andrews down to the lowest civilian, was intensely interested in avoiding any possible blame for what had happened.

Nonetheless, one man courageously decided to take command of the situation, even though he was hardly the highest-ranking officer present. And during the next ten hours he made a determined, imaginative, even heroic effort to save the ship.

He was Captain Clayton M. Simmers, the DMO—District Materiel Officer—of the Third Naval District. While overseeing the conversion, he'd studied *Normandie*'s plans and blueprints exhaustively. As of February 9, 1942, no one else in America, not even *Normandie*'s former master, Hervé Le Huede, knew as much about the ship as he did.

Simmers wasn't terribly concerned about the fire. With all of the water the fire engines and the fireboats were pouring into *Normandie*, he knew she couldn't keep burning much longer. Furthermore, he knew the fire damage, however widespread it might be, was essentially superficial. After all, *Normandie* was made of steel. So long as the ship's engine spaces were untouched either by fire or by the water used to put it out, she could be quickly restored and refitted. In fact, the fire might very well turn out to be a blessing in disguise, because it would permit more extensive alterations to the ship, better fitting her to troop-transport duty, because her superstructure would now be removed, giving her greater stability, and because Coman's crew would now have a chance to thoroughly master her operation.

What did worry Simmers was *Normandie*'s list. He managed to convince the other officers that this was a very serious matter. At about 3:25, forty-five minutes or so after the fire had started, they began to concentrate on the problem.

Simmers expressed surprise that the ship was listing despite the water ballast and fuel in her double-bottom tanks, which should have counterbalanced the water trapped above. Commander Philip Lohmann told him that both sets of tanks had been emptied for cleaning.

Annoyed that his orders had been disobeyed, Simmers ordered the tanks filled immediately, using fire hoses. But Fire Commissioner Walsh pointed out that the tanks were too deep within the ship. The hoses wouldn't reach.

Lieutenant John German, the Coast Guard's chief engineer aboard *Normandie*, then told Simmers that the tank manhole covers had been removed. That meant that the tanks on what was now the high side of the ship couldn't be topped off.

Simmers suggested putting the manhole covers back on, but German said that the thick smoke made that impossible.

Simmers then asked Fire Commissioner Walsh to have holes cut in the Promenade bulkheads with acetylene torches to let out the trapped water. Walsh went off to see that the job was done.

Then Simmers had another thought. He asked the group if there were any open cargo doors or portholes on the port side. If there were, *Normandie* could ship water through them, further increasing her list.

Boatswain Oliver Rahle, the Coast Guard security officer on *Normandie*, said he'd seen one open port forward on D Deck. He left the room to get someone to close it.

Admiral Andrews, remembering the *Europa* fire, raised the question of scuttling *Normandie*.

Lieutenant German said that this could be done, but it required going into the bowels of the ship to open the sea cocks or remove the condenser plates. Unfortunately, the dense smoke made that impossible.

Captain Le Huede pointed out that *Normandie* had twenty-nine sea cocks. These had to be opened simultaneously by a trained crew. He said that he doubted the Coast Guard or Navy could have done the job even if there had been no smoke.

Andrews asked about pulling the condenser plates, which would have the same effect. This was heavy work, but it required no special training. Lieutenant German said he'd gather some men and give it a try, despite the smoke.

At 3:27 the third city fireboat pulled into *Normandie's* slip. She was William Francis Gibbs' famous and powerful *Fire Fighter*. She'd steamed up from her Battery Park berth at nearly 20 knots.

With her two sixteen-cylinder diesel engines pumping, each developing 1,500 horsepower, and her nine separate water turrets, she began to deluge *Normandie* with almost as much water as the other two city fireboats combined.

There were now five fireboats in *Normandie's* slip—the three city fireboats and two private fire tugs. Together, they were turning the ship's portside upper rooms and cabins into reservoirs. As a result, *Normandie's* list slowly increased to 8 degrees.

At the same time a team of firemen climbed over the edge of the Promenade Deck, high up on the port side of the ship. Hanging by ropes, they lit up their acetylene torches and started burning holes as low on the Promenade Deck bulwarks as they could.

After a few minutes one torch broke through the steel plating. First a trickle, then a torrent of water poured through the hole. It put out the torch. The same scene was repeated at two other locations. The attempt to release the water trapped high up on *Normandie's* decks had failed. One of the firemen told Commissioner Walsh what had happened, and Walsh slowly walked back to the command post to inform the others.

Deep inside the ship, Fire Chief George Geller, Assistant Commissioner McCarthy's righthand man, inspected the lower decks, looking for fire or water damage. He was accompanied by a single aide, who carried a two-way radio for communication with Fire Department headquarters on shore.

Together, the two men groped through the dark, smoky and

unfamiliar maze of the ship, lighting their way with flashlights. Then, somehow, they got separated. The more Geller searched for his aide, the more lost he became. "I thought I was a goner," Geller recalled. "There was a hell of a lot of smoke. I got to the water side to signal the fireboats, but they were hitting me with their water streams—freezing water—and they didn't see me. I even stuck out my white helmet, but they didn't see it." Eventually Geller found his way to the upper decks and to safety, but he realized something had to be done to improve communication between the ship and the pier.

Normally, shouted orders would have done the job. But *Normandie* towered several stories above the pier level. Besides, the noise was terrific. Firemen were finding it hard to make themselves heard by colleagues standing right next to them, much less several hundred feet away.

For that reason Geller arranged for two Navy semaphore men to relay messages between the fire fighters on the ship and their commanders on the pier. One stood on the ship's forepeak, the other on the pier. Until night fell, these two sailors served as a link between the ship and the shore.

While Geller was struggling in the darkness to get back to *Normandie*'s upper decks, a number of Robins employees were still evacuating the ship. Among them was Frank Trentacosta, Gemma's husband. He was working with George Deighan, another member of Robins' fire watch.

"We were up forward on D Deck when we were ordered to go to the top deck aft," Deighan later recalled. "It was all smoke. I was going down a ladder, with Trentacosta behind me, when there was an explosion. There wasn't much flame, but there was a terrific concussion. I think it was one of the feeder tanks for the torches. Trentacosta was blasted right off the ladder and he fell past me to the deck below. I clambered down the ladder, picked him up and carried him off the ship, unconscious."

At the pierhead Trentacosta was given last rites and then loaded into an ambulance. In a ghastly coincidence, the driver was Trentacosta's brother-in-law, Albert de Marco—the very man who'd gotten him the job on *Normandie*. De Marco, tears in his eyes, rushed his brother-in-law to Roosevelt Hospital, where he was immediately taken to the intensive-care ward.

At the command post Captain Simmers was working on other ways to shift weight from *Normandie*'s port side to her starboard side, to reduce the list in any possible way. He asked about the port wing tanks, under the portholes. Brooks told him that at least seven were empty.

Simmers suggested using the ballast pumping system to fill them. Brooks went out to the ship to get the job done.

He'd hardly left the room when Walsh returned with the news of his failure to cut holes in the bulwarks.

For a few moments Simmers and Walsh argued about shutting down the fire tugs. Simmers wanted them stopped so no more water would accumulate in *Normandie*'s upper decks. Walsh refused, saying his job was to put out the fire and make sure it didn't spread to the rest of the waterfront. He agreed to reconsider the idea later when the fire was under better control.

At this time Lieutenant German returned from the ship, coughing, his face blackened from the smoke. He and his men had been unable to get through the heavy smoke to the condenser plates.

It was now about 3:30. *Normandie*'s top three decks were burning briskly. The fire had reached its peak. At this moment two more private fire tugs chugged into the slip and started spraying. There were now seven fireboats deluging the ship from her port side with more than a dozen streams of water.

Lieutenant Commander Brooks now returned to the command post with more bad news. He'd been unable to shift the ballast because the ship's power was out.

Simmers thought a moment, then suggested that fire hoses be used to flood the starboard wing tanks, pulling *Normandie* back toward an even keel. The fill holes for these tanks were much higher than those in the ship's double bottom and there was at least a chance the hoses would reach.

Commissioner Walsh agreed to give the idea a try, although Admiral Andrews feared that if the wing tanks were suddenly filled, *Normandie* might flop over in the opposite direction and crash against the pier. Simmers mollified him by telling Walsh to have the tanks filled slowly.

By this time the entire area surrounding Pier 88 had turned into one vast, macabre carnival.

□   Thirty-five fire engines of all descriptions, and their crews. All of their hoses were spread out along 12th Avenue like hundreds of snakes, pulsing and writhing with water being pumped from the hydrants;

□   Dozens of police cars, vans and horses, plus the emergency squads, the traffic-control squads, the precinct detectives, the patrolmen and the mounted policemen they brought;

□   Dozens of FBI agents, men from the District Attorney's office, Naval Intelligence agents, etc.;

□   Dozens of ambulances, plus doctors, nurses and other medical aides;

□   More than 10,000 patriots, fire buffs, sightseers and waterfront derelicts, all braving the cold, the wind and the smoke, pushing forward into 12th Avenue between 45th and 50th Streets, cheering, yelling and screaming as firemen brought survivors out of the fire or succeeded in putting out part of the blaze;

□   200 helmeted black soldiers called out to contain the crowds, each one of them equipped with a loaded rifle, its bayonet fixed;

□   Hundreds of air-raid wardens, fire wardens and auxiliary fire fighters, who, excited by radio news of the blaze, had donned their white armbands and demanded passage through the fire lines, where they stumbled over hose lines, crowded onto the pier, gaped, took pictures in areas forbidden to news photographers and prevented many of those who had good reason to be there from reaching their assigned posts;

□   Dozens of newspaper reporters and photographers, all of them complaining about the endless number of times they were forced to show their credentials to anyone and everyone with any kind of badge. One reporter claimed that he counted at least twenty different types of badge, some tin, some enamel, some goldplated, most of them carried by people with no authority at all;

□   Hundreds of civilian disaster volunteers, including Red Cross workers, Salvation Army volunteers and ninety members of the American Women's Voluntary Services. Before the day was over, they dispensed 10,000 doughnuts, 8,000 sandwiches, 10,000 cups of coffee, 1,000 pairs of wool socks, 5,000 blankets, 1,000 sweaters and untold numbers of cigarette packs;

□   Dozens of hot-dog and ice-cream vendors, their carts pushed as close to the fire lines as possible, doing a land-office business not only among those who had reason to be on the scene but also among hungry onlookers;

☐   Hundreds of Coast Guardsmen, Navy personnel and Robins Dry Dock employees who'd escaped from the fire and smoke on *Normandie*.

Add to all of this the noise and smoke, and the result was almost total confusion. In all, about 15,000 people crowded around Pier 88 to watch the fire. But it is likely that almost everyone in the New York metropolitan area witnessed the spectacular blaze.

Tens of thousands of spectators watched from the skyscrapers and office buildings of Manhattan. Among them was a passenger on *Normandie*'s last voyage, Sir John Wheeler-Bennett, assistant to William Stevenson of British Intelligence—the man later known as "Intrepid." Wheeler-Bennett saw the fire from 30 Rockefeller Plaza.

Thousands more watched from the New Jersey shore. Hudson Boulevard East, which ran along the top of the Palisades, was jammed with cars from Weehawken to a point three miles north. There were so many people with cameras and binoculars on the shore itself, especially near West New York and Weehawken, that Weehawken Police Chief Edward Kirk had to assign nine policemen to keep order.

Millions more residents of Manhattan, Queens and Nassau County experienced the event indirectly, through the sight and smell of the acrid black smoke that slowly drifted eastward over Long Island, over a distance of twenty-five miles. Radio announcers interrupted afternoon soap operas, cooking hints and children's stories with bulletins about the catastrophe.

At about 3:40 Mayor La Guardia, Admiral Andrews and Captain Baylis decided to board *Normandie* to see how the fire fighters were doing. They were crossing a gangway when the ship suddenly lurched several feet to port. They leaped aboard the ship, barely managing to avoid being dumped into the water.

Even before this latest lurch *Normandie*'s hawsers had been stretched as tight as piano wires. Now, as she fell farther away from the pier, her list increasing to 12 degrees, the hawsers tugged loose the steel bollards by which the giant vessel was secured to the concrete pier.

Unknown to any of the men in the temporary command post, water began pouring into *Normandie* through several openings on her port side—a garbage chute, two open cargo doors and a few portholes that hadn't been permanently blanked out.

High up on the port side, firemen lowered the last of *Normandie*'s lifeboats. It was filled with exhausted firemen, a few Robins workers and a sailor. The moment it touched the water, it was taken in tow and pulled to the pierhead.

In the command post Simmers now heard more bad news. The Fire Department hoses could not reach the starboard wing-tank fill holes. The problem was the length of hose needed inside the ship to snake down her corridors and down several flights of stairs.

By now Simmers was extremely concerned. He asked Baylis to order tugboats into the slip to push against *Normandie*'s port side, hoping they could hold her while he found another way to attack the problem.

Now Hervé Le Huede, *Normandie*'s former master, suggested that flooding the forward hold would at least get the bow down firmly into the silt. He said that the fire hoses would have no trouble reaching the hatch, since it was on deck. Simmers okayed the idea and asked Commissioner Walsh to see to it.

At this point Lieutenant Commander Brooks spoke up. He told the group that a number of mooring lines had snapped and suggested that new ones be strung.

Baylis was doubtful. He was worried that the pier might be pulled apart by *Normandie*'s mooring lines if she continued to list.

Simmers decided the mooring lines were needed, but he ordered that half be strung taut and half be given some slack. He also ordered that men be stationed beside the taut lines with axes, to cut them if pier damage seemed imminent. Brooks took on the job.

Baylis also raised another point. High tide would hit at 4:49. *Normandie* would be pretty much afloat then. Would she right herself? Or, stripped of the silt's support, would she topple over? There was just no way to know.

Now Captain Le Huede again raised the issue of shutting down the fireboats and the water hoses. The water, not the fire, was killing the ship, he said.

But Commissioner Walsh pointed out that *Normandie* was only listing 12 degrees, not a very dangerous list. As soon as the fire was out, he said, he'd shut down the water. Mayor La Guardia agreed, saying he simply couldn't let a mid-Manhattan fire burn out of control.

That ended the argument.

And while this discussion was taking place, two more private fire tugs appeared in *Normandie's* slip and began spraying her port side with even more water.

In the command room, the persistent and determined Commander, Simmers returned to the subject of draining the excess water from *Normandie's* upper decks. He asked Scott about opening the portholes, but Scott reminded him that most had been covered with steel blanks.

Once more Simmers brought up the scuttling idea. Once more Lieutenant German volunteered to give it a try.

Near the ship the smoke was so thick that it was impossible to see the gangways leading into the vessel. High up on *Normandie's* funnels, great blisters began to form in the camouflage designs so recently painted onto them. After a while they opened and began to peel, once more revealing *Normandie's* bright red-and-black civilian colors.

To some of those standing on 12th Avenue it was a horror movie, complete with extraordinary and inexplicable special effects, an event that would be remembered and related to their grandchildren.

To others it was a vicious, self-inflicted blow at America's capacity to prosecute the war against Hitler and Tojo.

To still others the fire was an impossible and unexpected tragedy. After all, this was no ordinary ship, no freighter, no minor warship, no nameless, characterless lump of steel and wood. This was *Normandie*, perhaps the greatest ocean liner of all time, one of humanity's stunning technological achievements, one of France's greatest artistic triumphs.

This was the *Normandie* of Cole Porter, Marlene Dietrich and Ernest Hemingway, the *Normandie* of vacationing movie stars and escaping Jews, the *Normandie* of the Abraham Lincoln Brigade, the *Normandie* of a Russian emigrant named Vladimir Yourkevitch, of a master seaman named René Pugnet, of a dreamer and doer named Pierre de Malglaive, the *Normandie*

of Emile-Jacques Ruhlmann, the first 1,000-foot ship, the first
to cross the Atlantic at better than 30 knots. She had lived a life
unequaled in glamour and majesty, and now she was dying.

At this moment one of *Normandie*'s chief creators, Vladimir Yourkevitch, was sitting at his desk in his New York office
in lower Manhattan, unaware of the disaster that had befallen
his beloved ship. Then the phone rang. An old friend from Russia
was calling. "Vladimir Ivanovitch, your *Normandie* is burning!"
his friend cried out, speaking in Russian.

For a few moments Yourkevitch could not understand what
his friend was saying.

"Your *Normandie* is burning," the man repeated. "I am
watching it from my office window. The smoke is coming out
thick and black."

Yourkevitch didn't know what to think. He knew all about
Normandie's superb fire-fighting system. He also knew about the
vigilance with which her fire brigade patrolled. The fire must have
stopped by now, he told himself. It just couldn't be serious.

He sat down to work again. But he couldn't work. He kept
visualizing his ship ablaze. Finally, at about 3:45 he rushed out
of his office and took a taxi to Pier 88.

Several blocks from the pier the taxi bogged down in traffic
and Yourkevitch got out, half walking, half running toward the
ship. Even before he caught a glimpse of *Normandie*, the noise,
the smoke and the crowds told him that his ship was involved
in a catastrophe of major proportions.

Coming around the corner of 48th and 12th, he saw her,
listing, smoking, draped with fire hoses. He knew she was in
terrible danger.

Three times Yourkevitch tried to get through the police lines,
trying to explain his special knowledge in heavily accented English. Three times policemen turned him back. Then he spotted
a Navy officer and tried again.

"The Navy is in charge," he was told. "Don't you worry about
it. We know what to do."

Unable to get the attention of anyone in authority, Your-
kevitch simply gazed at *Normandie*, his eyes filling with tears.
Finally, he left, unable to bear the sight that confronted him.
He went home to his apartment at 317 West 99th Street on the

corner of Riverside Drive. From his window he could see his ship dying.

Gemma Trentacosta was working at local #89 of the ILGWU on West 40th Street. She'd heard the sirens and fire engines, but hadn't thought much about them, since that kind of noise was common in New York. Then she found out *Normandie* was burning. She got her boss's permission to see what was happening. "I decided to go to a nearby police station," Mrs. Trentacosta later recalled. "An officer there informed me in a very kindly way that Frank had been taken to Roosevelt Hospital. He gave me no details about his condition. I hailed a cab and went there."

At 4:00 a fifteen-year-old Chicago boy named Ellis Bell got home from school. "Your *Normandie* is burning out of control," his mother told him. The boy was horrified. Ever since he was very small, ever since he'd seen films of her maiden voyage, he'd loved the great French ocean liner. A travel agent had sent him all of the ship's brochures and they'd become his most treasured possessions. Now his love was going up in smoke.

Ellis listened tensely to the radio news. When he heard that she was listing 12 degrees, he couldn't contain himself. "That's too much," he said aloud. "Scuttle her! She's already on the ground. She won't even look sunk!"

"So far," the radio announcer said, "the experts are working on ways to rid the ship of all the water that seems to be accumulating in her portside staterooms. Once that's done, she should be safe."

Bell was practically apoplectic. "Blow holes in the top decks and dump the water out quick!" he shouted at the radio. "They've got gunboats. Let them use the gunboat! Blow open the decks now, before it's too late."

It was a good idea. Appropriately placed explosive charges—or even some well-aimed cannon fire—would have accomplished what the Fire Department had been unable to achieve with its cutting torches. But even the resourceful Commander Simmers, cool-headed though he surely was, perhaps because he apparently never considered this idea, thought the ship could be saved by less drastic means.

At 4:01 flood tide hit the Hudson—the moment of maximum water flow toward the Atlantic, a current of 1.5 knots. If anything, this current helped *Normandie* because it, along with several tugs, pushed against the ship's port side. But soon it would slacken, stop, then begin running in the opposite direction.

Lieutenant German, his face blackened by soot, returned to the command post. Once more he and his men had failed to get to the condenser plates. The smoke had even penetrated their gas masks.

Normandie was now listing at 13 degrees.

Simmers again asked Walsh to shut down the water. Maybe in an hour, he was told.

Simmers' thoughts returned to the empty starboard wing tanks. If they could only be filled, they would counterbalance the water on the portside upper decks. The fire hoses couldn't reach the fill holes inside the ship, but perhaps holes could be cut in the hull and the tanks filled from the outside. He suggested the idea to the group, which enthusiastically approved.

Simmers, Le Huede and Agnieray made a sketch of the starboard wing-tank locations, there being no exact plans available. When they finished, Simmers called in Herman Minikine, the Robins vice president and supervisor of the *Normandie* job, showed him the tank locations and asked him to cut five four-inch-square holes in the ship's shell plating. Minikine went off to gather a crew and do the job.

Moments later a Coast Guard ensign entered the command post and delivered some startling and disturbing news. There were several open doors on *Normandie*'s port side.

The high officials were livid. They'd been told there was only one open door and that it would be closed. Baylis, Brooks and Scott decided to take a dinghy out into the slip to survey the ship, despite the freezing cold, the icy spray from the fireboats and the brisk winds.

By this time there were thirty-six fire trucks on the scene, from as far north as 102nd Street and as far south as Spring Street. All of this apparatus, plus the city fireboats, plus the private fire tugs (there were six of them on the scene by now) was inundating *Normandie* with at least forty-five streams of water.

Out in the slip Baylis, Scott and Brooks found one open cargo port on E Deck aft. It was already partially submerged. Another open cargo port on D Deck was still above water. There was also an open air port amidships and an open manhole directly under stack number one, neither one submerged—yet.

The three men rowed back to the pierhead, where they were met by Lieutenant German. German organized two working parties. He sent one to the receiving ship *Seattle*, which was docked nearby at Pier 92, to get wooden plugs and high-top rubber boots. He led the other party into the ship, carrying bagging to plug the leaks.

German's men closed the air port, the manhole and the D Deck cargo port without much trouble. They also found an open galley chute and closed it off as best they could. The partially submerged cargo port on E Deck was another story, however. Not only was water rushing in, but the strongback braces were gummed up with paint.

After a titanic struggle, half a dozen men shoving against the door simultaneously, they managed to close it most of the way and brace it fairly well. But in an unsuccessful effort to put the strongbacks in place Lieutenant German broke his thumb. He played no further part in the day's events.

At the same time Minikine's men managed to cut five holes in the starboard shell plating. Minikine told Simmers the tanks could be filled any time. Walsh said he'd see to it.

Hoses were now fed into the holes. Unfortunately, no one had known the tanks' exact position, so the holes were cut well below the tank tops. Also, two holes were cut in one tank—so only four of the five tanks were actually cut open and those four only partially filled.

However, the water pumped into these empty tanks did partly counterbalance the water trapped in *Normandie*'s portside staterooms and public areas, actually reducing the list a bit, to about 11 degrees.

For a few minutes the men in the command post thought the worst might be over. Then someone remembered the tides.

At 4:49 *Normandie* was afloat once more. For a few minutes the list remained at 11 degrees. There were cautious smiles in the command post. Then, at about 5:00 the giant ship heeled farther away from the pier, snapping the already taut hawsers, taking up the slack of the others. When her movement stopped, she was listing at 15 degrees.

At Simmers' urging, Admiral Andrews approached Commissioner Walsh and once again asked that the fireboats be shut down. This time Walsh agreed. He sent for Fire Chief Geller and told him to signal the fireboats. "I think we can hold her now," Walsh told La Guardia.

A few minutes later Geller gave the signal, then went about his business. On the other side of the ship Simmers and his colleagues thought the fireboats were shutting down. But the fireboats either missed the signal or ignored it. They continued to deluge the vessel as before.

High up on *Normandie*'s main mast, the crow's nest, which had been baking in the flames for more than two hours, now began to smolder, then smoke, then burn. The little platform burned itself out just as the sun set, at about 5:23. Shortly afterward Walsh announced that the main fire was "under control."

As darkness fell and suppertime approached, the crowds around Pier 88 began to thin. A Fire Department searchlight truck arrived, its huge beams throwing an eerie light on the ship.

Back in the command post, Red Cross workers brought in sandwiches for all the high officers. Simmers now summoned Lieutenant Commander McCloskey, who'd been one of his assistants during the conversion, and asked him to somehow get that last wing tank filled. McCloskey succeeded, but filling the tank had little effect on *Normandie*'s list.

At about 6:15 someone noticed that the fireboats were continuing to pump water into *Normandie* despite Walsh's orders. Fire Chief George Geller tried to get their attention, but without any luck. Semaphore signals were sent, but in the darkness they went unnoticed.

Finally, Mayor La Guardia got on the radiotelephone. "This is the Mayor," he said. "And I am giving all the city fireboats a direct order. Cease pumping as of this moment. I repeat: Cease pumping immediately. This is Mayor La Guardia and I am speaking for myself and Fire Commissioner Walsh."

One by one, the fireboats began to shut down. Recently, Chief Geller offered a possible explanation as to why they'd kept pumping: So long as they were on duty, the fireboat crew got extra pay. The moment they shut down, their pay scale dropped.

So greed played a role in *Normandie*'s fate, as well as misfortune.

La Guardia's radio message shut down the city fireboats, but the private fire tugs were not on the same radiotelephone circuit. They continued to pump for nearly a half-hour more, every gallon increasing the threat to the ship.

The gauges of the three city fireboats showed that they had pumped about 3,506 tons of water onto the ship. The private fire tugs probably pumped twice that much, for a total of about 10,000 tons from the water side. The land-based fire engines added another 6,000 tons, for a grand total of 16,000 tons—or 32 million pounds, or 4 million gallons.

Most of this water sloshed over to *Normandie*'s port side, where it was trapped inside the ship. Observers estimated that less than 10 percent of the water ever found its way off the vessel. No ship ever built, before or since, could have remained upright in those circumstances.

At 6:30 Commissioner Walsh pronounced the fire "under control." The firemen began the cold, laborious job of coiling up miles of half-frozen hose.

Normandie's list was holding at 15 degrees. Andrews sent his aide, Lieutenant Ernest Lee Jahncke, Jr., into the ship to see if she'd sustained any serious fire damage or water damage to her boilers, generators or motors. Jahncke returned with the news that the engine room was in fine shape and "dry as a bone."

Andrews and Walsh congratulated themselves. The fire was out. The ship was holding at a 15-degree list. It looked as though *Normandie* would be carrying troops after all, although her maiden voyage would be delayed for a few months.

But Simmers, a more experienced and deeper-thinking man, was worried about low tide, when the ship would hit bottom again. He didn't know if the silt would hold her.

Then another thought occurred to him: Why not beach *Normandie* on the Jersey shore? He voiced his idea, only to be told that her propeller linkage had been disconnected.

At Roosevelt Hospital a Paulist priest met Gemma Trentacosta outside of Frank's room. He did his best to prepare her for tragedy. In his fall Trentacosta had fractured his skull, broken a number of ribs and suffered several internal injuries. He was dying.

The priest then took Gemma to her husband's room, where he lay unconscious. She kissed him, told him how much she loved him and begged him to live. He did not respond. He died at 7:10.

Until now all published sources have reported that he was the only fatality in the *Normandie* disaster. Actually, another man died as a result of injuries received during the fire: Larry Trick. But his death did not take place until several days after the event.

At 8:20 Admiral Andrews held a brief news conference. "*Normandie* has been saved by the splendid and heroic efforts of the New York Fire Department," he said.

The crowd was drifting away from the scene. The ambulances had long since ceased making shuttle trips between Pier 88 and the various city hospitals. The Red Cross, the Salvation Army and the American Women's Volunteer Service began packing up. Most of the fire engines pulled out. The West Side Highway was reopened.

At around 8:30, with the list still holding at 15 degrees, Simmers, still thinking, came up with a new idea. Perhaps pumps could rid *Normandie* of the water on her upper decks.

But where could he get pumps at 8:30 in the evening? He mentioned the problem to one of the fire marshals, who told him that the Fire Department could supply as many as he needed.

Within a half-hour the Fire Department had brought twelve 250-gallon-per-minute Homelite self-priming pumps to the fire scene. Firemen and sailors lugged them into *Normandie* and positioned them in the flooded rooms of the Promenade Deck. Then they began looking for exit holes for the pumps' outlet hoses.

Here was the rub. The pumps worked, but the outlet hoses had to be stretched such a distance to reach an exit—a porthole or other opening—that the pumping pressure fell off to almost nothing. The water could not be pumped out.

Simmers could scarcely believe it. Time and again his best efforts had been frustrated. No matter what he did, no matter how determined he was, no matter what he thought of, there was some reason it wouldn't work. It almost seemed as though fate had made up its mind about *Normandie* and there was nothing he could do to alter the decision.

Throughout the day, while the firemen had fought the blaze and Simmers and others had tried to correct the ship's list, the FBI, the New York District Attorney's office and the police had been more concerned with another issue: Had the Germans succeeded in pulling off one of the most damaging acts of sabotage in living memory?

This was more than just an idle question. If German saboteurs were this determined, efficient and well organized, they had to be caught. Otherwise, the entire New York waterfront, the Brooklyn Navy Yard, the warships anchored on the east coast and perhaps America's entire industrial might were at risk.

The FBI, the police and the District Attorney's men had already questioned everyone who'd been in the grand lounge. Events immediately before and after the fire had pretty much been determined. But many questions remained:

Who'd ordered the life preservers stored in the lounge? Had they been soaked in gasoline or any other inflammable liquid? Had fires simultaneously broken out elsewhere on the ship? Had the fire-fighting equipment or the alarm system been tampered with? Were Derrick and his crew loyal to the United States?

Most of these questions could not be answered immediately. Investigation and lab work would reveal the truth. But the FBI needed two pieces of evidence immediately: a first-hand look at the fire scene and some samples of the life-jacket bales.

At 9:30 that night, with the fire still smoldering, a team of FBI agents boarded the ship to gather the necessary evidence.

On *Normandie*'s Main Deck they found that the portside cabins had been turned into swimming baths. Trying to reach the Promenade Deck, however, they were surprised to find that the stairwells were also flooded.

When they finally got to the Promenade Deck, via a long and circuitous route, the agents discovered that many of the life preservers were still smoking. Several firemen were wetting down the burning embers.

Checking up on Derrick's story, the agents made their way to stanchion #4. A semi-circular metal shield two feet wide and five feet high was still standing erect beside the stanchion, its top six inches below the spot where the cutting had taken place. The stanchion itself was just as Derrick and his men had described it. The tip of the tower was lying on a bit of charred carpeting, the end still attached, albeit barely, to the stanchion base. Burned-out life preservers lay as close as a foot or two from the base. An agent took one of them for laboratory testing.

In the command post Simmers refused to stop thinking about the situation. Another idea occurred to him: using the fireboats to pump the water out of the ship by connecting hoses to their uptakes. He discussed the idea with Chief Geller. Geller said the idea might have worked except for one thing: The uptakes weren't threaded. There was no way to attach hoses to them.

For nearly five hours Simmers had been struggling to correct Normandie's list, convinced that the ship was in desperate danger. Now his options were exhausted.

At 10:00 p.m. Admiral Andrews held another press conference. "I am pleased to report that fire damage to the ship has been comparatively slight."

"How long will it take to repair the damage?" asked a reporter.

"Well, I don't want to minimize this," Andrews said. "Normandie's departure will be delayed. But we'll have her ready to go in a few months."

"Sir, is there any danger that she might capsize?"

Admiral Andrews smiled tightly. "At this point, I doubt it. Her list has only increased one degree or so over the last few hours. Still, there are the tides to worry about. Low tide is at 10:37. If there's no further list then, I think she's safe."

Meanwhile, the tidal current had reversed itself, flowing from the Atlantic into the Hudson, pushing against the starboard side of the ship. At 10:26 the current flow reached 2.1 knots. It was ebb tide. In her slip Normandie groaned and eased over to port another degree.

Low tide arrived at 10:37. On this day that meant that the water's surface had dropped more than three feet below the high-tide mark. Normandie sank lower and lower until her bottom rested firmly on the silt that had built up during her enforced idleness.

As she hit bottom, the giant liner lurched again, snapping

hawsers like old rubber bands, pulling down some of the pier's stringpieces. She stabilized at a list to port of just about 20 degrees. In the command post the atmosphere turned grim.

A few blocks away the Broadway theaters began to let out. Despite the brisk, chill winds, theatergoers and actors, the former dressed in evening clothes, the latter still in greasepaint, headed toward the fire scene.

At Pier 88, partly illuminated by the Fire Department's searchlights, a begrimed and sooty *Normandie* leaned toward the water at a crazy angle, like some mortally wounded prehistoric monster. On her upper decks a few firemen tended to some burning embers. Down below, searchers prowled the darkened hull, looking for men who'd been injured or trapped.

The pier itself was practically empty, most of the emergency vehicles having pulled out long ago. There were only two sounds: the relentless drumming of the emergency lighting generators and the sporadic creak-pop of the starboard-side hawsers parting under frightful stress.

At 11:30 Commander Lohmann, who had expected to be the chief engineer of this great vessel, somehow found his way down to the engine room and back. "We're starting to take water down there," he told his colleagues. "It doesn't look good."

By midnight *Normandie* was listing 23 degrees—as much as she'd ever heeled over in any Atlantic storm.

The gangways had been extended several times. But as the list increased, they became more and more precarious. At Coman's suggestion, nets were strung between the ship and the pier so that no one would be trapped in the ship if the gangways were pulled away from the pier.

His order came just in time. At 12:22 *Normandie* pulled even farther away from the pier, her list increasing to 25 degrees. Two of the remaining three gangways fell away with a crash, remaining fastened at one end to the ship.

Concerned about his crew members still aboard the ship, Coman implored Andrews to give the abandon-ship order. A moment later Andrews complied. "Admiral Andrews has ordered all hands to leave the ship," the loudspeakers on Pier 88 blared out. "The Admiral has ordered all hands to abandon the *Normandie* and all boats to clear out of the slip."

Now, for reasons still unknown, the police swept through the area, ordering all the newspaper photographers to leave the scene. No further pictures were taken of the ship until after the climax of the catastrophe.

Admiral Andrews was sitting in his car, which was parked at the head of the pier just opposite the oblique perpendicular of the ship's famous uprearing bow. Reporters surrounded the car and peppered him with questions. "The men have been ordered to evacuate the ship by reason of a dangerous list," he explained tersely.

"Do you think the ship might topple over?" one of the reporters asked.

Admiral Andrews, the commander of the Third Naval District, an officer with more than thirty years of Navy experience, simply shrugged.

Other reporters cornered Fire Commissioner Walsh. "Is the ship in danger?" they asked.

"I'm inclined to doubt it," he replied. "Her keel is already pretty deeply mired in mud."

At that moment *Normandie* moved again, heeling over, her port side slipping toward the water, the silt beneath her completely pulverized. When the motion stopped, she was listing at 33 degrees.

A few moments later the relative quiet was shattered by noise—banging, clattering, thundering, booming, rumbling. All the loose gear aboard the ship, tools, cranes, life rafts, tanks, standee cot frames, even the tower of stanchion #4, began tumbling across *Normandie*'s decks and smashing into her portside plating or dropping into her slip.

It was the same sort of sound that had been heard thirty years earlier, out in the cold Atlantic, near some icebergs that had drifted farther to the south than expected. It had come from the *Titanic* when her stern was raised high, just before the final plunge. It was a death rattle.

At 1:40 the last of the three gangways connecting *Normandie* with her pier pulled away and crashed against the ship. Almost simultaneously the last of the ladders left leaning against her bow fell to the ground. The two nets tied between her and the pier were now her only connection to land.

Still, a few brave men went back into the ship again and

again, looking for trapped survivors. About a dozen of those who'd been on the ship when the fire broke out were still unaccounted for.

Among the searchers was Father Peter Baptist Duffee. He and several sailors moved through the depths of the ship. Accompanying them was Dr. Edward R. Maloney, president of the medical staff at St. Vincent's Hospital. They climbed down a stairway to the engine room.

Suddenly, *Normandie* lurched again, and the searchers were thrown violently against the generators. Dr. Maloney's eyeglasses were shattered and his face cut. Father Baptist tore several muscles in his stomach and seriously strained his back. Both men tumbled into the water collecting in the engine room.

Father Baptist was the first up. He helped Dr. Maloney to his feet and guided him out of the ship, since Maloney could barely see. They exited *Normandie* at 2:15, the last men to leave the ship.

At 2:37 p.m., almost exactly twelve hours after Derrick's torch had ignited a bale of life jackets, *Normandie* slowly rolled over into the ice-caked shallows of her slip.

Only a few people remained on the scene. Among them was a man who would play a large role in *Normandie*'s future: Captain John I. Tooker, a salvage expert from Merritt, Chapman & Scott.

At the moment *Normandie* capsized, he saw something no one else seemed to notice: When the giant vessel finally fell, she dipped a full 90 degrees into the water, half submerging her thirty-eight-foot-wide funnels, water pouring in and drowning internal fires in a hiss of steam. But as she touched bottom, her buoyancy reasserted itself and she staggered back upward a bit and held, spotlighted from the shore, at an angle of 79 degrees.

What did it mean, that 11 degrees? Tooker knew. It meant that *Normandie* didn't want to roll over, that she wouldn't have done so unless she'd been forced. It meant that her natural buoyancy might someday be used to refloat her.

For everyone else who witnessed *Normandie*'s fall, there were no redeeming aspects to the scene. What they saw was a once magnificent vessel now transformed into a lifeless hulk, a dead dinosaur trapped in the tar pits.

In the final moments *Normandie*'s bow had leaped toward

Pier 90, sending her rudder up under the corner of Pier 88. It had pulled loose five pilings as the ship toppled over.

In Chicago a young boy named Ellis Bell listened to *Normandie*'s final catastrophe on the radio. "No," he said to himself, "not *Normandie*, not *Normandie*." He cried himself to sleep.

18

HER FUTURE IN doubt

Before the war, as a little girl in Connecticut, Patricia Nielson loved driving into Manhattan with her parents for the day. She especially loved the trip down the West Side Highway, past the gigantic ocean liners at their Hudson River docks, disembarking passengers from Europe or taking on Americans bound for the Continent.

On the ride back home she often saw the beautiful vessels at night, their portholes sparking like stars, some with their names spelled out in lights on their topmost decks, like great theater marquees.

Once in a while she'd even see a midnight sailing, with taxicabs and big limousines lined up at the docks below, people and porters pushing baggage carts trying to board the ship all at once, music floating out over the highway.

When the war broke out, the great liners vanished from the piers one by one, until only *Normandie* remained. Patricia came to love her, and to depend on seeing her every time she came to Manhattan, because the beautiful ship reminded her of the carefree days before World War II.

"If my father passed *Normandie* at more than fifteen miles an hour," Patricia later recalled, "I voiced strong protest." Eventually *Normandie* became a kind of symbol for the entire Nielson family

"The day after *Normandie* burned and capsized," Patricia remembered, *we drove in to see her. No one was sure what was going to happen to her or how soon, and we wanted to say goodbye.*

As we rounded the curve under the bridge, we could see the great hump of her, lying on her side, and as we came closer, the hoses still stretched across her and steam and smoke were wisping up into the clear air. We seemed almost close enough to touch her as we drove past, caught in the traffic jam with all the other people who had come to see her.

It broke my heart, that great, beautiful, beautiful creature, so tall and proud and stately, lying there all smoky and stained, mortally wounded. She looked so hurt and so helpless and so awful I cried and cried and cried. . . .

Eventually, after several accidents on the West Side Highway, one of which injured three patrolmen standing guard, Police Commissioner Valentine had a board fence constructed at the pierhead to prevent passing motorists from seeing the ship. But during the first few days after the fire *Normandie* was visible to all.

At street level, according to the *New York Times*, some 30,000 spectators flocked to the sight on the day after the fire. Police, black soldiers with rifles, and sailors restricted sightseers to the sidewalk on the east side of 12th Avenue.

Thousands of office workers, arriving at their jobs in Manhattan's skyscrapers, found they could see exactly what had happened to the enormous ocean liner simply by looking out of their windows. "It was as though the Empire State Building had slowly teetered and fallen sideways into the street," John McClain wrote in the *Journal-American*.

Normandie lay on her port side, a colossal beached whale. She'd come to rest slantwise in her slip, her aft end wedged under the offshore tip of the pier, her forward end canted toward Pier 90, the tremendous naked sweep of her upturned flank swelling out of the partly frozen slip.

Her huge oval funnels, which once had towered high above the elevated highway, were now parallel with the water, their

(Top) City fire boats and railroad fire tugs concentrate their spray on Normandie's port side. (Bottom) Smoke from the burning French liner drifts out over Manhattan, toward Queens.

As Normandie *begins to list, her gangways are pulled away from the pier.*

Normandie *lying on her side at Pier 88, in 40-odd feet of water. Her rudder is wedged under the pier, her bow canted toward Pier 90, next door.*

The grand stairway after the fire. The statue at the top had been put in storage a month earlier.

A re-creation of the fire scene, staged by the FBI at the Brooklyn Navy Yard. The burlap bags contain kapok life jackets from the same batch that had been in the grand lounge.

"Normandieville," the village of carpentry and metalworking shops set up on a temporary pier built beside the capsized vessel. The superstructure has already been removed from Normandie. Note the barges on the right. Divers brought up debris from inside the ship and loaded it on these barges for weighing and disposal.

*Divers entering
the capsized ship.
Down below, they
worked in total
darkness, in "mud"
often over their heads.*

*Normandie afloat and being towed to a "secret location" for repair,
after the largest salvage effort in history succeeded in raising her.
Her sides are stained with oil, showing the rise and fall of the tides.
The two water spouts on her starboard side show that pumps were
still at work keeping the interior as dry as possible.*

Normandie in dry dock following salvage. Photo shows how her hull was battered by rocking back and forth on the rocky pinnacle at Pier 88. There were many cracks and holes in this area, all patched from the inside with concrete.

Sound again, after her hull was repaired and repainted below the waterline, Normandie was taken to the Brooklyn Navy Yard for an inclining experiment to determine her center of gravity, etc., prior to further repairs and refitting. They never took place.

Normandie *being disassembled at Port Newark. Note "LIPSETT" painted on her starboard side in large white letters.*

The last piece of Normandie *is lifted out of the water—a section of her double bottom.*

lower rims separated from the murky ice by only a hand width or two. The bulbous tip of her famous, flaring bow was revealed for all to see.

Her vast, sloping side, gray and stained, was thinly ridged with scaffolding. Amidships, a gangway lettered in the mannered red script that had become a French Line trademark lay against the naked steel, still fastened at one end to a passenger entrance. Across a great stretch of gray, two of her enormous four-bladed propellers, pathetically useless now, broached the water, ugly and awkward.

Inside, *Normandie* was an incredible mess. Many passageways were blocked by debris and some were mashed together by the impact of heavy equipment against the lightweight bulkheads.

Mud had begun to seep through open portholes, filling up the cabins and corridors. Furniture, tool chests, life jackets and other objects floated about aimlessly in the colloidal mixture.

As the ship had fallen over, passageways had been turned into crawl spaces and elevator shafts into passageways. The complex switchboard mounted on *Normandie*'s engine-room walls was now overhead. Half of the theater's red plush chairs, bolted to the floor, hung above the water.

Normandie's hull was as sound as ever. But, deep inside it, her engines and generators were slightly more than half submerged in the brackish, dirty water. The tides rose and fell within her engine compartment, over a daily range of almost six feet.

The huge vessel lay in a bed of soupy mud. But at a point about a third of the way down from her bow, toward her stern, she was supported by a sharp rock ledge under the mud. This ledge had been created when the slip was dredged before *Normandie*'s maiden voyage, seven years earlier.

The cheers and celebrations of that great day were long forgotten now. *Normandie* was as still as death. In the hospitals 229 officers and men of the United States Navy and 283 contractors' employees were being treated for the injuries and burns they'd suffered.

America was furious.

"It is not alone a ship that has been damaged," the *New York Times* editorialized. "Men may have to die on the other side of some ocean because help cannot now get to them in time. The investigation should be relentless."

Government officials at all levels—but, most of all, President Franklin Delano Roosevelt—were deluged with angry letters and telegrams.

"First Pearl Harbor and now the *Normandie*, one a disaster that may yet cost us the war, the other a dismal tragedy of tremendous cost," Stephen Bowen telegraphed FDR. "Is this the type of performance for which you think America will pour out its blood and sweat and tears?"

A *Times* editorial writer struck a more sentimental note. "It requires an effort of the imagination to realize that the great hulk of a once proud ship lying on her beam in the Hudson River at the foot of 48th Street is not suffering humiliation," he wrote. "The sight of her hurts the human eye and heart."

There was also pain and anger in France—poor, truncated Vichy France. But there was something else altogether in Germany. "The Nazi propaganda machine seized upon the *Normandie* disaster today as a club to weaken the United Nations' morale and tried to pass off the fire as the work of its own saboteurs," the *World-Telegram* reported.

Every morning-after news story about the *Normandie* disaster addressed the question of what—or who—had caused the fire. And they all reported that New York Attorney General Frank S. Hogan and Admiral Adolphus Andrews were sure that a welder's carelessness was the immediate cause.

Nonetheless, sabotage rumors spread across the New York waterfront, through the city and through the nation as fast as the fire had raced through *Normandie*. Her fire hoses had been slashed, or her sprinkler system had released gasoline, or fire had broken out in many places simultaneously, or several bombs had exploded in various parts of the ship—so said the rumors.

Several radio commentators suggested that Frenchmen owing allegiance to the Vichy government were responsible for the fire. So did Drew Pearson in his famous newspaper column, "Washington Merry Go Round."

Barnett Hershey, a commentator on WMCA radio, said, "The unofficial representatives of Vichy, who traveled back and forth when Clippers still ran between Lisbon and New York, often declared that the *Normandie* would never serve the United States as the *Leviathan* had served during the last war. None of them ever explained the statement, except for a smile and a shrug."

All of this amounted to a public outcry, and the government responded the way governments have always responded and probably always will—with investigations. There were six different inquiries in all: the FBI, the Navy, the House, the Senate, the New York Fire Department and the office of the New York Attorney General. All had exactly the same purpose: to place blame on someone, anyone—preferably not one or more loyal Americans, but a nefarious alien saboteur.

Roosevelt himself suspected sabotage. "Dear Frank," he wrote to his Secretary of the Navy the morning after the fire, "will you let me know whether any enemy aliens—or other aliens—were permitted to work on the *Normandie?*"

Knox passed FDR's inquiry on to J. Edgar Hoover, but the FBI had already begun investigating the men who'd been aboard *Normandie* at the time of the fire. A close study of the Robins employee lists revealed that they included 105 people claiming birth in the United States without proof; 2 Allied aliens; 3 neutral aliens; an enemy alien who claimed naturalization; 3 Allied aliens with first citizenship papers; 4 enemy aliens with first citizenship papers; and an enemy alien who'd been cleared by Naval Intelligence.

These 119 men were questioned and investigated thoroughly, as were 30 people with similar backgrounds who'd worked for the various subcontractors. None had been in the lounge when the fire began, and all were subsequently cleared.

The FBI also thoroughly investigated the circumstances of the fire. In fact, on February 12, just three days after the actual event, it restaged the whole thing at the Brooklyn Navy Yard.

A steel column very much like the one Derrick had been working on was erected in a large, high-ceilinged storeroom. Some life-preserver bales from the same batch that had been on *Normandie* were brought in and put around the column at the same distances as on the ship. To this scene was added welding gear that duplicated the equipment used by Derrick and his chain gang—a torch, a metal shield, a piece of asbestos board.

Then Derrick and his entire chain gang were brought into

the room. So were all of the others who'd been in the grand lounge at the time of the fire, plus Lieutenant Commanders Brooks and Scott—twenty-four people in all, not counting a platoon of FBI agents. A Navy fire truck was stationed nearby as a precaution.

The FBI gave Derrick the green light. He turned on his torch and started burning operations. Despite all precautions, the sparks from his torch flew, some of them bouncing past the two shields and into the bales of life preservers. A roaring fire broke out immediately.

All the men in the room reacted to this fire just as they'd reacted to the one aboard the ship. They beat on it with their hands and jackets. They tried to separate the burning bales from those that hadn't caught fire. But the flames spread with breathtaking rapidity. Eventually the fire truck was called in to put out the blaze. It was almost necessary to call in the city Fire Department.

After the fire was out, the FBI separately questioned each of the twenty-four witnesses. Did the fire on board the ship happen the same way? Did it spread with the same speed? Did it look the same? Did it smell the same? Was the smoke the same color? All the witnesses agreed that the *Normandie* fire and the Navy Yard fire were identical.

At the same time the FBI Technical Laboratory in Washington examined the specimen life preservers that had been taken off the ship on the night of the fire. The vests were subjected to every test the chemists could think of, yet none of these revealed any inflammable foreign materials on the surface of the life jackets or inside them.

The *Normandie* disaster dominated newspaper headlines for only a few days. Too many terrible events were happening elsewhere in the world.

On February 14 the Japanese invaded Sumatra and seized its chief oil refinery. The next day "impregnable" Singapore fell to a Japanese assault. On February 19 carrier-based Japanese aircraft attacked the Australian city of Darwin, killing 140, sinking many ships and cutting the supply line to Java. On February 22 Roosevelt ordered MacArthur to leave the Philippines. Five days later the United States lost the Battle of the Java Sea, giving Japanese forces free reign in the southwest Pacific.

The United States had now been at war for less than three months and every day had brought more bad news. Lying on her side at Pier 88, *Normandie* was a striking reminder of America's vulnerability.

"While the fire-ravaged liner *Normandie* lay grotesquely on her side in her West 48th Street slip," the *New York Times* observed, "Naval authorities remained non-committal on the one question everybody was asking: can she be salvaged?"

Certainly this question was on the mind of young Ellis Bell. He wrote Yourkevitch in New York, asking if *Normandie* could be refloated. "Emphatically yes," the answer came back. "*Normandie*'s own buoyancy can do it. She can definitely sail again." Yourkevitch even sent the boy a salvage-plan sketch. Jubilant, Ellis tacked it up on his bedroom wall.

No one in authority made any immediate decisions about *Normandie*'s ultimate fate, but preliminary salvage operations actually began the very morning after the fire.

Captain Simmers asked Merritt, Chapman & Scott, the largest marine-salvage firm in America, to immediately remove everything valuable from *Normandie* that could be easily reached (especially guns, searchlights, winches) and to determine the ship's exact position.

At daybreak on Tuesday morning the MC&S tugboat *Courageous* pulled up to *Normandie*'s stern and anchored. Workers clambered over the hulk, taking depth soundings and measuring the charred superstructure. Two MC&S barges also tied up at the end of the pier, one laden with lumber (for walkways and scaffolding), the other with diving equipment.

The next day Commander William A. Sullivan, the Navy's Supervisor of Salvage, gave Merritt, Chapman more formal marching orders:

1. Do a preliminary weight and buoyancy study of the ship as she lay.
2. Draw up plans for a scale model for use in salvage studies.

3. Have divers inspect the part of the ship that was submerged.
4. Make daily reports of any settlement or shift.
5. Remove all guns, winches, boats, stacks, masts, propellers and other appendages, as specifically requested by Simmers.

A word about William Sullivan is in order here, for from this moment on he looms large in *Normandie*'s story. Sullivan was the U.S. Navy's leading salvage expert. He'd been concerned with salvaging vessels ever since 1917, when he graduated from MIT.

When Nazi submarines began to sink British ships, the British Navy established its own salvage operation. Sullivan managed to get himself assigned to it. Later, just before the war, the U.S. Navy authorized Sullivan to establish a salvage school at Pearl Harbor. Then came December 7. Sullivan and his three master divers went to Pearl Harbor to work, not to teach.

Immediately after the fire Merritt, Chapman workers removed what they could from *Normandie* and began cutting off her funnels. This was a logical first step, whatever the ship's final fate. If she were to be scrapped, her funnels would be the first part of her to go. If she were to be salvaged, her funnels and even her superstructure were excess weight, a barrier to restoring buoyancy.

By the third week in February all three of *Normandie*'s gigantic funnels had been cut up and hauled away to the smelters, as had most of her two elaborately divided smoke uptakes.

Sullivan ordered the salvagers to begin removing *Normandie*'s superstructure, including her beautiful curved bridge bulkhead and her lovely tiered aft decks. This also meant removing the decks, walls and ceilings of her best-known and most impressive public rooms: the winter garden, the theater, the first-class smoking room, the grand lounge, the café grill.

This did not represent much of a change in plans. After all, even before the fire Washington had almost delayed *Normandie*'s sailing to remove this very superstructure in order to increase her stability.

Ellis Bell, seeing newspaper photos of *Normandie*'s superstructure being dismantled, was horrified. He realized that this part of the ship was not being lovingly preserved, unlike the art works that had been removed during the conversion. Workmen with cutting torches swarmed over the ship, many of them in diving suits this time.

Those who ventured inside had to walk on thin, shaky partitions that had been intended as walls, not floors. With each step they took the chance of stepping onto a door that would swing open and drop them into who knew where.

One man stepped onto a partition of gray-painted glass. It broke under his weight and he fell seventy feet down a passageway, as if it were an elevator shaft. Another opened a door above his head and, with the beam of his flashlight, picked out a tremendous steel safe hanging in mid-air, one leg hooked into an electric cable.

As workmen were cutting away *Normandie*'s superstructure, she caught fire again and on many different occasions, as torch sparks ignited debris, cork decking or insulating materials.

But now, of course, everyone was ready for fire. A new professional fire watch—fourteen retired New York firemen, headed by a retired battalion chief—kept all but the largest blazes well in hand.

While the Navy was taking the first necessary steps to salvage Normandie or scrap her, the FBI was tracking down and following up on every lead that even hinted at sabotage, despite all the evidence against it.

Leads poured into FBI offices by the hundreds—letters, phone calls, telegrams. Agents canvassed their informants. Motion-picture film of the fire taken by amateurs was developed by the FBI and studied, just as the Zapruder film of the Kennedy assassination was dissected in 1963.

Criminals and underworld characters of every kind were questioned, as were diplomats, foreigners, international travelers, union leaders, longshoremen and anyone else anywhere in the country who might know anything at all.

For instance, on February 12 one South Carolina man sent a telegram to his Senator, and the Senator passed it on to the FBI. He claimed he'd overheard a poolroom conversation on February 7 in which one man told another, "There is one vessel in the United States which will not be used and that is the *Nor-*

mandie. Before Monday night it will burn to the waterline, and there will be another important ship which will burn before very long and that one is the aircraft carrier *Wasp*. We have a man on board who will take care of it when the time comes." The man asked his Senator for $40 "to cover his expenses."

FBI agents flocked to South Carolina. When pressed, however, the man admitted the whole story was a hoax. He was a wino who needed some refreshment money.

Dozens of people called the FBI with similar information: "I overheard my neighbor say, 'Just see what happens to the *Normandie*.' " Or, "Someone in a bar told me, 'I'll bet she'll never sail.' "

Others had even more vague information that nonetheless, to their way of thinking, was ominous indeed. "My nextdoor neighbor speaks German with his friends," said one informant. And, "People with a foreign accent always congregate in so-and-so restaurant."

There were many such reports: "So-and-so, who is a foreigner, suddenly seems to have a lot of money." And "So-and-so is 100% pro-Nazi. He runs a welding business and he had 40 men working on the *Normandie*." And "So-and-so read reports of the *Normandie* disaster and seemed absolutely gleeful."

Other informants alleged that *Normandie*'s conversion workers included members of the IRA, the Falangista or the Fascisti.

Several informants wrote the FBI to note that Milton Caniff's comic strip, "Terry and the Pirates," included a character named Normandie (a pretty girl, as it happened). One comic-strip reader pointed out that during the week before the fire the cartoons included the words *harbor*, *fire* and *sabotage*.

Another informant told the FBI that an astrologist had told him *Normandie* would burn before she sailed. And an American Airlines stewardess notified the FBI that a passenger had taken "several pictures" of the ship on a flight just days before the fire.

All in all, the FBI exhaustively investigated every last one of these leads—760 in all—to no avail. All it found were liars, mentally impaired persons, attention seekers or people who'd misconstrued something that was totally innocent. Not the slightest trace of sabotage came to light.

Nonetheless, the FBI did conduct some fascinating interviews. Perhaps the most interesting was with Admiral Andrews. He was delighted to answer all the questions about the fire Agent Foxworth could think of, since he knew nothing about it firsthand and couldn't be blamed.

But when Foxworth started asking him why *Normandie* had capsized, Andrews was instantly outraged. "Wait a minute," he sputtered. "Do I understand that you, as FBI, are inquiring into how the ship was handled and how the water came on board? Is that a function of the FBI or is it a function of a Navy Court of Inquiry?"

Foxworth replied mildly that the FBI wanted to inquire into all the circumstances of the disaster since they might be interconnected. Andrews still insisted the FBI was responsible only for determining the cause of the fire.

Foxworth then terminated the interview and reported the results to Hoover. Hoover instructed Foxworth to inform Andrews that he must either answer all FBI questions or face the possibility that the FBI would publicly bow out of the inquiry, blaming Navy obstruction. Andrews gave in.

In New York's Dannemora Prison mobster Charles "Lucky" Luciano thought he knew more than the FBI. He thought Albert Anastasia had arranged the *Normandie* fire as part of a complicated scheme to get him out of jail. Anastasia might well have contemplated such an act, but a close reading of the recently declassified FBI reports on the fire and capsizing proves that neither he nor any other mobster nor any saboteur had anything to do with it.

Nonetheless, the blaze may have played an indirect role in Luciano's release and eventual deportation. The Navy and the office of Attorney General Frank Hogan concluded they could use underworld leaders to help the war effort, particularly to guard against waterfront sabotage in the New York area, since the mob had very close ties with the various waterfront unions.

Lieutenant Commander Charles R. Haffenden of Navy Intelligence was given the job of carrying out what came to be known as "Operation Underworld." He went to see Joseph "Socks"

Lanza, the notorious semi-literate czar of the Fulton Fish Market and its fishing fleet. Lanza told him to see Luciano, who was transferred to Sing Sing for the meeting.

Eventually, according to Luciano, a deal was cut. Luciano would help the Navy with its waterfront security problems and Luciano would immediately be freed from prison, but deported to Italy.

At that point Luciano was transferred out of Dannemora, one of the more unpleasant penal institutions, to Great Meadow Prison in Comstock, New York, a country club by comparison. But he was not released until after World War II ended, at which time he was sent to Sicily.*

While Luciano sat in prison and the FBI dealt with the deluded and the deranged, the war news continued to be gloomy.

On March 2, 1942, Japanese forces landed on Mindanao. On March 8 they took Rangoon. The next day the Dutch formally surrendered Java. Two days later MacArthur left Corregidor, saying, "I shall return."

Halfway around the world, the British were worried about the German battleship *Tirpitz*, which was trapped in Norway. What damage it could do if it broke out into the Atlantic was obvious to all. To forestall that possibility, the British decided to attack and destroy the only dry dock on the Atlantic that could service it: the enormous lock at St. Nazaire, which had been built for *Normandie*.

In the early morning hours of March 28, nineteen ships—260 British commandos in eighteen coastal craft, plus the former American destroyer *Campbelltown*—sailed into St. Nazaire harbor. Their intent: to ram the lock with the destroyer, which had been loaded with explosives, and to blow it to smithereens.

On the way in, the force was severely mauled. All but two of the small ships were sunk. In all, 170 men were killed or captured. But somehow the old American destroyer, with its de-

---

* All of this comes from *The Last Testament of Lucky Luciano*, his as-told-to autobiography, written just before his death. How much of it is true, we may never know. But the confidential FBI reports indicate that he was either mistaken, misled by his mobster buddies, or lying in hopes of inflating his importance and influence.

layed-action fuses, rammed the lock. In the consequent explosion the lock simply disappeared.

Each of the six investigations that followed the *Normandie* disaster did its job in a different way and came to somewhat different conclusions about who was to blame for the catastrophe.

The Navy Court of Inquiry, presided over by Rear Admiral Lamar Leahy, U.S.N. (retired), began its work on February 14, meeting behind closed doors at the Federal Office Building at 90 Church Street in Manhattan. It took 2,270 pages of testimony and examined 2,000 pages of exhibits.

On April 21 the court announced its findings. The fire, it said, was caused solely by "gross carelessness and utter violation of the rules of common sense by employees of the Robins Drydock and Repair Company. The training of fire watchers . . . was superficial. No evidence of sabotage was discovered." The court recommended that Robins be sued for the resulting damages, but a clause in the Robins contract limited its liability to $300,000.

The court also made some rather nasty remarks about Lieutenant Commander Brooks, who'd commanded the Coast Guard detail, and Lieutenant Commander Scott, who'd represented the District Material Officer on board the ship. "Brooks," said the court, "did not on his own initiative keep himself completely informed whenever work on the vessel either presented a serious fire hazard or placed out of commission facilities installed on the vessel for detecting, reporting and fighting fires."

The court said that Scott hadn't kept Brooks informed about conditions on board the ship which would have let him carry out his duties, especially the safety part of them.

The Secretary of the Navy, Frank Knox, who had the final say-so on what to do about the court's recommendations, took a rather fatherly attitude toward the two officers. "They failed to take adequate steps to insure *Normandie*'s safety," he said, "but because of mitigating circumstances, no disciplinary action will be taken at this time," other than to place the court report before any selection board which may consider the officers for promotion.

"Two unfortunate junior officers get a black mark on their records and that is that," commented the *New York Herald Tribune*. "Nobody puts a black mark on the Secretary of the Navy, the Navy Department, the Commandant of the Third Naval District or anyone else responsible for the over-all fact that no one was in charge of this immensely valuable ship, no one saw that proper precautions were observed, that officers and crews were trained and alert to their duties. Pass the whitewash bucket."

But what of the *laissez-faire* Rear Admiral, Adolphus Andrews? He was not cited in the Court of Inquiry, politics being what it was. However, he did not emerge entirely unscathed. While the court was in session, he and three other admirals came up for promotion to vice admiral. The Senate delayed his promotion until the court's findings could be published. In March, Andrews was relieved of all responsibilities except for directing the effort to combat German submarines off the east coast.

As for Captain Coman, who'd innocently asked that the lighting standards be cut down and who'd lost his command as a result, he was transferred to Washington and eventually to the Pacific.

The House Subcommittee, which was chaired by Representative Patrick Drewry (D—Va.), started out as the Court of Inquiry had, hearing witnesses (fifty-eight of them) and taking testimony (5,000 pages of it). House members even visited the sunken ship.

In the midst of their investigation, however, Representative Samuel Dickstein (D–N.Y.), who was not a member of the subcommittee, publicly charged that "the nation's #1 Nazi" had "put more than 30 foreign agents to work on the *Normandie*. This man, he said, was William Drechsel, former official of the Hamburg-Amerika and North German Lloyd steamship lines.

Dickstein hadn't pulled Drechsel's name out of a hat. He knew the man well. In 1934 Drechsel had admitted before the McCormack-Dickstein Committee that he had supplied $125,000 in bail for Nazi agents who'd been arrested in the United States. Later he'd proclaimed his allegiance to Hitler.

Now Dickstein charged that this man was responsible for the *Normandie* fire. "If Naval Intelligence made any kind of investigation, if the Government had checked the men put on that ship, they would have found the true cause of the fire to be sabotage," Dickstein said.

Captain Drechsel, as he was known, had been a U-boat commander in World War I and a transatlantic-liner captain after that. After a period as a shipping-line executive in Germany, he came to the United States, where, with the help of money from the W. Averell Harriman interests, he helped to found the Oceanic Patrol Service Corp., which furnished uniformed and plainclothes guards for the piers.

It was even discovered that Oceanic had provided guards for *Normandie*. Was this a case of the fox guarding the henhouse? Had the real cause of the *Normandie* fire been found?

When reporters questioned the House Subcommittee about the Drechsel business, they were told that the subcommittee would look into it if that seemed warranted. So the newspapers went to work on the story themselves.

They soon found Jeremiah A. Sullivan, a "big, bluff, well-dressed man" who was president and one of the founders of Oceanic. He said Drechsel wasn't even part of the firm anymore and hadn't been since October 4, 1939. Furthermore, he said, Oceanic hadn't had a man on *Normandie* since November 1940. And at the time of the fire the company had had a single man guarding the pier gate, an American citizen who'd been with the firm for more than a decade.

The papers also interviewed Drechsel himself, who confirmed Sullivan's story. Drechsel lived in Englewood, New Jersey, with his wife and two children. He'd been an American citizen since 1938. "I don't want to say anything about Mr. Dickstein's charges," he told the newspapers, "except to deny them." Further investigation confirmed every detail of Sullivan's and Drechsel's stories. It was another dead end.

In the end the House Subcommittee agreed with the Navy Court of Inquiry, saying there "was no evidence to support the widely held theory that the fire was caused by enemy agents or fifth columnists—even though opportunities for sabotage were abundant." But the subcommittee disagreed with the Navy about Commanders Brooks and Scott.

Brooks, the subcommittee said, "made a sincere effort to protect the vessel to the best of his ability, but was hampered

[by] the lack of experienced personnel and capable assistants. [He] is not guilty of any offense nor can he be charged with serious blame."

Scott "placed too much reliance on the Robins employees. This is an error in judgement rather than a commission of an offense."

The subcommittee also raised another issue the Court of Inquiry hadn't considered: responsibility at the top.

According to Drew Pearson, in his "Washington Merry Go Round" newspaper column, "Isolationist Reps. Mell Mass of Minn. and James M. Motto of Oregon did their utmost to pin the chief blame on FDR. Rep. Patrick Drewry of Virginia, the old guard Democratic chairman of the Subcommittee, almost let them.

"The man who blocked the political sceme was Rep. Ed Izac, of California. But before the report was agreed on, there was almost a riot in the hearing room when Izac and Mass exchanged verbal punches."

Evidently Mass and Motto attempted to blame Roosevelt for setting *Normandie*'s sailing date at February 14. There was much confused talk about the delay and about its cancellation, all leading to the notion that the fire was caused by the rush.

But, although the rush was certainly a contributing factor, the subcommittee found that the disaster was caused by "carelessness, confusion, divided authority, lack of supervision and command."

The Senate Naval Affairs Committee decided after its hearings that the *Normandie* fire was caused by the careless use of an acetylene torch close to inflammable life preservers "without the protection of adequate safeguards, in violation of all rules and sound judgment."

As for the capsizing, said the committee, that was caused by "the undue amount of water placed on board the ship by the New York City Fire Department, in the act of extinguishing the fire."

The next investigation to be heard from, of course, was that of the Fire Department. It congratulated itself on putting out the fire promptly and absolved itself of any responsibility for the capsizing. Commissioner Walsh contended that 90 percent of the water poured onto *Normandie* "was washed overboard."

The New York Attorney General's investigation added little to what had already been reported. After Frank Hogan and twenty assistant district attorneys questioned some seventy witnesses, Hogan concluded, "There is no evidence of sabotage. Carelessness has served the enemy with equal effectiveness."

During these investigations the Japanese continued to sweep through the Pacific islands. They captured Bataan on April 9, Corregidor on May 6 and, on the Asian continent, completed their conquest of Burma on May 15.

But the war news was not all bad. In the middle of April, Jimmy Doolittle led sixteen B-25 bombers on America's first raid on Japan, hitting Tokyo, Yokohama, Kobe and Nagoya. The Doolittle raid didn't do much damage, but it shocked Japan and boosted American morale.

In the first week of May the United States and Japan fought the Battle of the Coral Sea, the first naval engagement in which neither fleet saw its enemy—carrier aircraft carrying out the attacks at great distances from their mother floats. It was a costly battle for America, which lost the aircraft carrier *Lexington* and several other ships. But Japan, in its first serious setback, was forced to cancel its planned invasion of Australia.

Three weeks later 1,000 Royal Air Force bombers launched a devastating night raid on Cologne. Eighteen thousand buildings were destroyed, another 10,000 heavily damaged.

Inside Russia, Stalin's armies finally broke the German siege of Leningrad, which had lasted so long and cost so many lives. A rail line was opened to the city and food finally began to pour in.

In America the question regarding *Normandie* remained: What would be done with the hulk of that great ship? Would she be left in her slip for the duration, a visible reminder of American carelessness and vulnerability? Would she be cut into scrap, the scrap melted down and made into new weapons of war? Or would she somehow be set aright, refitted and drafted once more?

The answers depended on many factors: American war needs, public relations and propaganda, technical difficulties, resource priorities, morale.

There was also the matter of Roosevelt. His mother had often traveled aboard *Normandie,* and he'd taken a personal and sympathetic interest in her, as New York's Mayor La Guardia discovered when he visited the President on February 12 to discuss the catastrophe.

"I told him about the terrible fire," La Guardia said, "and I asked him what he thought could be done. And, you know, he took pencil and paper and drew a diagram for me of a ship's side, showing a division into compartments and explaining how a pumping operation could be carried out."

The American public also wanted her raised, and many citizens thought they knew how it could be done. More than 5,000 salvage suggestions poured in to Commander Sullivan, forwarded by half of America's Congressmen, all of its Senators, Governors, Cabinet officials and Navy officers on every level.

Some of the suggestors wanted money in advance, some wanted it after *Normandie* was righted and some wanted nothing at all. Some promised to raise the ship in a week; others said it would take as long as four months. Some sketched out their ideas on wrapping paper; others provided professionally drawn blueprints. The most frequent suggestion: Dig a trench beside *Normandie,* fill it with water (as if the Hudson wouldn't), then shove the ship into the trench.

An engineering firm came up with an amusing variation on this idea. It proposed digging a tunnel directly underneath the ship, filling it with water, then blasting away the tunnel top. *Normandie* would drop into the resultant trough right side up, the company imagined.

The next most frequently suggested plan was to inflate balloons (either inside the ship or suspended above it with cables). After that came the notions of putting thousands of Ping-Pong balls (or sealed tin cans) into the hull to make it float, using derricks to lift the ship, or attaching pontoons to the outside of the hull.

A New York woman proposed that *Normandie* be frozen in a block of ice, which would then be chopped free of the slip and floated upstream to the George Washington Bridge. The ice block would be attached to the bridge with cables. When the ice melted, *Normandie* would be drawn upright.

One of the letters Sullivan received came from none other than Vladimir Yourkevitch. Yourkevitch had been designing ships for the Pusey & Jones corporation of Wilmington, Delaware, and serving as a consultant to the ship division of the War Department.

Yourkevitch said he knew all of *Normandie*'s specifications and had already worked out a way to raise the *Paris*, which had capsized under almost identical conditions in April 1939. Sullivan invited him to Washington.

Before he left, the *New York Times* interviewed the Russian emigrant. How could *Normandie* be raised? "The first step," Yourkevitch replied, "is to seal the 2,000 underwater openings—portholes and doors. Then the main deck must be reinforced, to resist water pressure. At this point," the slender man told the reporter, "the water could be pumped out. *Normandie* would gradually begin to float—on her side. Then, carefully calculated amounts of water would be pumped back into specific ballast tanks. The ship would then slowly swing upright." Yorkevitch estimated that the job would take about five months.

Throughout February and March, Sullivan studied the salvage problem with the help of Yourkevitch and many other experts. He reported his findings to Admiral van Keuren, chief of the Bureau of Ships:

Yes, said Sullivan, *Normandie* could be salvaged. Yes, she was worth saving. Her hull was in fine shape and some of her machinery was okay, too. Yes, it would be the largest, most difficult salvage job ever attempted anywhere. But it would offer a unique opportunity to create a salvage school of great potential value to the American war effort.

Van Keuren was convinced, but he had to sell the idea to his boss, Frank Knox. It was true, he wrote the Secretary of the Navy, that it would probably take two years and cost $5 million to do the job, but he cited three good reasons for going ahead with it:

1. It would cost almost as much to scrap the ship as to salvage it.
2. The ship could be salvaged now and its use determined later, according to U.S. war needs.
3. At the least, a salvaged vessel could be used to help repay the French for the original seizure—after the war, of course.

Knox suggested to FDR that a committee be appointed to make a recommendation. FDR agreed.

On April 15 Knox announced the appointment of a nineman committee to decide the question, consisting of the president of the National Council of American Shipbuilders, the president of the Moore-McCormack Shipping Line, the administrator of the Webb Institute of Naval Architecture, a professor of marine architecture from Yale University, the director of the David Taylor Model Basin in Washington and a couple of rear admirals. The committee also included the famous naval architect William Francis Gibbs. Commander William Sullivan was appointed secretary.

Knox asked the committee to answer three questions:

1. Should *Normandie* be scrapped as she lies or should she be raised?
2. If she should be scrapped, what's the best way to do it?
3. If she should be raised, should she be scrapped after she's afloat or should her disposition be decided later?

Meanwhile, Sullivan developed a salvage plan essentially similar to Yourkevitch's: Use divers to make the ship watertight and reinforce her top deck, then pump her out and let her natural buoyancy bring her to an upright position.

Theoretically, this proposal was foolproof. But it was time-consuming and expensive. Captain Thomas A. Scott of Merritt, Chapman & Scott, which would have to provide most of the equipment and the workmen, was dead set against it. He thought the whole project was a waste of money and a poor use of MC&S's valuable resources. Several committee members agreed with him.

Sullivan pointed out that although it might cost $5 million to raise the ship, it would cost at least $2.5 million to scrap her where she lay. And raising her would produce a large, seaworthy hull, while scrapping her would only produce scrap.

Sullivan's most powerful ally on the committee was William Francis Gibbs. He not only wanted *Normandie* raised, he also wanted the committee to recommend that she be turned into an aircraft carrier. "She'd have a longer and wider flight deck than any carrier in the fleet," he pointed out. "That means she'll be able to launch bombers against Japan."

The committee wasn't enthusiastic about Gibbs' carrier plan. The idea had been rejected before, with good reason. On the other hand, the committee was impressed by *Normandie*'s engines and hull. And, at least at this time, America's need for more ships was undeniable. "Nothing is more important than the fact that we must have ships to carry things—guns, airplanes, cargo or whatnot," one of the admirals said. "Here is a ship which, for an expenditure of five or six million dollars, can be put back afloat and on her feet. I think the idea of scrapping would come very low, so long as we are in the war."

Most committee members were moved by the fact that the operation could be used to train salvage divers for work in the European and Pacific war theaters and by the propaganda value in France of doing everything possible to save her "floating colony." But some wanted to know what Mayor La Guardia thought, since, whatever was done with *Normandie*, all of New York would witness it.

"I do not claim to be a naval architect," La Guardia told the committee. "But it seems to me that the logical and sensible thing is to float the hull and then decide what is to be done with the ship." The committee then voted to do precisely the logical and sensible thing.

On May 21 President Roosevelt gave the report his enthusiastic stamp of approval. Late that afternoon the Navy announced that it planned to raise *Normandie* from the muck of the Hudson River floor and bring her back to life.

In Chicago a teenage boy named Ellis Bell wept tears of joy. In New York a Russian emigrant named Vladimir Yourkevitch felt as though his only child had been saved from execution.

19

GULLIVER VS. THE LILLIPUTIANS

Since the disaster the Navy had treated *Normandie* like a state secret. She'd been surrounded by swarms of Navy Shore Patrol police, city cops and Coast Guardsmen, cut off from view by a plywood fence and placed off limits to unauthorized personnel. Civilians caught taking pictures of her had their film confiscated.

But when Washington decided to raise her, the Navy decided to publicize the feat, hoping it could turn what had been an enormous public-relations catastrophe into at least a modest public-relations triumph.

Step one was to invite New York's leading newspapermen to visit the capsized ship so that they could see just how monumental a task the Navy was about to undertake. This shipboard press conference took place on May 26, 1942, four days after the salvage decision was announced.

"For the first time since she yielded to the irresistible weight of tons of water and rolled over to her side, the *Normandie* was visited today by others than Navy officials and civilian workers engaged in salvage operations," Robert Wilder wrote in his *New York Sun* column.

> *Convoyed by Commander William Sullivan, reporters and photographers crowded over the great ship's side, peered into open hatchways, dodged workmen and slings of debris and watched the painfully slow process of preparing the vessel for righting.*

There is no glamour now about what was once the pride of France. Her superstructure has been cut away to the promenade deck. Her sides are rusted and seaweed creeps over the sheer of her bows. Catwalks run the length of her side and small, electrically driven "donkeys" haul and tug at the loads of charred and twisted scrap which come up from below.

There is, though, a certain impressive dignity about the ship, the dignity of a leviathan which has threshed away its life in the shallows.

From a catwalk high on the side, it was possible to look down a great expanse of checkered rubber matting. This was once the promenade. Scarlet-coated page boys darted along here. Passengers lolled in deck chairs while what was the most luxurious liner in the world raced on its Atlantic crossing.

Today, the promenade is an ugly thing without a hint of life. Now and then, a workman will scramble down a rope ladder and disappear into a dark hole cut there. Far below, tugs and cranes snort and haul. But nothing moves on the promenade, centered as it is to almost a 90 degree angle.

About 500 civilian workmen are engaged in the job of salvage, but not half that number are to be seen outside. The others have burrowed deep inside and there they slowly gather together the loose furniture, splintered boards, everything moveable and bind their gleanings together for the slings, which are hoisted by whirring electric winches.

Responsible authorities have estimated that it will take at least 18 months to prepare the vessel for reflating and another year to clean her up and be ready for sea. There has never been a salvage job of such magnitude undertaken before.

Gerold Frank of the *New York Journal-American* found the experience "appalling, overwhelming, incredible."

Like ants swarming over a beached rowboat, we climbed and peered and teetered on high catwalks 80 feet above the water. We peered into the subterranean depths from which echoed the hollow sound of men's voices as they worked out of sight below, the screech of electric cranes, the rasp of drills boring into solid metal.

Three of Normandie's *decks have been sheared off at the water's edge. She is marked and scarred and ravaged by fire, wind and rain. An elevator shaft is now a dark tunnel and those who walk down it pass all of* Normandie's *decks.*

"What we're doing now might be called a general housecleaning," said Commander William A. Sullivan. "You open a door and you might find a big bed, say, suspended in air from a telephone wire. We've got to remove everything moveable."

An anonymous *New York Post* reporter wrote,

The reporters were admitted to the pier and the ship this morning, after a thorough inspection, which included three separate checks on their credentials and two friskings by sailors.

To date, Sullivan and his crew have accomplished the following: stripped the entire ship above the water, including most of the superstructure above the promenade deck, pumped about a fourth of the mud that oozed into the hull back where it belongs, closed the ports and started putting in new bulkheads.

Besides giving the reporters a guided tour of the wreck, Commander Sullivan explained how he intended to raise her.

"There are at least twenty different ways to raise the liner," Sullivan told the reporters. "The most difficult part of the job was choosing the least expensive one."

The method Sullivan had selected, he said, was something called "controlled pumping." As Sullivan described it to the gathered reporters, controlling pumping seemed simple enough. Salvage experts merely had to:

1. Make the submerged part of the ship watertight, by sealing all openings;

2. Subdivide the interior into watertight compartments so some parts could be flooded, while other parts were emptied out, thereby controlling the ship's righting motion;

3. Gradually pump water out of the submerged part of the hull until the vessel slowly rolled back to an even keel.

"It's a cut-and-dried job," Sullivan told the newsmen.

Of course, salvaging *Normandie* was anything but a cut-and-dried job. Never before had anyone attempted to raise a ship this large. None of the German warships scuttled and then raised at Scapa Flow after World War I, nor any of the American battleships sunk at Pearl Harbor and then salvaged, even approached *Normandie* in size.

Commander Sullivan, a lean, blue-eyed man in the prime of life, was in charge of the entire operation. His second in command was Lieutenant Commander C. F. Chandler, who was given charge of Pier 88 and was responsible for security.

The salvage superintendent was John Israel Tooker, Merritt, Chapman & Scott's premier salvage man. Captain Tooker, as he was known, had more than twenty years of ship-salvage experience, most of it as a diver. His father, Captain "Izzy" Tooker, was the man who had masterminded the salvage of the *St. Paul*, a small liner that had capsized at its New York pier in 1918— and father and son had worked together.

The technical expertise was supplied by A. C. W. Siecke, Merritt, Chapman & Scott's chief naval architect and engineer. He was responsible for all the stability and strength calculations, for determining shoring requirements and figuring out the final pumping schedule.

But raising *Normandie* was only half the job. What would be done with her once she was upright? Rear Admiral C. L. Cochrane, new chief of the Bureau of Ships, told a House Appropriations Committee that he expected *Normandie* to be refitted as a troop transport, a project that would take nine months and cost $20 million (as opposed to $60 million for a comparable new ship).

A week after New York newsmen visited the fallen *Normandie*, American warships did battle with Japanese warships near Midway. The Japanese lost four aircraft carriers, the Americans one. The Japanese lost 332 planes, the Americans 147. Few realized it, but the war in the Pacific had reached a turning point. Before the summer was over, U.S. Marines would land on Guadalcanal and four other Solomon Islands. In Russia the German offensive was grinding to a halt. Soon the Red Army would go on the offensive.

In North Africa, however, the brilliant German General Erwin Rommel destroyed 230 of the British Eighth Army's 300 tanks in what was known as Black Saturday. Shortly afterward Rommel captured Tobruk and advanced all the way to El Alamein.

The traitorous Pierre Laval, Prime Minister of Vichy France, took the occasion to proclaim his faith in Germany's ultimate victory. But a new force had entered the fray. On July 4, American-built and manned bombers flew their first mission, attacking four German air bases in Holland.

Through it all, *Normandie* lay in the muck of the North River while scores of men clambered over, around and even below her, like Lilliputians trying to free Gulliver.

Practically everything about her situation presented one kind of problem or another, problems Sullivan had managed to avoid discussing during the May 26 press conference.

Problem one: the underwater surface on which *Normandie* was lying.

According to Harvard Professor Karl Terzaghi, whom Sullivan had hired to study the situation, *Normandie* was resting on a fine, firm bed consisting of three strata: a twenty-foot layer of black, highly organic and almost liquid "mud" (actually, sewage); a second stratum of "hardpan" or gray, siltlike organic clay; and a third stratum of fine gray sand.

These strata were underlain by bedrock, at least underneath the forward third of the ship. Beyond that, the mud-silt-clay mixture was hundreds of feet deep.

But at frame 237, the blueprint number of one of *Normandie*'s gird-like ribs, just about where the middle of the first funnel would have been if the ship had been upright, a hard ledge of rock reared upward. As the tides came and went, *Normandie* pivoted, fore and aft, on this rock. What worried Sullivan here was the potential for hull damage. Somehow the stern must be lightened, he decided, to keep the pivoting to a minimum.

Problem two: the mud and silt on the bottom.

Because of *Normandie*'s enormous weight, she'd sunk into this semi-liquid mixture to a depth of forty-six feet (the rocky knob probably preventing her from sinking even more deeply). This settling was harmless enough, but when the ship went down, most of the 350 portholes and some of the sixteen large cargo ports on her port side either were already open or were forced open by water pressure. As a result the mud-silt mixture had poured into the ship, sometimes to a depth of twenty feet.

Problem three: the murky water in the slip.

One city sewer line emptied directly into the slip between Pier 88 and Pier 90, another emptied into the Hudson at the end of Pier 90 and a third emptied into the Hudson at the end of Pier 86. The waters in the slip were also filled with oil and gasoline that had leaked out of *Normandie*'s fuel tanks. The result: water that was nearly opaque, even in the most powerful underwater lighting available.

This made it impossible to inspect the hull for damage, impossible to see which ports were open and which were closed, impossible to accomplish very much at all from the outside of the ship.

Problem four: as *Normandie* rolled over, the scaffolding that had been hung on her port side for workmen to stand on while blanking off the portholes had been crushed like matchsticks. Now splintered two-by-fours had been rammed through many of the portholes, making it practically impossible to close them.

Despite the problems, the Navy took the first necessary steps in the salvage process. It began by buying Pier 88 from New York City for some $2.6 million.

The Navy needed the pier as a headquarters and material-storage site for the salvage operation. Also, salvage crews intended to disassemble part of the pier at the north side of its outboard end so it wouldn't damage *Normandie*—or vice versa—when the ship began to roll back upright. (This was the area under which *Normandie*'s stern had wedged itself at the moment of capsizing, destroying five pier pilings in the process.)

At the same time the Navy began to build on the north side of the wreck what came to be known as "Normandieville," a miniature industrial park of workshops, offices and storage rooms to meet salvage-crew needs.

Closest to the ship and running from bow to stern, Navy engineers built a catwalk broad enough to carry electric trucks. Lining the catwalk were office shacks, an elaborately equipped firehouse, concrete mixers, air compressors, tool sheds, portable power generators, welding machines, small derricks, banks of gas cylinders for acetylene torches and power and water lines.

A number of barges were moored more or less permanently alongside these buildings. These contained the blacksmith shop, the carpenter shop, the machine shop and the engineering office.

While the Navy was building Normandieville, a model-maker at the Brooklyn Navy Yard, Charles Bollot, was constructing two scale replicas of the ship.

One of these, 10.5 feet long, was built of copper and wood, with transparent celluloid decks and sixty-three separate removable sections. This was made for the divers to study before going underwater so they could understand where they were headed before they disappeared into the murk.

The other model was four feet long. Built of solid North Carolina pine, this one turned on its axis, lengthwise, so that the underwater parts of the ship could be quickly located as she was being righted.

Most of what had to be done before *Normandie* could be pumped out had to be accomplished underwater—closing the ports, compartmentalizing the ship with new bulkheads, reinforcing the decks so that they could withstand pumping pressures. That meant divers—many more divers than America possessed. But the salvage school took care of that.

Actually, Sullivan and his men established *three* schools: a divers' school for Navy enlisted men, a divers' school for civilians and a salvage school for Navy officers. Many volunteered, but Sullivan selected only men who already had ratings as carpenters' and machinists' mates, shipfitters and the like.

The divers' schools were set up on the south side of Pier 88. There was a "nest" for divers' suits and suit repair. A float was put into the water alongside the pier so that inexperienced divers could be helped into their heavy suits and helmets before going down.

Diving students were trained twenty-four hours a day, seven days a week, sailors and civilians working side by side. As they gained proficiency, they were given underwater tasks of increasing complexity.

The student divers had to pass a number of tests. One of the simpler ones was to dive to the bottom of the river with some pieces of lumber, some nails and a hammer. The assignment: to build a box.

Beginners almost always failed the first time out. They'd put two pieces of wood together and reach for the hammer—releasing the rest of the wood, which, of course, would shoot to the surface. The diver not only had to return to the surface to retrieve the floating lumber, he also had to endure the jibes of more experienced colleagues.

Some 30 to 35 percent of those who attended the schools failed to graduate because they lacked the necessary mechanical ability, the physical stamina or the emotional makeup. But, thanks to these two diving schools, it was possible to keep an average of seventy-five divers working on *Normandie* twenty-four hours a day.

Sullivan also ran a salvage school for Naval Reserve officers who'd been graduate engineers. They were first qualified as divers to depths of seventy-five feet, then given a two-month course in naval architecture to teach them the basics of ship stability and trim and the stability of damaged vessels.

In all, these three schools trained about 2,500 men, who became the core of the Navy Salvage Service. On the east coast alone this service rescued ships and cargoes worth a total of $750 million, more than justifying the $4.5 million cost of raising *Normandie*.

Sullivan and his men also cleared more than fifty harbors abroad—Palermo, Salerno, Naples, Cherbourg, Le Havre, Toulon, Marseilles, Manila and many others. They removed the wrecks of more than 1,000 ships of all sizes, plus thousands of small craft. They also brought up thousands of tons of harbor-blocking debris and vehicles. The value of what they salvaged and reclaimed was more than $2 billion.

Perhaps the most outstanding example of their work was at Naples, where Nazis had blocked every dock, fouled every channel with a sunken ship and scuttled cement-laden (and booby-trapped) ships in all the important berths. Four months after the Allies took Naples, Sullivan and his team had the port leading the world in the amount of tonnage received, thanks in large measure to their training on *Normandie*.

While they worked on *Normandie*, civilian divers were paid $25 to $30 a day, while enlisted men got the usual pay for their rank, plus $10 a month for the diving qualification. They weren't given the diving premium of $5 per underwater hour because diving in the waters of a river slip simply wasn't considered dangerous enough to justify the extra money.

But it was very dangerous. Even in the clear blue waters of the Caribbean, diving is dangerous. If something goes wrong with the air supply, a diver can suffocate quickly. Even too much air is a problem. If the air exhaust valve on the helmet goes on the blink, the diving suit blows up like a balloon, the diver shoots to the surface, his suit bursts and he plummets back down, anchored forever by 200 pounds of canvas and steel.

If a diver descends too quickly, he may face something divers call "the squeeze." In this situation, air can't be pumped down fast enough to counteract water pressure on the suit, and the diver is crushed to death.

Then there's the bends, caused by too fast a rise from the depths. This causes bubbles of nitrogen to form in the blood. If these bubbles reach the brain, the diver can die. If a diver happens to hold his breath while surfacing, he faces still another danger. As the outside pressure lessens, his lungs may suddenly burst.

In the best of circumstances, then, diving is no picnic. At Pier 88 in 1942 it was a nightmare.

First, there was that water. It was like ink, ink mixed with sewage and oil and mud. Divers couldn't see where they were going or what they were doing. They had to feel their way into the hull, risking snagging or tearing their suits on some sharp projection. They also had to work inside the hull entirely by their sense of touch. They had to hammer and nail and saw in utter darkness.

Normandie herself presented another hazard. Lying on her side, as she was, her decks had turned into bulkheads and her bulkheads into decks. As a result, divers found themselves walking on partitions that were built to carry nothing heavier than a layer of wallpaper.

Salvage experts also worried about the possibility that toxic or even explosive gases might accumulate within the hull, the result of rotting foodstuffs. To keep this hazard to a minimum, gas-analysis equipment was brought in and conditions inside the ship were checked frequently.

Then there was the mud. Mountains of it had oozed through open portholes and cargo doors. With one step a diver might have a solid footing, with the next he might find himself sinking over his head into mud the consistency of butter.

And there was the spun glass which had been used to insulate *Normandie*'s electric wiring. Fine particles of it floated about underwater, penetrated the seams of diving suits and worked into the pores. It took months for the filaments to "grow out," with accompanying itching and infections.

Finally, there was the fire danger, exacerbated by the flammable gases and the oil floating on the water in many compartments. To reduce the risk, a three-shift fire watch was put into effect. Extra lines for the divers were strung in every compartment, and emergency air hoses and face masks were attached to the divers' air lines. Rescue breathing equipment was cached in a shack on a float beside the ship, along with resuscitation gear. A round-the-clock medical watch consisting of a doctor and two assistants was on duty.

The surprising result of all these precautions and the thorough training given to each diver was that there were *no* fatalities during the entire operation and few serious accidents.

What there was was an enormous amount of difficult and tedious work.

The work began at the main New York offices of Merritt, Chapman & Scott. There, A. C. W. Siecke calculated *Normandie*'s buoyancy, metacentric height, center of gravity and every other important measurement, for the ship as she lay and for every angle she'd assume as she was pumped dry and began to right herself.

At the same time divers were removing the tons of scorched, sodden rubble that filled the wreck, including smashed grand pianos, twisted Army cots, broken glass by the barrelful, spoiled food, kitchen utensils, ruined wiring, rusty tools, blankets, damaged fittings, plywood bulkheads, ship's piping and practically everything else imaginable.

Each load of debris had to be dragged to an accessible place, lifted onto a sling, winched out of the wreck, deposited on a barge, marked with the exact location from which it was taken, then painstakingly weighed so that Siecke's center-of-gravity calculations could be adjusted.

"Looking back on it, it was a truly horrible job," Leonard Greenstone, who worked as a diver, recalled. "But at the time it seemed very exciting."

In all, about 6,000 tons of rubble were removed from the ship, plus 4,000 tons of broken glass.

While some divers were removing debris, others were working on the mud problem. Before the portholes could be closed— one of the most important steps in making the hull watertight— most of the mud had to be removed.

To accomplish this, divers installed "air lifts"—eight-inch pipes through which air was pumped at about eighty pounds per square inch. The rising air bubbles were supposed to push water and mud up over the side of the ship, but before the debris was fully cleared, the pipes were constantly plugged by such objects as glass shards, lumber and metal scraps. One air-lift unit almost strangled itself trying to swallow a grand piano.

Eventually the mud began to flow out of the bowels of the ship. But fresh mud flowed in to replace it. After a while, however, it caked up and formed inverted clay domes, stopping further inward flow.

The next order of business was to make *Normandie* as watertight as a bottle. Among other things, that meant somehow sealing up the 356 portholes that hadn't been blanked off during the abortive conversion attempt.

If *Normandie* had sunk in an upright position, divers could have put the sealing patches on the outside of the hull. But *Normandie*'s port side was *lying* on the mud, its portholes pressed against the bottom. It might have been possible to dredge some mud out from underneath the hull, but, as it was, the mud was barely solid enough to support the ship's weight.

Somehow, divers had to enter the ship and, working from the *inside*, put a patch on the *outside* of the porthole, covering it and a bit of the surrounding area so that water pressure would tighten the seal. But how could divers push a patch through a porthole that was smaller in diameter than the patch itself?

Captain Tooker found a way. He invented what came to be called a "Tooker patch." This was a piece of wood three inches thick, cut in a circle large enough to cover a porthole. Around the inside edge Tooker tacked a rubber gasket about a quarter-inch thick. Then he cut his wooden disk from one edge to the other and attached the two pieces together with barn-door hinges. Through it he put four long toggle bolts, two to a side.

Placing Tooker patches over *Normandie*'s portholes was a tedious process indeed. A diver would start by studying the model to figure out where he was going. Then he'd climb into his heavy suit, rubber seals clasping his wrists to make the sleeves water-tight, his feet shod in iron, a heavily weighted belt around his middle, his head inside his round iron mask warmed by a woolen cap and his hands covered with a pair of cotton work gloves.

Then he would ease into the opaque water, slowly sinking out of sight, a Tooker patch under one arm. Down below, he'd climb through a small hole into the ship's bowels, proceeding by touch and memory. He couldn't see a thing.

Eventually he'd find the porthole he was looking for. He'd unhinge its brass fitting, the frame that held the glass. Then he'd fold his Tooker patch in half (the reason for the hinges), thrust it through the porthole into the mud and open it out. After that he'd feel for the bolts, pull them through the porthole, fit strongbacks on them and tighten them.

Then he'd feel his way back through the inky labyrinth of tilted passageways until, with a burst of foam and a bubble of air, he'd break the water's surface, still inside the ship, and grope, like a sloth, for the ladder.

Finally, panting and exhausted by the weight of the metal which had kept him upright and able to work underwater, he would reach his tender, who'd take off his helmet and give him a chance to relax and smoke a cigarette.

Placing one Tooker patch might not be much of a task, but divers had to seal 356 portholes with Tooker patches. Sometimes they had to excavate ten feet of solid mud to do it, working an entire week to close just one porthole.

In addition to the portholes there were sixteen cargo ports, each large enough to admit a first-class passenger's Hispano-Suiza or Rolls Royce. Then there were the even larger funnel openings, now exposed by the removal of the superstructure. Besides all this, there were 4,500 smaller openings, all of which had to be sealed, plugged or otherwise closed.

Tooker patches served well enough for the portholes, but the larger openings had to be closed by enormous covers built with twenty-one inch girders, sandwiched between layers of heavy lumber and surrounded by thick rubber gaskets, the rubber being taken from Normandie's own rubber decking.

The largest of these patches weighed 52 tons, was 54 feet long, 22 feet wide, and 3 feet thick. It covered a huge cargo port. Such patches were built on barges tied up alongside the wreck, then lifted into place by derricks. Each one fit with the accuracy of a watch crystal.

The smallest patches were wedged into place like a cork in a wine bottle. But everything else was bolted down, then sealed with concrete from a concrete mixer and pumper mounted on a nearby barge.

All of this patching accomplished only one of the tasks necessary to ready Normandie for raising. Before there could be any "controlled pumping," the entire interior of the ship had to be divided into watertight compartments. Otherwise, when she began to roll and the vast quantity of water within her began to shift from port to starboard, there would be nothing to prevent her from capsizing to starboard.

So now Normandie, which some had thought insufficiently compartmented for military service, was compartmented with a vengeance deck by deck, all the way up to the top.

Working underwater and by touch alone, divers constructed the new bulkheads of grooved eight-by-twelve timbers joined together by two-by-fours.

As work progressed, a crane pulled each new timber upward against the underside of the lowest one previously laid, holding it there while divers bolted the ends into place. After the main surface was completed, wooden pockets were built along the corners and the lower edger of each bulkhead, and concrete was piped into these pockets to add strength and assure watertightness.

Many new watertight compartments were created by this process, the walls made out of bulkheads while decks served as the floors and roofs. And each time one of these compartments was finished, divers measured it carefully so that Siecke could calculate its volume for various water levels and angles of inclination. Into this labor went 240,500 board feet of eight-by-twelve timbers and 1,685 tons of concrete.

Still more lumber and concrete went into the next task: shoring up the decks. *Normandie*'s decks were built to withstand the vicissitudes of ocean travel, but not the enormous hydrostatic pressures of controlled pumping. Therefore, they had to be strengthened. Divers accomplished this task by placing a mile and a half of shoring timbers between the decks—working, as usual, by their sense of touch alone.

Other divers did their best to rustproof *Normandie*'s machinery and everything else liable to rust. They dipped, swabbed or sprayed turbines, motors, gyroscopic controls, pumps, lighting fixtures, kitchen equipment, laundry machinery and ice-making devices first with a preservative, then with a rust-preventing compound.

Unfortunately, nothing whatever could be done to protect the thousands of miles of wiring within the hull. Before *Normandie* could sail again, all of it would need replacing.

In addition, there was the matter of the pier. Since the bottom of *Normandie*'s rudder and skeg extended under Pier 88 for five feet, Sullivan knew that rotating the ship to an upright position could damage the pier. For this reason he had workmen cut away 300 feet of Pier 88, lengthwise, at the outboard end. Also, twenty-eight pile clusters were installed along the ship's aft area, between the hull and the remaining pier structure, to serve as a bumper when the huge vessel rose from her muddy bed.

On October 13, 1942, seven months after the fire, with salvage work well under way, Commander Sullivan once more invited the press to view the scene.

Censorship was lifted completely and nothing was held back as the reporters, who had been warned to wear old clothes, were permitted to crawl wherever they dared—and they dared to crawl practically everywhere. Helmeted workers stepped aside to allow the visitors to pass, sometimes warning them to be careful of the rubber air lines that fed oxygen to divers who worked silently in the ship's interior.

As the party proceeded, the newsmen realized that all obstructions, cabins, plumbing and everything except permanent bulkheads had been cleared away between decks. And it was between decks that the party alternately walked, climbed and swung from one footing to another.

A day later stories once more filled the newspapers of America's largest city, extolling the Navy's efforts and expressing awe at the magnitude of the task. Both *Normandie* and the Navy's reputation were being salvaged here.

These newspaper stories inspired novelist Walter Havighurst to write a short story about *Normandie* for *Collier's* Magazine.

"They say the war has finished off the great liners," it began.

> *Soon, transatlantic planes will take 12 hours from New York to London and Paris. Maybe the big ships will go and people won't hear again the great voice roaring over New York at midnight and the docks will be empty where the bands used to play while last minute passengers hurried up the gangways and thousands lined the tiered decks. Maybe that won't be again. But there is one ship that will never be forgotten.*
>
> *What was she like? France. She was like France before the anguish and she is like France now. She was a ship with destiny around her; we knew that when she first steamed out of Le Havre in '35, all her pennants stiff with the wind of her own speed. She was like France—*

the verve and the valor and the chichi too. There was enough nonsense about her, but she also had grandeur and whether you traveled in the fabulous 'Trouville' suite or only watched from a Hoboken ferry as she came up the river, you didn't forget her.

Now, in the littered slip where the tides are murky with mud and oil, they are turning her over. Slowly. Slowly. I guess you couldn't see it, standing at the dockside or watching from the elevated highway. But you could feel it, the deep life stirring in her, the beginning of buoyancy again.

There was some living spirit in her, like the breath of France. She was like France and she would rise again. . . ."

But France was not rising. Quite the contrary. On November 8 British and American forces landed at Algeria and Morocco in North Africa. Unfortunately, they were opposed by the Vichy French, with much bloodshed.

Three days later the German Army marched through Vichy France, occupying everything except the Mediterranean coast and essentially emasculating what remained of the French government.

But in many other ways, the war was going well for the Allies. Shortly after landing, the Allies captured Casablanca. Soon afterward British troops reached Tobruk. In Stalingrad, Soviet forces began to throw back the Germans. And at an abandoned football stadium on the campus of the University of Chicago on December 2 a team of American scientists achieved history's first nuclear chain reaction.

As 1943 began, events took an even more positive turn:

☐ The Allies scored their first land victories over the Japanese, first in Papua, then on Guadalcanal.
☐ The RAF launched its first daylight attack of the war on Berlin.
☐ The Germans surrendered at Stalingrad.
☐ Roosevelt, Churchill and the Combined Chiefs of Staff met at Casablanca to plan future strategy (Roosevelt ar-

riving on a Pan American Airways Clipper flying boat, the very first air journey by an American President while in office).

☐ That spring and summer the Allies finally solved the U-boat problem, sinking thirty-eight in the Bay of Biscay alone during the month of May. At the same time all German forces in North Africa surrendered.

On May 25 Roosevelt and Churchill met again, this time in Washington. (Churchill crossed the Atlantic on the *Queen Elizabeth*.) They decided that France would be invaded on May 1, 1944.

All of this might have happened months earlier, had *Normandie* been available to carry 15,000 troops from America to England in four short days.

Her nearest equivalent, the *America*, the largest liner ever built in the United States, carried more than 450,000 troops to and from a variety of war zones during World War II, traveling the equivalent of fourteen times around the world. She shortened the war by giving America the ability to thrust a substantial number of troops into a distant battle within a few days' notice.

Such might have been said of *Normandie*, had it not been for Clement Derrick's acetylene torch.

While Sullivan's salvagers worked to raise *Normandie*, much of what had been taken from her during the conversion attempt was sold off in thirteen separate public auctions—works of art, Art Deco paneling, furniture, silverware, dishes, bed linen, even the wine that had been aboard her on her last arrival in New York in August 1939.

These auctions were conducted at the U.S. Customs Seizure Rooms at 210 Varick Street, in lower Manhattan, under the auspices of Harry M. Durning, Collector of Customs. The auctioneer was Edward G. Collard.

Originally, the U.S. government had intended to return everything it had taken from the liner, fully restoring her to her prewar glamour. But the disaster made those plans moot.

The first auction was held on May 26, 1942, just five days after Washington announced its decision to salvage the ship. It disposed of some 18,000 magnums, bottles, splits and so-called "nips" of wine, liquor, beer and other beverages, including soft drinks.

These items brought a grand total of $20,723.50—just $110 under appraised value. Two hundred people attended, and sixty-six made purchases.

Charles Sichel, of H. Sichel & Sons, the international wine dealers, had the remarkable experience of seeing some wine he had sold *Normandie* auctioned off for a much higher price—in some cases 40 percent above retail value. Even *Normandie*'s stock of Coca-Cola went for eight cents a bottle!

The second auction took place on August 25. This one disposed of 1,800 mattresses, 700 woolen table pads, 2,500 pillows, 1,324 woolen steamer-chair blankets, plus assorted books, cigars, perfumes, lingerie, jewelry, phonograph records, crates of beads, crabmeat packed in Japan, ebony elephants, trays decorated with butterfly wings, Polish postcards and one leopard-skin rug. The auction brought in another $12,000.

The leopard-skin rug was purchased for $60 by Louis Marchiony, the spumoni manufacturer. John Krupsaw, a Washington mattress dealer, bought 650 *Normandie* mattresses for $7.50 apiece. "I plan to sell them to new housing developments in Washington," he told the newspapers.

The third auction occurred on October 28. Most of *Normandie*'s large carpets were sold, including the huge hand-knotted Aubusson carpet that once graced the grand lounge. It went for $800.

The auctioneer's gavel was heard once again on December 9. This auction was to include the eight-by-eleven-foot French flag that had once flown from *Normandie*'s mast, but a few days before the auction a Navy officer gave it to Henri Morin de Linclays, the resident director and general manager of the French Line.

Some 500 people showed up for the December 9 auction, including former passengers seeking mementos, shoppers for bargain Christmas presents and various wholesale dealers. Altogether, they paid $47,952 for what the catalog called "a great variety of articles of extraordinary value and artistic merit."

Among these articles: 492 deck chairs, 19 round tables, 600 dining-room chairs, 100 tourist-class dining-room chairs, 34 porthole curtains, 27 metal folding serving tables, 5,000 pieces of draperies and bedspreads, 3 baby-grand pianos, 2 folding-keyboard pianos, 40 sets of card tables and chairs, 1 prayer rail, 75 baggage hand trucks, 11,000 hangers, 31 vacuum cleaners, 11 boxes of clay pigeons (some damaged) and 250 thermos bottles.

A particularly determined man who arrived early and refused to leave for lunch was Henry Stolow of Fifth Avenue. He paid $710 for a wood Aubusson tapestry-covered 12-foot settee, appraised at $400. He also bought some dining-room chairs. "I know the price is no bargain, even though the settee is a beautiful one. But I liked it and so I bought it," he told a newspaper reporter. "You see, I came to this country on the *Normandie* on one of her first trips and I felt I ought to have some of the chairs, too."

A Cherry Street wholesaler, David Wener, paid $310 for 4,000 life preservers, some donut and some jacket style. He advertised them in newspapers all over the country and sold all of them by mail order for $2 each. One order, for fifty of them, came from the Belgian Congo.

For a time, in fact, Wener based practically his entire business on merchandise from *Normandie*. He had great success with a lot of cane-seated, red-framed deck chairs with innerspring cushions and linen tickings, which he retailed for $25 apiece. And when he advertised some silver-plated pint thermos decanters engraved with the French Line insignia for $10 apiece, he got $5,000 worth of mail orders, more than he could fill.

There was yet another auction on May 13, 1943. This one disposed of 500 barrels of wine, wearing apparel, jewelry and skis left by forgetful passengers, chinaware, rifles, bales of cotton, embroidered satin drapes, tapestry-covered chairs, 279 electric clocks, 293 French telephones (not compatible with AT&T equipment), 696 teaspoons, 209 ice-cream molds, 9 pairs of boxing gloves, one gymnasium bucking horse, 100 metal ladders, 57 small bulletin boards, 1,830 opal glass bathroom shelves, 55 office cabinets, a dozen silver-plated trophies, 47 cuspidors.

And so it went, this diaspora of *Normandie* artifacts. All told, the Customs Appraiser auctioned off $134,191.15 worth of *Normandie* effects, which amounted to between half and two thirds of what was removed from her.

On July 27, 1984, paintings by Duclos de la Haille, depicting the province of Normandy in war and peace, were sold for $200. Vestments and other ecclesiastical paraphernalia from the chapel went to the Shrine Church of the Sea, at 10th Avenue and 21st Street in New York. Her lifeboats were sold on March 28, 1945, "as is, where is," at the Navy's 35th Street pier in Brooklyn. B. Altman acquired fifty one-by-three-foot squares of pink-mirrored, hammered glass, which it used to set off jewelry displays.

Most of the rest was returned to the French Line, turned over to the French embassy or retained by the Navy for its own use or for other government agencies.

The French Line, for instance, took a statue of François I, the papal benediction, some of the sports trophies, various gift flags, two Sevres vases given to the ship by President Lebrun, as well as 52,000 pieces of silverware, 52,000 pieces of china, 32,000 pieces of glassware and 26,000 pieces of linen, all bearing the CGT logo.

Also returned to CGT: 5,369 books from the ship's library, the Dunand lacquerwork panels and the bronze doors from the smoking room and various paintings. These items were all shipped back to France in 1946. Some were later used on the *Liberté* and the *Ile de France*.

The French embassy in Washington got a good bit of furniture from the grand lounge and from the Trouville, Deauville and Bayeux Suites.

In November 1942, with the *Normandie* salvage work well under way, Commander Sullivan and twelve members of the first class to graduate from his salvage school were sent to Casablanca, whose harbor was clogged with sunken shipping.

Sullivan never returned to *Normandie*. Instead, he and his men spent the rest of the war clearing out harbors in Europe and in the Pacific. His *Normandie* responsibilities were turned over to Captain Bernard E. Manseau.

By summer 1943 America and her friends seemed to be advancing everywhere. In Russia, the Red Army was forcing the Nazis farther and farther away from Leningrad, Stalingrad and Moscow. In the Southwest Pacific, U.S. forces were attacking such Japanese-held islands as New Georgia, Rendova and New Guinea. In Europe, U.S. and British forces were invading Sicily.

Toward the end of July, 739 RAF bombers bombed the German port city of Hamburg, killing about 20,000 and creating firestorms with temperatures close to 1,000° and winds of more than 150 miles an hour. One of the casualties: Vladimir Yourkevitch's first and only German passenger ship, the *Vaterland II*. Bombs set it on fire and buckled its plates beyond repair.

Back in New York City, at Pier 88, work on *Normandie* was progressing more quickly than expected and the Navy brass in Washington and New York were salivating at the thought of the favorable publicity the ship's coming resurrection would bring. So, toward the end of June 1943 workmen were ordered to build a 400-foot-long canvas-canopied observation deck facing the slip where the fallen *Normandie* lay, so that the press and various other VIPs could watch the ship rise from the depths.

This platform ran from 48th Street to 50th Street and extended for ten feet onto the southbound lanes of the West Side Highway. A broad stairway connected it to the pierhead.

At the same time other workmen began dismantling Normandieville, which would be in the way, both physically and visually, when the big moment came.

On August 1, the day before pumping was to begin, a few newsmen were given one last look at the prostrate vessel. Among them was Bruce Bliven, of the *New Republic*. "It was an impressive experience to walk along the dock and see the vast grey hulk towering above us 60 feet into the air, knowing that she extended a roughly equal distance below the water," he wrote.

> *A workman busy on the big curving hull looked like a fly on an elephant.*
>
> *At one point inside the hull, a huge half circle of white was painted with numbers around the edge and over it a ten-foot red pointer. It indicated the exact degree to which the ship had rolled and would serve, as she rolled slowly back, to record progress exactly.*

> *To me, the most poignant thing of the whole trip was*
> *something I saw in one of the offices on the pier—the great*
> *painted panels removed from the ship. Each panel bore*
> *the name of a French city—Toulouse, Bordeaux, Nantes,*
> *Rennes.*
>
> *Looking at the names of those proud cities, it sud-*
> *denly seemed to me that the ship was a symbol of France*
> *herself. The fact that she was rising from her humiliation*
> *and degradation was a good omen that France, too, would*
> *someday rise again.*

Even now salvage workers were completing the last job necessary before "dewatering" could begin: they were installing gigantic gasoline-driven salvage pumps inside the hull—an extraor-
dinarily difficult task.

Some ninety-eight pumps, ranging in weight from 1,000 to
2,760 pounds and in size from three by two by one feet to eight
by five by two, had to be lifted by derricks into the ship and
shoehorned through the maze of corridors to the right place on
the right deck. After that, they had to be bolted onto platforms
hinged on one end, with pulleys at the other, so that as *Normandie* slowly swung upright, the pumps could be kept within
15 degrees of horizontal.

As the ship lifted, the pumps continually had to be moved
lower within the hull, since they needed to be within twenty
feet of the water's surface to work properly. Each time they were
moved, their exhaust lines also had to be shifted. Altogether,
these pumps were capable of emptying 10,000 tons of water an
hour out of the hull. At that rate she could have been dry in
less than ten hours. But *Normandie* couldn't be dewatered too
quickly. If she were, there was every chance she'd suddenly snap
over and capsize in the opposite direction, smashing against
Pier 88.

But Tooker, Manseau and Sullivan had already taken such
matters into account. They'd decided to pump out the ship very
gradually so they could control her movement absolutely.

There were two things they couldn't really control, however. First, there was the rocky knob on which *Normandie* rested,

about a third of the way back from her bow. She would pivot on this point of rock as she came up. Unless her bow was light enough, the rock would batter her hull plates.

Second, there was her muddy bed. If this mud created suction against the hull, *Normandie* might suddenly lurch to starboard when the suction broke, leading to a frightful, uncontrolled flop against Pier 88.

The salvage team did its best to take these difficulties into account. It worked out a pumping plan that would keep the bow as light as possible. It tunneled beneath the hull and installed water and air jets to break the suction even before the pumping began.

On August 2, 1943, all of the pumps were tested. The ship appeared bottle-tight. Tooker, Manseau and their team confidently believed that *Normandie* would be upright within a week.

At 5:30 p.m. on August 4 the water within the hull was lowered about nine feet. *Normandie* showed definite signs of straining to right herself. The next day was spent on further tests and calculations. Every test was positive.

At 8:00 a.m. on August 6 Tooker and Manseau ordered the pumps turned on again, likewise the air and water jets. At 9:15 *Normandie* trembled, then almost imperceptibly began to roll toward an upright position, a fraction of an inch at a time.

But at this point a problem presented itself—long anticipated but still a problem: the reappearance of the outboard bulkhead of what used to be the Promenade Deck, the part of the superstructure that, buried under tons of mud, couldn't be removed earlier.

The salvage team feared that this wall, weighed down by mud, might peel back, taking with it a vast area of *Normandie*'s hull plating. For that reason, at about noon, when the bulkhead began to appear, the pumping was temporarily halted and divers attached wire stays between the bulkhead and the Promenade Deck. At 10:00 p.m. the pumps were turned on again. After fifteen minutes *Normandie*'s list had decreased by about 4 degrees, a fairly substantial amount.

On the next day, August 7, the pumping continued without incident, the salvage team controlling *Normandie*'s righting movement with great precision. By the end of the day the ship was holding at a 67-degree list, 12 degrees more vertical than at the start.

At this point *Normandie*'s stern was more or less afloat. In fact, from a practical standpoint, the ship was aground at only one point: that rocky knob about a third of the way back from her bow.

Before the pumping process began, the salvage team had decided to raise *Normandie* to a 45-degree angle, then began clearing out the wooden bulkheading, shoring, concrete. Now, on the morning of August 8, with the operation proceeding exactly as planned, they decided to bring *Normandie* up to the target inclination without further hesitation.

The pumps were turned on again and this time left running until they'd removed more than 11,000 tons of water, chiefly from compartments 14, 15 and 16, all three of which lay directly above the rocky knob.

When *Normandie* reached an angle of 49 degrees, the pumps were shut down once more so they could be moved to a lower level. This took the remainder of the day. It seemed now that the great liner would be fully afloat in a day or two. Then cleanup could begin and, after that, rebuilding.

By this time thousands of people had begun to gather on both shores of the Hudson, on Manhattan rooftops and as near Pier 88 as policemen would let them get, hoping to see the phoenix rise.

One of the those watching was a naval officer who'd been aboard *Normandie* when she caught fire and capsized. "When she went over," he told reporters, "I had a feeling that nothing humans could do could stop her or set her right again. Now I feel there's nothing humans cannot do if they set their minds to it."

As the afternoon wore on, the observation platform quickly filled up, jammed with the wives of Navy officers and Merritt, Chapman & Scott employees. The VIPs the Navy intended to invite had not yet been summoned, but Admiral Adolphus Andrews was there.

There was a holiday spirit to the day, but most of the spectators eventually went away disappointed. *Normandie* was moving toward an even keel even more slowly than a minute hand on a clock.

Among the members of the salvage team, however, there was a very real sense of confidence. Everything had gone exactly as planned. *Normandie* herself was responding eagerly.

That night the *New York Sun* carried a slightly premature ode to *Normandie's* revival, written by a man named W. I. Phillips. In part, it said:

> *Nice work, old girl!*
> *Just one more grunt or two*
> *And you'll be right side up*
> *Or nearly so!*
>
> *A little longer, baby;*
> *Chin up, kid,*
> *And they'll be saying*
> *"Look what Normie did!"*
> *Then, radiant and bright,*
> *You'll sail again*
> *With joy erasing all*
> *Those months of pain.*

The Navy brass, impressed by the untroubled progress, scheduled a ceremony for a few days hence. Reviewing-stand invitations were printed up and distributed to a broad cross-section of government and civilian VIPs.

Then, early the next morning, August 9, the salvage effort turned sour. The pumps in compartment 16, directly above the rock ledge, were unable to lower the water beyond the existing level, even operating at peak capacity for twenty-three and a half hours. An extremely serious leak had developed. Divers were sent down to find it, but the mud and rock prevented them from reaching the area.

Tooker and Manseau were not unduly worried, and so decided to go ahead with the dewatering. On August 10 the pumps were turned on again and *Normandie* continued to rise. By the end of the day her angle of inclination was just 42 degrees—37 degrees less than when the operation had begun. But nine ten-inch pumps operating at full capacity in compartment 16 were unable to gain more than a foot or two headway.

Just after midnight on August 11 divers finally located the source of the trouble. The tank-top seams forward of the first row of boilers in #2 fire room, in what the salvage men had designated compartment 16, had been split open five feet horizontally and two feet vertically. At one point the gap was an inch and a half wide. With the ship now listing at "only" 42 degrees, it was possible for divers to inspect the hull for the leak from the outside.

While one group of divers went down to inspect the hull, another group began to stuff rags and sawdust into the tank-top seams, hoping to seal them at least partially until *Normandie* could be towed to a shipyard.

At 2:15 a.m. a diver reported a split hull plate on the port-side bilge, at about frame 240, in the middle of compartment 16. More rags were called for and stuffed into the crack.

By the end of the day *Normandie*'s list was just under 40 degrees. The salvage team decided to hold it there for a day or two while the full extent of the hull damage was determined.

Sure enough, on August 13 divers found a hole in the port wing tank about three and a half feet in diameter. This one was at frame 237, in the middle of boiler room #2. It was sealed with a custom-made Tooker patch.

Tooker and Manseau knew what had caused the leaks. It was that rocky knob on which *Normandie* had pivoted. Evidently the liner had teetered on the high, sharp pinnacle when she capsized, while the tides rocked her back and forth as she lay there for months, helpless, and especially as she began to move during the righting. As a result, some of her hull plates had been badly dented, even punctured—how badly, the salvage team did not yet know.

By the morning of the 14th Tooker and Manseau thought that their divers had found all the ruptures in compartment 16. They decided to seal the leak by laying some 100 cubic yards of concrete in the corner between the wing tanks and the double-bottom tanks. On the 18th pumping resumed.

At first compartment 16 held tight. But suddenly, with the

water level down ten feet from the previous day, water began pouring back into the ship. Divers quickly found the problem: There was a new rupture in the tank tops, beyond the patched area.

Tooker and Manseau decided to reduce *Normandie*'s list to 25 degrees by pumping out the compartments on either side of compartment 16. Then divers were sent down with large bags of rags and sawdust. Using poles, they pushed them up against the hull, in the hope some would be sucked into the cracks and partially choke off the leaks.

Now, for the first time, the divers could examine the infamous rocky knob. What they discovered was a large, rocky ledge full of jagged projections. They also realized that if *Normandie* were righted any further before she began to float, she'd roll right into some of the sharpest pinnacles.

The pumping was now brought to a halt—except in compartment 16, where it was necessary to run the pumps continually to keep the water at its current level. Manseau told the Navy to cancel the forthcoming celebration. The observation-deck invitations were quietly withdrawn and the platform itself was eventually torn down.

Between August 22 and 30 Tooker, Manseau and Siecke made new calculations and sent divers down to examine the hull again and again. They discovered damage far beyond their original estimates.

The rocky knob which fate had placed in Pier 88 had hurt *Normandie* almost as badly as the fire and the capsizing. It had created a network of cracks over an area fifty-four feet long and twenty-seven feet wide, centering on compartment 16.

The salvage team decided to attempt to stem the leaks by pouring more concrete—800 cubic yards of it, enough to fill all the wing tanks and double-bottom tanks in the area. The experts hoped this would provide a dam against which bags of rags, sawdust, mats, etc., could be pushed from the outside.

The concrete pouring began on September 7 and continued for four days. On September 12 a pumping test seemed fairly successful. By the next morning, though, compartment 16 was leaking again. It took thirteen ten-inch pumps to keep the water just seven feet below its previous level.

The salvage team had put winches on Pier 88 and Pier 90 and strung mooring cables between the ship and the winches. This system was intended to straighten *Normandie* in her slip as she came afloat, to prevent further damage to the pier or the ship.

Now, with *Normandie* partly afloat, the electric winches were turned on, putting a heavy strain on the mooring cables. Inch by inch, the bow of the ship was pulled toward Pier 88, an action which simultanously dragged the ship's stern away from it.

The purpose this time, however, was not to protect the pier or even the ship. It was to position the cracked hull plates over some 3,000 bags of rags that divers had pushed into the muddy bottom, in the hope they'd be sucked into the hull cracks.

During the next two days *Normandie*'s bow was moved about sixteen feet toward Pier 88, bringing the bilge keel over the bags of rags which were waiting for it. This worked exactly as intended. But, to make sure they held, another 800 cubic yards of concrete were poured into the ship, in and around compartment 16. The leaks were reduced to a trickle.

At 4:30 a.m. on September 15, 1943, the salvage team agreed that *Normandie* was fully afloat, even at low tide. Even in compartment 16 the pumps were holding their own.

To make sure the leaks didn't open up again, the salvage team ordered a collision mat made to cover the cracked hull plates. A number of standard collision mats were assembled and sewn together, making a cover about sixty-five square feet. This was securely fastened over the damaged area.

Normandie was a ship once more.

Originally, Commander Sullivan had estimated that the job would take two years and cost $5 million. It was actually accomplished in sixteen months, at a cost of $4.75 million, not counting the pier repair.

On shore, Leonard Greenstone gazed at the ship in awe, practically speechless and almost overcome with feelings of triumph and pride. He could see some of the Tooker patches he'd placed underwater by touch, and he knew that he had helped bring this great vessel back to life. "It was like being a member of a winning Superbowl team," he said years later.

Said the *New York Times* on its editorial page, "The *Nor-*

mandie went down in defeat. She comes up in victory. She will sail again—on war duty—and someday, with all her flags and all her lights, return triumphant to her old port."

For one New Yorker, *Normandie*'s resurrection was a very personal event. "When they told me the ship might be broken up instead of salvaged, I felt as though my heart had been torn out of me," Vladimir Yourkevitch told a reporter. "Now I have the feeling of having just got over the crisis of a serious operation."

At this time Yourkevitch was serving as a go-between in the transfer of Lend-Lease ships between the United States and the Soviet Union, his knowledge of ships and his Russian language making him the perfect man for the job.

It was a heady period for the designer. His son remembers a steady stream of Soviet and American naval officers coming to the family home in Yonkers and his father taking frequent trips to Washington.

The Russian émigré was also working on a visionary ship project, a plan for cable-linked convoys of tubelike concrete "ships," which, submerged just below the water's surface and filled with oil or other liquid cargo, would be towed by submarines. Eventually a few were built in South America.

He also designed a new shipyard in San Pedro, California, plus the world's largest and most powerful dredge, several cable ships, some cargo ships and a ferry boat. In addition, he supervised the construction of eight ocean-going wooden tugs for the U.S. Maritime Commission.

Yourkevitch also made an involuntary contribution to the American war effort: the hull shape he'd developed for Czarist Russia and brought to its final form in *Normandie*. Paying no attention whatever to his patent, the Navy appropriated the idea and used it in practically every new American warship. In fact, even today's warships (and cruise liners, for that matter) use a version of Yourkevitch's hollowed-out bow.

During this period the Allies continued to advance on almost every front. They conquered Sicily. They bombed German V-bomb experimental bases at Peenemunde, signed a secret armistice with the Italians, landed at Salerno, and occupied Naples. Italy declared war on Germany. And Hitler abandoned his effort to capture the Ukraine.

At Pier 88 most of the salvage men were packing up their gear and departing for other assignments, making room for another kind of work crew altogether—clean-up men, some 300 of them, hired by Merritt, Chapman & Scott at sixty-five cents an hour.

Their task was to remove all the concrete, wooden bulkheads and patches that the salvage divers had installed with such great difficulty. This clean-up was necessary before *Normandie* could be turned over to the Navy for refitting or whatever. The job took six full weeks.

Lester Holmes, who helped remove some of the lumber shoring, recently recalled that the quality of the work equaled anything he'd ever seen done on dry land in broad daylight. "It was amazing to think that this had been done underwater by men in diving suits, in total darkness."

On October 27—Navy Day—some twenty months and eighteen days after she'd caught fire, Captain Manseau turned *Normandie* over to Captain H. V. McKittrick, captain of the New York Navy Yard, Brooklyn, in a brief ceremony at Pier 88.

Scarred by fire, stained by oil, shorn of her superstructure and her glamour, *Normandie* was nonetheless afloat on a nearly even keel. Her dignity—and her life—had been almost miraculously restored.

dESTINATION UNkNOWN

In the best of all possible worlds, *Normandie* would now have been quickly transformed into a combat aircraft carrier which launched the war-ending blow, or, possibly, into a troopship whose soldiers arrived just in time to turn the tide.

Then, in this best of all possible worlds, she would have been lovingly restored to her former glory, to resume her career as one of the world's greatest passenger liners.

But this was not the best of all possible worlds. It was America in 1943, America at war, her resources strained to their maximum. Military expediency would dictate whether or not *Normandie* was brought back to life in this world, not sentiment, not even economics.

In January 1943, with the salvage work ahead of schedule and the war at its peak, Washington realized it had better decide what kind of warship *Normandie* was to become, so the design work could be finished by the time she was back on an even keel.

By February 8 the Bureau of Ships had come up with two designs. In one, *Normandie* would become a troopship. In the other, she'd become an auxiliary aircraft carrier. Either way, the Bureau expected to restore half of her original power plant, giving the ship a speed of about 24 knots at 80,000 horsepower.

On May 8, while *Normandie* was being patched and shored, her conversion was approved at the Navy's highest levels. She was to become a troop transport that could carry not only men and vehicles but aircraft which could fly onto and off of the deck. She would be equipped with standard aircraft-carrier arresting cables and catapults and the familiar aircraft-carrier island on the starboard side, complete with crane.

The Brooklyn Navy Yard was ordered to prepare preliminary contract plans and specifications. Todd-Erie and Bethlehem-Hoboken both expressed interest in the job. They were expected to hire either Gibbs and Cox or Cox and Stevens to produce the detailed design.

General Electric, which had worked with Als-Thom in France to build *Normandie*'s engines in the 1930s, was asked to recondition them. GE was also told to decide if new boilers would be needed.

Bit by bit, while the salvage men worked to raise the hull, the details of APV-4—*Normandie/Lafayette*—were worked out. Incidentally, one of the men who worked out the plans was Captain Hyman G. Rickover.

According to these plans, APV-4 would be able to carry a grand total of 14,750 men—600 troop officers, 2,000 enlisted personnel, 150 ship's officers and 12,000 troops.

The ship's 850-foot runway would be able to accommodate 31 B-25 bombers or as many as 169 F4F-4 fighters, or various combinations of other aircraft.

She'd be armed with eight five-inch 38-caliber guns, fifteen 40-mm. AAG quad mounts, thirty-six 20-mm. AA guns and the appropriate number of gun directors, plus huge quantities of ammunition for all of these weapons.

She'd also have facilities for fueling at sea, a new 1,800-seat cafeteria, new, larger fresh-water tanks, new longitudinal bulkheads, new transverse bulkheads, reinforced deck plating, new freight elevators, blanked-off cargo ports below the waterline, torpedo-protection bulkheads, searchlights and hundreds of smaller changes.

By the middle of August, after pumping had begun at Pier 88, the rebuilding plans were far enough along to begin model tests. These continued throughout the month and into September while *Normandie* slowly staggered up out of the mud, definitely the worse for wear.

The estimated cost of all these changes: about $20 million On September 16 the county of the Bronx offered to pay for it all in the Third War Loan Drive, announcing its intentions in a large *Daily News* display ad paid for by Alexander's Department Store. The county promised to come up to its quota of $38 million.

By early November 1943 *Normandie* was ready to leave Pier 88 on her first trip since 1939. She was fully afloat now, but was maintained at a 1-to-2-degree list so that any leakage would collect in the port bilge, where the three six-inch pumps still in place could get rid of it.

All of the temporary bulkheads, shoring, mud and debris had been removed. All of the concrete was gone, except for that used to patch the damaged part of her hull.

The various cracks and gaps in her plating were now stuffed with thousands of bags of rags and sawdust and covered by hemp collision mats—which were already beginning to dissolve in the highly polluted waters of the Hudson.

Some new items had been added to the ship: gasoline and oil tanks for the pumps and generators, dozens of new fire extinguishers, a temporary head for those who worked on board, a drinking water tank, a temporary wooden structure to support anchor lights and a temporary wooden bridge, complete with a bell to be used as a fire alarm or fog warning.

In the early morning hours of November 3 about sixty reporters and photographers gathered at Pier 88, at the Navy's invitation. A squadron of Meseck, Brady & McAllister and Dalzell tugs hovered in the slip or under *Normandie*'s stern at the ends of hawsers fixed to special towing rings which had been bolted into the ship's hull near the waterline.

Aboard her were 200 civilian Navy Yard workers, a small Coast Guard detail and 25 civilian salvage officers who manned her pumps. These men were commanded by Captain H. V. McKittrick, who'd accepted the ship at the ceremony a week earlier, telling reporters, "I can say this ship will be in service as soon as possible."

At a signal from McKittrick, the tugs began to back *Nor-*

mandie away from her pier, easing her stern into the incoming tide. Her rudder was locked dead center and her engines were silent. As she began to move, there was an enormous cheer from the workmen on the pier and on the ship. It was the culmination of the greatest salvage effort in history, and every man there must have felt that a miracle had been accomplished.

The reporters and photographers boarded a variety of small boats and set out to accompany the huge vessel. Thousands of other New Yorkers saw her as she moved slowly downriver, but many did not recognize her. She was flat-topped, her superstructure, masts and funnels gone. Her sides were streaked with rust and oil stains. She did not even fly a flag.

She looked like a vast hearse being pulled along at a funereal pace by a swarm of tiny tugs, or a dead elephant being dragged by a regiment of pygmies.

Navigating the big ship was a noisy, if simple, process. McKittrick stood first on one of the temporary wooden wing bridges and then on the other, signaling the tugs with a whistle and a hand wave. If he wanted full speed, he blew a series of sharp blasts. The tugs signaled back with their own whistles.

Normandie passed the Battery at 11:30 a.m., where a small crowd gazed and waved. A few minutes later she slid by the Statue of Liberty, "reminiscent, like herself, of a freedom-loving France," as one writer put it. The newspapers later said she was going to an undisclosed east-coast dry dock, but any keen-eyed young boy on the Staten Island ferry could have seen where she was headed: the Navy Yard Annex, a finger of filled land more than two miles long which projects into the upper bay, eastward from Bayonne, New Jersey.

On its tip was a tremendous new dry dock, the existence of which was kept a secret during the war. At 2:30 p.m. *Normandie* entered the dry dock. She was the first ship to use it.

The Navy expected *Normandie* to remain in dry dock for three weeks. She'd been taken there for inclining experiments to determine buoyancy and stability. These were required before the rebuilding could begin.

It didn't turn out as expected. The hull damage came as a nasty surprise. Nevertheless, the Bureau of Ships Chief, Admiral Cochrane, ordered it fixed.

Then came an even nastier surprise: Inspection revealed that practically *all* of *Normandie*'s propulsion machinery had been ruined by the eighteen-month submersion in the Hudson. Boilers, motors, generators, turbines, auxiliary equipment were all beyond repair. If *Normandie* were ever to move again under her own power, she would need new engines, new boilers, new everything.

That meant diverting propulsion machinery from other warships then under construction. It meant greater expense. It meant substantial delay. It meant severely straining already overburdened manufacturing plants. It meant further aggravating the manpower shortage.

On November 10 Cochrane recommended reconsidering the decision to rebuild *Normandie*. The ship wouldn't be ready for wartime service for about eighteenth months, he said in a letter to the Chief of Naval operations. Furthermore, with new machinery, ordnance and other equipment, it would cost about $50 million.

Ten days later the Secretary of the Navy directed that no money be spent to refit *Normandie*. The airplane catapults built for her were earmarked for another ship, a fleet aircraft carrier.

Of course, if there'd been a real military need for *Normandie*, she surely would have been rebuilt, whatever the damage to her hull and engines, whatever the cost in men and materials, however long it took. But in the fall of 1943 the Washington high command knew that by the time *Normandie* could carry troops or airplanes or both, there'd be no need for her. Hundreds of thousands of Americans would already be fighting in France, Italy and, it was hoped, Germany. The Russians would be pushing Nazi forces back through Eastern Europe. Similar success was expected in Asia.

It was at this time that William Francis Gibbs entered the fray.

When *Normandie*'s rebuilding had seemed a certainty, Todd-Erie had hired Gibbs and Cox to do an engineering study on the ship. Gibbs had reopened the question of just what sort of warship *Normandie* should become. He examined three alternatives: combatant aircraft carrier, troop transport with flight deck, or straight troop transport.

Normandie could be a carrier equal or superior to the new *Essex*-class carriers, Gibbs said. She could be built with a 43-percent-larger flight deck and 39 percent more hanger space.

But Gibbs thought she'd do even better as a troop transport. Without a flight deck, he said, she could carry as many as 18,800 troops at 30 knots. With that capacity and that speed she could transport 338,000 troops a year—five times as many as any other American troopship.

Gibbs also dealt with the stability question. *Normandie's* stability, he said, was equal or superior to any comparable ship—and he did the math to prove it. He specifically compared her to the *Aquitania*, the *Leviathan* and the two British *Queens*.

With new engines and new watertight subdivisions, Gibbs said, a *Normandie*-based troopship would have better fuel economy, greater cruising radius and fireproof troop accommodations than either the *Queen Mary* or the *Queen Elizabeth*.

It was a very convincing study. There was only one problem with it: America no longer needed *Normandie*—not for military purposes, anyhow.

While *Normandie* was in dry dock and the navy was digesting Gibbs' report, the Russians recaptured Kiev and American Marines landed at Tarawa and Makin in the Gilberts. Stalin, Churchill and Roosevelt met at Tehran to talk about the forthcoming invasion of Europe. Tito formed a government in Yugoslavia. Eisenhower was appointed Supreme Commander in Europe.

By January 1944 *Normandie's* hull was sound once more and there was a trim new black stripe at her waterline.

On January 11 the giant vessel was once more taken in tow. This time her destination was the Columbia Street Pier in Brooklyn, a part of the New York State Barge Canal Terminal that was leased by Todd Shipyards and, in turn, rented to the Navy. The pier sits at the mouth of the Gowanus Canal, at the southern shore of Red Hook.

To avoid cutting across the busiest part of the bay, which was crowded with ships taking on cargo for the invasion of Italy scheduled for the 22nd, *Normandie* was towed in a great loop south toward the Narrows, then north past Bay Ridge and the Bush Terminal. The tow took about two hours.

Nothing much was scheduled for *Normandie* in Brooklyn. Todd was told to "preserve the liner" until the Navy gave further instructions.

Ship designers are a persistent lot, however, if Gibbs and Yourkevitch are typical. Gibbs' initial report had been practically ignored. The Navy had made it clear to him that nothing would be done with *Normandie*, at least for now. But on February 6 he delivered a second report.

This time he compared *Normandie*, the *Queen Mary* and the *Queen Elizabeth* in detail, as troopships. In his report Gibbs proved, to his own satisfaction anyhow, that *Normandie* would be the world's best troop transport.

He also produced figures showing that her hull and useful equipment were worth $18 million, making it possible to outfit her completely for a total expenditure of about $33 million.

"It would seem," Gibbs suggested, "that the United States should have at least one ship the equal or superior to the Queens, in order not to be outclassed by the British."

This report caught FDR's interest. He asked Gibbs to submit a memo about building *Normandie* back into a passenger liner after the war.

In his reply Gibbs told the President that if *Normandie* were made into a troopship, she could easily be reconverted into a passenger liner. And then *Normandie*-size ships would be good competitors to the airplane, "which will require one day [in transit], present greater risk and cost and will not offer the social and vacation advantages of a sea voyage."

While Gibbs' memo was heading toward Roosevelt via the Navy Department, the *New York Herald Tribune* broke the news that all work on *Normandie* had been stopped. A few days later Secretary of the Navy James Forrestal admitted that *Normandie*'s future was in doubt.

On April 5 Forrestal delivered Gibbs' memo to FDR along with three buckets of cold water in the form of memos from himself, the Commander in Chief of the U.S. Fleet and the

Chief of Naval Operations. All strongly opposed any further government action on *Normandie*. Forrestal asked FDR to approve the delay.

But Roosevelt still had a soft spot for the great French liner. Though practically everyone in the Navy was ready to forget about her, he ordered Secretary of the Navy Forrestal to begin conversion work immediately unless it could be shown *Normandie* had *no* wartime or postwar value to America.

Unfortunately for *Normandie*, Forrestal proceeded to show exactly that. He got negative statements about the ship from the Navy Department, the War Department and the Maritime Commission. As for wartime use, they said, any money spent to convert *Normandie* would be better spent on new ships. As for peacetime use, they said, *Normandie* would be an economic liability, just as the *Leviathan* had been after World War I.

This was specious reasoning. The *Leviathan*'s troubles were caused not by the ship herself, but by poor management, by her anti-alcohol policy during Prohibition (while ships of other nationalities had bars aplenty) and by the depression.

But there was no one in high places to defend *Normandie* except the President himself. He decided not to defy his advisors' universally unfavorable opinions and gave Forrestal permission to cancel the *Normandie* refit. This action was announced on June 19, 1944.

Roosevelt, still uneasy about the whole thing, asked Forrestal to prepare a detailed report on *Normandie*'s American history, explaining the reasons for each and every decision. "I should like to have the record clear," FDR said, "as to what change made it advisable to seize her and raise her but now makes it inadvisable to convert her for any use." He also asked the Secretary to tell him how the Navy planned to preserve the ship for her "eventual return to her French owners."

While her fate was being decided, *Normandie* lay quietly in her berth at Columbia Street, Brooklyn, rust-coated and mossy at the waterline. Occasionally a passing tug or barge would accidentally and harmlessly ram her.

During this period *Normandie* was staffed by a single Navy officer, Lieutenant George Haeffner. A few Coast Guardsmen, trucked in every morning, served as her fire and security watch.

Half a dozen workmen or so continued to remove the concrete that had been poured into some of her tanks, paint her pipes and decks, coat her machinery with preservative. Among them, ironically, was Clement Derrick, whose torch had set her afire more than two years before, and Jack Panuzzo, who'd rescued several of those who'd been overcome by smoke.

Normandie's interior was a cavern of yawning holes. Voices echoed strangely and footsteps stirred up clouds of rust. But for the dim lights strung down her companionways, she could have been a death trap or an impenetrable maze for someone who didn't know her well. To make sure no one got lost, workmen had chalked arrows on the steel bulkheads.

Only her swimming pool, with its mosaic tiles, was still recognizable. In her engine room some curious tinker had partially dismantled her damaged turbine and scattered parts all over the dusty floor.

On the naked, flush-cut Promenade Deck an improvised wooden rail skirted the edge and wooden hatches covered her funnel uptakes and elevator shafts. Two of her four propellers and her four tail shafts were chained to her deck. A nearby sign said, "DON'T TAKE—WANTED."

She drew about twenty-six feet of water, compared to the original thirty-seven feet.

She was a hulk, a derelict.

Meanwhile, on June 4 the United States Army entered Rome. Two days later, in the most massive invasion in modern history, the Allies landed on the beaches of Normandy and began to push through the hedgerows of France.

A week later the Germans launched the first V-1 rocket—the buzz bomb—against England. V-2 rockets, forerunners of the ICBM, began descending on London a few months later.

On the Pacific front, United States Marines invaded Saipan, then Guam. At the same time China-based B-29s bombed Japan. The Japanese lost 470 planes in the Battle of the Philippine Sea. Tojo was dismissed as Japanese Premier, War Minister and Army Chief of Staff on July 18.

Throughout Eastern Europe, Red Army troops were forcing back their German counterparts. During the summer of 1944 the Russians swept into Poland, then crossed the Danube into Rumania.

Simultaneously, Allied forces rolled through France, the Germans falling back in retreat. In his novel *The Young Lions*, Irwin Shaw described some of the action.

One of Shaw's three protagonists, Noah Ackerman (who was played by Montgomery Clift in the movie version) found himself in a French farmhouse with his unit, surrounded by German troops. The Americans spread out inside the farmhouse, took up positions at the windows and began firing at the Germans.

> *Upstairs, in the bedroom of the master and mistress of the house, Rickett, Burnecker and Noah covered a lane between the barn and the shed where a plow and a farm wagon were kept.*
>
> *There was a small wooden crucifix on the wall and a stiff photograph of the farmer and his wife on their wedding day. On another wall hung a framed poster from the French Line showing the liner* Normandie *cutting through a calm, bright sea.*
>
> *There was a prolonged burst of firing from outside. Rickett, who was standing next to one of the two windows, holding a Browning Automatic Rifle, flattened himself against the flowered wallpaper. The glass covering the* Normandie *shattered into a thousand pieces, the picture shivered on the wall, with a large hole at the waterline of the great ship, but it did not fall.*

Later the company's CO, Lieutenant Green, came into the room.

> *. . . He looked vaguely about the room. "Isn't that the* Normandie?" *he asked.*
>
> *"Yes," said Noah, "it's the* Normandie."
>
> *Green smiled foolishly. "I think I will sign up for a cruise," he said.*
>
> *The men did not laugh.*

On September 8 British airplanes spotted a large ship in Trieste Harbor, inexpertly and haphazardly disguised as an island. They bombed it and it sank. It was the *Rex*, the gaudy Italian super-liner, *Normandie*'s immediate predecessor in the Blue Ribbon sweepstakes.

Back in the United States, somebody—quite possibly William Francis Gibbs—was spreading rumors about *Normandie*, saying American shipping men were seriously considering buying her, rebuilding her and putting her into postwar service as a passenger liner.

"Shipping men were said to favor using the vessel as a cabin class ship with a small number of exclusive accommodations," the *New York Herald Tribune* reported on October 1. "The vessel's superstucture will be smaller than before," the paper went on. This is "designed to lighten the vessel and permit greater speed and stability."

The Maritime Commission made it clear that someone might buy *Normandie* and turn her back into a passenger liner, but it would not be the United States.

"The airplane will supersede giant liners like the *Normandie, Queen Elizabeth* and *Queen Mary*," said Admiral Emory S. Land, Commission chairman.

And Frank J. Taylor, president of the Merchant Marine Institute, who was considered a spokesman for east-coast shipowners, agreed. "There will be no place for the superliner in the postwar era," he said.

Almost as proof of the proposition, *Normandie* was now shifted once more— towed away from the Columbia Street Pier in Brooklyn and back to the Navy Yard Annex in New Jersey. The purpose: to save dockage fees. No one, it seemed, wanted to waste any money on the once spectacular ship.

This was the moment that MGM chose to hold the premiere of *The Lady Fights Back*, a short film about *Normandie*, covering her French beginnings, the catastrophe that more or less finished her off and a wildly optimistic vision of her postwar future.

Normandie languished in New Jersey, more or less forgotten, while World War II drew to a close, the Allies sweeping through Europe and reconquering the Pacific islands one by one.

Allied offensives continued through the spring. On April 12, however, Franklin Roosevelt died. America lost a man who many believe was her greatest modern leader and *Normandie* lost her most powerful supporter.

FDR's death was followed by a series of climactic events in Europe. On April 18 all German resistance in the Ruhr came to an end, with the surrender of 325,000 troops under Field Marshal Model. A few days later Himmler offered to surrender to the U.S. and Britain, not the Soviet Union.

On April 26 Marshall Pétain was arrested. On the 28th Mussolini was shot and killed by Italian partisans. On the 30th Hitler committed suicide. On May 2 a million German troops surrendered in Italy. Two days later another million surrendered in the Netherlands, Denmark and northwest Germany. On May 7 the German high command surrendered unconditionally. As one result the United States took possession of the former German superliner *Europa*, a onetime *Normandie* competitor.

And on May 8 Winston Churchill and Harry Truman proclaimed V-E Day—Victory in Europe.

Now the Navy sought permission to declare *Normandie* surplus property and to dispose of her. Congressman Carl Vinson, of the House Committee on Naval Affairs, agreed, but, according to internal Navy memos, there was some opposition from other members of the House, "the origin of which we do not know, but possibly [it] stems from labor elements or Mr. Gibbs."

To the Navy's surprise, the Army now expressed an interest in the ship. "It has come to my attention," wrote a high Navy official, that "the Army is seriously considering sponsoring the conversion of *Normandie* to a fast troop ship. One might conjecture that a certain far from unknown Naval Architect, despairing of Naval acquiescence, has turned his sales pressure on the Army . . . looking for work for his firm and fees."

But *Normandie*'s time was rapidly drawing to a close. On June 13, 1945, Admiral Land, head of the Maritime Commission, offered to resell *Normandie* to France, " . . . in view of the unconditional surrender of the German government and the impracticability of using the *Normandie* in the prosecution of the war against the Government of Japan."

On August 6 an American B-29 dropped an atomic bomb on Hiroshima. Three days later Nagasaki was hit with another nuclear device. Five days after that, Japan surrendered. World War II had come to an end.

As America's battle-weary warships came home, some needing repair, some ready to be scrapped, *Normandie* was towed back to Brooklyn to free the Navy Yard Annex for other work.

On September 20, 1945, on Truman's orders, the Navy officially declared *Normandie* surplus property. Under maritime law she became the property of the Maritime Commission, which had taken over her title when she was first seized.

Admiral Land spoke uncertainly of her future. "All plans are in the hands of the French government," he said. "Nothing can be indicated about the disposal plans until we know the French government's desires."

On October 11, 1945, *Normandie—Lafayette*, as she was always called in official documents—was struck from the list of Navy ships.

The next day the *Washington Times-Herald* declared that this ship, once the most glamorous and beautiful of all ocean liners, was being considered as an A-bomb target. "Experts declared it would be highly important to determine the extent of destruction by an atom bomb on a floating target the *Normandie's* size," the newspaper reported. "It would probably have an important bearing on design and construction of naval craft of the future."

On October 29 the French Ambassador replied to Land's offer. CGT, he said, does not intend to repurchase *Normandie*, but was "ready to contemplate with the American authorities a legitimate compensation in suitable tonnage."

From this moment forward *Normandie's* story split in two.

One part involves the negotiations between France and the United States over compensation for *Normandie*. The chief American negotiator was Carl Vinson, who had become Secretary of the Treasury. His French counterpart was Léon Blum, the former Premier.

The U.S. government wasn't exactly thrilled about being asked to pay for *Normandie*. After all, America had spent billions on Lend-Lease to De Gaulle's Free French without getting anything in return. It had spent billions more—and also hundreds of thousands of lives—liberating France.

The new French government thanked America for these great gifts, but insisted that it was legally entitled to substantial monetary compensation for *Normandie*. In the interests of international harmony, and in line with the strong American desire to rebuild Western Europe, Washington reluctantly gave in.

On May 28, 1946, an agreement was signed. America paid the French $13.5 million, which the French agreed to spend on U.S.-built Liberty ships.

The *New York Times* was sympathetic to the French. "The United States is in the awkward position of the householder who borrows his neighbor's best china for a party and then smashes it. The French loved their *Normandie* and it would not be inappropriate to send a little apology to them, along with the cash payment."

Actually, America did send a little something extra along with the cash—not an apology, exactly, but something even better: the German superliner *Europa*, which U.S. troops had seized when Germany surrendered. The *Europa* was officially awarded to France by the postwar reparations Commission, thanks in part to American influence. France rechristened her the *Liberté*, an unusually appropriate name. She enabled the French to compete with the Cunard–White Star Line for the luxury passenger trade.

The second part of the story involves what finally happened to *Normandie*. During the long compensation negotiations the Maritime Commission offered her to every North or South American shipping line that might have any use for her. There were no takers. She was too big, too expensive to run and too far gone.

On July 17, 1946, about a month after the negotiations with France were concluded, the Maritime Commission announced that, because of the critical need for scrap steel, several hundred surplus ships were being made immediately available for scrapping. Among these was *Normandie*.

At this time *Normandie* was languishing at the Columbia Street Pier in Brooklyn, under the charge of a certain Lieutenant Jacobs. She was an empty hulk—all evidence of the salvage carpentry and concrete removed, along with all wiring and almost all piping and ventilating ductwork.

In Washington, Maritime Commission experts estimated that, as scrap metal, *Normandie* was worth about $174,000, a far, far cry from the millions it had taken to build and outfit her, to begin her conversion and to raise her.

The *New York Times* was struck by the *Normandie* tragedy. "All she is good for now is to relieve a shortage of scrap metal. But when she goes she should have whistles and cheers again. She was a great and unfortunate ship. And an age, a period in history that will not return, dies with her."

Once more Johnny came marching home. In Europe the displaced people began finding their way back to their native lands, while those still there counted the dead.

New governments sprang up throughout Europe, many of them Communist. The United Nations held its first General Assembly session. The Nuremberg Tribunal sentenced twelve leading Nazis to death.

The first fully electronic computer went into operation at this time. An engineer at Ford coined the word "automation." Douglas Aircraft introduced the DC-6. Kaiser-Frazer automobiles were put on the market, as was the Crosley compact car (list price, $250).

There were severe housing shortages in America, along with a pent-up demand for consumer goods leading to runaway prices and rising wage demands. More than 4.6 million U.S. workers went on strike during 1946.

And at Westminster College, in Fulton, Missouri, Winston Churchill, no longer British Prime Minister, said that "From Stettin in the Baltic to Trieste in the Adriatic, an iron curtain has descended across the continent."

On September 7, 1946, *Normandie* was put up for sale as scrap, "as is, where is." Bids from scrap dealers were solicited.

Interested parties had to put up 25 percent of their bid in advance and pay the balance within ten days if they won. The winning bidder had to dismantle the ship completely within eighteen months. He would not be able to sell it as a ship, only as scrap metal. The scrap had to be sold to American firms.

Potential scrappers got busy figuring out how much to offer for the hulk. In the meantime, the government was flooded with all kinds of odd offers for the ship.

Someone thought she should be grounded on some beach and turned into a kind of land-based carrier, an airport of sorts. Others suggested she be made into a plane ferry. The Time Oil Company of Los Angeles, without officially bidding, offered to buy *Normandie* for use as a stationary oil tanker tied up in inland waters. An astrologer in Brooklyn offered his services as consultant if it was decided to refit her as a liner, and a Connecticut man offered to sell stock to raise the money needed to restore her as a liner. A San Francisco promoter wanted to buy the ship, tow her along the coast from port to port and charge admission, ending up at the Golden Gate, where she would become a permanent exhibit (a similar fate eventually befell the *Queen Mary*, only she ended up at Long Beach).

There were also suggestions that she be made into a floating apartment house for veterans, a floating nightclub, a floating memorial to Franco-American friendship, a gambling ship twelve miles off San Pedro, California, even a floating hotel with a flight deck on the New York–Bermuda air run.

A certain Alfred Gordon of New York wrote President Truman suggesting that *Normandie* be converted into a showboat. He offered to apply for a twenty-five-year lease. "As an impresario," Gordon said, "I have toured the world and would be thoroughly competent to judge the possibilities of such a showboat."

One man did everything in his power to see her restored to her former glory. He was Vladimir Yourkevitch. Ever since the Navy had announced its decision not to rebuild the ship, he'd lobbied for her restoration. Hoping to get some backing, Yourkevitch sent a wire to the Transport and Communications Commission of the United Nations Economic and Social Council:

SS NORMANDIE DEMOLISHING AND SCRAPPING BEGINS IN TWO WEEKS STOP AS FORMER DESIGNER HAVE INSPECTED VESSEL FOUND GOOD CONDITION HULL AND MACHINERY STOP FOR SIX MILLION DOLLARS MAY BE RECONVERTED IN TEN MONTHS AS TRANSATLANTIC LINER 2000 PASSENGERS WHICH WOULD COST NEW NOW 26 MILLIONS AND REQUIRE THREE YEARS TO BUILD STOP MAY BE USED BY UNO FOR TRANSPORT DISPLACED PERSONS OR AS UNO TROOP CAR-

RIER FOR 15,000 MEN STOP CAN SUBMIT DESIGN AND ES-
TIMATES IF UNO APPROVES IN PRINCIPAL STOP IF DESIRED
CAN COME PERSONALLY.

Of course the U.N. wasn't interested. It was the wrong organi-
zation, the wrong time and the wrong project.

The Maritime Commission got just five bids. Newport News
Shipping and Drydock offered $25,000. The S. F. Dow Co. of-
fered $42,500. Patapsco Scrap came in with $63,070. Boston's
Metals' bid was $125,000. Lipsett, Inc., a junk firm with a Wall
Street address, offered $161,680.

On October 2 the Maritime Commission accepted the Lipsett bid.

Normandie had been quite an expensive proposition for
America. The Navy spent $11.19 million on the ship—$4.4
million on the original conversion, $5.89 million on her sal-
vage and hull repair and $900,000 to clean and maintain her
thereafter. To this should be added the $13.5 million the U.S.
paid France in compensation for the ship.

There were some small subtractions, of course—the $134,191
realized from the auctions and the $161,680 paid by the win-
ning shipwreckers, a total of, $295,871. That means the U.S.
was out only $24,394,129.

On the other hand, the salvage experts trained on *Normandie* saved ships and cargoes worth many, many times the amount
the United States spent on her, so America actually ended up
with a handsome profit. It would have been far better, however,
if *Normandie* had served her war duty as scheduled, then been
restored to her prewar glory.

Now her troubled life was about to come to an end at the
hands of the Lipsett company. Lipsett had already junked, among
other things, the 2nd Avenue and Fulton Street (Brooklyn) els,
the twenty-five-block site of Stuyvesant Town and Peter Cooper
Village (said to be the biggest wrecking job in history), Boston's
North Station–South Station el and, during a steel shortage early
in the war, some 100,000 tons of abandoned railroad tracks all
over the country.

"On the basis of our bid," said Morris Lipsett, one of the
two brothers who headed the firm, "we paid the government

$3.80 a ton for the scrap steel in the *Normandie*. There are about 40,000 tons of it in the ship today. But when you stop to consider the costs of scrapping her, you get an idea of the gamble involved.

'We have to pay steel workers and steel burners from $1.38 to $2.25 an hour for the twelve months it will take to break her up. Then there's the cost of installing pumps, dynamos, temporary bulkheads and other items, besides lighterage and tug bills."

When the Lipsetts bought the ship, the OPA ceiling price on scrap steel was $18.17 a ton. The Lipsetts were hoping that either they could dismantle the ship for less than that or that the price would go up.

The Lipsetts were thinking of more than just immediate profits, however. They knew many ships would be scrapped. The *Normandie* job was a good way of getting the necessary technical and business experience.

Lipsett now set about looking for a wrecking site. Dry-dock space was prohibitively expensive, so Lipsett decided to do the job while *Normandie* was still afloat. Even so, it was difficult to find pier space that was both sufficiently large and inexpensive.

After quite a search the wrecking company finally found a location: Port Newark, New Jersey. It was large enough, it was more or less just across the bay from Brooklyn, it was city-owned (and therefore inexpensive), it was equipped with two fifty-ton gantry cranes. Best of all, perhaps, rail spurs led directly to the side of this pier, while there was space for sixty open railroads gondola cars—perfect for loading scrap steel and sending it off to the open-hearth furnaces of nearby Pennsylvania.

Before the actual dismantling could begin, *Normandie* had to be towed once more, from Brooklyn to Port Newark. It would be her final journey.

The day before the move, painters working from scaffolding on both sides of the ship emblazoned the name "LIPSETT" on her hull in large white letters. "Just like every other contractor," Julius Lipsett recently explained, "we were looking for recognition. We accepted the challenge, so we decided to play it for all it was worth."

At 3:00 a.m. on Thanksgiving Day, November 28, 1946, a time and date chosen by the tide charts, twelve tugs, led by the most powerful tug in America, the *C. Howard Meseck*, tied up their lines to the huge hulk at Columbia Street. There was a thirty-five mph wind from the northwest.

The tugs gingerly put on the steam and began to pull. What was left of the great liner slowly eased away from the pier, stern first. Then, just 1,000 feet out, the whole operation came to a stop. The winds were just too strong to proceed. *Normandie* was redocked.

As the dawn came up, bright and clear, the wind slowed to fifteen mph. A little after 7:30 a.m. the tug lines went taut and the giant, lifeless hulk headed out into the bay.

Slowly and smoothly the tugs pushed and pulled the dirty, rusty, slab-sided vessel away from Red Hook, past Buttermilk Channel and across the upper bay, where not a whistle was sounded and scarcely any ferryboat passengers recognized her (although a French Line official, dressed in mourning, watched from a Coast Guard cutter).

With the help of a fast ebb tide, she glided through the oily Kill van Kull, past Sailors' Snug Harbor, on its hill, and past Shooters' Island. Soon she was at Bergen Point, the entrance to Newark Bay, where the tugs brought her to a complete stop before attempting to turn her more than 90 degrees to starboard for the final stretch.

"As the *Normandie* approached the Jersey Central Railroad Bridge," according to Stephen Gmelin, who witnessed the event, "two trains came to a halt on the span to await her passing and many passengers left their cars for a better view."

As the tide slackened, the tugs steered her toward the west draw of the bridge—a span just 200 feet wide. Since *Normandie* herself was more than half this width, it was a tight squeeze indeed.

Now the lead tug shifted its towing line to *Normandie*'s bow. It backed underneath the bridge. At the same time the steering tug moved its line to her stern. She was pulled through the span.

"We've moved the *Normandie* twice before and have towed the country's largest battleships, but, we have never before attempted to move so large a ship through such confined waters," said Joseph Meseck, Sr., the tug-company president.

A half-hour after the operation began, *Normandie* was safely through the bridge and in open channel. Not long afterward she was tied up at Port Newark without incident. She had found her last home.

The twenty-mile trip, the last *Normandie* would ever take, had lasted just five hours and cost $20,000. In her five seasons on the Atlantic the great liner had traveled 445,000 miles. In the last eight years of her life she traveled less than fifty miles, all in New York harbor and all in tow.

As soon as *Normandie* was safely tied up, Lipsett workers drove four nineteen-pile clusters into the bottom of the bay on her offshore side to prevent her from going adrift in the event of high winds. This turned out to be a wise precaution, since on one occasion the winds were high enough to snap some of her mooring lines and pull out a few of the bollards on the pier.

Lipsett's men swarmed over the ship, studying her, doing calculations, making plans.

At the same time Vladimir Yourkevitch continued his devoted attempts to save his brainchild. He called a press conference and told reporters he'd drawn up plans for a shrunken version of the liner. He also said that the French government had sent Philippe Deros, an advisor to the Merchant Marine Ministry, to investigate his plan. Deros, said Yourkevitch, liked what he saw and had cabled France recommending that the government get involved.

The new design, Yourkevitch said, called for retaining *Normandie*'s existing hull and engines and building a new superstructure. The ship was to be shortened by 220 feet by removing the center section and its two boiler rooms, reducing her gross tonnage to 32,000. Two of her four propeller shafts would be removed, Yourkevitch said, but the ship would retain power enough to make 28 knots.

During this period Yourkevitch visited Port Newark and begged Morris and Julius Lipsett to hold off on the dismantling until the French gave him a final answer. And, shortly, they did. The answer was no.

Yourkevitch then tried to get American financing to save *Normandie*. But this idea got nowhere. It wasn't as though he had no influential contacts—he knew some very important people, such as Igor Sikorsky and Armand Hammer. But he was neither a diplomat nor a salesman. He failed at this attempt, too.

The Russian emigrant gave up. He never again returned to Port Newark. "I think it broke his heart," Julius Lipsett said.

There was another unhappy party: the city of Newark. City fathers didn't like seeing their front yard turned into a junk heap. They mustered all of the legal pressure they could to make Lipsett abandon the operation.

In the end a compromise was struck. Newark agreed to give Lipsett eight months to do the job. Lipsett promised to pay Newark $500 a day for each day the wrecking operation went beyond the deadline, which was July 22, 1947.

Because of labor disputes and Yourkevitch's last attempt to save his ship, the actual dismantling did not begin until January 7. By then everyone was feeling the urgency of the Newark deadline.

It was a relatively simple job to dismantle the ship down to the waterline or thereabouts. Workers just cut her apart, plate by plate. The plates were hoisted onto the pier, where they were cut into chunks about eighteen inches wide by five feet long, small enough to fit into the waiting gondola freight cars.

Once the operation got under way, the wreckers filled six to ten gondolas a day. When they were loaded, they were hitched up to a locomotive and hauled off to steel mills at Coatesville, Pittsburgh or Bethlehem, to be melted down.

At the mills the *Normandie* scrap was classified as #1 steel (its chemistry was identical to that of most structural steel) and dumped into the open-hearth furnaces, along with odds and ends of scrap steel from many other sources. Virgin metal was added to the scrap, in the then usual mixture of 55 percent scrap, 45 percent new metal. All of this was melted together, then turned into structural steel for buildings, sheet steel for the automobiles, refrigerators and gas ranges American consumers were demanding, and forms of steel for every other purpose imaginable.

In a very real way, then, *Normandie* is still with us, spread out all over America, being recycled again and again, her identity gone forever.

When the wreckers approached *Normandie*'s waterline, their work became very tricky indeed. The ship was, after all, afloat.

One wrong cut could unbalance her, cause her to capsize and sink.

The Lipsetts developed an interesting method of dealing with this problem. They would pump thousands of tons of water out of Newark Bay into *Normandie*'s bow to raise the stern almost out of the water. Then they'd build a temporary bulkhead about forty feet from the fantail.

At this point the burners would cut off the cantilevered rear portion of the ship. Cranes would lift it onto the dock, where it would be cut up into chunks small enough to fit into the gondola freight cars. Then the process would be repeated on the other end. Back and forth it went, *Normandie* shrinking now at the stem, now at the stern.

To watch the stresses on the hull that developed during the scrapping process, the wreckers placed some 200 Whittimore stress gauges all over the hull. They were capable of detecting deformations of as little as ten one-thousandths of an inch.

These stress gauges reflected Morris Lipsett's fear that the hulk might cave in or break apart. "Believe me," he later remarked when he was invited to address a National Safety Congress about his firm's masterwork, "if we'd used a stress gauge on our minds, it would have shown a greater elongation than ten-thousands of an inch."

About 170 men worked on the wrecking crew. It was not a pleasant job, especially for the burners. When they worked on painted steel, they often found themselves breathing lead fumes. For protection they wore respirator masks and drank pints of milk at 10:00 a.m. and 3:00 p.m. (calcium creates resistance to lead poisoning). If they got sick, they were given doses of a medicine containing calcium carbonate, bismuth subcarbonate, tincture of ginger, tincture of camphorate opium, milk of magnesia, and pepsin.

Despite the lead fumes and other hazards, however, not a single worker was seriously injured during the wrecking process, although there were some very close calls.

On one occasion a burner was leaning on his lifeline (a rope tied to a steel member, required by Lipsett's insurance company) when another burner, forgetting the purpose of the line, cut right through it. The other worker fell into the bay, but was promptly rescued.

Initially, safety experts insisted that the entire crew wear life jackets. Then one of the life jackets—which was stuffed with kapok—caught fire. That ended the life-jacket requirement.

While the wrecking crew dismantled the ship and cut up her seven-eighths-inch-thick hull plates, the OPA did exactly what Lipsett had hoped: it raised the price of scrap steel, first to $30 a ton, then, gradually, to $45 a ton.

The hulk's non-ferrous metals, totalling about 1,700 tons, brought higher prices. The turbines, elevators and other machinery were lifted onto the pier and torn apart there, and their component metals were segregated in a yard next to the pier— aluminum, lead, copper, brass.

In addition, there were about 2,000 tons of Belgian paving blocks in the ship's bow, put there as ballast when her stern section was reinforced to prevent vibration back in the winter of 1935–6. These were sold to a New Jersey contractor, who used them to pave the streets of various nearby towns or as stone fronts for houses. They netted about $2,500.

The Lipsett brothers had taken a calculated risk when they bid on the *Normandie* job, but the risk paid off. In all, they made about $100,000 on the job. More importantly, it led to other ship-scrapping jobs.

After the firm finished with *Normandie*, it scrapped four of America's largest battleships—the *Wyoming*, the *Utah*, the *Oregon* and the *New Mexico* (ironically enough, a ship which had been commanded by Robert Coman, *Normandie*'s prospective captain).

In later years, when it came time to scrap the French Line's *Liberté*—the former *Europa*—Lipsett did the job through an Italian subcontractor. And when the *Queen Mary* was retired, brought to Long Beach, California, and made into a museum, Lipsett removed some of her interior structure to make room for the display area.

On July 22, exactly on deadline day at Newark, four tugs towed the remains of the great liner three quarters of a mile down the channel to a U.S. Navy dock Lipsett had rented. By then the hulk had been reduced to a total weight of 15,000 tons and a length of 762 feet. Her plates were only fifteen feet above the water and her ribs rose into the air like those of cattle long dead on the Western desert.

At the Navy dock the dismantling continued, the hulk shrinking daily. By October 7, the day after the Yankees beat the Dodgers in the 1947 World Series, only a single piece of *Normandie* remained in the water: a seventy-five-ton section of steel that had been part of her double bottom. In midday the giant traveling crane lifted it out of the water and onto a gondola car, where it was hauled away to Lukens Steel Co., Coatesville, Pennsylvania.

Normandie was gone.

But she was not forgotten. In fact, six weeks later *Normandie* once again made headlines.

The story broke on November 16, 1947, in the New York French language weekly *France-Amérique*. "C'EST UN ESPION ALLEMAND QUI INCENDIA LE 'NORMANDIE' ", read the main headline: A German Spy Says He Burned the *Normandie*. A subhead added, "UNE RÉVÉLATION SENSATIONELLE," which it certainly was.

According to the story, the spy was one Fritz Scheffer, an erstwhile New York hairdresser, Bund member and SS officer who'd recently been arrested in Western Germany on a murder charge. He'd chosen the moment of his arrest to make his confession to an Allied intelligence officer. Scheffer claimed it was he who'd directed the entire job of setting the ship afire.

Scheffer's story was full of local color. He'd belonged, he claimed, to a Nazi spy ring that worked out of a seamen's mission in Hoboken. He got his instructions at a Harlem café which the spy ring used as a meeting place, from an emissary of Admiral Wilhelm Canaris, Hitler's spy chief.

Bribing the union with $50, he got one of his men hired as a stevedore working on *Normandie* Then he and other Bundsmen got similar jobs. The ship, he said, was not guarded by the Army, the Navy or the Coast Guard. Also, among the contractor's guards were a number of former Bund members and sympathetic White Russians.

"My men put life preservers around in key spots, after having stuffed them with kapok," he said. And when he gave the signal, a dozen of the stevedores touched off the heaps of preservers simultaneously with their acetylene torches. "When these were afire, my men turned their torches on the woodwork of the grand salon, being careful to light those portions nearest portholes so the draft would be good."

It was he who gave the alarm, Scheffer said—but he waited until the flames had spread throughout the grand lounge.

When the firemen arrived, Scheffer and his minions, he claimed, gave contradictory instructions to the firemen. Then they quickly left the ship. "When the hoses finally went into action," he said, "my men and I were far away. May I add that we also did a little sabotage on the fire plugs and the hoses?" Scheffer said that he went immediately to Argentina, then back to Germany.

Scheffer seemed to know a lot about the fire scene—the life preservers, the acetylene torches, the grand salon, the delay in giving the alarm, etc. But his story also contained a lot of nonsense.

He said the fire took place on February 10, 1942. Actually, it happened the previous day. Practically everything he said about the guards was wrong. Robins had furnished no guards, but there were Coast Guardsmen doing this job, and also New York policemen.

There were no stevedores at work in the grand lounge at the time of the fire. The life jackets were manufactured with kapok filling, not stuffed later. There was no woodwork in the grand lounge nor any porthole.

Jack Panuzzo, who was at the scene, said, "To me, this guy Scheffer is nuts. The fellows that started that fire were some hardworking Brooklyn boys who had some hard luck with a blowtorch."

Alderman Sullivan, another witness, agreed. "The story is nothing but lies," he said. "I saw it all. I originally proved it was not sabotage. It can be considered a closed book now."

Still, almost every major American paper picked up the story and headlined it, to the great discomfort of J. Edgar Hoover.

According to recently declassified documents, Hoover put out the word to his lieutenants: Find this man Scheffer and put his story to the test.

FBI agent Edward Scheidt searched FBI files for any record of Scheffer. There was none. He cabled the U.S. Army high command in Germany for details of Scheffer's arrest. The Army knew nothing.

In New York other FBI agents questioned the reporter who'd broken the story in America, a man named Gustave Estrangin. It turned out that he'd picked it up from an item in *Sud Ouest* a French paper.

In Germany no record could be found of the man, however. Inquiries were also made at *Sud Ouest*, without result.

In the end the FBI concluded that Fritz Scheffer did not exist. He was almost certainly a bored newspaperman's invention. There was no confession, no spy, no shocking revelations, no story at all.

Nor was there a *Normandie* anymore, except in the memories of those who had been associated with her in one way or another. Her story had come to an end.

But this great and beautiful ship, this remarkable human achievement, had affected too many to disappear without further trace. As the years passed, she was heard from occasionally until, like a famous human being who has passed away, she became something of a legend.

21

THE NORMANDIE LEGEND

It's been fifty years since *Normandie* first sailed out of Le Havre, ready to conquer records and capture hearts. Now she's gone, along with most of those who built her, served on her, traveled on her or played some other important role in her story.

In a very real way, however, *Normandie* is still with us. Practically everyone who ever had any connection with the ship took a small piece of her away as a keepsake: crewmen, passengers, conversion workers, Coast Guardsmen, divers, salvage men and scrappers. Today these fragments are stowed away in attics and basements, mostly forgotten. But some parts of *Normandie* are available for all to see.

Her steering wheel, charred but whole, resides in the South Street Seaport Museum in New York, thanks to the detective work of John Maxtone-Graham.

Baudry's statue of "La Normandie," which stood at the top of the stairs leading to the smoking room, now stands in the Fountainebleau Hotel in Miami Beach, Florida. No one seems to remember how it got there, but the hotel is built on the site of the Firestone estate, which had acres of formal gardens. It's quite likely that the statue was purchased for those gardens in the mid-1940s.

Normandie's other statue, De Jean's bronze "La Paix", which once towered over the elegantly attired diners in the main dining room, now presides over the "Garden of Normandie" in Pinelawn Memorial Park, in Farmingdale, Long Island. Pinelawn's owners purchased "La Paix" from Our Lady of Lebanon Church in Brooklyn. That church's former pastor, Monsignor Mansour Stephen, had bought it at a *Normandie* auction in 1945, along with the two sets of bronze doors that led to the main dining room and the huge cloissonné panels which led to the chapel. These panels were decorated with an image of a Norman knight by François-Louis Schmid.

The bronze doors with medallions designed by Dupas and executed by Dunand now serve as the front and side doors of the church (which is at the corner of Henry and Remsen Streets).

The cloissonné panels, which were mounted on a number of cast-iron plates and measured twelve feet by twenty-five feet, were sold by the Church of Our Lady of Lebanon at auction at Sotheby's on June 13, 1981. Monsignor Stephen had paid $380 for them. They were auctioned off for $31,000.

The beautiful wood double doors that separated the main lounge from the first-class smoking room and the panels that surrounded them—jungle scenes carved, richly colored and lacquered by Jean Dunand—found their way into a private dining room in an elegant New York restaurant, Mr. Chow's, on East 57th Street.

The owners of this restaurant, who are among America's leading Art Deco collectors, have also managed to find quite a bit of *Normandie*'s Christofle silverware and serving vessels. All of these pieces are in daily use.

Two of the ship's stone bas-reliefs, one by Saupique, which was mounted in the wall of the upper entrance hall, and one by Bouchard, which was mounted in the lounge vestibule, are embedded in the outside walls of Packard's supermarket in ckensack, New Jersey.

Recently, Bruce Newman, president of the Newel Art Galleries in New York, located—in the hands of a private European collector—the grand lounge side of the sliding wall between that room and the smoking room. This consisted of thirty-two smallish stucco panels lacquered in gold and silver by Jean Dupas and Jacques Dunand (the other side of the panels in Mr. Chow's restaurant).

These panels, which are only a quarter of an inch thick, measure 18 feet high by 26 feet wide. The mural etched upon them is called "Dawn, the Four Winds and the Sea." It consists of heavenly figures, floating around a brilliant sun.

At the war's end, these panels were returned to the French Line, which installed them on the *Ile de France* during her post-war refit. The European collector who owned them purchased them at a 1962 auction for $500. Newman put them up for sale at $2.5 million and reportedly sold them for more than $1 million—an astonishing price, considering the fact that Schmidt's cloissonne knight brought only $31,000 at auction in 1981.

Other *Normandie* artwork has also recently been "discovered." Gertrude Stein, of New York's Gertrude Stein Gallery, and Evan Blum and Miriam Novallo, of Irreplaceable Artifacts, also in New York, have located, in the hands of another private collector, the two paintings by Ducos de la Haille that had hung in the lounge vestibule near the grand lounge and the ceiling mural by D'Espagnat, that had decorated the dome of the banqueting room at one end of the main dining room. A price of $1 million was put on these three pictures. As of this writing, they have not been sold.

Perhaps the most interesting *Normandie* remnants—the most important art works salvaged from the ship—are the magnificent glass panels which lined the grand salon. These panels, which depicted the story of navigation in mythological terms, were designed by Jean Dupas. In all, there were four main designs, each fifty feet wide and twenty feet high, each composed of 100 smaller panels four feet high and two and a half feet wide and weighing about fifty-six pounds.

About half of one main design—fifty-five panels—resides in the Metropolitan Museum of Art, in New York City, mounted on a wall in much the way it was originally mounted on the ship. Nearby are several pieces of *Normandie* furniture. The section is complete except for the top row of panels, which the museum ceilings weren't high enough to accommodate. These panels were discovered in relatively good shape, in an antique shop in Cold Spring Harbor on Long Island by Penelope Hunter-Steibel, a museum curator, and Dr. Irwin Berman, who purchased them and gave them to the museum.

Another 150 panels were purchased in the early 1950s by Marco Behar, an antiques collector and dealer, for a total of

$1,500. Some sixty-five of Behar's panels were later purchased by Hilliard Rentner, a retired New York financier.

Nine of Rentner's panels, two contiguous rows of eight and one unattached panel, were sold at Christie's auction gallery in New York on March 21, 1981. The eight-panel set was graveled down to Malcolm S. Forbes for $90,000, who bought them as a wedding gift for his son.

One of the remaining *Normandie* panels is owned by James Garner, the movie star. And another four or five are in the hands of other private collectors. As for the rest—about 190 panels—their location is unknown.

But the location of certain other etched panels is known. The Dunand bar panel, for instance, is in the Gare Maritime in Le Havre. And an Ingrand bar panel is in the hands of a private collector. Two paintings by Degallaix, which once adorned one of *Normandie*'s small, private dining rooms, now "fill my study with sunshine," according to Max Pluss, who lives in Switzerland. Mr. Pluss purchased the paintings at auction in 1942.

Most of the rest of *Normandie*'s art works—the paintings, carved stone panels, bas-reliefs—vanished. No doubt much of this material survives somewhere, but its present owners probably are not aware of the provenance.

The same can be said for much of *Normandie*'s spectacular Art Deco furniture. A lot of it was auctioned off, piecemeal, during the 1940s. One generation considered it memorable or valuable. The next may have stowed it in basements or attics or discarded it.

Some of this furniture, retained for military use, was dispersed and its identity forgotten. For instance, some furniture was taken to a warehouse at Camp Shanks, at Orangeburg, New York. After the war, when Camp Shanks became a student housing project, the furniture was auctioned off.

Other *Normandie* furniture was bought by about 100 officers at the U.S.N. Reserve School for WAVEs at Hunter College in the Bronx. But these officers moved on, one by one, until only a few were left. The furniture was divided among them.

Some *Normandie* furniture retained its identity for quite a while. Many of the armchairs and settees of the grand lounge, all of which would be museum pieces today because of their almost microscopically stitched tapestry upholstery and fabulous colors, ended up adorning "The Normandie Lounge" at the Conrad Hilton Hotel in Chicago.

Fifty other Aubusson tapestry-covered *Normandie* chairs went to the Stevens Hotel, also in Chicago. That same hotel also bought quite a few of the black macassar-wood armchairs from the main dining room. Where they are now, no one seems to know (although an example can be seen in front of the glass panels at the Metropolitan Museum of Art).

Some *Normandie* furniture, along with most of her silver, glassware, china and linen, was returned to the French Line, which used it on the *Ile de France* and the *Liberté*.

When the *Liberté* was scrapped, most of the furniture in her grand lounge, some of it originally from *Normandie*, was purchased by the Sagamore Hotel in Lake George, New York, where it remains in use to this day.

As for the china, silver, glassware and linen, most was auctioned off in Europe in the summer of 1981 at Monte Carlo, Biarritz and Geneva. These auctions included Daum crystal glasses, sheets, towels, steamer rugs and 25,000 pieces of silver-plated cutlery (out of the original 45,000 pieces delivered by Christofle), as well as chafing dishes, porringers, finger bowls and champagne buckets of several sizes.

Some of the crystal and glassware found its way to Bloomingdale's department store in New York City, which sold it, along with reproductions from the original molds, in the fall of 1983.

As for the thousands of brochures, deck plans, passenger lists, booklets, etc., the vast majority has been lost—thrown out as trash, burned up in house fires, destroyed by floods caused by broken pipes, incinerated in World War II bombing raids and the like. Some however, has been lovingly preserved by collectors and ship historians.

And, of course, much more no doubt exists in scrapbooks and albums in attics throughout America and Europe.

Normandie has often been remembered in literature. In 1981 and 1982 no less than four *Normandie*-based novels were published—two spy thrillers and two romances. *Act of War* by Leonard Sanders (Simon & Schuster), convincingly postulates that *Normandie* was sabotaged while she lay interned at Pier 88. *Normandie Triangle*, by Justin Scott (Arbor House), would have us believe that the Nazis managed to stash a miniature submarine within the capsized *Normandie* hull! Its mission: to sink the troop-laden *Queen Mary*.

As for the romances, *Normandie Affair*, by Elizabeth Villars (Doubleday), an interesting story, uses the ship as a background, always accurately. A best-seller called *Crossing* by Danielle Steel (Delacorte Press) is very entertaining but contains several minor inaccuracies about *Normandie*. For example, *Normandie* is said to *weigh* eighty thousand tons—but gross tons are a measure of enclosed space, not weight. Second, the benches and lamps behind the café grill are described, even though the novel is set in 1939; the benches and lamps had been removed in the winter of 1935–6 and replaced by the tourist-class lounge. The novel also places Captain Thoreux aboard even though he had retired by then. And, *Normandie* is said to have regained the Blue Ribbon though in fact she'd lost it for the last time to the *Queen Mary*.

World War II was hard on superliners. The first to go was the *Bremen*, which saboteurs set afire as she lay at her pier at Bremenhaven in March 1941. The Italian superliner *Conte di Savoia* burned and sank when attacked by Allied planes in September 1943 while anchored off Venice. The *Rex* was sunk in the harbor of Trieste a year later, also by Allied aircraft.

But some important ships did survive the war: the *Ile de France*, the *Aquitania*, the *Queen Mary*, the *Queen Elizabeth* and, on the Axis side, the *Europa*.

Following World War II, three great superliners were still to be built: the *United States*, the *France* (III) and the *QE 2*. The first and the most remarkable of these was the *United States*, a ship designed by William Francis Gibbs.

The *United States* was about a third smaller than *Normandie*, with a gross tonnage of 53,329, a length of 990 feet and a breadth of 101 feet 5 inches. When she was built in the early 1950s, the public was told that she'd have 158,999 shaft horsepower and a cruising speed of about 30 knots.

Actually, her engines produced 240,000 horsepower—80,000

more than Normandie. During her trials she hit a top speed of 42 knots—10 knots faster than Normandie's best trial speed and more than 48 mph.

On her maiden voyage, on July 3, 1952, the United States cut an amazing 10 hours and 2 minutes from the Queen Mary's fourteen-year-old record, averaging 35.59 knots. On her return voyage she crossed the Atlantic at an average speed of 34.51 knots in 3 days, 12 hours and 12 minutes.

It was the first time since Normandie's maiden voyage in 1935 that a transatlantic liner had captured the Blue Ribbon in both directions on her first round trip. And in many ways this is the way it should have been, for the United States was a kind of successor to Normandie; Gibbs had studied the French ship with great care and had been strongly influenced by her.

In 1959 CGT commissioned its own new superliner, to be named not after a single province, like Normandie or her projected sister, the Bretagne, but after the country itself.

The France's maiden voyage began on February 3, 1962. Although the ship had hit 35 knots during her trials and some thought she might challenge the United States, CGT officials knew their ship stood no chance against the mighty American vessel; hence they made no attempt to win the Blue Ribbon.

Though she wasn't a record-breaker, the France was in some ways reminiscent of Normandie. Her flaring prow, spoon-shaped stern and whaleback at the bow were similar. What's more, she was 1,035 feet long—the longest passenger liner ever built, although not the largest. Her gross tonnage was 66,348, about 16,000 tons less than Normandie.

Unlike Normandie, she had conventional engines, conventional—not divided—funnel uptakes (so she had a number of small public rooms, not the vast open spaces of her predecessor) and conventional decor, which many critics detested.

According to the poet Turner Cassity, the France was still overshadowed by memories of Normandie:

> The Channel clouds; the ships merge utterly;
> Our faith now is in the France, for good or ill.
> But when the bored forsake the guarding rail,
> The life preserver, spotlit, still reads Normandie.

Like her ancestor, the *France*'s timing was bad. *Normandie* had to deal with the depression. The new ship confronted the dawn of the jet age.

In 1958 more people crossed the Atlantic by ship than ever before—1.2 million. But an even greater number crossed by plane.

And on October 26, 1958, the Pan Am Boeing 707 Jet Clipper *America* departed New York for Paris, inaugurating regularly scheduled transatlantic jet service. It made the trip in six hours.

Suddenly the Blue Ribbon was a dead issue. The amazing technological advances that had created the *Mauretania*, the *Bremen*, the *Normandie*, the *Queen Mary* and even the *United States* had been superseded by a spectacular new technology. Ships were no longer the only way to cross. Most people thought they weren't even the best way.

There was one person who didn't feel that way, however, and never had—Vladimir Yourkevitch. He still dreamed of creating another superliner, a ship even greater than *Normandie*.

In 1955 Yourkevitch announced that he'd drawn up plans for a 90,000-ton passenger liner that could carry 6,000 in tourist class. It would be 1,150 feet long—the largest and fastest passenger ship afloat. Best of all, it could be converted into an aircraft carrier practically overnight.

No one was interested.

In 1958 Yourkevitch created plans for a ship 1,140 feet long, with a 132-foot beam and a gross tonnage of 100,000 tons. With engines generating 280,000 horsepower, it would cruise at 36 knots and carry 4,000 single-class passengers across the Atlantic in a little more than three days.

This time Yourkevitch got the backing of H. B. Kantor, president of the Carter Hotels Operating Co. and former owner of the Governor Clinton Hotel in New York. Kantor wanted to build two ships, the S.S. *Peace* and the S.S. *Good Will*. He said he planned to charge $50 one way, with food available at extra cost.

Kantor was a businessman of substance, but even he couldn't come up with the $240 million needed to build the *Peace* and the *Good Will*. Bills were introduced in Congress to help finance the ships, but nothing came of them. The world had its eye on the skies, not the oceans.

While Yourkevitch dreamed and the passenger jets multiplied, the doughty old *Queen Mary* and the *Queen Elizabeth* continued to ferry passengers back and forth across the Atlantic, but their clientele was gaining in years and shrinking in numbers.

In the mid-1960s Cunard decided to order a new ship, not to supplement the *Queens* but to replace them—a vessel that could provide transatlantic passenger service and also serve as a cruise ship.

Built at a cost of $72 million, Cunard's new ship went into service on May 2, 1969. She was the *QE 2*, a vessel of 65,863 gross tons, 963 feet long, with a breadth of 105 feet—slightly smaller than the *France*, but with equally modern lines and an interior that most critics liked better.

The *Queen Mary* retired on September 27, 1967, after an astonishing thirty-one years on the Atlantic, having steamed more than 3.79 million miles in 1,000 crossings—a record *Normandie* might have equaled or surpassed had the fates treated her differently. The *Elizabeth* followed her sister's example on November 29, 1969.

The *Mary* was purchased by the city of Long Beach, California, for the rather remarkable sum of $3.45 million, for use as a maritime museum, hotel and convention center. She opened her doors on May 10, 1971, and she is there still, conveniently close to Hollywood, where, when the script calls for an ocean liner, she is the only setting available.

The *Elizabeth* was purchased first by Fort Lauderdale, Florida, which hoped to use it as a floating hotel, then resold to C. Y. Tung of Hong Kong. He punningly rechristened her *Seawise University* and made plans to use her as a floating university off the Hong Kong coast. But on January 9, 1972—thirty years minus one month after the *Normandie* fire—the largest passenger ship that had ever been built burned and sank. She was a total loss.

There was now only a single true transatlantic liner in service—the *France* (the *QE 2* was a dual-purpose ship, not purely a liner). Very shortly, even this last example of the art found herself in trouble.

The problem was economic—a passenger shortage, rising fuel costs, unmeetable crew wage demands. On October 9, 1974, the *France* was permanently laid up. She was first sold to a Saudi Arabian financier who planned to use her as a floating hotel. When his plans fell through, she was purchased by Knut Kloster, a Norwegian.

Kloster had this last transatlantic express steamer towed to Bremenhaven, where $100 million was spent to convert her into a cruise ship. Among other things, her forward engine room was shut down and two of her four screws were removed.

On May 16, 1980, this beautiful ship, now rechristened *Norway*, steamed into New York harbor and tied up at a pier in the Hudson River, almost exactly where *Normandie* had made her second home.

Standing some distance away and squinting into the sun at this beautiful 1,000-foot ship, with its soaring prow, its whale-back breakwater, its name in lights between its funnels, it was almost possible to project oneself backward in time.

It was almost possible to imagine another ship in another era, to imagine Captain Pugnet up on the bridge, brimming over with pride, to imagine Madame Lebrun, the French President's wife besieged by newsmen, to imagine the steamer trunks being noisily carted out of the lower ports to waiting yellow cabs, to imagine Colette or Noel Coward or Ernest Hemingway striding down the gangway and waving, to imagine Vladimir Yourkevitch bursting his buttons.

It was almost possible to imagine the crowds of curious by-standers, anxious to get a glimpse of this fantastic vessel, to rub shoulders with the movie stars, the intellectuals, the financiers, the sports figures and the merely wealthy who traveled aboard her.

It was almost possible, but not quite. For *Norway* was not *Normandie* and 1980 was not 1935. The ocean-liner era was over. It had lasted about seventy-five years—no more than a moment in human history.

To be sure, ships still tie up on the Hudson, big ships, handsome ships . . . cruise ships. Cruise ships, for all their similarities to the vessels which once crossed the Atlantic, are not ocean liners. They are vacations. They are floating resorts. They are not transportation.

So, ships there are, but not transatlantic liners. Those are long gone, all of them. And once something has been gone long enough, we tend to romanticize it. Even those of us who never really knew or experienced the thing delight in its memory. We're entranced by every detail. We join groups like the Oceanic Navigation Research Society or the Titanic Historical Society. We simply cannot know enough. And this is as it should be, for without this impulse, our past would slip through our fingers.

The great passenger ships were real and meaningful, part of life. They brought generations of immigrants to the United States. They were the only link between the Old World and the New. They were the stage sets on which millions of stories were played out. Finally, they were a truly remarkable human achievement, one that deserves to be remembered and honored.

And once upon a time human imagination, knowledge and ambition joined together to produce a vessel that was more beautiful and more daring than all the others, a vessel known as *Normandie*.

INDEX